Acknowledgements

D1406226

Thanks to my husband, Ed Burwell, for his patience and understanding during the year in which this book has been "under construction."

Thanks also to my patient editor, Peter J. Weber, and my understanding publisher, and to those who offered suggestions along the way. Their assistance was invaluable.

Finally, thanks and applause to those generous colleagues who help each other constantly by sharing tips, suggestions, and URLs for further exploration of the wonders of cyberspace via lists for librarians, the Association of Independent Information Professionals, and other "space stations."

— Helen Burwell

Before You Start . . .

Why Another Competitive Intelligence Book?

In recent years, the corporate world and the broader business community have increasingly acknowledged the value of using information to obtain a competitive advantage in business situations. Some companies have created special departments or units charged with this mission. Working independently or assisting other parts of the organization, these units gather data, information, and knowledge regarding the company's competitors, the industries in which they compete, and industries that affect their own.

Job titles like 'Chief Information Officer' or 'Director, Business Intelligence Unit' now appear in corporate telephone directories. Membership rosters of organizations like the Society for Competitor Intelligence Professionals (SCIP) have grown rapidly. Books on CI strategy are available in the business books section at most large bookstores.

But an article in *The New York Times*[1] reported the following:

> A survey of about 50 large corporations by Fuld & Company, a consulting firm based in Cambridge, Mass., found that 20 percent of responding companies had shut down their corporate intelligence departments at a time when membership in a trade group, the Society of Competitive Intelligence Professionals, is reported to be growing by 25 percent a year.

The article goes on to speculate about possible reasons for the demise of those CI departments. The fact remains, though, that with or without an official CI department, the company still needs business intelligence to succeed and move ahead! If there is no organized CI department, then the various departments within the company must call on their librarians for assistance, or fend for themselves. An answer: use this book.

Attendees at seminars I have led have indicated the need to become experts on information sources — from researching privately held companies *to* learning more about doing business around the world *to* identifying trends and locating industry forecasts. Some companies have sent a half dozen analysts to class, while others have requested special sessions tailored to the needs of their organizations. Among these people there appears to be a real hunger for tools that will help them find the answers they seek. An answer: use this book.

---

[1] *The New York Times*, April 25, 1999; Page 4, Column 1 c. 1999 *New York Times* Company.

For some, searching online is something quite new, while for others the quest is for new or better sources of data that has eluded them. Some bemoan the fact that they cannot find reference tools that describe and source the required information from the perspective of the various departments within their organization. While Research and Development may be interested in a competitor's potential new products, Human Resources may be interested in a competitor's benefits package or executive's salaries. Meanwhile, the Sales and Marketing Department wants to know how other companies are attempting to gain market share through advertising or other promotions. An answer: use this book.

How To Use This Book

In meeting with many potential users of the information in this book, we have learned that their needs are at different levels, depending upon the nature of their work, their computer skills, and the project immediately at hand. For that reason, the book addresses the topic of online information by presenting material that can be used by beginners and advanced searchers. Beginners should start with Parts I-III. Advanced searchers may wish to start with Part IV.

The book is organized as follows:

- An overview of CI in general, with some guidance in addressing CI research conceptually, to put the reader in tune with the thought processes necessary when selecting sources for searching online.

- An analysis of key information sources intended to explain how to use them to best advantage.

- An Industry Checklist and several different Company Checklists that help the searcher to gather all of the relevant data that should be included when compiling reports for different CI applications.

- A collection of more than 1700+ bookmarks can be used by those who wish to search the Internet, going farther and wider than the resources mentioned above. These are also available at the Online Competitive Intelligence page on the Burwell Enterprises website at www.burwellinc.com.

- A group of appendices and resources keyed to subject matter contained in the various chapters in Parts I-III. This is a selective list, which describes a few good sources for each topic, and explains where the source can be obtained or reached. Both commercial and Internet sources are mentioned here.

The reader may note that certain websites are discussed in more than one chapter or section. Generally, these sites combine various types of intelligence or the data they provide may be used for several different purposes. The author has no connection with any of the vendors or sites mentioned in this book, other than that of Burwell Enterprises at www.burwellinc.com.

Whether the reader is strictly a World Wide Web searcher, uses only commercial sources, or works with a combination of the two, he or she must be confident that information used to make the company's crucial business decisions is timely, accurate, and suited to the purpose for which it will be used. The tools necessary for such a task can be found between the covers of *Online Competitive Intelligence!*

Contents

Identifying a company's competitors is a much more complex undertaking than merely generating a list by classification code, however. The challenge comes in finding more and more details about companies so that you can identify your company's *true* competitors. That is one of the reasons for this book – to assist in that identification! See Chapter 4 for identifying competitors.

Finding Leads Outside of the U.S.

One way to keep a business growing is to increase the customer base and volume of sales. How can a company in middle-America, for example, find leads in places like Asia or Eastern Europe?

The Traditional Approach

A few years ago, you might have contacted a local or regional "incubator" or similar organization. Organizations like the U.S. Department of Commerce offer various programs designed to assist businesses interested in importing or exporting goods and services.

Another option was to join a trade mission to a particular country or region. This approach, however, costs time and money, and you might have found yourself competing with other members of the trade mission for contacts in the target country.

You might have hired a consultant. This also costs money, and finding a consultant with good contacts and knowledge of your company's industry presented a challenge.

Perhaps you searched the *Journal of Commerce* or a comparable publication. To get timely leads, you needed a subscription to the publication or access to an online service that licenses the publication. This meant paying for a subscription to the online service. Also, specific searching skills had to be learned in order to use this service correctly.

The 21st Century Approach

Those old strategies still are useful, but today you have a powerful tool in cyberspace that provides additional, less-costly possibilities. You can meet, greet, and learn using the Internet. The World Wide Web is rife with trade-related sites, where information abounds on how to do business in various parts of the world, who-has-what to buy or sell, and more. Electronic mailing lists and discussion groups are a popular means for sharing news, leads, and tips on these subjects, though they usually require a subscription or registration. Those who wish may participate in such lists actively. However, many subscribers prefer to "lurk," which means reading selectively and ignoring items of no interest rather than contributing frequently to the discussion. This provides an excellent way to keep up with what is being said by others without becoming entangled in lengthy discussions. For more information on discussion groups and monitoring them, see *Usenets/Listservs* in the *Bookmarks & Favorites* section of Part 4. After identifying organizations, companies, or individuals via the Internet, contacting them by email is fast and inexpensive.

If something is a "hot topic," then it generates a volume of written material. By that measure, CI is definitely hot. A search of the magazines/news segment in the Gale Group's *Business & Company Resource Center* located 150 mainstream and scholarly articles about CI. Where can you find Gale's *Business & Company Resource Center* service? It is marketed to libraries, many of which allow their cardholders to search their collections via the Internet. The Gale databases are also licensed to various vendors in cyberspace.

CI articles now appear in general business publications, news magazines, publications aimed at the "techies" in the Information Systems Department, as well as in the profession's own journals. The authors of these articles are not just practitioners "preaching to the choir," as the following screen capture from Gale Group will attest:

Mark	Document Title
☐	**How your competitor sells, helps you sell...more.** Jeffrey Gitomer, *The Business Journal-Milwaukee* , 0740-2899, May 3, 2002 v19 i33 p14(1) Abstract
☐	**Bribes and trash archaeology: COMPETITOR INTELLIGENCE by Jimmy Burns: Even some of the more respectable companies have been known to use shady tactics occasionally.** Jimmy Burns, *The Financial Times* , 0307-1766, April 11, 2002 p5 (798 words) Text
☐	**Characteristics in information processing approaches.** Johan Frishammar, *International Journal of Information Management* , 0268-4012, April 2002 v22 i2 p143(14) Abstract
☐	**Spies Like Us: Creating a competitive-intelligence shop is easier than you might think.** Daniel Franklin, *Time* , 0040-781X, March 25, 2002 v159 i12 pB12+ (478 words) Text
☑	**Competitor intelligence appointment made by ASPACE.** *M2 Presswire* Jan 22, 2002 pNA (409 words) Text
☑	**Business Intelligence Using Smart Techniques: Environmental Scanning Using Data Mining and Competitor Analysis Using Scenarios and Manual Simulation.** Bala Subramanian, *Competitiveness Review* , 1059-5422, Wntr-Spring 2002 v12 i1 p115(1) (333 words) Text	1 page PDF
☐	**Strategic factor market intelligence: an application of information economics to strategy formulation and competitor intelligence.** Richard Makadok, Jay B. Barney, *Management Science* , 0025-1909, Dec 2001 v47 i12 p1621(18) Abstract

A representative list of additional CI books and articles may be found in Part IV in Appendix E. These will provide further information on the practice of competitive intelligence for those new to the field. In addition, specialized works can be found on individual topics like market research or benchmarking.

Increased awareness of the need for actionable business intelligence has been fed by a continuous flow of books and articles on the subject. There are books of success stories detailing the results achieved by CI task forces formed at major U.S. corporations, as well as "how to" books which address all aspects of competitive intelligence work, including telephoning, interviewing, manual research techniques, or online searching.

Most of all, online tools have made CI tasks easier – whether on a large or small scale – by oneself or in concert with the company decision makers and managers.

Part I

An Introduction to Competitive Intelligence

Chapter 1

What Is Competitive Intelligence, Anyway?

It's Not What You Call It, It's How You Use It That Counts

Competitive intelligence. Competitor intelligence. Business intelligence. These terms describe one of the hottest areas in business-related information research, and while the concepts may be related, each of these terms has a different connotation:

Competitive Intelligence: the analysis of publicly available information on competition and competitors to help your company use strategic decision-making to gain an advantage in a line of business.

Competitor Intelligence: information on specific companies or organizations, including such critical factors as financial performance, productivity, market position, and strategies about another specific company or group of companies.

Business Intelligence: broader than Competitive Intelligence, Business Intelligence encompasses information that is not necessarily "competitive" in nature but which helps complete the picture in a CI undertaking, for instance, an analysis of industry trends.

Why CI?

No matter what you choose to call it, the important thing to remember is that the use of such information has become a strategic necessity in today's competitive, global business environment.

Some authorities have stated that ninety percent of the information needed in a company's CI program is available from publicly available sources, and that the other ten percent can be deduced.[1]

The best rationale for gathering and using competitive intelligence might be to find "What's in it for me or my company."

Gathering and applying competitive intelligence not only results in a more successful and profitable company, but it may be crucial to that company's survival.

The Difference Between Two Millionaires

To illustrate the benefit of collecting competitor intelligence on an industry, here is a story of two millionaires. Both of our millionaires are self-made. They are about the same age. In truth, they grew up very near to each other. Tom made his fortune in a single industry over a span of fifteen years, starting with a one-room workshop. He turned it into a 40,000 square foot furniture factory – all his own. Meanwhile Dick, whose high school interest was in cameras and electronics, progressed up the ladder of success by going from company to company in Silicon Valley. Beginning in sales, moving to development and marketing, he finally drew his big hand in computer microprocessors. In fact, both of our millionaires drew big hands – well beyond $50 million each.

By the time both men reached 45 years of age, they were virtually retired. Both rode the wave crest to success in their respective industries.

There is one major difference between our two men. The first, Tom, had his success in one industry – manufacturing alternative furniture. In part, he succeeded due to his perseverance and to weak competition in the marketplace. He did not have to do much competitive intelligence – what is to be concerned about when your competitors are found hanging out at rock concerts?

Our computer industry millionaire, Dick, *did* have to use competitive intelligence. When it came decision-making time in his fast-paced competitive industry, he had to have up to the minute information about the competition; what Apple was planning; who the companies in Singapore were selling to; and who had factories in what country; and how many salespeople worked for the competition. These precious tidbits of information helped him make informed – and correct – decisions, winning decisions.

Let us turn the clock ahead. How are our two multi-millionaires doing? After selling off his factory, the furniture millionaire decided to help his son launch a racing bicycle manufacturing business. They neglected to investigate what they were getting into – and promptly ran afoul in the new, competitive environment. Costs far out-stripped returns. The people they chose to assist them in the venture – largely friends from the former venture - could not and did not perform. Next, Tom tried a return to furniture manufacturing, but the new product lines did not catch on.

Meanwhile, in year 2000, Dick retired from his seven-figure job with the microprocessor mega-manufacturer. Had his own in-house competitive intelligence warned him to get out before the dot.com crash? He's not saying. Because so much of his experience involved competitive

---

[1] Combs, Richard E. and Moorhead, John D., *The Competitive Intelligence Handbook,* Metuchen, NJ & London, Scarecrow Press, 1992, p.13.

intelligence, now, after his daily golfing, he makes his living consulting with mutual fund companies, advising them on the plusses and minuses of the electronics and computer firms the fund managers might consider for investment. His wealth continues to accumulate.

Let us re-examine these the careers of these two men. One rode the wave of the waterbed craze and later believed he could successfully manage any business. Success followed by two failures. The other was in a field where he had to learn to use competitive intelligence. He continues to succeed at whatever business venture he chooses to engage in today. Whether you are riding the wave of success or not, business intelligence and its application may be crucial to your career, now and into the foreseeable future.

Use CI to Turn a Weakness Into an Advantage

One mark of the successful competitor in the business world is the ability to triumph over adversity. All companies are faced with difficult decisions from time to time. How well these important decisions are handled makes the difference! Here is an example:

From Fire Sale to Cyber-Sale – A Successful Turnaround

Because of tight money and a mild winter, Acme Manufacturing was stuck with a warehouse containing a million dollars worth of expensive skiwear that had not sold. Acme hired a consultant to devise a way to sell the merchandise without holding a "fire sale."

The consultant, Jane, began to research the problem. As part of her online research, she found several useful pieces of information:

- Omega Inc.,a much larger competitor, was planning a major advertising campaign for next season. They would introduce a new line of mid-range priced skiwear aimed at the teenage market, and the "big money" advertising campaign would support this.

- Several new e-commerce sites on the Web now focused on selling sporting goods.

Armed with Jane's findings, this new plan was formulated for Acme: rather then try to match the competition's ad campaign dollar for dollar, it would be possible for Acme to establish a web page to tout the high quality and good looks of Acme's ski clothes, complete with graphics showing the product line. The e-commerce site owners would process orders. By eliminating the middleman, i.e. the retailer, it would be possible to sell the goods at a reduced price using the Internet and avoid taking a loss on the merchandise.

When the decision-makers at Acme were presented with this recommendation, they quickly decided to jump into e-commerce.

Instead of losing money, they were able to turn the situation around to their advantage. This near disaster taught them several things:

- Given her valuable advice, paying Jane $2000 to be their consultant was clearly worth it.

- They could be successful in a new marketplace — the Internet.

- They could learn what competitors were planning, and get into the new marketplace well ahead of Omega Inc. and perhaps other old-school industry players.

After expenses for their consultant and paying costs incurred using the e-commerce service on the Web, Acme still realized a profit. At the same time they learned a valuable lesson!

Use CI to Predict a Competitors' Next Moves

Ah, using CI to predict a competitors next move can give you a big advantage, as Acme Company learned in the example above. Knowing early what a competitor is up to allows you to respond more quickly to that competitor's plans, and adjust your own. The right response could mean greater market share, which translates into greater revenue, or saving you from a major loss.

For most, that is what they think competitive intelligence will do first and foremost - it helps you determine what the competition is doing. Finding what they are doing and planning to do is not so difficult if you go about it correctly. Consider the following:

Use CI to Become Aware of Change as It Happens And Before It Is Too Late to Act

Librarians call it Current Awareness. Others may call it an alert service. Whatever you call it, the ongoing monitoring of events in an industry, of preferences in the marketplace, or of staffing changes that could take a company in new directions is crucial if your company is to be a leader rather than an "also ran." What follows is the story of one company that successfully used CI to stay on top of change.

Use CI to Manage Potential Problems Proactively

MegaCorp, a large multinational corporation, was planning some major changes that would impact employees around the world. Several departments in the company were interested in how these changes would be covered and presented by the media, as well as how the changes would be perceived by the employees and stockholders.

Early in the game, special monitoring was undertaken to detect and measure the reactions of these groups, as the various announcements were made over a period of a few months. Bill was assigned to coordinate this activity.

MegaCorp needed to monitor the media in a dozen different countries in addition to the U.S., so Bill arranged for automatic "alerting services" with LexisNexis and signed up for AccuClip Express, offered by CyberAlert. As a precaution, MegaCorp also decided to monitor broadcast news in the event that enterprising radio and TV personnel got the story and decided to interview employees. To that end, they signed contracts with the Video Monitoring Service, www.vidmon.com, and The Financial Times, www.ft.com, for coverage within and outside of the U.S. See Chapter 6 for more detail on these services.

To put an ear to what employees and stockholders were saying, they used another service offered by CyberAlert to monitor the major internet message boards on a daily basis. The findings of this message board monitoring service would provide a running commentary on what was being talked about in cyberspace by employees, stockholders, and other interested parties. Each day, Bill received an email that told him which message boards contained new discussions regarding MegaCorp. He read the messages and identified areas that could be cause for concern.

As a result of the intelligence developed during the message board monitoring, several beneficial results were achieved:

- The Human Resources Department learned what employees were thinking. The result: several detailed articles were published in employee newsletters, expanding the data that had been included in the company's official announcements, and defusing what could have been a negative situation regarding employee morale.

- The Public Relations Department developed a series of press releases stating the facts concerning potentially negative situations. The press releases were designed to anticipate queries by the media, and to avoid misinterpretation or publication of only half of the story.

- Investor Relations used the input from the message board monitoring as a "heads up" to add explanatory documents to the company website. In addition, they were able to better prepare their company president to respond to shareholder questions from the floor at the next annual meeting.

MegaCorp also could have gone to Google, at www.google.com. Google's *Groups* segment assists in searching the contents of online message groups. Search results can be sorted or limited by date. *Groups* lacks the email convenience, but it does provide the necessary functionality for keeping up with what is being said. See Chapter 13 for additional discussion of alerting and monitoring services.

Use CI to Gain Competitive Advantage and Beat the Competition to Market

Uncovering what the competition is planning provides an opportunity for offensive or defensive measures designed to gain or retain competitive advantage or market share. The story that follows illustrates the concept of CI being used to gain competitive advantage.

Alpha Company discovered that Beta, Inc, a small start-up company, had apparently begun clinical trials of a new drug. Alpha company had invested significant money and personnel in the development of a similar drug, believing that they had a unique product in mind. Alpha Company also discovered that Beta, Inc's CEO was Mr. X, who was formerly employed by a large international pharmaceutical company. They were very concerned about possible ramifications of this connection, as well as some other "coincidental" facts that had surfaced regarding connections between Beta, Inc and large drug companies.

Alpha Company's researchers undertook a RUSH online research project to determine (1) the progress of Beta, Inc's clinical trials, (2) what stage the clinical trials had reached, and (3) whether any connection could be established between the small start-up company and one of the large international companies. As the research progressed, they also were interested in collecting more information about some of the other people whose names began to appear.

The searchers combed the Internet and several specialized commercial databases and quickly learned where the clinical trials were taking place as well as the stage that had been reached. Scholarly articles from the commercial sources provided solid scientific information. On the Internet, they identified several websites that track clinical trials, as well as home pages for many pharmaceutical companies, both large and small. Data found here was useful to telephone researchers who conducted interviews with key personnel at several companies.

Additional information regarding Beta, Inc's activities was located at the website of the U. S. Food and Drug Administration, where calendars provided information regarding the subject matter of meetings, attendees' names, etc. Alpha also established a connection between Beta, Inc. and a former FDA employee who apparently was a Beta lobbyist.

By putting together the information retrieved online, and combining it with the results of telephone interviews and other research, Alpha Company was able to determine what Beta, Inc. was up to.

Alpha Company moved quickly in its own efforts to complete trials, obtain the necessary FDA approvals, and bring the product to market long before Beta was able to, thus gaining a crucial competitive advantage.

Thanks in large part to the nearly instant availability of information, and the broad range of resources available in electronic format, Alpha Company was a winner in this battle in the highly competitive pharmaceutical marketplace. Alpha Company's cost to conduct the competitive intelligence project was $10,000. The estimated profit returned from their new product was in excess of $1,000,000.

Who Gathers Competitive Intelligence?

Now that we have discussed the importance of CI, its uses, and reviewed some examples of these uses in actual cases, it is important to discuss who gathers competitive intelligence information. Some who search for CI may not think of the information in those terms, nor do they realize they are participating in gathering competitive intelligence, and the company may not use the name CI for what these people do, even though they spend a great deal of time doing it. The boss asks his secretary to "create a list of email addresses for all suppliers in town," and the secretary becomes part of the CI process.

In-House Specialists and End Users

Who handles the CI chores in your office? It can vary, and gathering information may be assumed to be part of anyone's job. A person's competitive intelligence role may be to identify a question or need, or to go about gathering information for creating a workable CI plan. After the CI process passes through the development stage, others may be assigned tasks of answering questions or researching, such as finding information and answers about competitor companies or about an industry, or combing the Internet for the necessary statistics, experts, and news items. Others may administer the CI plan, organizing and analyzing the data. Or, all tasks may be handled by one person.

The official or unofficial job titles held by your main CI role-players may include:

- **Key Player**. In a small company or in a start-up company, the Key Player is charged with certain responsibilities for helping the company to grow.

- **Professional Librarian** responsible for supporting the information research needs of various people or departments in the company. Librarians often call this the Reference function, when describing their work.

- **Executive** engaged in sales, marketing, research and development, human resources, planning or other areas. The executive may need certain information to fulfill responsibilities that are part of his or her job description.

- **Sales Person** competing with dozens or hundreds of others, some of whom may work for the same organization. Your sales people's CI role may be to compile lists of potential buyers for products or services. Sales people are, of course, good sources of CI information due to their direct access to customers, and what those customers know and say about your competition.

- **Entrepreneur** starting a new business, trying to create business and marketing plans. The entrepreneur may turn to an outside CI professional for tasks too time-consuming to handle on their own.

- **Independent Information Professional**, sometimes known as an information broker, who is hired by the project or on a contract basis to gather information required for use in-house by the client.

- **Independent CI Professional**, someone who worked in CI. Often, the Independent CI Professional has worked for a large organization where he or she gained the experience that they now offer to clients on a consulting basis.

CI Practitioners – A New Breed

More and more these days, we see job descriptions or meet people who describe their position at work as involved *chiefly* in the area of competitive intelligence. CI practitioners help businesses gather and analyze data to create information, which is combined with what is already known, to create the *knowledge base*. Words like "interpret," "deduce," or "intuition" are sometimes mentioned in the context of their work, since the knowledge base involves human interaction and taking advantage of what is already known by those within the organization. This knowledge base is used when studying companies or industries or making various decisions that are crucial to a company's growth or survival.

CI professionals come from varied backgrounds, most frequently building upon experience in some area of the business, or from working in information research. In general, they fit one of these profiles:

- Their background and education is in business or a business-related field. Experience in one or more areas of a company's activity such as sales and marketing, research and development, planning, or other areas, has led to an assignment working in CI.

- They have a degree in library or information science and have worked in the company's library or information center, fielding research questions from others in the company. They are now part of the company's CI team, or they receive research requests from that group.

- They are a manager, with an understanding of the "big picture" of the company's information needs and challenges. They are expected to have, or to gather, the knowledge required for making decisions that are in the company's best interests.

Additionally, some CI practitioners have had experience working for the government, often in some intelligence-related capacity.

CI Teams Come in All Sizes

In the past ten years, more and more large companies have staffed CI teams to support other departments in the organization. These CI "groups" provide the research and analysis needed by the decision-makers. Just as often, smaller businesses have recognized that they, too, cannot thrive unless they use CI information to their advantage, so time must be budgeted for CI research.

Business magazines are full of articles about small companies that grew into large ones because they figured out how to do something better or faster. This "figuring out" required awareness of what was happening, of what was needed, and of how other companies were handling the issue.

CI activity in your company may be the responsibility of a CI group, or the task may be in the hands of a nucleus of research-oriented people within your department. Likewise, the CI department may be a "one person band" - translated, that means *YOU*. What is important is that within your company, the right information must reach the right people at the right time. In the case of factual information, you probably have a deadline. In the case of trends, consumer behavior, or new competitors, however, this means to collect useful information as early as possible and as continuously as possible. Old information is not much better than no information – as usual, timeliness is crucial.

Learning More About CI – Join the Pros

One of the most significant events in the evolution of business intelligence gathering was the founding of ***The Society of Competitor Intelligence Professionals (SCIP),*** in 1986. Since that time the organization has grown to fifty chapters, with members all over the world. As described on the SCIP website, www.scip.org, this organization provides its members with networking, educational opportunities, and a Code of Ethics that is taken very seriously by the membership. SCIP's annual conferences in the U.S. and in Europe provide additional opportunities for members to expand their knowledge and understanding of the field.

Many SCIP members have backgrounds in market research, government intelligence, or science and technology. The Frequently Asked Questions page at the SCIP website - click on "FAQ" - makes it clear that CI is not industrial espionage, digging through trash bins, or warfare. It is an ethical business practice carried out by those who are smart enough to learn what information to go after, and how to do so.

Chapter 2

Is Everything Really on the Internet? If So, Where?

Online Searching Can Yield Valuable CI

The popularity of the Internet, coupled with the increased use of personal computers, means that databases – those storehouses of information on just about everything – are no longer mysterious programs used by "computer geeks," but a basic tool used by many of us to manage all kinds of information for business or personal purposes. Thanks to developments in technology over the past twenty years, there is a much greater awareness of online databases in the business community these days, and an increasing reliance on the availability of them.

The Tools Have Changed

Only a few years ago, online searching presented two options – the Internet or the modem – for reaching other computers where information was stored. Using the Internet meant learning about File Transfer Protocol (FTP), Telnet, or something new and promising called the World Wide Web.

Commercial electronic information sources used modems and communication software to reach servers the size of a room. Large aggregators like Dialog, Dow Jones, or Orbit licensed databases and made them available to those who could learn to use arcane search languages specific to each vendor. Searchers had to be "techies" in addition to their "real" jobs as librarians, market researchers, scientists, etc.

With improved technology and increased awareness of the Internet as an information source, the emphasis is now on the World Wide Web. Most searchers no longer have the occasion to use FTP or Telnet. Commercial databases are accessed via the Internet through a website. We have more choices as traditional commercial database vendors have adjusted to this new environment and new internet-based vendors have appeared. Now the options look more like this:

- Commercial databases from aggregators, formerly accessed via modem.
- Commercial databases from new, entrepreneurial sources.
- Commercial databases, direct from the source.
- A universe of documents and graphics made available on or through individual websites.

Traditional Commercial Vendors

One great way to keep up with trends or events that will impact your company is through searching online using commercial databases or the Internet.

For business intelligence, Dialog, Factiva (formerly Dow Jones Interactive), and LexisNexis are the U.S. survivors among the large commercial online services that were created years ago as dial-up systems. Other services such as DataStar and FT Profile are popular for coverage of non-U.S. parts of the world, while specialized online services serve the needs of specific areas such as the scientific or legal communities worldwide.

These vendors have mounted increasingly sophisticated websites to take advantage of improved technology and to supplement their subscription-based clientele by tapping into a new market – end users who access the services from their desktops on an as-needed basis using credit cards.

New Players With New Offerings

New commercial vendors with names like Alacra, Skyminder, and dozens of others, have aimed at recognizing the internet's potential as an information tool. In developing their features and services, these modern commercial companies have taken advantage of internet technology to give the old-timers a run for their money - or for ours. The newcomers offer some of the same database files available on the major services in addition to files that the major vendors might not consider cost-effective. As mentioned previously, their sites offer credit card access for pay-as-you-go customers or the traditional deposit accounts where users charge against a pre-deposited amount.

- **Producer/Vendor Web Offerings**
  Database producers have created their own web-based commercial services that compete with the big major vendors. Some database producers such as Reuters removed their files from other vendors' systems as license agreements expired. Others, like The Thomson Corporation, have commercial services of their own, but also allow their files to remain available through major vendors.
- **Internet sites intended to inform or educate**
  These World Wide Web sites have been created by entities such as trade associations, industry groups, academic institutions, businesses, the media, or individuals. Some of these contain searchable databases and provide copies of documents, usually for free. Many of them are crowded with advertisements that offset the cost of providing the searcher with "free" information. They may also contain documents that you might not otherwise locate because a larger database producer did not pick them up.

Accessing competitive intelligence online involves tradeoffs. One benefit of this new competition is pay-as-you-go pricing from vendors whose products and services were traditionally only subscription based. The pay-as-you-go plan allows you to search files that you may have been denied in the past because you could not justify the cost of a subscription that would be used only occasionally. It has also meant faster availability of new information, and graphics than could not be provided via the older dial-up mode of delivery.

On the negative side, however, the newer technology means that database producers may not have to rely on large aggregators such as Dialog or LexisNexis to market their products. Some of the long-time search favorites must be accessed through individual websites. Removal of files from the major services means the loss of some of the cross-file searching ability that the big vendors formerly touted. For example, you can no longer search Reuters files along with other favorite business or news files simultaneously on Dialog or LexisNexis. Nor can you eliminate duplicates, and pay one vendor for the documents retrieved from different producers' databases. In addition, there are the pitfalls inherent in any open environment – anyone can create a website and publish on the Internet. So certain key questions arise: is the data complete? When was it last updated?

Free Sources – Are They What They Are Cracked Up To Be?

Greater awareness of the existence of online information, coupled with increased options for accessing it, makes it easier to justify using online research as part of your CI activity. However, because of a popular misconception – that it is all on the Internet for free – some people find it difficult to warrant subscriptions to commercial services.

Why spend money when you can get information or documents for free? The answer depends upon what you are getting. It is important to examine the differences between the types of free online information sources, then to make informed choices. For this purpose, the possibilities break down this way:

- Free sources on the Internet, sponsored by recognized, reputable sources.

- Free sources on the Internet, maintained by companies, individuals, or organizations with whom you are *not* familiar.

An old saying comes to mind when considering free competitive business information - "Never look a gift horse in the mouth." According to an online search, the exact quote was first written by John Heywood, who said in the 16th century: "No man ought to looke a given horse in the mouth." That was long before the Internet. Some of what we obtain at no cost on the Internet may be useful. On the other hand, taking it at face value may be less than acceptable, and perhaps fraught with peril.

Paying For Information Has Its Advantages

Some comparisons between using commercial online sources and free sources for obtaining business intelligence are in the *Comparing Features: Commercial Databases vs. Free Internet Sources* comparison chart later in this chapter. Those comparisons are important, but should be considered only after understanding what to expect from free versus fee-based sources. Here are some advantages to paying a vendor:

Ease of Use –
One search with a powerful search engine covers all relevant data on a subject or category. Multiple files can be searched simultaneously. Some well-known database publishers provide free searches on their websites. However, as with free sites, there are often tradeoffs. Their search engines may not be as powerful as those used by commercial vendors for searching the same data, so getting the desired information without spending money could mean spending extra time searching, switching databases, following hotlinks, or reviewing lengthy unstructured search results.

Timeliness – Commercial vendors update data on a regular schedule.
Free sources may provide lists of companies, sales figures, product lines, or other attractive data, but it is very possible that the information is out of date. Although a website's offerings *sound* good, it is important to remember that it costs money to keep this information timely. Constant maintenance may not be a high priority. To get the most recent data, it may be necessary to go straight to the source – the organization that collects and compiles the data. At the very least, look for information on the website regarding the date that the database was last updated, or contact the organization sponsoring the site and inquire.

Amount of Data Available – When you pay, you search the entire database.
Some vendors do not include their entire databases when providing searches via their website. The full database is found *only* in the commercial versions of the product. If you are willing to pay for the information, the commercial versions of their products can be searched using services such as Dialog or LexisNexis, or must be purchased from the database producer in CD or DVD format.

Control Over Output –
Using commercial products, you can search more widely, sort the results, and limit results by factors such as company size, geography, etc. You also have flexibility regarding which pieces of data will be included in the records that you download or print.

Dun & Bradstreet's database products are a good example of the points mentioned above. There are both free and fee-based Dun & Bradstreet files available, and records contain varying amounts of information with varying degrees of timeliness. The trick with databases like those of Dun & Bradstreet is to figure out which of the many reports, available on their websites or from their commercial sources, will provide the information you need at the best price.

CD-ROM or DVD Products – An Alternative Approach To Searching

Many popular databases are now available in CD-ROM or DVD format. When multiple users have to access the data, these CD-ROM and DVD products may be loaded on local area networks and made available at the various desktops. CD-ROM or DVD works well in some environments, but not so well in others. Consider these points:

- For heavy use, they may be extremely cost-effective.
- A user-friendly interface may be included.
- Search engines are often comparable in power to those used by online versions of the database.
- Searchers using CDs are not pressured to search quickly because "the meter is running."

But, there are tradeoffs to using CD's and DVD's:

- CDs or DVDs are purchased for a flat fee, which is sometimes substantial. For only occasional use, this may not be a wise choice.

- The purchase price may or may not include periodic shipments of updates.

- These products are only as current as of the cutoff date indicated by the publisher. You may still have to go online to update search results.

To sum up, the commercial versions of online databases provide greater power and flexibility in searching and sorting, but may be more expensive, since CDs, DVDs and online subscriptions cost money. On the other hand, the database producer may make some, but generally not all, of the information available on the Internet at no charge. Two old adages apply here: "Time is money" and "You get what you pay for."

It Is *Not* All On the Internet, Free

You may have heard someone in your company say, "Everything is on the Internet, and it is free." While it is true that we can access a great deal of valuable data there, getting expert business intelligence from the Internet at no cost can be a perilous undertaking for the unwary. Considering which sources to search, which ones to trust, and which approach will be most productive can be complicated.

There are some very positive things about the Internet. It presents us with opportunities for researching new and different bodies of information, such as the archives of discussion groups where people with common interests express opinions or share ideas. It also provides us with access to some materials that were previously unavailable in electronic format or that were obtainable only through subscription-based online services. In addition, we now have more rapid access to a large body of government information that was formerly out-of-date by the time it appeared in print.

Since it is not managed or regulated by any central body, you may find information on the Internet that is out-of-date, incomplete, thoroughly biased, or just plain inaccurate, or worse. It is important to understand this – or to get The Boss to understand – and to consider a combination of commercial and free internet sources for gathering business intelligence.

Several years ago, *The New York Times* published a lengthy article in *Circuits*, one of the newspaper's weekly supplements, titled "Whales in the Minnesota River? Only on the Web, Where Skepticism Is a Required Navigational Aid."[1] The article provided a lengthy discussion on the issue of whether or not to trust what you find on the Internet. Special sidebars mentioned websites that tell you what to look for when seeking reliable information on the Web, and how to separate good data from bad. Accuracy is still important, and subsequent chapters in this book address this topic. You will learn how to decide when to choose the Internet, and when to go to commercial sources for business intelligence.

---

[1] "Whales in the Minnesota River? Only on the Web, Where Skepticism Is a Required Navigational Aid" *New York Times*, March 4, 1999. Page D1.

Be cautious in choosing sources if maintaining your anonymity is important. The host at that "free" site can track the identity of computers that search the site, and which pages are searched. Someone might deduce information about your product development activity by seeing what patents or other types of files you have searched on their site.

TIP - It is possible to waste a lot of time on the Internet trying to find a free source for data that is readily available in a familiar commercial online source. Yet, the Internet provides a wealth of valuable information not available from commercial services. By having a clear understanding of the possible pitfalls inherent in the use of internet sources, you can combine the best of both worlds.

How to Ensure That You Are *Really* Getting What You *Think* You Are Getting

Your goal is to stay ahead of the competition, to learn what they are doing or planning, and to keep abreast of developments, trends, and forecasts in the industry. You want to access intelligence that is both as timely and as comprehensive as possible. To be sure of what you are getting, it is helpful to understand the "nuts and bolts" of the types of available sources.

The table below outlines the issues that should be considered when comparing commercial sources with free ones.

Comparing Features: Commercial Databases vs. Free Internet Sources

	Commercial Sources	Non-commercial Internet Sources
Standardized Language/Indexing **(Authority Control)**	Articles in the database are indexed using an official list of index terms. Can check the vocabulary list. If you search on the proper keyword, you will retrieve all relevant articles.	Documents not indexed; there is no controlled vocabulary. One document may refer to "car," while another mentions "automobile." You must enter synonyms to retrieve as many articles as possible.
Access To Full Text Databases **(Available from some vendors and many websites)**	Full text availability means instant gratification – not a trip to the magazine shelves with a citation in hand. Vendor may provide segment searching to limit searches to specific areas of documents, for greater precision. The importance of full text searching varies with the goal of the search.	These files are searched using a variety of search engines, which use different sets of rules in searching. Document format may mean less flexibility in printing, copying, etc. Combining documents into an organized report may take more time.

	Commercial Sources	Non-commercial Internet Sources
Quality Control	Articles come from published sources, with attribution. Source lists are generally available. The database producer can be contacted for questions regarding quality of information.	There is no supervision of data loaded on the Internet. Out-of-date material rarely removed. Dates on documents retrieved by a search engine may refer to date loaded on the Internet, not date of document itself. It is difficult if not impossible to contact the responsible party.
Consistency of Format	Content may vary across databases, but records generally contain basic information such as title, author, publisher, and date. The pattern is consistent for all records within one database.	Search engines retrieve documents from sites all over the Internet. No uniform set of standards is followed when loading documents to websites. You must organize search results for consistent appearance.
Continuity/ Timeliness	Updates are loaded on a regular schedule, which is published. Subscribers are given notice if a database is going to be removed or is not being updated.	Websites come and go without notice. Sites frequently include the date the site was last updated, but this may apply to design, and not necessarily to content.
Objectivity	Most documents come from named sources. You can consider the source when you read a document or article. Commercial vendors do not usually have a political or social agenda.	Not all documents are attributed. You may not easily realize that the site belongs to someone with a particular bias.
Accountability	The online vendor is accountable for the material retrieved using their service. You will not be provided objectionable material by accident.	You may innocently link from an innocuous site to something that offends you or which you would not consider appropriate for certain audiences.
Navigation Between Files	Search across multiple files simultaneously or use "in and out" approach to move between databases.	Fast hotlink access to related topics or other sites of interest.

To make your intelligence decisions about online sources easier, ask yourself these questions when making choices:

1. Is there a "free" source that contains the same documents available from a fee-based source?

Many publishers have now made current issues of their newspapers, magazines, or journals available on their websites at no cost. Some publishers have even loaded searchable archives.

Suppose that your company is planning to add to its Board of Directors. Perhaps the time has come to include someone who happens to be female among the candidates. You need to identify some qualified female candidates. You could, of course, search a large file like the Dow Jones Publications Library, or one of the business publications on Dialog or LexisNexis. You would decide on appropriate search terms, and receive a list of articles. By scanning the titles, you might zero-in on one or more documents that you wished to purchase in full text.

You might, of course, have been told or remember that business magazines often publish lists whose names begin with words like The Top 100…. By checking the Fortune website, you would find references to a list ranking The 50 Most Powerful Women. You might even have located that information because you looked at the *Bookmarks & Favorites Section* in Part IV. When you hotlink to the right document, you may print it for free. This is the type of question that is handled well using free sites on the Internet, provided the site is one that you trust.

2. Can I trust that the free source will continue to be available at no charge?

With major publications like *Forbes*, *Fortune*, etc., you can probably assume that current material will be available free. It is part of the publisher's marketing plan to allow such access to recent issues in hopes that you will become a subscriber or patronize their advertisers.

Certain other internet sites that provide free reports, company profiles, or other material today, may announce next week that you must pay for the material that was formerly free. In these cases, the "introductory" period is over, even though the "introductory" part was not previously made clear. Other websites provide a brief report at no charge, but the "good stuff" is available only to those with a subscription.

The worst-case scenario here would be that you are under a time constraint, you need to locate some crucial information, and you plan to use that great internet site that you found a couple of weeks ago. Lo and behold, the introductory period is indeed over, you have spent fifteen minutes and have nothing to show for it.

Or you use your favorite internet search engine and locate a reference that sounds promising, but the pieces of data that you need are listed in the "For Members Only" column on the site's homepage. Unless you have your credit card handy or plan to sign up for a subscription, you may have to look elsewhere for the information. Meanwhile, the clock keeps ticking away.

3. Do I need one specific article? Or am I looking for everything that can be found on the subject?

You want to check all possible sources for references to your company. This includes searching many types of materials such as newspapers and magazine articles, scientific or technical sources, trade publications, etc. You need to search widely and deeply in a reasonable amount of time.

This is not the time to rely on your favorite internet search engine and to begin to wade through the 4,929 hits retrieved. For this type of search you need to choose tools that will cover the greatest number of sources, for as far back as you choose to go, or as far as possible.

In this type of search you may not rely on one commercial online service, either. No commercial service has everything. To be as thorough as possible, you need to search across the offerings of several vendors. If you do not have the subscriptions to do this, consider outsourcing the project to an information broker.

Commercial vendors do send out press releases every week, announcing that this or that book, journal, or tool has been added to their service. Sometimes these announcements brag about an "exclusive." Do watch for special features offered by commercial sites.

By considering these questions you can make some decisions about handling choices when it comes to searching in cyberspace instead of in the stacks at the library. In general, you will probably conclude, as many professional searchers have, that it is wise to have a variety of search tools at your disposal, if possible, and to think the question through before turning on the computer.

Trusting Your Sources — If It Matters, Verify and Validate!

If your doctor suggests radical brain surgery for a pain in your foot, you would be wise to seek a second opinion. The same holds true when making business decisions based on something you have read or heard.

Commercial database services are an excellent tool for verifying information because many vendors allow you to quickly search and retrieve articles from a number of sources simultaneously, with provisions for removing unnecessary duplicates. This makes it easier to compare and verify data.

Document the Information Source

Database files usually consist of individual records, each containing discreet fields of data. For each record retrieved in the search result, the source, date, and other important information needed for credibility and accountability are presented up front. Usually the vendor's Customer Support telephone number is easily visible should additional questions arise.

If you were looking for market share data in the PC industry, the sample database record shown below would appear to be a "dream come true." It appeared in Business & Industry, available as File 9 on Dialog, at www.dialog.com. It also could have been retrieved directly from the database producer, which is now Gale Group, at www.gale.com. Note that the article's title, the name of the publication, and the date of the issue containing the article are readily available. Within the article, the table's caption probably identifies the source or sources of the figures presented. You can go to those sources, if desired, to verify that the figures are correct.

```
01758204 (THIS IS THE FULLTEXT)


PC Market Share, By Vendor
( PC market share by vendor is tabulated for 4th qtr-1995
and 4th qtr- 1996; shipments for 4th qtr-1996 are 6.8 mil units, vs 7.7 mil in 4th qtr-1995 )


Information Week , n 620 , p 37
March 03, 1997
Document Type: Journal ISSN: 8750-6874 ( United States )
Language: English Record Type: Fulltext
Word Count: 53


TEXT:
                    4Q 1996     4Q 1995
Compaq                14%         12%
Packard Bell          10%         16%
IBM                   10%          8%
Dell                   7%          5%
Gateway 2000           7%          5%
```

▶▶ The title of the article cited above is indicative of the detailed data available online. This article could be printed immediately in full text without requiring a trip to the library. ◀◀

Use Caution on the Internet

Internet sources vary greatly as to credibility and reliability. If you located the article regarding PC market share on a well-known publisher's website, or found figures on a U.S. government agency site, you might feel comfortable in using them. What if you located them by doing a search using a popular search engine, and the information was found on something called "Joe's Home Page"? Who is Joe? How can you be sure he knows anything about the subject? Would you be comfortable citing Joe as a source if The Boss asks where the data came from?

Remember that quality control is crucial. As mentioned above, there is a bit of a built in comfort factor when using commercial databases, but, if the free source is one that you know and trust, then you may save money. For a deal worth thousands or even millions of dollars to your company, it is possible that both types of sources will be useful.

Chapter 3

Good Online Search Strategies Help Get the Job Done

A successful online search does not just happen. Thinking the project through in advance will help ensure the best possible results. It is important to understand the question or assignment and the type of result required - is what is asked for a few numbers, or statistics, or a detailed report? Once you set your goal, then it is time to think about the search.

Remember these two keys to successful searching:

- Careful Preparation is Crucial;
- Your Strategy Depends Upon the Question At Hand

Careful Preparation Is Crucial

The purpose of the needed information defines the search. The approach to finding answers will differ, therefore, depending upon the requestor's type of work and how they intend to use the information. If you do your own research, or work with the person making the request, you are probably familiar with the subject matter, relevant publications in the field, and the names of key players in your industry.

If you are doing online research for someone else, ask the person making the request for any additional background information, titles of important publications on the topic, and what exactly will satisfy their need. This information will be useful in determining how and where to search. You would waste your time and money to gather reams of statistics and dozens of articles if what was needed could be found in a recent issue of a trade publication that the requestor could have mentioned.

If you are the requestor, you can improve the quality and turnaround time for a request by providing accurate information and possibly briefing the searcher on what you *really* need, or how the data will be used. Remember: good preparation before going online will save your company time and money during the search process.

Strategy Depends Upon the Question At Hand

One factor in deciding whether to search free or fee-based services is the desired outcome. If you are attempting to answer a question of fact, the answer may be readily available from a particular source or type of source. The various types of sources are covered in more detail later in this book.

Having zeroed-in on the type of source to search, the next step is to find that source online on one of the commercial services or in free sources such as government files and internet sites. Here are some examples of the types of projects:

1. The Compilation Project –
"Get Me A List of Companies That..."

List building questions often require using one or more directories in electronic format. Many of these directories are industry specific, but others may cover a wide range of businesses or industries. As discussed earlier, timeliness and comprehensiveness of the directory data included in your search result is crucial since companies come and go, change addresses, add or drop product lines, etc.

Suppose that you need to create a list of manufacturers of PVC pipe within a particular geographic area. You are looking for basic information - company name, address, and contact information. One of the first places searchers go is to the Thomas Register of American Manufacturers. The Thomas Register website, www.thomasregister.com, is a good source for this type of information because it allows searching by company name, product/service, and brand name. The database is user-friendly and will let you search on common product names such as PVC without knowing that the full name for PVC is polyvinyl chloride. Searching on "PVC pipe" retrieves a number of hits, as seen in the following screen capture:

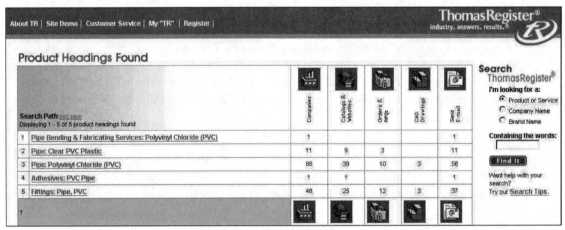

▶▶ The Thomas Register of American Manufacturers website identifies products and services offered by listed companies, which saves the searcher both time and effort. ◀◀

By clicking on one of the five product headings, you can access a hotlinked list of company names and addresses. Another click, and a company record is displayed, providing you with an individual company name, address, and possibly a description of their business activity.

Remember that the print or CD versions of Thomas Register will likely contain more companies that meet your search criteria than will the internet database. As a crosscheck, try searching a file like *Duns Market Identifiers* (Dialog File 516), using an SIC or NAICS code to identify companies that provide a given product or service.

Is Your Mission Accomplished?

At this point you can print a group of company records. But is this a list or a pile of printouts? Using free sources on the Internet, you may first find a site with a series of hotlinks, then you must click on each hotlink and display or print records one at a time. You might print out a pile of individual company descriptions, or create a list by cutting and pasting information into a list in a word processing program.

By contrast, performing this search in a commercial database would usually provide an answer in the form of a number indicating how many companies in the database contain your search terms, perhaps expressed as "(PVC or polyvinyl chloride) and pipe)". If the number of results is too high, you could narrow the search results using other criteria such as geography or annual sales. In some commercial databases, a smaller number of hits will reduce the expense. While any search in a commercial database will cost money, you can refine the search result in advance, and can print out a list of possible companies, including all or part of each record retrieved. Plus, you can sort the list in a number of ways.

2. The Survey Project – "Get Me An Overview of XYZ"

Suppose you want to determine some of the trends in an industry over the past several years. This may mean you want an overview — something general, like a survey article in a trade publication. Either commercial or internet sources may work well for this type of question.

Check the Publisher's Website

If you are relatively certain that a particular magazine is likely to have covered the subject matter, you might go directly to the Internet to locate the information you need, free of charge. Lots of magazines or newspapers are available to you online even if you do not subscribe to their print version. Even for publications that are not free, print subscribers may receive a price break if the website requires a subscription.

Popular business publications such as *BusinessWeek*, *Forbes*, *Fortune* and many others have built sizeable websites that often include links to other useful information sources. Internet addresses for business publications and other important business information sources can be found in *Bookmarks and Favorites Section* of Part IV. Also, a search engine may allow you to access recent issues or search an archive by entering keywords, and to quickly locate one or more articles on your topic. The *Forbes* website, at www.forbes.com, shown below, is a good example:

▸▸ Business publications such as Forbes have created websites that include a variety of useful financial or research tools in addition to articles from their current or recent issues. ◂◂

To quickly locate business publications by industry or by topic, try the Michigan Electronic Library website at http://mel.org/viewtopic.jsp. Choose the Business, Economics & Labor link, and then click on News. This is an excellent site that contains hotlinks to take you directly to the website of the titles listed. Web addresses sometimes change. A site like the Michigan Electronic Library is generally kept up-to-date, so it may be more reliable than bookmarks that you saved weeks or months ago.

Download Articles from Commercial Online Services

To determine where a magazine or journal is available in either commercial online services or on the World Wide Web, you might also consult Information Today Inc.'s *Fulltext Sources Online*, found at http://books.infotoday.com/directories.shtml. *FSO* provides commercial database locations or web addresses for periodicals, newspapers, newswires, newsletters, and TV/radio transcripts. Special codes indicate publications where a fee is charged for online access to back issues and also where no archives are available.

A list of publications considered essential reading for those who keep up with online information sources is found in Appendix E of Part IV. These publications typically contain carefully researched reviews of important database files and websites, news about developments in the field, research tips and hints for searching specific topics, and more.

Look For A Trade Association Site

Trade Associations exist for most major industries or professions. These organizations were quick to grasp the advantages inherent in an internet site that could promote the industry or profession represented, and their online offerings have grown exponentially in recent years. Now, online, you will find a plethora of references to trade publications, articles, graphics, statistics, news, and other material related to the group represented. Speeches included on the site point to key players in the industry or profession. Many such sites will include relevant laws and regulations. Of course, issues and initiatives important to the field will be well covered here. Hotlinks may point to the websites of key members of the association.

3. The More Complex Project – "We Need Some Facts and Figures..."

An example of this type of question might be something like:

"What is Company X's share of the widget market, and what were last years sales figures for their new electronic widget?"

Another variation on this theme might sound like this:

"We're considering the manufacture of electronic widgets to our product line, possibly expanding into new markets. We need to know who else manufactures these products, whether they market them in California, or Croatia, or China, and what the size of the world market for electronic widgets is now and will be in five years. By the way, we'll need to investigate patents and trademarks regarding electronic widgets. Oh, and find out if we have any trade restrictions or regulatory matters to consider."

To answer this type of request, you need facts and figures. The results will most certainly impact an important decision that could determine the company's future.

Although some useful information may be found in trade publications, there are also other types of sources that could be treasure troves of intelligence, containing the data that you need, or providing clues to that illusive data's whereabouts. Here, briefly, are some possibilities that will be expanded upon later.

Statistical Data Compiled by Government Agencies

Government files containing reams of statistical data, spanning hundreds of subjects, are available from agencies such as the U.S. Census Bureau, the U.S. Bureau of Labor Statistics, and the U.S. Department of Commerce, among others. These sources will supply the demographic data needed to determine whether there is a market for our sample product – electronic widgets – and the size of that market. If you contemplate actually manufacturing those electronic widgets in a new area, you will be concerned with labor-related matters such as wage rates, availability of skilled labor, etc. Some of this government data can be downloaded and imported into spreadsheets or other software for additional massaging or analysis later.

Laws, Regulations, and Intellectual Property

Doing business in new markets means that the company may be subject to the laws and regulations promulgated by individual states or provinces, or to entire legal codes for foreign countries. Much of this data is now available on the Internet at little or no cost. It is important, of course, to check for recent updates to any law or regulation, as your lawyer or company Legal Department will attest. Several university websites offer both U.S. and non-U.S. laws in searchable electronic format. See "Legal Information" in the *Bookmarks & Favorites Section* of Part IV. Increasing availability of laws and regulations in electronic format does not mean that we should all begin doing our own legal work. *Always* consult your attorney when making important business decisions involving the law, especially when it comes to *interpretions*.

Ownership of intellectual property such as patents, copyrights, or trademarks also must be considered before developing new products or moving into new markets.

Public Records Information

A variety of public records may be used when researching new products or markets. You must decide the name under which to do business in the new jurisdiction, and may find that your first choice is in use, or reserved by a competitor. You may wish to research real estate records, particularly if considering buying property in the proposed new market area. This also will help identify competitors' real property. It may be important to identify the officers and directors of a company or to determine parent-subsidiary information. You may wish to read a company's bylaws or to investigate its corporate filings. Ultimately, your Human Resources Department may use public records if hiring is undertaken and background checks are required.

Do Not Forget The Scientists and Engineers

Competitive intelligence includes much more than searching business databases. As a matter of fact, scientists and engineers were the earliest users of computers for their work, and identifying them by searching online is relatively easy. Business applications came years later. As the use of computers became more common, technology improved and search interfaces became more "user friendly."

Science and technology still rely heavily on computerized databases. STN, that cyberspace bastion of scientific knowledge, is found on the Web at http://info.cas.org/stn.html. STN also offers *STN Easy* through their site, allowing an easy interface for accessing what could otherwise be rather complex material. Access is also available by direct dial-up.

Other scientific or patent database services like Questel-Orbit, www.questel.orbit.com, or Thomson Scientific, now including both the Derwent material, at http://thomsonderwent.com, and the Delphion database at www.delphion.com, also are found on the Web. True web access is still a thing of the future for Questel-Orbit subscribers, but its subscription based QPAT service, www.qpat.com, allows you to search the full text of all U.S. patents issued since 1974 and to retrieve 100%-secure images. MicroPatent, shown below, is another popular source among patents and trademarks websites.

The ability to download from the Internet intellectual property documents and drawings from around the world has been a boon to the science and technology communities.

Scientists and engineers often need specifications and standards, patents, and similar information that can now be located quickly and easily in electronic format. Examining specifications and standards early in the product development process may result in good choices that reduce or eliminate potential problems later. Examining existing patents could result in a decision to license technology rather than invest in research and development. In our sample, these types of decisions may have a dramatic impact on whether the company develops those electronic widgets *and* on whether they compete successfully with other products on the market.

Online services or websites intended for general use may be less comprehensive than the vendor's "professional" collection. In-depth online searches on scientific and technological subjects should be undertaken only by experienced searchers – those familiar with the subject matter and the best electronic sources for the material.

Scientists may also be interested in what is in the pipeline. This is when the Internet becomes a crucial and valuable tool that may yield material not readily obtained through commercial sources. However, as discussed previously, it is important to be sure that what you find can be trusted.

TIP - Each search strategy will be different, just as each request is. You may wish to create your own database, or list, of search strategies, keeping track of how well each worked, the time involved, and other important details - how you constructed the search, the questions and people involved. Use this stored information when constructing search strategies for new CI tasks.

Chapter 4

Begin At the Beginning

Test Driving Your CI Vehicle

Who Is Your Competition?

Having defined competitive intelligence and identified information sources available in electronic format, it is time to begin the task of gathering business intelligence, and we will start by knowing the competition. This is one of the keys to competing successfully in business, and it is not always as easy as some people might think.

How can you identify the competition and retain or increase your company's market share? Begin by creating a realistic list of competitors. Suppose that there are five major manufacturers of remote-controlled electronic gizmos in the country and your company is one. Your company's competitors are the other four companies on the list. Right?

Not necessarily! You may think that you know your competitors, but with some online sleuthing, you may find that your list of companies gets longer. New companies may be entering the industry, or other companies venturing into new markets - markets you thought your company had "sewed up." Perhaps that new competition is introducing new products that will make your company's gizmo as obsolete as buggy whips.

Competitors usually fall into three categories: **Direct Competitors, Indirect Competitors**, and **Potential Competitors.**

Direct Competitors

Identifying a company as a direct competitor depends upon how you describe what that company does. Are their products or services the same as your company's? Are you competing in the same marketplace, either by geography or type of customer? Generally your company's direct competitors are those who sell the same products or services that you sell, to the same customers, in the same geographic area.

Indirect Competitors

Identifying indirect competitors takes a bit more thought. Those companies may offer products or services that are quite different from your own, but which can be used for the same purpose. If customers buy their goods instead of yours, your company loses sales revenue. For example, their hair-removal cream competes with your electric shavers.

Potential Competitors

A third group to consider is potential competitors - companies that could become direct competitors - other companies who may consider entering the same business arena as yours. The rumor mill may provide a tip-off in this situation. As consumer trends change, you may need to identify different companies as potential competitors. Could their products grab market share while yours become endangered species?

To make the picture even more complex, you may determine that a company in another country, with much lower labor costs, has become a direct or indirect competitor. Your competition may be over the border or on another continent, so be sure to think globally when deciding where to search for competitors.

As important as identifying them is weighing, evaluating, and then analyzing what is found about these organizations. Some of the answers may be found close to home...

Practice Good Defense, CI Style

Once we begin our research, questions arise: Are we finding information that helps us deduce their plans or strategies? Should we believe what we read about that company? Have we searched in the right places? Have we found everything? Did we ask the right questions?

One good way to answer these questions is to research your own company first, going online and using your company's name, key personnel, trade names, or products as search terms.

This helps you to:

- Identify sources for researching your competitors. Search broadly and deeply, and see where information on your company is found - trade publications, marketing materials, newspaper business sections, government sites. It is likely that the competition will be mentioned here as well.

- Determine what the competition knows about your company.

Practice - Validate the credibility of online sources by asking in-house personnel to verify the information found on your own company.

How can you be sure that you have found everything? You cannot be sure. By thinking creatively and correctly using online tools, you will find most of what is available. You may be surprised at what others can learn about your company.

Here are some tips to use when performing defensive CI using online sources:

Can You Trust the Author?

Consider who is responsible for each online article or document about your company. Did someone who specializes in your industry write the article? Look at several of this person's articles to get a feel for whether the writer's work seems fair and unbiased, whether it appears to be well researched and whether the author appears to have access to credible sources. You may discount articles written by this person based on how he or she measured up when you read about your own organization. You may, on the other hand, decide that the writer is generally credible, and use articles by the writer as sources of information about your competition. The next time you search for information on a competitor, take your conclusions about this source into consideration.

The Trap of Thinking Too Narrowly

Is your company frequently mentioned in certain publications outside your industry? It is possible that something triggers an article or reference within the trade press of another industry. If you produce raw material used in that industry or, if you purchase that industry's goods and services, your company may be discussed in that industry's trade publications. Service industries often mention their clients as part of their marketing effort, so you should consider whether companies that think of you as a client have bragged about it.

Let us call your company MegaCorp. MegaCorp is mentioned in a public relations/advertising trade journal. It is easy to envision headlines like:

GAB Wins MegaCorp Account

Any reference like this about your company indicates that there may be similar references to your competition in the advertising and public relations press as well. There may be a discussion of the new direction your competition plans to take in its advertising and marketing program. An excellent source is the *Advertising Age* website at www.adage.com, which has a searchable archive back to 1995. You must register, but there is no charge for searching or for viewing the results.

A warning, however: you are informed that the print and online versions of the periodical are not the same. Only a few stories from the print publication are put online each week, and that most of the daily news appearing on the AdAge.com website is original reporting that has not appeared in the print edition. It would be wise to read the detailed explanations provided on the website to clearly understand what is and is not available. A master search page is available for those who wish to use Ad Age Pay Points to purchase articles. To access the entire contents of *Advertising Age* in searchable electronic format, we are referred to NEXIS at www.nexis.com, or to Factiva at www.factiva.com.

In addition to learning who has won an account, you also can gain some interesting insights into what is happening internally within a competitor's organization by searching these files. As an example, by searching on the name of one of the players in a major corporate merger several years back, it is possible to discern what may have been happening in-house regarding their advertising accounts:

» In June of 2000 we learn that ABC Advertising of New York City has won the mega-bucks global marketing account for certain products of merged US-THEM Corp., formerly US Corp. and THEM Corp. ABC had previously had the THEM account, and had been in hot competition with XYZ Advertising's office in another part of the country for this huge piece of worldwide business. XYZ is given a small piece of business involving another product line.

> » Fast-forward six months. Now we learn that PQR Advertising, a non-incumbent based in Europe, has won that megabucks account for the merged company, which has consolidated marketing efforts for both product lines mentioned above. The consolidated account is now up for grabs.

> > » Two years later, however, XYZ is back in the picture as US-THEM Corp. awards them a huge global account. Included in the review but not the winner was, who else? – PQR!

Advertising Age attaches a QwikFIND code I.D. to each story found on its website. We can search the site's QwikFIND database using the code attached to the story of the PQR award win and retrieve additional related stories that have appeared *only* on the internet site.

The *Advertising Age* website also takes advantage of new technologies that have become available since this book's first edition was published. In their *TV Spots of the Week* segment, you can watch the video of highlighted television ads, playable online as Microsoft Media Player files. The agency doing the work is identified, so you can evaluate the work of various agencies. An analysis of this material may tell a savvy employee of an US-THEM competitor that there has been some internal jockeying for position within the marketing department of the merged company. Of course it may mean simply that US-THEM was not happy with ABC's work. It also provides a list of PQR's wins and losses in the advertising account wars during the past year, describing several wins in the United States and Europe, but also indicating the loss of a major account in America – that of another major corporation involved in a merger with a key player in its industry.

Jack O'Dwyer's Newsletter or *O'Dwyer's PR Services Report*, both available on LexisNexis, are also good places to undertake this type of searching. The O'Dwyer website, at www.odwyerpr.com, provides for interesting searching if you are willing to purchase. A one-week subscription is available at minimal cost, but if an ongoing subscription is what you need, it is also available.

Let us say, at O'Dwyer's, you pick up another kernel of intelligence – the name of a company's PR counsel. These are the people called in for assistance when a company does not have the skill set or possibly the staffing to handle situations like these:

- Crisis management – a product recall, for example

- The launch of a new campaign or product

- Handling a project somewhere in the world where a public relations effort might help further the company's business objectives

A search of the current online version of *O'Dwyer's Directory of Corporate Communications* provides the names of a number of company employees – more business intelligence that could be useful. An online search for *Home Depot*, one of the more than 6000 database records, including all 2800 companies listed on the New York Stock Exchange, yields the following:

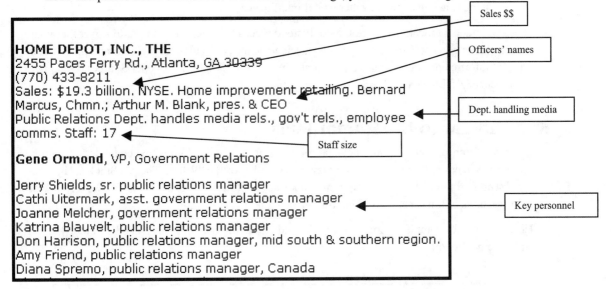

HOME DEPOT, INC., THE
2455 Paces Ferry Rd., Atlanta, GA 30339
(770) 433-8211
Sales: $19.3 billion. NYSE. Home improvement retailing. Bernard Marcus, Chmn.; Arthur M. Blank, pres. & CEO
Public Relations Dept. handles media rels., gov't rels., employee comms. Staff: 17

Gene Ormond, VP, Government Relations

Jerry Shields, sr. public relations manager
Cathi Uitermark, asst. government relations manager
Joanne Melcher, government relations manager
Katrina Blauvelt, public relations manager
Don Harrison, public relations manager, mid south & southern region.
Amy Friend, public relations manager
Diana Spremo, public relations manager, Canada

Labels: Sales $$ · Officers' names · Dept. handling media · Staff size · Key personnel

Alternatively, you could search O'Dwyer's by one of 39 industry categories from Advertising to Utilities. For example, the database shows 159 such records for the Food Processing industry. What an easy way to find direct contacts - by surveying people in corporate public relations across an entire industry.

Even though you may think of a website as limited, a little examination shows that it can be a source of a great deal more valuable data, including some often-elusive facts on privately held companies.

An additional database at the O'Dwyer's site lists "Worldwide Fees Of Independent Firms With Major U.S. Operations." Here the number of employees and percent of revenue change from the previous year are included in tabular form. This is useful, but it is the hotlinks to the lengthy directory entries for each company that provide a wealth of detail, including corporate philosophy, areas of specialization or expertise, details on all branches, and lengthy client lists.

The name of the advertising agency that represents a particular company is an isolated fact that may not seem significant to you, but it may mean a great deal to the folks in your company's marketing or public relations departments who are familiar with the agencies and can possibly predict the direction that a competitor's advertising is likely to take based on the track record of the agency concerned.

Search Using News and Trade Publications

Even if you are not "mega" in size, check the advertising industry publications both online and off for columns that might contain valuable news. If you are located in or near a large city, watch major newspapers for weekly columns covering the local public relations/advertising scene. In this way, you may pick up information regarding which agencies work for what companies in your geographic region, changes in personnel, or other useful intelligence.

News and trade publications are not the only good places to search. You might discover that your company is cited in conference proceedings, scientific or technical reports. These and many other types of information sources that are discussed in detail in Chapter 7 - Deeper Sources – Finding Intelligence Off The beaten Track.

Keep an Ear to the Rumor Mills

Did any references appear in internet chat rooms or print media columns that contained words like "rumor"? We have all seen these. You may be a member of the "Where There's Smoke, There's Fire" school of thought, or you simply may not trust such rumors. A rumor may, however, be worth a few seconds of time spent searching for verification or corroboration.

Here is a classic example where the rumor started on the Internet and was picked up in the press. It is an "oldie but goodie"

KRTBN KNIGHT-RIDDER TRIBUNE BUSINESS NEWS (DALLAS MORNING NEWS)

August 03, 1998   16:46

JOURNAL CODE: KDMN LANGUAGE: English RECORD TYPE: FULLTEXT

WORD COUNT: 1414

   Aug. 3 - More than six weeks before Texas Instruments Inc. announced plans to sell its memory chip operations, rumors about a potential deal were buzzing on the *Yahoo! Finance* message board on the Internet.

   One late-night entry on May 4, from an anonymous participant who said he is "a manager for TI," reported that the Dallas-based company would be "very interested" in selling its Richardson memory plant to Micron Technology Inc., if the Idaho chipmaker could swing the financing.

   Another contributor to the site, identified only as a 36-year-old man

---

In the story referenced above, the rumors turned out to be true. The story was found using the Dialog commercial online service.

If you do not have time to watch the internet message boards like Yahoo! Finance and Motley Fool yourself, consider using an internet monitoring service such as eWatch at www.ewatch.com, a service offered by PR Newswire, a reputable player in the electronic information world. The eWatch website sums up the value in this activity: "In today's fast-paced business world, the buzz starts on the Internet. Information (or worse yet, misinformation) can spread at breakneck speed through cyberspace. Rumors and hoaxes are ubiquitous, companies and products are lambasted, often resulting in loss of a company's reputation or serious financial damage." See Chapter 13 for discussion of similar monitoring service products.

Check What Is Coming Out of the Horse's Mouth

Broadcast transcripts are now searchable on several major online services, including Dialog and LexisNexis. Search these for transcripts of interviews given by CEO's or other members of senior management. These people are well prepared for such interviews, so they are likely to quote numbers and other useful facts. Depending upon the interviewer's questions, you might pick up such useful tidbits as production figures, the company's focus for the next five years, comments on where the industry is going, or similar statements.

If you do not subscribe to the services mentioned above, consider checking eLibrary at www.eLibrary.com. This site is also subscription based, but the cost is relatively low and a free trial is available. The eLibrary maintains licensing agreements with a number of publishers of newspapers, magazines, transcripts, pictures, maps, and books. Transcripts can be ordered here for a long list of network shows.

The TV News Archive at Vanderbilt University, at http://tvnews.vanderbilt.edu, offers a database of more than 30,000 news broadcasts from 1968 to the present. Searching on a company will retrieve both commercials and news stories regarding your target. Tapes of entire broadcasts or compilation tapes of individual news stories specified by the borrower are available for a fee. Searching is free, but registration is required. A search here could tell when and where a company employed television advertising during a particular period, and if, when, and how they made news. You may also receive some interesting insights into contrasting coverage of a story over several electronic media sources.

For starters, use these sources to create a CI folder on your company, then check these sources for CI on competitors. By searching the media, you will learn the names of the VIPs and those who act as company spokespersons - search using words or phrases like "mega corp and interview." The results may help you fill in some of the blanks in the information you are gathering about that company, or validate information gathered from other sources.

The example below shows search results using the keywords "bill gates and interview."

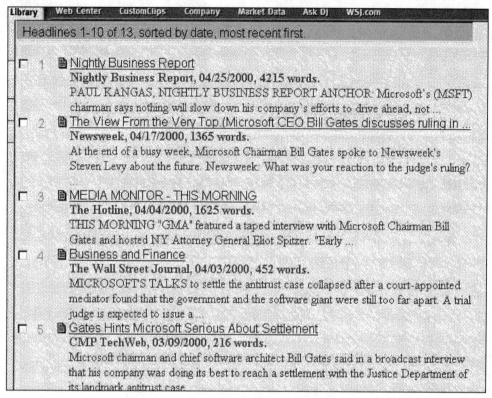

> ▶▶ The search shown above from Dow Jones Interactive, returned 13 hits, all of which included the phrase "Bill Gates" within 5 words of "interview" in the headline or lead paragraph. Search results were limited to the current year, and were sorted to show the most recent article first. Longer time periods or different types of sorts are also possible. ◀◀

Did Your Sources Miss Anything?

Call the person who handles public relations for your company to determine what interviews company VIPs have given, to which media outlets. Search online for these. If your search does not turn up these transcripts, then you may wish to re-think and widen your search strategy.

Loose Lips Sink Ships

Perhaps management is considering closing a certain domestic plant and moving the operation to another location outside the country. They have a team preparing a "top secret" study on the subject. Suppose that your online search turns up a message on the Internet, or one of the "rumor columns" in a trade publication, mentioning that such a study is underway, or that the company is planning to close the plant. Company insiders generally know what would be, and has been, officially released. There may have been a slip-up or leak. If you do find something along these lines, consider monitoring the same source for news on competitors. After all, your competitors make mistakes too.

Taking the Next Step Toward Effective CI

After searching exhaustively for your company, analyze the information you have found and note the places where you found it. Create a checklist for future use, including the following categories of sources to search. Within each category, note individual services or types of sources.

As an example, suppose your company is in the apparel industry. The checklist might include the following among sources mentioning your company:

General Publications and Mass Media
The New York Times (center of US fashion/apparel industry)
Other national/international newspapers that cover business news – especially those from places where you import fabric, for example, or places where you outsource work.

Various directories that cover the apparel industry

Local newspapers wherever there is an apparel-related plant

Industry trade publications
Apparel Industry Magazine
Bobbin
Women's Wear Daily

Business oriented mass-market publications
The Wall Street Journal
Business Week, Forbes, Fortune
Businessworld (Philippines) (Perhaps you have factories there.)
Indonesian Commercial Newsletter (If you do business there.)

Trade publications for related industries that referenced "your" industry
Discount Store News
Fibre Organon
Footwear News
Textile World

Names and contact information for useful individuals or organizations

Government agencies that regulate the industry

Other categories or sources where you expected your company to be mentioned …
but they were not.

Each item on this checklist should not be overlooked as potential information sources. Check them periodically – set a schedule – or select one or more as a last resort when all else fails.

The processes discussed in this chapter should get you thinking more creatively about other places to look for information on your competitors. However, we have just seen the "tip of the iceberg." We will see more of the "iceberg" in the following chapters.

Part II

Choosing and Using Online Sources for Gathering CI Data

Chapter 5

The Key to Choosing Online Sources - Ask the Right Questions!

All Online Sources Are Not Created Equal

Searching for competitive information, whether in relation to companies or industries, is serious business. Missing an opportunity or making a bad decision can cost your company millions of dollars, or worse!

Whether considering subscribing to a commercial online service or treasure hunting on the World Wide Web, it is best to be an informed shopper. You cannot assume that a given source has all available information on the subject, is accurate and timely, or that there is not a better source available. There might even be an alternate source that offers more at a lower cost. If your intranet offers links to online databases or selected sites, keep in mind that those are not the only choices out there, though the boss might prefer that you try intranet sources first.

In the commercial online environment, when you are selecting a service, remember that sales representatives are naturally going to present their product in a favorable light — that is their job. Your job, as a consumer, is to make informed buying decisions.

When it comes to searching the Internet, your task becomes more complex. With the exception of commercial vendor sites, there is no salesperson trying to convince you to choose this site or that site. Word of mouth, magazine articles, swapping bookmarks, or following links on other websites tend to be the common ways to identify useful or interesting internet material. The problem is that more and more internet material is *not* free. In addition, there is not always a responsible party to contact if questions arise regarding the information on a site; on a commercial service, there is usually someone available to answer questions.

Whether paying to use a source or searching a source for free, it is crucial to know *beforehand* what to expect from that source, otherwise you may waste time and money or, worse yet, get bad data that leads to the wrong business decision.

Choosing the Online Services Closest to Your Needs

The time to sign up for commercial online services is *not* when you are under a deadline or when others are waiting for results. Examine your company's needs before visiting websites or telephoning online services for information about their products. The few minutes spent organizing your priorities and needs will be well invested as you proceed. Start out by answering the broad questions over the next two pages, then move on to the more specific items in the Twelve Guidelines For Evaluating Online Sources.

Are your company's online information needs varied or focused?

Will online resources be used to search for many types of information or for only a few?

When considering subscribing to commercial online services, you will find that there are both "boutiques" and "supermarkets" available. If there is a single department or a small group of key personnel making CI requests, it may be possible to zero in on an information boutique that covers the appropriate subject matter, perhaps outputting the data in the desired format.

Specialized Subscription-based Online Services

The table below includes a representative group of specialized subscription-based online services. Although they may offer some general files, the majority of their offerings are in the subject areas listed. Some of the databases found on these services may be licensed to other vendors and may be available from other sources on the Web. Further details about these services and many others may be obtained by contacting the vendors, using the information provided in the Vendors List in Part IV of this book, or by using URLs provided in various chapters or in the *Bookmarks & Favorites* Section.

Boutiques-

Subject Matter	Vendor Name
Credit/Company Information	Dun & Bradstreet Experian
Financial / Securities	Factiva Investext Multex
Legal	Lexis Westlaw
Market Research	Profound Markintel

Medical	Ovid
Patents/Trademarks	Derwent Questel-Orbit
Public Records	ChoicePoint Lexis Public Records Merlin Information Services

If you are not the only searcher, or if several different departments will use online services for research, a supermarket may be the best choice. The list below includes some of the commercial online vendors whose services cover a variety of subject matter.

Supermarkets-

Description	Vendor Name
Business Subjects	Factiva
Multiple Subject Areas	DataStar Dialog Nexis SkyMinder
Science/Technology Subjects	STN Internet Database Service (IDS)

For those occasions when you need additional sources, services from these lists of these could be supplemented with pay-as-you-go services or subscriptions to services available on the Internet.

More Broad Questions...

Who will use the data?

The sales team needs different types of material than the research and development department. Consider whether your company users are rocket scientists or someone who generally requires a fast overview on a topic that may come up in a meeting with a client. In some cases a company-wide subscription to a major database vendor's service may meet the needs of many different departments, while other users may require very specialized database sources. Essentially, the online source chosen should complement the end users, i.e.: those who will ultimately use the information to make decisions.

How frequently will you or others in the company search?

You should consider whether the service would be used frequently enough to justify the expense of set-up and/or subscription fees. If the source that meets your needs is high-priced and your need for it would only be occasional, you may want to consider a cheaper alternative such as hiring an independent researcher also known as an information broker. To locate an independent information researcher, search the *Burwell World Directory of Information Brokers*.

Is online access really the best choice for your needs?

Searching the Internet can be time consuming. With some online services, per-minute communication charges are incurred. If receiving only monthly or quarterly updates is not a concern, you might wish to consider subscribing to certain databases in CD-ROM format. This will alleviate worries that the clock is ticking and costs are mounting.

12 Guidelines for Evaluating Online Sources

1. Examine the type of subject matter offered — you cannot find what isn't there!

It is important to learn what subject matter is offered by a service before committing to a subscription. Some online services contain large numbers of databases covering a wide range of disciplines.

Dialog at www.dialogweb.com, one of the services used frequently by librarians and professional searchers, is good example. More than 1200 databases are found on this service, which includes its European sister company Datastar and Profound, the market intelligence service. Databases are grouped into topics such as Biotech, Chemical, Engineering, Marketing, World News, Business Intelligence, Energy, Intellectual Property, and Pharmaceuticals.

In addition, the Dialog service provides the full text of articles from many newspapers and an extensive group of market research reports on dozens of different products and services discussed further in Chapter 7. Call this type of service an "information supermarket" since it is geared toward a wide variety of users whose searches require access to a wide range of subject matter. Thus, if the needs of your company vary, Dialog or a similar service would most likely meet your needs.

By contrast, Factiva, at www.factiva.com, is more business oriented. News, stock quotes and other company/industry financial data are the core of the material offered, with a large library of online publications available as well. Factiva offers what is described as "an intelligent collection consisting of high-quality business and news sites" that have been reviewed by Dow Jones staffers. The combination of the Dow Jones Interactive files with those of Reuters Business Briefing serves to broaden the scope of material available to former DJI subscribers. If a company's searching needs focus on business-related data, Factiva is a good choice.

Some services, such as LexisNexis are appropriate for both focused and varied needs. LexisNexis is available on the Web at www.lexisnexis.com. These services are offered as separate components (Lexis or Nexis) and as a package. The Lexis portion is focused on the legal market, covering extensive case law, statutes, regulations, and other legal matters. The Nexis part of the product contains news and financial, medical, and other general sources.

2. Know the age and amount of the available information...

...and decide whether the database will work for your most frequent search questions. Does the database file contain recent information only or is historic data included? What is the time period covered? Does the publisher offer a searchable archive online? Be aware of any lag time that exists for databases that will be important in your research. The publisher may restrict publication of the most recent data for a fixed period of time in order to preserve its sale of print products. Remember the Thomas Register example mentioned in Chapter 2, and know whether you are searching a partial database or the entire offering of a given vendor.

3. Determine frequency of updates or reloads

If all you need is a little bit of information on the trends in the mousetrap industry, perhaps an article published three months ago will be sufficient to give you an overview of what is happening in that sector of commerce. If you *must* have the most current information possible on what analysts are saying about a competitor's company, then last month's newspaper would not suffice.

The same applies to online data. The frequency of update varies with type of, availability of, and demand for the information as well as other factors. Certain sources are updated annually, while others --like newswires and stock market quotes -- are available in real time or with only very brief time lags. A vendor may offer databases licensed from a number of sources, so do not assume that all files on that vendor's site are updated with the same frequency.

It is possible that the same database is available on multiple online services, with different lag times, and different update or reload schedules. If very timely data is crucial to your choice of vendor or file, it is a good idea to call each database vendor to determine current availability and make your search decision based on what you have learned. The list of vendor contact information in the Resource List Section of Part IV will prove helpful for doing this.

Check those web page update claims. Database documentation usually indicates how often the file is updated. Many commercial vendors provide update messages on the search screen before you perform a search. Sometimes those "site last updated on…" messages are not specific enough to tell you *what* was updated. It could have been the entire database, a portion of its content or even the background color of the homepage. If you cannot determine when the database was last updated, a telephone call to the provider should produce answers.

On the whole, commercial sources tend to be updated more frequently than free sites. Why? Commercial sites have a responsibility to keep things up-to-date to meet the demands of paying customers. Free services are under no such obligation. To determine how frequently and/or regularly updates occur on an internet site, try inquiring by email, or use a commercial source because of the "comfort factor." Regardless of the services you choose, be aware of the update frequency of the databases you use, and choose those that meet your requirements for timeliness.

4. Examine the format of the results

Most people expect to obtain full text documents when retrieving intelligence information from online sources. However, it is important to realize that some older databases contain only abstracts or, worse yet, merely citations that provide title, date, and source of publication. The latter is often true of internet sites that provide citations and offer to email PDF files of the full document. Sometimes additional work is required to obtain the full text of older documents, which are often necessary to establish a historical perspective. If abstracts are available, this may be sufficient for your needs. More is not always better.

If time is not limited, and you have a large library at hand, you can simply take your list of citations to the library, locate back issues of publications containing the cited articles and head for the photocopy machine — keeping the copyright laws in mind, of course.

Whether citations, abstracts, or full text, it is much more effective and efficient to know the database format in advance than to discover at the last minute that the service you are searching does not offer data in the format you require! Even worse is having your boss question why you did not know beforehand how inadequate the source was when you try to explain why he or she must wait a bit longer.

Increasingly, you may encounter websites offering searchable databases full of information such as company profiles, for example. They may provide very basic information at no cost. In exchange, you will probably have to register, providing information that may include your email address and telephone number. The site may indicate that there is additional information available, *for their subscribers*. In this case it is important to look for a link to sample a "full" record before investing in a subscription or providing your credit card information in order to proceed. It is almost like the old joke about buying a used car – if you want wheels and an engine, you will pay extra!

The important thing to remember is that you do not need unplanned surprises or delays when competitive information is concerned. If you know what to expect in a file or online service, you can plan accordingly. Ask yourself these questions: "Will the results be full text, abstracts, citations or a combination thereof?" and "Which will meet my needs?"

5. Consider both prepared and unformatted results

Does it make better business sense to pay money to download prepared (i.e. formatted) documents that are ready to use, or to download raw, unformatted data at no cost from the source with the intention of cleaning it up later?

If the information is for your own use, you may not mind extraneous characters and lack of good formatting. If, however, you need to take copies of a competitor's 10-K report to an important meeting, obtaining a professional-looking report from a commercial vendor such as Public Register's Annual Report Service (PRARS), www.prars.com, may be the best approach. If short on time, seek out one of the sources that will allow downloading of reports and other lengthy documents in PDF format.

A financial professional recently described his online source requirements as follows:

- Companies must be searchable by criteria, such as SIC or NAICS codes.

- Data must be downloadable in tagged format.

Once information has been received, each "tagged" field is imported into a specific cell of a computer spreadsheet. Then, the data is exported from the spreadsheet into ASCII delimited format and loaded into an in-house database.

Essentially, this financial professional downloads information on dozens of companies at a time, and by following the above restrictions, he is able to build a database without re-keying a single word. The whole process takes only a few minutes, and does not require clerical assistance. Without establishing and adhering to these very specific format requirements, a lot more work would be involved, and the possibility of errors increases.

By selecting a database source that offers an adaptable format, this man automates what could be a tedious process. He is free to spend the bulk of his time using his professional expertise, analyzing the data for use in his practice.

6. Determine the geographic coverage of the source

Is the information in the database worldwide in origin or country-specific? It is important to ask this question carefully. Some vendors provide a few sources from only a handful of countries and then claim they offer "worldwide coverage." The increasing availability of English language versions of databases coming from websites based in foreign countries may present some interesting opportunities, if you have the time to locate these sites., but keep in mind that these translated sites, like machine translations offered by some search engines, may miss nuances or seem puzzling.

With some online vendors, geographic coverage is apparent from the name of the service. *Asia Pulse*, for example, is the joint venture of a number of Asia's major news and information providers, all experts in their own countries. *Asia Pulse* covers one hundred industries, from *Accounting* to *Utilities*, plus topics like *Education* and *Leisure*. Specialties on this service include sections called *Business in Asia Today* and *Business Class Travel.*

It is important to determine if the geographic areas of interest to your company are included in the product or service *before you subscribe*. As an example, here is a list of those countries covered by *Asia Pulse:*

Australia	Bangladesh	Cambodia	China, Hong Kong
Vietnam	India	Indonesia	Japan
Kazakhstan	Kyrgyz	Laos	Malaysia
Mongolia	New Zealand	Pakistan	Pacific Islands
Papua New Guinea	Philippines	Singapore	South Korea
Sri Lanka	Taiwan	Thailand	Uzbekistan

7. Ask about languages in which documents are available

While the search results of online services are usually in English, it is important to know whether you can expect to find articles in other languages as well. If you work in a field where major contributions are made in other countries, you or your company may profit from valuable new developments sooner if you can read them in the language in which they were written, rather than waiting for translated versions to be published. Furthermore, translations can be problematic. Various nuances disappear in translation, or errors creep in because of multiple meanings for words. Major commercial online sources such as Dialog, www.dialog.com or DataStar, www.datastarweb.com, offer documents in multiple languages. At the DataStar site even the interface is available in German or Spanish as well as English.

The language issue is very evident on the Internet. One can easily locate foreign websites. Sometimes they even appear in unfamiliar alphabets. Some of these sites are available in multiple languages. If available, English speakers should look for and click on the word `English` on the site to access an English language version. See Chapter 11 for a list of search engines in languages other than English.

The AltaVista search engine at www.altavista.com offers translation for some of the documents retrieved from its system. If the word "Translate" appears in the search results, a simple click will bring up the English language version. However, the feature is not available for *all* non-English material, and you may encounter some unusual results when you read the translation, which is machine-generated.

If you have located text on a website and simply *must* translate it, having absorbed the various warnings about trusting machine translations, the FaganFinder website, at www.faganfinder.com/translate, offers translations to or from 49 languages, not including dialects. If you have some foreign text but do not recognize the language, a handy link at this site offers to identify the language in which the text is written. Further details regarding the languages on the list, plus websites available in that language can be found at www.faganfinder.com/translate/language.php.

One application for this type of tool is to verify information provided from another source. You could possibly determine that facts or prices differ, depending upon whether or not you speak/read the local language where you are doing business. Determining that a vendor gives an advantage to the local populace might open the door to some bargaining.

8. Consider the interface

This is a very straightforward issue. Either a service's interface is complex, requiring experience and/or training, or it is simple and user-friendly.

Some high-powered database products require both training and extensive experience if one is to use them with maximum efficiency. Other services are easily and effectively searched using a simple menu interface. In the easier systems, the searcher often picks a category of information from a list on the screen. Next, the program prompts the user for information and gives an example of how it should be entered. Then the searcher enters something brief like the name of a company or individual, hits the appropriate key and the search is underway.

Interfaces are *always* evolving. Products that were originally offered only via direct dial-up connections are now available via the Web. Vendors recognize that this will help to expand their customer base.

Web interfaces, however, do not allow the same level of search capabilities as those offered by command-mode searching. While newer searchers may resist the need to learn command languages, the graphics, sounds and other forms of multimedia offerings available through the Web can greatly enhance the results that are provided to The Boss or the client. To meet the needs of both long-time hardcore command searchers and those seeking a simpler approach to online searching, Dialog (www.dialog.com) allows either a user-friendly internet interface or its original "command mode" searching at its website. A number of other vendors have phased out older means of access, hoping that the newer offerings will catch on with both groups.

Searching via dial-up mode offers some data manipulation functions not offered by internet search engines. In addition, searchers are not tempted to spend time "surfing." As a result, some vendors continue to offer both internet and dial-up service.

9. Shop for special features

Any feature that saves time and labor usually saves money, either directly or indirectly. What follows are some examples of features to watch for when looking at a vendor's offerings:

Useful Features Checklist

☑ Arrangement of downloaded data in tagged or ASCII delimited format for importing into another software program.

☑ Output available in PDF or similar format where applicable.

☑ Current awareness service (See Chapter 13 for more information).

☑ Interface and/or documents in multiple languages (especially useful for international companies).

☑ The ability to choose to see selected portions of database records, and to be charged less than full price per record.

☑ Sub-account billing, which categorizes your online costs by specified client or department.

☑ The ability to search simultaneously across multiple licensed database sources available on a vendor's website.

☑ The ability to examine the index to a field in a database and to pick entries to be searched.

▸▸ Some of these features are available only in more sophisticated traditional online services like the command mode version of Dialog. If you want the features but do not know how to use the version of the product that offers them, contact the vendor for advanced training, consult with your company's librarian for assistance, or hire an independent research professional who can assist you with the project. ◂◂

10. Consider all pricing options

Some vendors have a reputation for being expensive. This is a relative determination. What one company considers expensive may be considered worth it *at any cost* by another.

Also, acceptable payment methods vary. Some vendors require a credit card while others will invoice subscribers with established credit. Increasingly, vendors are adding secure servers to alleviate concerns about the misuse of credit cards on websites.

Several pricing options exist in today's market:

Subscriptions: Payment of a monthly or annual fee provides you with a password. Depending on the vendor, the subscription rate may include free access up to the equivalent of a certain dollar amount, at which point additional usage is billed at the published rates. A variation on this approach involves a subscription fee plus per-document costs.

Usage-Based Pricing: A flat monthly rate is agreed upon based on your company's previous or projected usage. This rate is renegotiated at the end of a specified period and then adjusted accordingly. LexisNexis and Dialog both include this arrangement as one of their pricing options.

Deposit Accounts: Search charges are made against an amount previously paid to the vendor and kept on deposit until used. Deposit accounts reduce the need for frequent check writing. KnowX (www.knowx.com), the popular internet public record service, uses this method for charging clients.

Enterprise Pricing: This refers to a pricing scheme that allows for use by large numbers of users within a single company. Enterprise pricing may be combined with some of the other pricing options. Most of the major vendors offer some form of this convenient arrangement. It reduces paperwork for both customer and vendor, and usually means lower per-search costs. The customer controls access in-house by granting network "rights" to those who need access to the service, or through the use of links on pages of the company intranet.

Pay-As-You-Go: A few online vendors allow access to occasional users who enter a credit card number before searching. Secure websites are generally in use for this type of access. With "Pay-As-You-Go" pricing, the credit card verification and charges apply only to the current usage session. Subsequent visits to the site will more than likely involve additional verification and charges. This payment arrangement is becoming more and more common as newspapers, for example, find that they can gain extra revenue by offering their archives for searching, at fees like $1.95 per article retrieved in full text. Some government entities, such as county tax assessors, have signed on with entrepreneurs who have mounted systems that charge for access to public records made available on the county's website. A source of free public record sites is available at www.brbpub.com. All online public record systems are detailed in the book *Public Records Online.*[1]

If you are part of a large company, talk with other online users in the company to see if you are paying for multiple subscriptions with the same vendor. Get together and negotiate a group rate that saves money for each department. Do not forget to include your offices in other locations.

11. Evaluate education and training opportunities offered by the vendor

With the possible exception of the simplest of menu-oriented interfaces described previously, most commercial online services require at least some level of user orientation before use. While basic training is usually free, some vendors charge for advanced level instruction. This need for training is reduced for online services that are searched using simple Web interfaces. Online tutorials may be all that you need. Be sure to watch for appropriate links or ask the vendor about workbooks, reference cards, or other tools that focus on CI subject matter available on their service.

---

[1] copyright 2004, available from BRB Publications. Tempe, AZ, 800-929-3811, www.brbpub.com

Some online vendors have moved away from printing extensive manuals, and often make such material available for download. This may range from a few pages to a 200+ page manual downloadable from the Internet! Adequate descriptions of database files, instructions for searching effectively, samples of output, and contact information for obtaining further assistance are a must. In general, the greater the cost of a subscription, the greater the number of printed tools and manuals available online

Web technology also allows commercial vendors to incorporate a great deal of useful, easy-to-locate help screens in strategic locations on web pages. Since searching on the Web is not time-based, searchers can take time to examine these materials if questions arise. In addition to tips about creating search strings, these "help screens" might include descriptions of databases offered by the service, lists of periodicals included, or even a glossary of special vocabulary. All are preferred by professional searchers.

Some vendors provide telephonic training. At a pre-arranged time, a vendor representative calls and walks you through the steps required to use their product successfully. This method provides a good way to get questions answered during the training process; it can last an hour or more.

Some of the largest online services maintain offices in major cities, with representatives who will visit high-volume clients, providing on-site training, new product demonstrations, etc.

The bottom line is: the amount and type of training should match the cost and level of sophistication of the service.

12. Ask about the availability and type of customer support

The quality and amount of service provided to users varies by vendor. Consider some of these questions when reviewing a vendor's customer support capabilities:

- What hours/days of the week is the customer service/tech support department available to assist callers? Monday through Friday service during regular business hours is the norm. But there are exceptions to the rule. The management of Alacra, a fairly new name in the online world, stresses service as part of its corporate persona. Its Customer Support telephones are staffed seven days per week, from 8 a.m. to 8 p.m.

- It is important to note whether the customer service is adequate for your time zone and the time zones of all other users in your company. If some of your people are located on other continents, ask whether support is available there, using local business hours.

- Does the vendor offer subject-specific specialists? It is comforting to be turned over to someone who understands your subject matter. At Dialog, for example, the automated telephone system instructs the caller to "Press 2 for assistance with science or technology…"

- Will the customer support representative recommend appropriate databases or help construct a good search for a tough question? At LexisNexis, it is not unusual for the support person to say, "Here's a search strategy that works for your type of question. Would you like me to give it to you exactly?"

- Does the vendor use the team approach? Nerac, at www.nerac.com, assigns an in-house specialist to each client. This person discusses your needs, suggests sources, or can run the search for you. Nerac's services are discussed further in Chapter 13.

Insider Tips of the Trade — Things the Pros Watch For

You can avoid costly mistakes or misunderstandings regarding online information by thinking like a professional searcher. In addition to the selection criteria described earlier in this chapter, professional searchers have developed a "sixth sense" regarding online sources.

Beware of a Deal that Sounds Too Good to be True

If a reference tool is sold in book form and/or CD-ROM format, is the publisher likely to make the same material available at no cost on an internet site? Maybe, but there may be tradeoffs. To provide the product free of charge on the Web, the loss of potential sales revenue must be offset. You may be bombarded with display ads on the web pages or the publisher may charge those people or companies included in the publication to make up for lost sales.

If neither of these options has been used, the publisher is probably giving away only a *portion* of the actual database. In some cases this is obvious because you are informed that you can only retrieve from a fixed number of records. Not all non-subscription sites make this clear, however. Here are a few additional things to watch for:

Sudden, Repetitive Error Messages

Let us say that you have located a website that promises to give you a very targeted list of something that you are looking for. It might be companies, industries, people, or whatever. A-Z hotlinks may be shown on the web page, and you click on "A." You are able to display a list and use your browser's "Copy" feature to copy the list to another file or to some other software program. Then you copy the "B" listing.

By the time you get to the letter "C," you may begin to receive error messages from the website that prevent you from going further. The messages do not say, "You cannot have any more free information!" In fact, you may not understand what the messages mean. In reality, they probably indicate that you had better consider ordering the publisher's CD-ROM or print product in order to have *true* access to the data. In other words, you have reached some sort of limit.

Search Results that Do Not Seem Right

Suppose that you are trying to obtain a current list of companies in a particular geographic area that manufacture a specific product. You may find "no hits" are retrieved when you have carefully followed the directions on a website search screen. Or, perhaps the search results seem rather small in an industry where you know that there are many more players. If something along these lines occurs, it can be another tip-off that the "free" data might not be the full version.

As a test, check the results for a company that you are confident should be on the list. If this name does not appear, you have reason to believe that the database being searched is a subset of the vendor's entire file. The next step is to call or email the vendor and ask whether the entire database is available free on the internet site or they have provided only part of the information, but failed to make that clear.

Suspicious Facts and Figures

If facts and figures that you retrieve do not go along with information you have retrieved previously, a warning bell should go off. Check yet another source to try to validate this new information. The data may be erroneous for numerous reasons.

One measuring stick for evaluating the quality of information retrieved from electronic sources is to search your own company or to perform a similar search where you can make informed judgments regarding your findings. You will quickly recognize "bad information". If this source is inaccurate regarding your company, question the source's credibility. If the source does contains accurate information on your "test case," then you may have discovered valuable new information. Either way, you should still verify the data using another source.

Obvious Errors Reveal a Number of Things

It is possible to find an obvious error in almost any database. Typographical errors or errors in dates are the most common. But considering the database size (millions of records), these occurrences are rare, especially in the online services mentioned throughout this book. These vendors stress quality control, and a loyal customer-base that lets them know if errors are found. When anomalies are discovered, the problem very likely lies with the database producer that provided the tapes.

Thinking Like a CI Professional — The Bottom Line

Whether using commercial online sources or those found free on the Internet, if you plan to search online, choose sources carefully. Follow the guidelines above to narrow down your choices. If you subscribe to an online service, choose among those with proven track records, and from those who will be responsive if you encounter problems.

Chapter 6

Getting the Scoop

Familiar Information Sources and Those You May Have Overlooked

Searching Newspapers

When it comes to business information, most researchers think of newspapers and wire services. Newspapers are usually divided into sections, however not all useful business information is printed in just the Business Section. If you hope to take full advantage of the intelligence opportunities newspapers provide, you must also remember to examine the other sections of the newspaper.

Look For Opportunities Hiding in the Headlines

Much has been said in the press about large U.S. companies and contracts for rebuilding Iraq after the war there during the past year. But some ingenious pea farmers from a small-town in the Texas panhandle have shown corporate America that *they*, too, can benefit from knowing their industry and spotting new opportunities. By translating what is going on in the world to their own environment, they turned news into new business.

This small Texas company is now a certified vendor under government contract to ship their product to Iraq. An Associated Press wire story quoted Deborah Nichols, of the Muleshoe Pea & Bean Company as having said, "We just stimulated some interest by reminding the federal officials that Iraqi people like black-eyed peas." Black-eyed peas are considered a specialty niche market in the U.S., and farmers are careful not to overproduce. California and Texas are the only two major sources of the legume. A spokesman for the U.S. Department of Agriculture Grain Inspection Administration indicated that this was only one of many facilities now shipping beans, peas, and other commodities to Iraq.

Do Not Overlook Columns

Nearly every section of the newspaper contains columns by reporters who cover a particular "beat." These writers become familiar with the people, places, and companies relevant to their assigned fields. In addition, their columns are often less formal than other parts of the newspaper. Columns also may contain items that are not lengthy enough to justify a full-fledged article.

A now-retired Houston librarian for a major international accounting firm once helped her firm's New York office impress an important client. It seems that the client was trying to locate an elusive man, who had left town suddenly, leaving no forwarding address. Apparently, he owed the client's company a large amount of money.

The client had heard a rumor that the debtor was in Houston, but had not yet hired private investigators or taken other measures to locate the man and collect the debt. He mentioned this situation to the New York accountants. The New York office librarian called the Houston office, asking for a search of the local newspapers. A search of the *Houston Chronicle* ensued.

Sure enough! One of the entries in the society column read something like this:

> **Mr. XXX**, Vice President of Sales & Marketing for YYY Co., celebrated his birthday Tuesday evening at XYZ [one of the local upscale restaurants where Houston jet-setters go to see and be seen].

Since features such as columns are included in the online version of the *Houston Chronicle* database, it took only a few seconds to locate the man's name. Presumably this information was enough for the client to re-establish contact, and possibly collect the money that Mr. XXX owed.

From the CI perspective, this news tidbit has several potential uses. Not only does it include name, job title and company affiliation, but it also provides information about the man's personal tastes, i.e. that he likes dining in upscale restaurants that serve gourmet food. This information could be plugged into a company personnel report (see charts for Intelligence Gathering in Chapter 17) or, if your company were planning to entertain the man, you would have a clue as to his choices in restaurants.

To make a favorable impression, it is a common practice in sales and marketing to try to learn something about a potential client's habits, preferences, etc. Similar information can be found in columns in the Business Section with titles like "On The Move . . ." that report on individuals' progress up their respective corporate ladders. These columns also may include photographs.

Finding Subtle Clues in Classified Ads

Prior to the advent of the Internet, it was common for newspaper databases to omit sections like the obituaries, display advertisements, or classified ads. The old technology could not handle these sections easily, and database size was a concern.

Now, the contents of the classified section is often included in the database and can provide valuable intelligence. For example, the Internet has revolutionized the process of finding a job. Online classified ad sites are proliferating. Both individual newspaper sites and specialized sites that focus on employment ads are easily located and searched for job openings in the U.S. and abroad. One such site, www.careerbuilder.com, offers these options:

- Search employment ads of the nation's leading newspapers
- Search job postings gathered from leading employers' websites
- Search job postings by industry
- Search Canadian jobs
- Search international jobs
- Post a confidential resume
- Apply online

Searches can be limited geographically, but an international search for jobs in the accounting field yielded listings for positions in Australia, Austria, Canada, China, Germany, Japan, Puerto Rico, Saudi Arabia, the United Kingdom, and the United States of America. A number of easily recognized names appeared as hotlinks in the tabular report. If one or more of these is your competitor, you have learned where that company is hiring, the type of position, and the number of openings being advertised. For Canadian jobs, it is even possible to limit results to those that include salary information, and to search within minimum and maximum ranges. This may be useful information if you plan to hire for similar positions. Other employment-related sites are included in the *Bookmarks & Favorites* section in Part IV.

Job search sites like these can help you deduce another company's plans. Suppose a company plans to develop a new product that, if successful, will revolutionize the market for a given product. They must hire scientists, engineers or other highly specialized employees who will engage in the research and development of the product when existing personnel may not have the necessary skills or may not be available for the assignment.

By monitoring the classified ads, you may discover that they are advertising for people with specific skills that are not required for their existing product line, or you may conclude that the company is somehow expanding or improving an existing product line. On the other hand they may merely have lost people with certain expertise and need to replace them. Further investigation will be needed to confirm your suspicions, but "the classifieds" can act as an early warning that competitors are up to *something*.

Checking Out Legal Notices Required by Law

Legal notices are usually published to meet the requirements of state or federal laws and regulations. They frequently pertain to applications for, or renewals of, permits for undertaking activities that are regulated. Alcoholic beverage licenses, zoning and building permits, and environment-related activities such as air and water discharge permits, are typical examples.

The law generally specifies where the public notice must be published and any time-related requirements. You can turn this legal requirement into a means of detecting the activities of competitors. Monitor the Legal Notices or Announcements section of your local newspaper or that of the county seat, and, depending upon your business, you will likely learn something useful.

More and more newspapers are searchable via the Internet. Searching this way reduces that likelihood that you will overlook a legal notice that was buried in the printed version. At some point in the future you may not need a newspaper subscription for this purpose. In 2003 a bill was introduced in at least one state that would eliminate the requirement that government notices be published in a newspaper. Instead, the bill calls for publishing these announcements *only* on the Internet. If the bill becomes law it may set a precedent that other states follow.

The excerpt below addresses an application for an alcoholic beverage license. A company applying for a new or renewed permit to serve alcohol would be obliged to place a legal notice in the appropriate newspaper, announcing that they have made such an application.

Public Notice

Notice is hereby given in accordance with the provisions of the State Alcoholic Beverage Code that Restaurants Unlimited LLC dba Joe's Bar & Grill is applying for an application with the State Alcoholic Beverage Commission for a Mixed Beverage Permit & Mixed Beverage Late Hours Permit to be located at 10000 Ranch Rd 999 South, City of Ourtown, County of Whatever, John Smith Pres; Tom Jones Sec/Treas., Elvis Presley Ent. Mgr.

Competitors or other interested parties, such as those living in a nearby residential neighborhood, are thereby provided notice of the company's intention and may respond by contacting the appropriate government agency, or by taking measures to counteract the effect that this license may have on their own businesses if the license is granted.

Other types of classified ads also may yield interesting news. An examination of the website of *The Salt Lake Tribune & Deseret News* turned up 176 Legal Notices. Subject matter of these notices over a three-day period included these business related items:

- Notice of an informal adjudicative proceeding to consider an application for administrative approval of the conversion of an oil well to a Class II injection well.
  Owners of other wells in this area may be able to draw some interesting conclusions from this action by the well owner.

- Invitation for sealed bids for trenching and the laying of utility conduit, including provision of all labor, materials, tools, equipment and insurance and bonding necessary…etc. etc.
  This may provide your company with a business opportunity – provided that the competition is not also reading the Legal Notices.

- On the 23rd day of April, 2003, the City Council of the City of South Salt Lake adopted an ordinance amending Title 17 of the South Salt Lake Municipal Code regarding the regulation of Mobile Vending Carts by amending Section 17.10.020 Approval Requirements and adding section 17.08.080 Mobile Vending Carts. *What surprises might this have for companies that sell hotdogs, drinks, or souvenirs? They had better check it out!*

- The Joint Commission on Accreditation of Healthcare Organizations will conduct an accreditation survey of a healthcare organization to evaluate the organization's compliance with nationally established Joint Commission standards. The survey results will be used to determine whether, and the conditions under which, accreditation should be awarded the organization. *Similar companies in the healthcare industry may be interested in determining the results of this survey. It may provide them with expansion opportunities or at least help in evaluating their own services.*

The Local Angle May Prove Useful

As seen through the eyes of the local population, an incident might appear quite differently than it would in the national or international press. Local reporters have their eyes and ears on the pulse of the community and report incidents from the local perspective.

Before I go back to the small town in the Northeast where I was raised, I visit the website of the local newspaper. Within a few minutes I am familiar with the latest issues before the City Council, state or regional topics of interest, what is going on at the high school, marriages, deaths, and even how many people were discharged from the local hospital on a certain day.

Now I am ready to interact with family and old friends. I know about upcoming events of interest, and am aware of what topics, such as layoffs or planned tax increases, should *not* be discussed in certain circles. By reading the local newspaper, I see these events through the eyes of the local population, which may have a different perspective than lawmakers in the state capital or in Washington, DC.

I discover who said what during a City Council meeting, which helps me determine on which side of an issue various Council members stand. This level of detail would not be found in the much larger newspaper published eighteen miles away, even though it covers news from my hometown.

This approach also has value as a CI tool. A few months ago a story appeared in the local newspaper describing the appearance of an entrepreneur before the City Council. The son of a former local resident, he described his plans to build a new motel/restaurant on the outskirts of town, with the financial assistance of a well-known professional football player. The project required that the city extend water and sewer lines, however, at some expense.

Had he read reports of Council meetings for the past several months, the entrepreneur might have realized that the city was short of funds due to additional costs incurred for snow removal during a hard Winter, and that the local tax base had eroded during recent years. This information might have been taken into consideration as he compiled his presentation. He might have couched his request for capital expenditure by the city in terms of the future benefits to the local economy. Anticipating the possible negative comments by certain Council members, he might have strengthened his arguments by researching the problem and locating examples of how other cities have addressed similar circumstances. It was not surprising to see that the article concluded with the fact that no further action was scheduled on this matter, at least not as of that meeting.

Viewing news through the eyes of the local reporter is important when gathering business intelligence, too, since many stories never make it to the national newswires. Consider an unfortunate incident such as an accident at an industrial plant. Even if this event is not significant enough to be picked up by national or international news outlets, it will probably be a front-page story in the local newspaper. The local paper or trade press may add details that were omitted by writers for the newswires or the local bureaus of large regional newspapers. The local story may take a different slant than the newswire or major newspaper, and this can be essential to getting the full picture.

The number of employees displaced by the incident may not be significant to the nation, but this information could have a significant impact on the local economy. Dozens or even hundreds of people may be out of work for an extended period of time, and their buying power may be reduced. Restaurants near the plant, where workers create busy lunch or after-work business, may notice a significant reduction in gross sales.

The implications in this information are well understood by the company's competitors. Supply and demand for the plant's products, and ultimately, the market price for the commodity, may be affected. To meet its obligations to supply customers, the affected producer may now have to purchase the product in question on the open market. This situation could continue for months, depending upon the severity of damage to the plant.

Competitors, meanwhile, have the opportunity to charge higher prices for their products, and may find this to be an opportune time to try to increase their market share by offering special deals to the clients of the affected producer.

For assistance in determining the availability of local newspapers on the Internet, examine the *NewsDirectory: Newspapers and Media* site – www.newsdirectory.com. Here you will find a list of hotlinks to states in the U.S. The individual state pages are arranged alphabetically or according to telephone area code, making it possible to search unfamiliar newspapers in nearby cities. The site links to more than 3,600 newspapers, more than 4,800 magazines, and hundreds of television stations from around the world. The newspapers and magazines must be maintained by a paper-printed publication and provide English language content online. Hotlinks to these publications are arranged by country. Many other excellent websites are included in *Bookmarks & Favorites* Section in Part IV of this book, under the heading News Sites.

Read Foreign Newspapers in Their Original Language

If at all possible, it is advisable to read newspapers or newswire stories in the language in which they were written. That suggestion might have resulted in hoots of laughter just a few years ago due to the lack of availability of foreign newspapers, but now it is possible to obtain publications from faraway places in a relatively timely fashion.

Keeping up with happenings in a place where one does business or plans to do so is a sound business practice. This strategy has saved many a business person from embarrassing situations that would have been caused by ignorance of another culture's customs. Equally important, foreign research can provide hints of political and social unrest or other factors that can cost your company millions, or make the company look like a hero.

When using translations, there is always the concern that some nuance may have been lost or a word misinterpreted by the translator. It is commonly said that the so-called "English language versions" of important non-English publications are not strict translations of what was originally published. Be that as it may, using them as one information source is probably better than ignoring them. If it is *really* important, then pay for a translation from a second source and compare the results. One major corporation even pays for a *third* translation if the first two do not appear to agree.

Thankfully, there is increasing awareness of the importance of searching in a variety of languages. Two good sources for reading in the original language of publication are ISI Emerging Markets, at www.securities.com, and the former Reuters Business Briefing, now part of Factiva, at www.factiva.com. The ISI Emerging Markets product provides full text of publications from dozens of cities and regions in countries in Latin America, Europe, Asia, Africa, and the Middle East. Publications are available in nineteen languages. If the publisher makes a translated version available, this is also searchable on the website. ISI also provides an email newsletter that allows subscribers to specify country or countries and search by words or terms. A sampling of publications available on the ISI site, which offers one week free trials, is shown below:

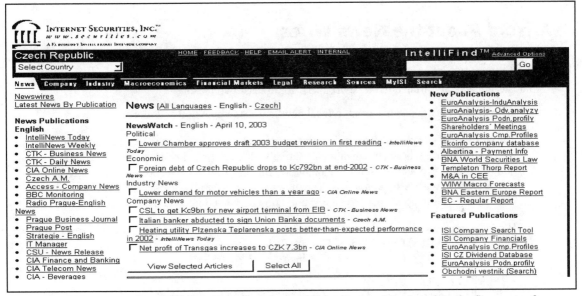

▸▸ Internet Securities Inc.'s website provides access to publications from far-flung parts of the world that might otherwise be difficult to obtain. The screenshot above shows the types of materials available for The Czech Republic. ◂◂

Sections of large services like LexisNexis are devoted to publications from Europe or Asia, and many sections available in multiple languages. Factiva offers nearly 8,000 sources from 118 countries in 22 languages, including more than 120 continuously updated newswires. Searchers can use English, Dutch, French, German, Italian, Japanese, Portuguese, Russian, and Spanish to perform searches of sites from around the world, both with English and without English-language content. Searches can be performed against a single site at a time, selected categories of sites, or from the entire collection available. However, you must be a Factiva subscriber to use these services.

Newstrawler, at www.newstrawler.com, contains dozens of news publications in English and other languages, plus information from broadcast outlets and other searchable information sites. You simply check off the titles to be included in your search in one country or across a group of countries. It is even possible to search ALL titles. Some Newstrawler documents are free, while some incur small charges. The site is based in Sydney, Australia.

The important thing to remember when searching a news publication is that, while an online service may have a huge collection of titles, no one service includes everything. It is important to identify the key publications for a particular market or subject area, and make sure that they are included in whatever online service or services you choose.

Services available through your company's intranet may cover *some* but not *all* of the geographic areas or publications that should be mined for data on competitors or industries. It may be necessary to convince the Webmaster in your company that the searchers need access to additional sources, either by adding links to pages on the intranet, or by providing them with specific bookmarks that can be used to search on-demand.

A Word About the News Wires

You may assume that since wire services supply news to the media, you will automatically pick up the newswire stories by searching the newspapers. However, not all stories filed by wire service bureaus are actually printed in all newspapers, for at least two reasons:

1. Wire stories may take a backseat to local news stories, which will sell more newspapers.

2. The newswire "story" may be a press release sent out by a commercial service like PR Newswire or Businesswire. These organizations routinely send press releases issued by companies that introduce new products or services, announce changes in executives, or to share other news that the company wishes to announce. The newspapers generally use some but not all of these stories, depending upon space available and upon perceived interest by readers.

```
DIALOG(R)File 258:AP News Jul
(c) 1998 Associated Press. All rts. reserv.

04495716 0318
Computer Associates drops $9.2 billion pursuit of Computer
Sciences
BY: ERIC R. QUINONES
DATELINE: NEW YORK  PRIORITY: Rush  WORD COUNT: 0691
THE ASSOCIATED PRESS  DATE: March  05, 1998  17:24 EST

04495692 0299
Computer Associates drops $9.2 billion pursuit of Computer
Sciences
BY: ERIC R. QUINONES
DATELINE: NEW YORK  PRIORITY: Rush  WORD COUNT: 0701
THE ASSOCIATED PRESS   DATE: March  05, 1998 16:53 EST

04495547 0173
Computer Associates backs off $9.2 billion pursuit of Computer
Sciences
BY: ERIC R. QUINONES
DATELINE: NEW YORK  PRIORITY: Rush  WORD COUNT: 0654
```

By searching a newswire's database, you may find that a story was actually filed several times. As reporters gather more and more information on a story, they may send corrections or additional detail in successive filings. Some of these may have arrived too late to meet the newspapers' deadlines, but they should be retrieved and examined for additional valuable intelligence facts.

The *Washington Post* website, at www.washingtonpost.com/wp-srv/searches/mainsrch.htm, offers search access to Associated Press and Reuters newswires as well as to the newspaper's archives. You may have to look at an ad on the search results page, but the information is free.

The example below demonstrates the evolution of a news story through multiple wire stores that appear during a given day:

Wal-Mart Sells Distribution Businesses (AP)
By CHUCK BARTELS   7:26 PM May 2, 2003
LITTLE ROCK, Ark. - Wal-Mart Stores Inc. is selling its distribution businesses McLane Co. and Merit Distribution
Services for about $1.5 billion to ...

Wal-Mart Sells Distribution Businesses (AP)
By CHUCK BARTELS   4:21 PM May 2, 2003
LITTLE ROCK, Ark. - Wal-Mart Stores Inc. is selling its distribution businesses McLane Co. and Merit Distribution
Services for about $1.5 billion to ...

Wal-Mart Sells Distribution Businesses (AP)
By CHUCK BARTELS   3:19 PM May 2, 2003
LITTLE ROCK, Ark. - Wal-Mart Stores Inc. is selling its distribution businesses McLane Co. and Merit Distribution
Services for about $1.5 billion to ...

Wal-Mart Sells Distribution Businesses (AP)
By CHUCK BARTELS   3:17 PM May 2, 2003
LITTLE ROCK, Ark. - Wal-Mart Stores Inc. is selling its distribution businesses McLane Co. and Merit Distribution
Services for about $1.5 billion to ...

Wal-Mart Sells Distributors McLane, Merit (AP)
                                                                                 12:23 PM May 2, 2003
OMAHA, Neb. - Wal-Mart Stores Inc. is selling its distribution businesses McLane Co. Inc. and Merit Distribution
Services for about $1.5 billion. ...

▸▸ At least five different versions of the story appeared within a few hours when Wal-Mart announced the sale of its distribution businesses in May, 2003. Note that the later stories contain the by-line of the reporter covering the story, while the initial story did not. ◂◂

Dow Jones Newswires may be accessed at www.djnewswires.com or at Factiva, which is now the home of the Dow Jones and Reuters newswires. For wider coverage, at least fifteen newswire archives from Africa, Asia, and North and South America, are available on Dialog. While the depth of these files varies, the vendor documentation usually lists inclusive dates. The LexisNexis service's "WIRES file" allows simultaneous searching across newswires, combining them with industry-specific services. LexisNexis and Factiva both provide searchable Associated Press *state* newswires.

Searching the Broadcast Media

Coverage of product releases, product recalls, changes in key personnel, and other useful information regarding competitor companies may be broadcast on radio or television. Only a few years ago, it was nearly impossible to track what was being said in the electronic media. At the end of some TV shows an announcer would remind us that "For a transcript of this show, call the telephone number on your screen ... etc," while an 800 number appeared. Listeners to public radio outlets such as *National Public Radio* (NPR) could not count the number of times they were offered taped transcripts of their favorite broadcasts. Unless you were watching or listening, and happened to jot down the ordering information, getting transcripts was not always easy.

Now, however, commercial online services such as Factiva or LexisNexis offer searchable, full-text, electronic collections of radio and TV transcripts. These can be searched individually if you know the name of a particular program. They can also be searched globally, so that you can search for all references to a word or phrase, from dozens of broadcast sources covering a long or short period of time. For example, the LexisNexis CNN transcript file is searchable from 1992 to the present.

Audio, video, and even DVD transcripts of network broadcasts can be obtained quite readily. For example, both CNNfn, at www.cnn.com, and CNBC, at www.cnbc.com, provide links to sources for transcripts of their programming. If you wish to undertake a monitoring program, consider a company that specializes in this service. The Transcription Company, at www.transcripts.net has an exclusive contract with ABC News, but also serves other clients. This organization offers transcription services, translation, and captioning services for over twenty audio and videotape formats. Their website states, "If you can hear it, we can transcribe it!" Each transcript comes with a cross-referenced index.

The Burrelle's subscription service at www.burrelles.com has been around for many years. Theirs may be a familiar name to someone in your organization who has used Burrelle's clipping services. Their offerings have expanded to include transcripts, on-demand research, and other custom services. Hotlinks available at www.burrelles.com/tt/ttothers.html will help you to drill down to specific broadcasts by date and name of show for the following:

CBS News	NBC News	CNBC
C-SPAN	Christian Broadcasting Network	The Discovery Channel
Fox News	MSNBC	MTV
PBS	WNBC-TV	Syndicated Programs
Council on Foreign Relations		

▶▶ Videotapes of a number of these programs
are also available from Burrelle's. ◀◀

A Message From Our Sponsor ...
Monitoring Broadcasts

The Twentieth Century saw the growth and development of a phenomenon unlike anything in history: advertising. Thanks to modern technology, consumers in nearly every part of the world are bombarded daily with advertising via a variety of media. The companies paying for these ads hope to reap rewards on their investment in the form of greater sales, brand loyalty, etc. Examining the past and present in this ocean of electronic and print messages can be useful as companies and their advertising agencies attempt to decide the directions to take in capturing the attention of the fickle viewing public.

Video Monitoring Service, at www.vidmon.com, offers some of the same services as the transcript services mentioned above, but they have a unique specialty: the majority of their clients are public relations firms, advertising agencies, and marketing departments who are interested in activities in a variety of media:

- Print - The contents of the VMS library of 1.5 million pieces of creative advertising dating back to the 1960s. Each day more than five hundred ads from over 90 markets are added to what is claimed to be the world's largest advertising database.

- Television - VMS also maintains a library of more than 1 million television commercials, adding more than 400 of these each day and making them available to clients via the Internet. Additional commercials from Africa, Australia, Asia, Europe, and South America can be obtained upon request.

- Radio - For radio advertising, centers throughout the U.S. monitor commercials airing on more than 100 major market stations. Radio ads in foreign countries or Spanish language stations in the U.S. are also available.

- Out of Home - This phrase refers to the ubiquitous billboards found along highways across America. This relatively recent addition is a library that contains not only copies of the advertisement's contents, but also photos of the billboard in context. This can help indicate whether the advertiser's message is mounted on a rooftop in an urban setting, planted in the countryside among cornfields and cows, or placed along the roadside on a busy interstate highway where thousands of motorists pass daily.

- The Internet - Banner ads and links from thousands of North American sites on the World Wide Web are available through an arrangement with Evaliant, www.evaliant.net. Access to Evaliant's entire library or occurrence data for internet ads is available, and geographic location of the target audience.

It is now possible to monitor a company's advertising on Canadian television, thanks to Eloda, at http://eloda.com. This subscription-based website allows advertisers to track and view competitors' commercials in a growing library of more than 5,000 ads that have been collected from thirteen stations in Toronto, Montreal, and Vancouver. The technology used by this site may represent a new trend in this field – a robot analyzes audio and video signals, distinguishes between commercials and programs, and automatically adds new commercials to the library without creating duplicates.

A search of these types of sources could be useful to your company's Marketing Department in determining the strategies used by competitors in various markets. The same product is likely to be marketed differently depending upon age, race, perceived income level, etc. Analyzing the strengths or weaknesses of ad campaigns launched by the competition can help your company to capitalize on their own investment in advertising, with the goal of increasing market share for its product or services. Additional discussion of this topic is addressed in Chapter 13.

Trade and Industry Publications

Nearly every industry has a group of magazines, journals, newsletters and directories that focus on its products, people, and corporate members. The contents of some of these publications may seem very boring to outsiders, but they are invaluable resources for those within the industry.

Staff members who are industry insiders monitor trends, report on news in the industry and, generally, keep up with intelligence regarding the industry. Some trade publications also report rumors in the field that may warrant independent verification. Browsing through a few issues of such specialized periodicals is a good way to get an instant education on some of the basic subject matter, terminology, and key players in the industry as well as the names of companies who are industry suppliers.

Competitors' activities, plans, and strategies may be more easily ascertained in this literature than by searching mainstream news sources, because trade publications focus on details of interest primarily to the industry that they cover. In other words, trade articles are likely to be much more in-depth and informative than what would usually be found in your local paper or even in a nationwide business newspaper.

The trade press is also a good place to identify and track the careers of executives. It may be possible to follow their employment path as they move up the corporate ladder, or from one company to another. This information may be useful to your organization's recruiters, in both identifying promising candidates for a position they wish to fill and for verification of certain facts on an executive's previous history *before* contacting him or her.

How can you identify the trade literature for a given subject or industry? Professional searchers turn to *Fulltext Sources Online*, mentioned previously in Chapter 2. *FSO*'s Subject Index uses nearly 100 topics to organize the thousands of titles under appropriate and useful headings. The list of titles can be long under categories such as Banking/Finance/Accounting, but it is a simple job to browse the list and select titles that suit your purpose. As an alternative, some websites focused on specific industries provide lists of pertinent journals and trade magazines.

At the time this chapter is being written, one-year subscriptions to certain trade publications are available free through Tradepub.com, at http://vertmarkets.tradepub.com/_brands/vertmarkets/main/fdpkg.html. A very long list of titles is available on subjects ranging from the predictable to the exotic, to "qualified professionals." This offer is probably aimed at building long-term subscribers, but it is a good way to look at publications in an industry that may be of interest, without blowing your publications budget. If you do not need it for a second year, you can cancel the subscription.

Some trade journals publish what are known as "special issues." These issues focus on a particular topic such as salary surveys, reviews and forecasts, geographic regions, lists of the "Top 100 Something-Or-Others," etc. They traditionally appear during the same month every year and are often retained by subscribers for future reference. This information is often offered in electronic format if the magazine or journal is available online in full text.

If you can locate it, Trip Wyckoff's *Directory of Business Periodical Special Issue,* published by Hoover's, is the place to go when you need to identify sources for such information. The subject index points to each publication that offers a special issue on your topic of interest. Although this book was published in 1995, it is still extremely useful if you locate a copy on library shelves.

Mr. Wyckoff's website, Special Issues, at www.specialissues.com, offers a searchable database of nearly 3000 magazines, their special issues, and website content. This is a subscription-based product that is an offshoot of his directory mentioned above.

Also see Appendix C, Periodicals Special Issues for periodicals containing trends, forecasts, and other crucial intelligence.

Gathering Customer Feedback Via the WWW

Your organization may have sophisticated tools and procedures in place for determining customer satisfaction with products or services. In addition, the Customer Service Department or a VIP may receive occasional communications from people who have taken the time to write letters – either commending something they like, or complaining about unsatisfactory products or services.

The advent of the Internet has provided a new tool for both the consumer and this situation. There are now websites that gather feedback from individuals who wish to register compliments, complaints, questions, or suggestions regarding companies from a long list of industries. Although this is not the most efficient way to gather such information on *your own* organization, it is possible to learn what competitors are doing – either right or wrong – and to react accordingly in your own environment.

Planet Feedback, at www.planetfeedback.com, is an attractive combination of tools for sale and free information, including a monthly newsletter. Sophisticated Customer Relationship Management (CRM) products are available here. Even if your company is not buying you can still make use of the site.

A click on the "Ratings" tab of the homepage brings up a search interface that allows searching by company name or by industry. Company or industry report cards are retrieved, showing percentages of complaints versus compliments and a detailed breakdown of types of complaints, compliments, and companies. Also found on this screen is a table listing the ten best and ten worst reported companies, according to consumers using the site. A symbol indicates companies noted for being good listeners to PlanetFeedback letters. Registration is free, but required.

Chapter 7

Deeper Sources

Finding Intelligence Off The Beaten Track

There are a number of treasure troves that may not come to mind when you think about searching for business intelligence. The Sales and Marketing Department may not think to use a source that the Human Resources Department uses frequently. Human Resources may not have discovered a source that is a basic tool for those in the Research and Development Department, and so on. Survey the different departments of your company. Find out what sources each department uses and compare. New sources may be discovered, increasing the efficiency and knowledge base for your company.

It is important to recognize that intelligence may be found in a variety of places. If you have searched in vain in the usual sources, try a fresh approach off the beaten path.

Trade Associations

For nearly every cause and industry, there is some sort of association or organization. They promote and represent the industry or cause for which they were formed. Typically, trade associations collect data from their member companies, compile statistics, and keep track of trends in the industry. As such, these organizations can be an invaluable source of intelligence.

Identifying the associations that represent a particular industry or market sector of interest is the first step toward using this resource.

Gale Research's *Encyclopedia of Associations* has long been a standard reference tool for identifying trade associations or other nonprofit membership organizations in the U.S. as well as internationally. The Encyclopedia can be searched on Dialog File 114 or through an electronic service from the publisher, called *Associations Unlimited*, which is marketed to public and academic libraries. The print version is often available at libraries. Subscription-based *Associations Unlimited* combines the Encyclopedia of Associations with a database of additional nonprofit organizations, making it a sizeable resource of 440,000 records. *Associations Unlimited* covers U.S. national, regional, state and local, nonprofit membership organizations in all fields, including US 501(c) nonprofit organizations.

Several good sites on the Internet can be used as alternatives to the *Encyclopedia of Associations*, but these alternatives are not as comprehensive. For example, Concept Marketing Group Inc., at www.marketingsource.com/associations, offers a subscription-based "Directory of Associations" that contains 35,000 records. Also, the American Society of Association Executives (ASAE) website, located at www.asaenet.org/Gateway/OnlineAssocSlist.html, offers a searchable database of 6500+ records that allows keyword searching to identify associations.

Occasionally, lists of associations turn up in unexpected places. For example, the Red Books Online site contains a hotlink for their list of advertising/media related associations at www.redbooks.com/Content/Associations/set_associations.html. This is in addition to the main focus of the website, which is to market their database of advertising agencies.

For locating trade associations in Canada, http://commercecan.ic.gc.ca/scdt/bizmap/interface2.nsf/ is useful with a long list of Canadian and international associations available. This site includes tabs for pages covering associations, companies, and links to other relevant resources.

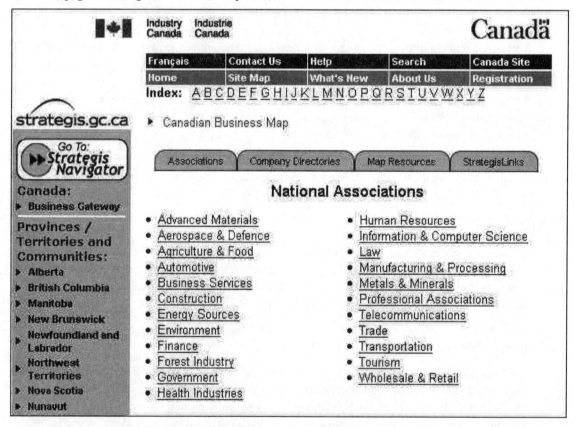

▶▶ Strategis, a service of Industry Canada, provides and attractive and useful site for locating information on Canadian business and industry. ◀◀

A number of other websites, including non-U.S. associations and directories of associations in specific fields, are listed in the *Bookmarks & Favorites* section in Part IV of this book.

Obtaining Trade Association Documents

A relatively new online goldmine, called Industry Insider: The Trade Association Database, is now available from Investext at www.investext.com. The database contains documents from more than 200 associations, covering more than 50 industries worldwide. The records contain benchmark data, statistics and forecasts that have been compiled by industry experts—information that can be extremely useful as you analyze an industry, examine your company's market share against industry figures, and learn what the experts are predicting for the next five years.

Some associations now have prepared information packages that cover "everything" they have on the industry, and they routinely provide these information packages to those who inquire.

Several years ago, a client called my company to request research on the dry cleaning industry. We identified a particular trade association and telephoned them, explaining what information we needed. The voice at the other end of the line said, "I have about five pounds of paper on the subject. It will cost you $50.00."

We sent a check immediately and in a few days our package arrived. We located the necessary statistics, prepared the report for the client, and provided them with the remaining material as an "appendix" of additional intelligence on the industry. The client could not believe that we had gathered so much useful data in such a short time. The price was right!

Industry Watchers and Activist Groups

Industry watchers and activist groups have an agenda or cause as a reason for their existence. In the process of researching an issue, they may compile a great deal of material that can be useful to researchers outside of their organizations. You can capitalize on that fact by knowing that this material exists in cyberspace and going after it! Be careful – remember that the material that you retrieve is probably biased.

Watching Executive Compensation

Executive compensation is a subject that may be researched for a variety of reasons. A company may wish to retain valuable employees by compensating them in line with or above the industry standard. In order to do so, the company must ask, "What is the industry standard?" By looking in the proxy statements of publicly traded companies in their industry, the company will find the information sought.

Top Five Data Services, at www.top5.com, produces annual reports on executive compensation in publicly held companies for the biopharmaceuticals and medical equipment and supplies industries. In addition they offer incidental papers such as *Board Compensation in Small, Publicly Traded, High Technology Companies*, which is available for download from the website.

In addition, the Dialog service offers these databases devoted to proxy statements:

- EDGARPLUS - PROXY STATEMENTS (File 780)
- SEC ONLINE - PROXY REPORTS (File 544)

If you need a free source for proxy statements or help on how to use them, one handy source is found in Executive Paywatch, at www.paywatch.org. Click on "The CEO and You" to reach a database for locating the CEO's total 2002 compensation for Standard & Poor's S&P Super 1500 Index; or choose and industry and examine a list of companies and CEOs in the industry, ranked by annual executive compensation amount. Along the way you will notice icons with labels like "Runaway CEO Pay" and "What You Can Do," which express the point of view of the organization that operates this website. You have already been warned about bias, but since compensation information comes straight from SEC filings, you are not in jeopardy.

A link labeled *The Executive Pension: Supplemental Executive Retirement Plans* brings up what are called "Extraordinary Executive Pension Case Studies" on fifteen well-known companies from across the spectrum of U.S. business and industry. For companies not included in their own searchable database, Paywatch recommends that you refer to the company's proxy statement, Schedule 14A, found at the U.S. government's EDGAR site, at www.sec.gov.

What was the organization that undertook the labor needed to create the Paywatch site? You guessed it – a labor union. The AFL-CIO has provided a resource intended for use by union members, but that union's Paywatch site is also useful to management as a resource for comparison with other companies in an industry.

Ecomp, at www.ecomponline.com, offers executive compensation data on more than 12,000 U.S. public companies and 50,000 senior executives. The information comes from proxy statements, 10-Ks, and Registration Statements. It can be downloaded into a spreadsheet for analysis using a variety of reports:

- Direct compensation
- Total compensation
- Long-term compensation
- Fiscal year-end option
- Exercised/realized option
- Unexercisable option
- Multi-year fiscal year-end option
- Three-year total compensation
- Company financial report

In addition, Ecomp offers executive compensation reports for the software and Internet, semiconductor, hardware, and biotechnology Industries. In other industries, detailed custom compensation reports for both executives and directors may be commissioned. There is a cost involved, but if you are looking for the level of detail offered here, it may be a good investment.

Director compensation can be an important research topic. If, for example, your organization is planning to add new Directors, it will be useful to learn how competitor companies compensate their Board members so that your organization is competitive in that marketplace. If a potential Director is someone your organization wants to attract, it will be important to offer an irresistible or at least competitive compensation package.

Forbes Magazine's People Tracker website at www.forbes.com/cms/template/peopletracker/
index.jhtml, is another useful source for executive compensation. Registration is required but the
database is free. Here a detailed history of an executive's education and employment history is
followed by salary, bonus, "other" compensation, and stock options, both exercised and unexercised.
A series of articles on executive compensation published since 1997 appears in the Lists section of
the Forbes homepage, www.forbes.com. Analyzing documents like these can shed light on trends,
new forms of compensation, etc. on a competitor company or an entire industry.

Tracking Competitors' Donations

Donations to political parties or candidates by individuals and businesses may be of interest to your
organization for a number of reasons. The Public Affairs Department or Legal Department may be
looking at whether a competitor received favorable treatment through action taken by lawmakers, for
example. Databases and the Internet make it possible to gather a significant amount of data on
donations, through government sites such as that of the Federal Election Commission, discussed in
Chapter 9, or through political watchdog groups.

Politics and politicians are frequent targets for interest groups. The Center for Responsive Politics, at
www.opensecrets.org, offers links to data on recent and upcoming elections; presidential and
Congressional races. State and local money maps also are featured on this group's homepage. An
interesting collection of data can be gathered here using the site's searchable databases:

- Donors Lookup
- Lobbyists
- Soft money donors
- Donations by Industry
- PACs
- Top individual Donors
- Top organizational Donors
- Donors by State or ZIP code

Donations made to political parties' "soft money" accounts are not subject any contribution limits, so
this is how many large companies give. If this site does not yield the information that you are
looking for, hotlinks under these group headings may prove useful:

PoliticalMoneyLine at www.politicalmoneyline.com/cgi-win/indexhtml.exe? offers dozens of
databases, some of which are free, while others require subscriptions. This site is a source for
determining a variety of facts including donations, lobbying activity, and punishment for illegal
activity. Someone in your organization may be interested in some of these facts useful in studying
competitors' activities, considering executives for employment, or for other reasons. Here are a few
highlights among the website contents:

- Federal Lobby Directory - Free
- Lobbyist Toolbox - look up donations by top lobbying firms and top organizations that lobby
- Top of Form

- Bottom of Form

- PAC / Party Profiles – donations to political parties by PAC type, such as industries, city/county, public employees, etc.

- PAC Names and Addresses - order by credit card

- Industry Total Donations - broken out by political party - FREE

- PAC Donation Leaders – by categories - FREE

- Top corporate PACs donations to Candidates – subscription based

- New corporate PACs – you may not know about these yet

- Labor Union Contributions – look up donations by 50 top international unions

- Illegal Corporate Donations - highlights a mixture of civil, criminal, and corporate actions relating to illegal corporate (for profit only) domestic money-in-politics activity. Includes executives' prison terms, executive resignations, and stockholder lawsuits.

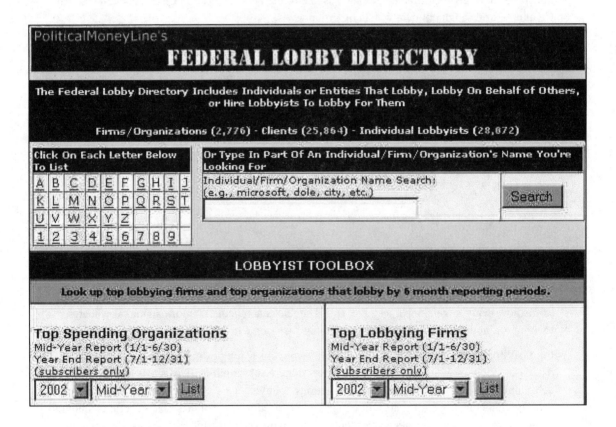

Other watchdogs may focus on specific industries or types of industries. For example, The California-based Marin Institute offers the Alcohol Industry & Policy Database at www.marininstitute.org, while CorpWatch, www.corpwatch.org, describes their activity as "holding corporations accountable."

A power search interface provides searching by political office, sector, business, or industry. The National Institute on Money in State Politics owns the Follow the Money website, at www.followthemoney.org/index.phtml. Here you might learn the amounts and beneficiaries of a competitor's political contributions by state and by election year. Another search allows you to examine that contributor's donations across all states by clicking on one of the election years under "all states in the database". Discovering that a particular company made hefty contributions to specific elected officials may provide a tip-off about future plans for expanding into new product or service lines. This type of advance warning may allow your company to use this information to its own advantage.

Additional intelligence may be gathered at Common Cause's *Soft Money Laundromat*, at www.commoncause.org/laundromat/. Searching can be performed by donor name, location, and industry. An interesting list on the Donor Profiles page shows the top 50 overall soft money donors to Democratic and Republican national party committees from 01/01/1995 through 12/31/2002. The site also includes, of course, a detailed definition and history of the concept of "soft money" as it applies to the political process.

Internet sites like these can be useful for more than what their names would indicate. Data gathered to prove this watchdog group's point of view may provide your organization with valuable facts and figures. For example, your Government Relations Department or Law Department may monitor what is being said about an industry. Pending legislation could be of interest to your Marketing Department, since it is likely to affect your company's sales or those of your competitors. These departments might also be interested in issues that will impact your industry indirectly by affecting your customers or suppliers.

Determining Who Is Polluting the Environment

Since the Federal government requires disclosure of emissions data, it is possible to look at what is coming out of the stacks or otherwise being disposed of over at Competitor X's plant. Scorecard, at www.scorecard.org, is an environmental information service provided by the Environmental Defense Fund. Hazardous air pollutants, criteria air pollutants (these include carbon monoxide, lead, nitrogen dioxide, ozone, particulate matter and sulfur dioxide), chemical releases from manufacturing facilities, and animal waste from factory farms are among the items tracked.

By clicking on a state map or entering the name of company in a search box dubbed the "polluter locator," you can retrieve "the dirt" about the emission of these materials. The Toxic Release Inventory of chemicals emitted from manufacturing plants, gas stations, etc. is all there, chemical by chemical, in pounds. By examining these figures, your company's scientists and engineers may gain valuable intelligence regarding what goes on behind those closed doors at Company X.

An additional site for searching the TRI is RTKnet, at http://d1.RTK.NET/tri/par.php. This site is the work of The Right-to-Know Network. This site also contains databases covering the following:

- Comprehensive Environmental Response, Compensation, and Liability Info. System (Cerclis)
- Emergency Response Notification System (ERNS)
- Toxic Substances Control Act Test Submissions (TSCATS)
- Facility Index System (FINDS)

- Risk Management Plans Search
- Docket (Civil cases filed by DOJ on behalf of EPA)
- Resource Conservation and Recover Act Information System (RCRIS)
- Accidental Release Info Program (ARIP)
- Permit Compliance System (PCS)
- Biennial Reporting System (BRS)

TRK's Master Search allows simultaneous searching of all of these databases.

Conference Proceedings

Papers delivered at conferences are an important and often overlooked source of valuable intelligence. They may discuss research in progress, market trends, customer case studies, and a myriad of other topics.

How to Use Them

Here are a few ways in which you can use information found in conference papers to accomplish tasks that may be crucial to your company's success:

Spot Patterns and Trends in the Industry

The same topics may appear in the proceedings of an annual conference for years in a row. Based on this fact, you can make some logical assumptions. The subject matter is of interest to practitioners in the field, who attend this conference.

Twenty years ago, a topic such as online information retrieval may have been addressed for an hour or two in a panel discussion with a title such as "The Company of the Future: Will the Computer Replace the File Cabinet?" A search of recent conference proceedings indicates that there are now entire three-day programs dedicated to online subjects, complete with dozens of presenters and crammed exhibit halls.

Let The Competition Tell You What They Are Up To

Industry conference proceedings usually include speakers' names, affiliations, and the text of the papers that they present. Speakers often share new things they have learned, brag about how well they do something at their company or show how knowledgeable they are on a topic.

By searching on a competitor company's name and locating papers presented by their employees, you may gain valuable insights into what is going on in their labs, planning departments or other facilities. At the very least, this information can help validate information or conclusions reached using other research methods.

Identify Experts

For recruiting purposes or for other reasons, you may wish to identify individuals with a certain expertise. Conference speakers present papers about new discoveries or other interesting information to their peers in a given profession. A person whose name appears again and again in such proceedings may be considered by some to be an expert in the field and worth recruiting.

Learn Names of Competitors' Employees

Your CI department may be gathering all data possible on a competitor. A search of recent conference proceedings may be useful for determining both job titles used in the competitor's organization and the names of the employees who fill those positions.

Locating Conference Proceedings Online

One obvious way to locate conference proceedings would be to enter the phrase "conference proceedings" into a search engine along with other relevant words or phrases such as "engineering" or the name of a professional or scientific association. For gathering business intelligence it might be smarter to conduct a search across a large database of these materials to avoid overlooking material that could be relevant.

The two most comprehensive sources are *Conference Papers Index*, from Cambridge Scientific Abstracts (CSA), at www.csa.com/csa/ids/ids-main.shtml, and the British Library Document Supply Centre's *Inside Conferences*, available on Dialog as File 65. Together these sources contain hundreds of thousands of citations and references to conference papers covering dozens of subjects, from as far back as 1982.

Inside Conferences contains details of all papers given at every congress, symposium, conference, exposition, workshop, and meeting received at the British Library Document Supply Centre since October 1993. Each year over 16,000 proceedings are indexed and more than 500,000 bibliographic citations for individual conference papers are added annually. As an alternative, it is possible to obtain this material through a subscription to *Inside Web*, at www.bl.uk/services/current/inside.html. This service allows you to search and order directly over the Web and receive articles within two hours. A subscription is required, so it may be wise to seek out a public or academic library that uses this service.

CSA's Internet Data Service, at www.csa.com/csa/ids/ids-main.shtml, provides citations to papers and poster sessions presented at major scientific meetings around the world. Subject emphasis since 1995 has been in the life sciences, environmental sciences, and aquatic sciences, while older material also covers physics, engineering, and materials science.

Another approach to locating conference material is to search industry or profession-specific databases that contain conference papers along with other types of articles or documents on the subject. Even though some of these databases may contain only summaries of documents, they serve a useful purpose by *identifying* conference papers. You have quickly found out what has been written or said, and by whom.

If all you want are names of presenters and an affiliation, using these resources allows you to do your sleuthing without actually reading the scientific or technical papers.

Identifying conference papers without bothering to read the full text of what is retrieved would not be recommended for some purposes. For noting names and affiliations, however, or for tracking the frequency with which a name appears, an abstract of the paper may be sufficient.

Getting Your Hands on the Real Thing

Having located references to conference papers, the fun begins! If you need to read the full text of the conference papers, try a large research library, such as those on university campuses or in large city libraries, or purchase the papers through sources described above. First it may be worthwhile to stalk your prey in cyberspace. Many associations now publish their annual conference proceedings or provide ordering information on their websites. To find these, try a site like that of the American Society of Association Executives, at www.asaenet.org or others mentioned in this chapter. You could also search the name of the association using one of the web search engines. You are very likely to locate some of the more recent material on the association site, on the personal website of a speaker, or on a company site.

Identifying Conferences and Tradeshows

For familiar industries or professions, you probably know the names of the important annual conferences or tradeshows. If you tried to create a comprehensive list of these events, however, you would probably be amazed at the length and breadth of the list. Several Internet sites provide searchable databases that will be useful in your quest. Consult under the heading "Conferences/Tradeshows" in the *Bookmarks & Favorites* Section in Part IV.

Product and Services Rollouts

Companies or services tend to announce new products at conferences or trade shows. Consult the trade press that covers the relevant industry to locate news on your competitors' offerings. Look on their websites for press releases, and other announcements as well.

Scientific and Technical Documents

There is no underestimating the role that science and technology plays in the business of many companies. Engineers work with codes, specifications, and standards. In manufacturing companies, the Research and Development Department creates inventions and better ways to do things. Everyone uses computer systems and networks put together by the Information Technology Department.

Obtaining the right information at the right time while this building, creating, or assembling is going on is crucial to getting ahead and staying ahead of the competition. Much of the necessary material is now available in electronic format, just waiting to be accessed. Scientific reports are one of the subjects now being made available to Internet searchers thanks to what has been dubbed The Invisible Web. Vascoda, a new site from Germany, available at www.vascoda.de/vascoda_en.html, is a good example. The site is sponsored by the Federal Ministry for Education and Research (BMBF) and the German Research Society (DFG). It includes four scientific networks among its many offerings. For further discussion, see Chapter 12, which discusses The Invisible Web.

Industry or discipline specific databases abound, both on the Internet and through commercial services. Librarians know that if you name an area of science or technology, there is probably an entire database on the subject available on Dialog, DataStar, Questel-Orbit, Ovid, and other commercial online services, most of which maintain searchable websites for subscribers.

Many organizations responsible for industry codes and standards have websites where you can keep up with new developments, order documents, and learn about educational opportunities. The Amer. Society of Mechanical Engineers (ASME) ASMENET site at www.asme.org and The Amer. Society For Testing and Materials (ASTM) at www.astm.org are two possibilities. Trade association sites like the American Petroleum Inst. (API) at www.api.org are also a good possibility.

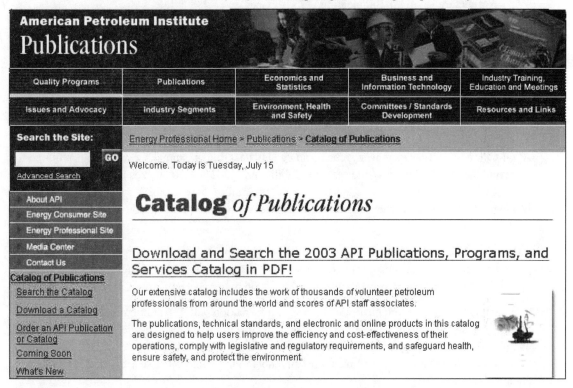

▶▶A wealth of technical data is available from trade associations
such as the American Petroleum Institute. ◀◀

WARNING: Not everything you find on the Internet should be trusted. Always be certain that the sci/tech documents that you use are authentic and up-to-date. Rely on recognized professional societies, reliable document delivery companies, or government sites for obtaining accurate data.

Government agencies are also good sources for scientific and technical documents. The *National Technical Information Service (NTIS)* is a U.S. government-related organization that many searchers have depended on for years. The NTIS website, searchable at www.ntis.gov/search.htm, can be used to locate and order government publications and other products issued by NTIS since 1990. Here you can find more than 2.5 million government information products such as technical publications, data files, CD-ROMs and audiovisual materials, more than 750,000 of which are searchable on the website. Searching capability is limited to titles and topics, and most records do not include abstracts. The "Featured Collection" hotlink provides better searching and browsing access to business, environmental, and health information.

For comprehensive subject searching of all NTIS collections, the GOV.Research Center website, at http://grc.ntis.gov/daypass.htm, provides access to a number of government databases, including:

Agriculture	Engineering	Science
Biotechnology	Environment	Space
Business	Health & Safety	Technology
Communication	Medicine	Transportation
Energy	Research & Development	

At GRC, the NTIS files may be searched using a Day Pass, but an annual subscription is required for searching the others. The cross-file search capability provided by GRC makes it an attractive alternative to commercial services, which may not offer all of these database files. For those who would not be frequent searchers, however, the annual subscription fees to individual databases may not be cost effective.

The National Research Council of Canada, at www.nrc-cnrc.gc.ca/main_e.html, is the principal science and technology agency of the Canadian federal government. NRC fosters regional economic innovation through sixteen research institutes located in major centers across Canada.

The Canada Institute for Scientific and Technical Information (CISTI), at http://cisti-icist.nrc-cnrc.gc.ca/cisti_e.shtml, is Canada's sci/tech and medical library, a leading scientific publisher and an information services provider in Canada and around the world. CISTI is an excellent place to start for ordering documents, searching databases, and obtaining various other services that give you a competitive "edge."

Science and technology materials from Japan are available on the STN commercial service mentioned earlier. The Japan Science and Technology Corporation Information Center for Science and Technology (JICST) JICST-E database is an English-language subset of a larger file that is available only in the Japanese language. Machine translation is used to convert citations and abstracts in areas of medicine, biological sciences, chemistry, and chemical engineering. Sources include journals, serials, conference proceedings, and technical reports.

Another file, JICST-E Plus, contains the items mentioned above, plus non-indexed versions of records that may appear later in JICST-E. This source also includes coverage of more than 400 conferences not included in JICST-E. Searching here might provide a "heads up" that will not be apparent for several months in JICST-E. This could give your company an edge over competitors if you locate information that the competition does not know about.

Using Sci/Tech Can Win the Case!

Use of technical information is not limited to the scientific community. Attorneys often use technical information when trying to convince the judge or jury that their client should prevail.

A law firm represented a railroad that was sued by a driver whose vehicle was involved in an auto-train accident at a rail crossing. The driver claimed that there should have been a better warning system in place. The case was being heard before a jury in a county where it was said that juries traditionally found *against* the railroads in this type of case, granting generous awards to the plaintiffs. An attorney described the charges to the law firm librarian, expressing his desire to find some authority on warning signs. The librarian thought of NTIS, and located a report that provided authoritative data involving the size of warning signs and distances at which they could be read satisfactorily. The information in that report was crucial to winning the case. When it was time for her next performance review, the librarian was praised for her work and rewarded accordingly.

In a manner similar to the previous discussion of conference papers, scientific and technical documents or articles may be used to identify both individuals who have certain expertise and academic institutions where certain research may be taking place. If, for example, you wish to identify venture partners for scientific research projects that might have possible commercial applications, this information could be very useful toward achieving that goal.

Information from Published Sources

Credit or Financial Reporting Services

The phrase "credit report" probably brings to mind names like Dun & Bradstreet, Experian, or Trans Union. Your company may have a direct-dial subscription to one of these services. Commercial credit report databases also are readily available on all the major online systems as well as on the Internet. These reports often contain more that just bill-paying information.

You may not need to check your competitors' credit, but what about learning about their collateral financial obligations? These appear in the commercial credit report under the category "Public Records." You may turn up assets such as real estate transactions, "UCCs," which are filings made under the state's Uniform Commercial Code, or adverse filings like lien records or tax liens. It is true that this information could be obtained using a public records online search, but this commercial service can be a real time and labor saver. Public records are discussed further in Chapter 8.

In Practice: From time to time, you may spot other interesting tidbits of intelligence in commercial credit reports. A few years ago, our company worked on a CI project where one company was interested in possibly buying another. Attempts to retrieve data on the CEO of the target, a small privately-held company, yielded minimal results. Retrieval of a company credit report was a "last resort." The report not only provided the company president's name, which was expected, but also the names of his alma mater and his previous employer! This background information helped our client to better understand how to approach that CEO. The leads found in the credit report helped create a successful research project out of one that earlier had looked rather bleak.

Other types of financial reports can be of great value in your search for business intelligence. The Dun & Bradstreet Business Information Report (BIR) can be retrieved on several of the major commercial online services, including Dialog and Factiva. Professional searchers consider this report to be a basic tool for getting a concise picture of what is happening to a company. It is invaluable when researching privately held companies.

Included in the BIR, you will find detailed data regarding activities such as these:

- Special events (Earnings update, changes of officers, restructuring/reorganization, changes in Board of Directors)
- Payment summary
- Financial statement
- Cash flow
- Net worth
- Public filings (litigation, UCCs)
- Banking information
- History
- Business type
- Management background (individuals)
- Subsidiaries
- Import/export activity

A third financial report to consider is Dun & Bradstreet's Financial Profile. This is the most costly of the reports discussed here. It contains detailed financial information covering several years, and would assist your company's experts in analyzing a target company's financial strengths or weaknesses.

Market Research Reports

Market research reports are compiled by a number of companies that make this material available both in print and via searchable databases. They also have licensed these files to major online vendors. Contents of the reports may be used to make decisions regarding new product development, sales and marketing strategies, or other areas where the preferences of the buying public are important.

Entire market research reports are considered "expensive, but worth it," by those who use them. Costs may range from $1000 to $3000 each, if you purchase the print version. It is possible, however, that you do not need all of the data in the document. By accessing the reports online, you may be able to view the Tables of Contents and purchase only the pages that meet your needs, paying a fraction of the cost of the entire report. Some online services offer reports from Europe, Asia or Australia in addition to North America.

Perhaps, your company's Sales and Marketing Department is interested in consumer preferences for a product like disposable dishware. They are trying to make a decision regarding advertising: Should the emphasis in advertisements be placed on convenience – use and then throw away – or should the ads stress environmental issues – they can be recycled? They would probably prefer to use the approach that is currently in favor with the product's consumers, so they may try to find material that addresses the issue of convenience versus recycling.

Perhaps the Research and Development Department is working on new product ideas. They might ask, for example, has there been any research to determine whether the public has color preferences for soft drinks? Would a drink that was blue in color find a market? Would it please the beverage-buying public or would it bomb?

Are there, perhaps, cultural or language-related reasons why a product would be the new favorite in the marketplace in one country while a "dud" in another? Many people have heard the story of the General Motors company's experience years ago. Their product line included an automobile that was popular in the U.S., the Chevrolet Nova.

People familiar with astronomy might have interpreted the model name, Nova, as "star." But what about the Latin American market? In Spanish, Nova might be interpreted as "no va," which translates to "it does not go." Would you buy a car that "does not go"? This story illustrates the fact that market research studies contain useful background information.

Two good places to find market research reports online are the Dialog service, www.dialogweb.com and Investext's Research Bank Web at www.investext.com, which includes its MarkIntel service. MarkIntel offers access to market research from more than 70 sources worldwide, including 27 exclusive sources. It is possible to purchase individual pages of your choice.

Both of these services require a subscription, but Investext offers a search-on-demand service for subscribers. This service will perform a search for you and charge accordingly, which is a convenience if you are in a hurry or short on staff.

Use a group file like Dialog's MARKETFULL to search across the market research reports of multiple vendors simultaneously. This saves time and may turn up material that you would otherwise have missed.

A competitive intelligence project from the Burwell Enterprises case files demonstrates the usefulness of market studies. A client wanted articles and other information regarding "interactive kiosks," including a list of vendors for the finished product, i.e. those companies that sold the electronic components already installed in the box or pedestal where the product was housed.

One of the most useful items retrieved was a report from Frost and Sullivan located using Dialog. The abstract of the report pointed to data regarding trends and forecasts in the market for these kiosks, as well as a list of companies polled in the study itself. The client, who was familiar with Frost and Sullivan, was very pleased with the research.

TIP - Be sure to look for *dates* on online market studies. You probably want the most recent data that you can find, so do not waste money retrieving reports that are out-of-date unless you want to observe the way that preferences change over time.

Product Manuals

The concept of buying a competitor's products, obtaining manuals, or purchasing in-house telephone directories has quietly existed in the sales and marketing world for years. What better way to learn about the competitor's product than to actually examine it, read instructions for operating it, or even discuss it with the inventor?

The Internet has brought the old idea of gathering manuals into the twenty-first century with the advent of websites like LiveManuals, at www.livemanuals.com/index.cfm. Searching is available by manufacturer, product, or product category, for product manuals, simulations, and support. The site is intended to market interactive manuals to other websites for marketing their products on the Web, but for the business intelligence sleuth it serves a different purpose. The list of products ranges from appliances to wireless devices. A detailed list of "makes and models" points the searcher quickly to a specific product – and the show begins.

Directories

Online directories are like lollipops. They come in all sizes, shapes, and colors. Many important business directories, such as Dun & Bradstreet products or the CorpTech Directory, have been available online or on CD-ROM for years. They are now available on the Internet.

Frequent searchers know that, using these tools, they can enter keywords or an SIC code to locate companies producing or offering certain types of products or services. Searchers also are accustomed to limiting results to a geographic area (all widget manufacturers in New York), if desired. They can even limit results to those companies with more than or less than X number of employees or with annual sales greater than or less than $Y million.

The CorpTech Directory specializes in high-tech industries. Corptech's website, at www.corptech.com, allows you to locate high-tech products, view demographics within high-tech industries and view projected employment trends geographically as well as by major product group, all at no charge. Subscribers get to see additional material.

Corptech defines what is "high-tech" very broadly. This makes the Corptech Directory an important source for hard-to-find company information such as data on privately-held companies.

Some directory databases, such as the many available from Dun & Bradstreet, have a financial perspective, providing varying amounts of data such as sales figures, credit history, even "complete financials," if your budget can afford the cost of the report. It is important to note that some sales figures are estimated (and are identified as such), and that the subject company supplies much of the data. Dun & Bradstreet products are available through most major online vendors, as well as directly at www.dnb.com.

The Industry Canada site, mentioned previously, contains links to both government and non-government Canadian websites that list Canadian companies in a wide variety of industries. Icons make it easy to distinguish between the two types of resources.

"Directory Assistance" Doesn't Always Come From the Phone Company

Depending upon their focus, directories can be a key tool for gathering a great deal of business intelligence. Here are a few examples of what you can learn

Plant Locations

A plant need not be a large manufacturing site. Certain types of companies may maintain work facilities that are not truly branch offices. These locations may not show up in a Dun & Bradstreet file, but may appear in a directory such as the one shown below, because mail is received at the site.

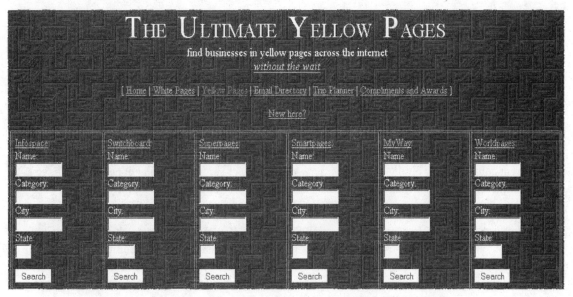

▸▸ This type of online directory file may help you locate plant sites.
If one source does not find it, another may! ◂◂

Some directories compile company data from a wide variety of sources, some of which may contain "old" information. Always search several sources and compare the results, and check the dates the files were updated when this information is available. The website shown above, at www.theultimates.com/yellow, provides the opportunity to search several online directories for company names.

Corporate Family Relationships

A "tried and true" technique for identifying corporate affiliations when using Dun & Bradstreet databases is to look at the Duns Numbers. Dun & Bradstreet assigns a unique number to each company entry in its business databases like *Duns Market Identifiers*, File 516 on Dialog.

In addition to a Duns Number, a company record may show specific numbers for retrieving Duns Corporate Number, Duns Parent Number, and Duns Headquarters Number. Searching on one of these numbers could turn up a holding company with a totally different name. In reverse, you could retrieve records for all affiliated companies by searching on the Duns number of the parent company.

The Directory of Corporate Affiliations, File 513 on Dialog, is a directory file produced by National Register Publishing Company, containing business profiles and corporate linkage for 114,000 public, private, and international companies. To gather even more intelligence, follow the trail up the corporate family tree to learn sales information, number of employees, names of directors, and stock-related information. This directory is also found on the LexisNexis service.

Descriptions of Products and Services

Using a Standard Industrial Classification (SIC) number is not a great way to describe what a company does. First, the company's list of products or services may be much wider than that which is identified with a particular SIC number. Second, the designated SIC number may be one of those extremely general designations such as "business services, nec" (nec means *not elsewhere classified*).

To make matters more complex, this is the age of the conglomerate. The "children" of the ultimate parent company may produce a wide variety of products or services that do not necessarily have a common thread. This means that each branch, subsidiary, or other corporate entity may be appropriately tagged with a different SIC code number than other members of the corporate family.

The North American Industry Classification System (NAICS) will provide much more specific categorization for businesses, and will cover many types of businesses not specifically included in the SIC system. Since NAICS is not entirely in use yet, some other measures should be considered when creating a list of companies in a specific field. Keyword searching a description of products and services may be a much better way to locate suppliers, create a list of competitors, or to see a clear picture of what a company actually offers.

The NAICS Association's Website, at www.naics.com/index.html, is an excellent place to gather information on the subject. Here it is possible to purchase various reference files and manuals pertaining to the 2002 NAICS, either on CD ROM or via immediate download. Earlier files containing the 1997 NAICS to 1987 SIC table or the 1987 SIC to 1997 NAICS table in html format for use on Websites may be downloaded free.

Using industry-specific directories, shown next at Ward's at http://wardsauto.com/sear ch/index.htm, keyword searching with industry jargon will quickly identify relevant companies faster than printing a long list from a directory like Yahoo! and scanning the brief description of each company in a general category.

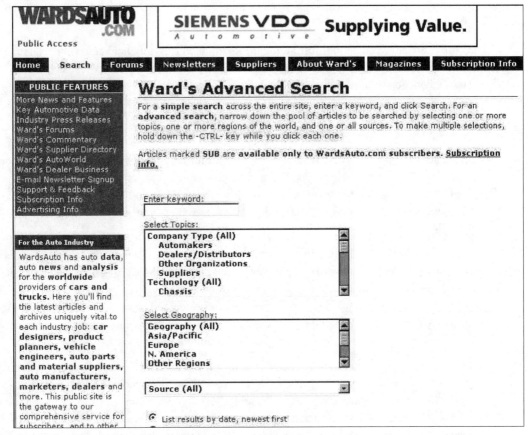

▸▸ Searching an industry-specific directory like Ward's is a way to quickly identify suppliers of specific items, such as custom molded plastic parts to the automobile industry, within a particular geographic area. ◂◂

Advertising

How and where do competitors spend their advertising budgets? *Advertiser & Agency Red Books: Advertisers*, DIALOG File 177, is a great source for answers. In addition to a great deal of detail about the company itself, its product lines and trade names, you will learn the advertising agency it employs, the agency renewal month, approximate advertising expenditure last year, and types of media used. For information on the CD-ROM version of the product, see www.redbooks.com/cd.htm.

Competitors' Service Providers

It is often very easy to learn what organizations a competitor company has retained for accounting services, legal counsel, etc. Dun & Bradstreet records, such as those in *Dun's Market Identifiers* mentioned previously, sometimes provide this information along with the name of the company's bank. In the case of very large corporations, this may be less useful because various departments, subsidiaries, or divisions may use the services of a number of such organizations. But, for smaller companies, you may have located intelligence that will help you to make a decision or to avoid a conflict-of-interest situation.

Directories are an excellent tool for finding information on privately held companies, large or small. For publicly traded companies, you may search SEC filings as your primary research tool. Be sure to see the explanation of these filings in Appendix A of Section 4.

New Playing Field, New Game Plan

With the advent of the Internet, the list of possibilities for intelligence gathering has mushroomed, and the strategy has also changed. Your company now has more resources available, and more options for choosing how to obtain the information they hold. Taking the direct route on the road to business success involves organization and planning, as well as implementation.

You can search an internet directory like Yahoo! to identify competitors, possible suppliers or to answer questions like, "Who are the players in the [fill-in-the-blank] industry?" Yahoo! gives a list of companies by category. You may be linked directly to company websites. On other websites, you may find a button that takes you to a product like Hoover's, www.hoovers.com or www.hoovers.com/global/uk to retrieve company profiles containing the data you seek. These types of sites may even offer to compile lists of competitors, though the results appear to be based on 4-digit SIC codes and may be a bit broad in their definition of "competitors."

Another approach is to search for an industry trade association to see if they have linked a directory of member companies to their homepage. These also may be hotlinked and take you directly to the company's website. It is important to check carefully, though: the internet list may include only that portion of the association's membership that has websites and *which want to be found*. Knowing that a company belongs to a certain association tells you something about their business or their interests, but remember that some companies may not wish to broadcast all their "connections."

When using an internet search engine to locate directories on a topic, include "directory" as one of the keywords to be searched. Some search engines require that this word be present in the search results by using a plus (+) sign. For example "+automotive +directory."

Brokerage House Reports

The information in the reports created by analysts at securities firms and brokerage houses is invaluable for keeping up with or studying an industry or individual companies. You may be accustomed to telephoning a broker and requesting information, which is an economical way to tap into this expertise.

What do you do when you are in a hurry? What if you need to compare the opinions of analysts from several different brokerage houses? How can you see if their opinions or predictions regarding a stock or an industry actually prove true months or a year after they were made?

The answer lies in searching the reports online. There are basically two good sources for analyst reports: MultexNet and Research Bank Web. MultexNet, at www.multex.com, is now subscription based. Multex reports cover more than 10,000 North America companies and include business description, name of officers and directors, and executive biographies and compensation.

What of the original vendors offering analyst reports online? They keep getting bigger and better. The Investext Group's Research Bank Web is now owned by Thomson Research, and found at http://research.thomsonib.com. Here you can search by ticker symbol, name, or industry group through thousands of reports, and combine individual pages into a single PDF document. Industry studies are also available.

If you are a Factiva subscriber you can search and view tables of contents free, and purchase either Multex or Investext by the page. Tables and pages are available on other major online services as well. The ability to tap into these high-quality research products and buy only those portions you need at reasonable prices makes them an invaluable resource in your arsenal of CI tools.

Your CFO – chief financial officer – will know whether your company's CEO has met with any security analysts and should be able to provide reports from meetings. Now you will know what your company is telling the financial world. You may be able to use the information in comparing your company with competitors, or to evaluate the credibility of various analysts.

Political Risk Services

If you are considering doing business outside the U.S., you may need to educate yourself quickly about a foreign country. In this rapidly changing world, laws, economic conditions, political and social factors contribute heavily to the potential success or failure of an undertaking. Calling the U.S. Department of Commerce or the U.S. Department of State will be of some help, but there are also sources in cyberspace that will prove to be very useful.

At the Economist Intelligence Unit (EIU) site, www.eiu.com, you can register free and receive monthly World Forecast summaries; a weekly newsletter containing to intelligence and analysis on key issues around the world selected from ViewsWire, RiskWire, Executive Briefing and Ebusiness forum websites; White papers covering EIU's latest research; or The Economist Intelligence Unit's Global Business Portfolio, which consists of all three.

For their subscription customers, EIU offers a variety of services, including country reports. These reports cover a general summary of events for the past quarter, political structure, economic structure, country outlook, an analysis of key political developments, and economic policies and trends, complete with statistical data. A list of their various reports can be found at www.eiu.com/catalogue/title/eiutit1.html. A trip to the EIU online store is another option.

Another website to access for this type of material is that of the PRS Group, at www.prsgroup.com. PRS provides political risk services in the form of country reports and forecasts covering 140 countries, market newsletters containing consumer demographic trends and analysis, and consulting services. Their various offerings can be purchased piecemeal and may be useful if you are getting acquainted with the subject.

It is not only the CIA that is interested in happenings in other countries. If your company imports, exports or otherwise does business in foreign countries, it may be in your best interest to know what is *really* going on there, and what is forecasted to happen in the foreseeable future. There is nothing like having people on the scene for sensing political upheaval or similar activities, then sending you a warning!

Chapter 8

Public Records

A Business Intelligence Bonanza

Public Record Versus Public Information

Strictly defined, **public records** are "Those records maintained by government agencies that are open without restriction to public inspection, either by statute or by tradition." They are records of incidents or actions filed with a government agency for the purpose of notifying others.[1]

Public information is information furnished by people and businesses to contribute to the flow of business and personal communications. Your telephone number is an example of public information, unless you have made special arrangements to the contrary with your telephone company.

Some public records are also public information. An example might be the clearly posted sign found in some eating or drinking establishments, indicating maximum occupancy restrictions or the fact that this establishment is licensed to sell beer and wine. The law says that the business must have this type of license, and in posting the license or sign the business is informing you that they meet this requirement.

There is a difference, however, between public record and public information. It is impossible to express a hard and fast rule about which is which. The fact is that access varies from state to state, county to county, depending upon the law. What is available in one place may not be available in another.

When researching public record information in a new geographic area, always ask the "availability question." If necessary, consult your lawyer for an interpretation of the law. To determine online availability of records for states in the U.S. or for certain non-U.S. locations, consult the *Bookmarks and Favorites Section* in Part IV of this book.

Local custom also can play a role in the accessibility of material that, legally, is supposed to be available. For example, old records that were never automated may be stored in a sub-basement or

---

[1] *The Sourcebook to Public Record Information*, BRB Publications, 2004, p. 7.

down the street from the courthouse. These records may be unavailable, not for any legal reason, but because the courthouse is short of staff or because the person in charge does not understand the value in researching old records. You are legally entitled to obtain these records, but doing so may require asserting your rights, or using that strategy that works so well these days: "You will hear from my lawyer tomorrow…" You may also do what the press does – use the Freedom of Information Act (FOIA) to file a written request for the items you wish to view.

Over the past several years, there has been a growing awareness of the value of using public data in the business decision-making process as well as for tracking the activities of businesses or organizations. This is especially true when researching privately held companies, about which it is often difficult to find accurate data.

You can avoid costly mistakes and gain a competitive advantage thanks to the increasing availability of this data in electronic format. If it is online, it does not matter if you are working late, on a weekend or during a government holiday — the "electronic courthouse" is open for business.

Using Public Records in Your CI Program

Whether part of a large company, a small one, or on your own, you can use public record information in your business intelligence operation. The type of records used, and their application, depends upon their function. Following are a few possible applications.

Identifying Corporate Relationships

Official filings with the government can be used as your primary source when determining corporate parent-subsidiary relationships, or you may use this information to verify data obtained from other sources.

Certain public record filings such as Secretary of State Corporation or Limited Partnership records are especially important when researching privately held companies, where you cannot just search for SEC documents as you can for publicly-traded companies. Accessing public record filings may be almost the only way to learn details on some privately held companies. A case in point:

A client called an independent research company requesting information on companies engaged in a specialized service aspect of the horse racing business. As an example, they cited a Kentucky company that is well known in the field. The researcher assigned to the project decided to search Dun & Bradstreet files for the Kentucky company, to gather available information, and to use the SIC code assigned to this company to search for others with the same code. To the researcher's surprise, the service company, which offers a detailed and very professional website, did not appear in Dun & Bradstreet's databases. However, a record for this entity was easily located in the Kentucky Secretary of State's searchable database. This record verified the names of the owners of the business and showed that the service business had been incorporated by one of the companies that specialize in that service. A likely explanation for this puzzling situation could be that the entity being researched is only one of several activities at a large horse farm and that revenues from these activities are combined into a single corporation's revenue stream.

In this particular case, the story gets even more complicated – the service company *did* appear individually in the database of another reputable credit report company's website. This, of course, proves the importance of checking multiple sources.

Identifying Affiliations of Officers/Directors of Companies

Public records are a good source for linking people with companies. Using the major commercial online public record services, you can search by an individual name to learn of all of this person's corporate affiliations in one state or across a group of states. Doing so sometimes turns up information that might otherwise have been overlooked, or which was not disclosed by that party.

Discovering Adverse Information

Some public record filings appear in commercial credit reports, but under certain circumstances it may be necessary to go to the "official" source (i.e. the government agency of origin) for information on liens, judgments, or bankruptcies as well as for possible pending litigation that could have a negative impact on the company or on its performance. In certain cases, a judgment may have been satisfied or a lien released, but the information does not appear online. This may not be the fault of the online vendor. Paperwork gets backlogged in many courthouses and the release may not yet have been properly recorded. An on-site search will usually clear up such confusion.

Finding Evidence of Debt

Uniform Commercial Code records – described later in this chapter – are a useful way to study a company's debt. Filings will indicate the name of debtors, creditors, and whether the filings represent a lease or a loan. In some states you can learn what was used for collateral, but other states may restrict this information.

Identifying and Locating Assets

Asset information is useful for determining the value of another company for merger or acquisition purposes, or in litigation. If your company plans to sue a competitor, it is important to know whether they have enough assets to make the effort worthwhile. Although your lawyer or legal department would handle the legal aspects of a situation like this, you may be the person charged with gathering the financial data. In some states individuals or organizations may be taxed on inventory, equipment, or other tangible personal property in addition to real estate. The first step here is to determine whether personal property is taxed in the counties where a company does business. Stock holdings are also assets, as mentioned later in this chapter.

Identifying A Company's Real Property Holdings

The value of real property may be useful not only because the property is an asset, but also in long range planning and other strategy matters. Determining who really owns a piece of real estate may involve some extra digging, especially if the owner is listed as a business entity rather than as one or more individuals. If that is the case, you will have to research the business entity to obtain the names of its officers.

The County Clerk's database will provide the appraised value of properties. When considering the value of a piece of property, remember that the *appraised value* and the *market value* may quite different, with market value frequently the higher of the two figures. To determine market value, consult a local realtor. If you know the state and county where you wish to search the real property tax records, there are a number of websites with links lists where you may look for that county, www.brbpub.com/pubrecsites.asp for one. The Real Estate Center at Texas A&M University offers some available county offices, state by state at http://recenter.tamu.edu/links/clappd.html. The XYZ Partnership may also be researched in your state's Secretary of State corporation records.

Real property information can have a variety of useful applications. Suppose your company is seeking a location for a new retail outlet. Assuming that you plan to buy property rather than leasing, you realize that it would be wise to check on ownership of nearby properties as part of doing due diligence. Suppose that a nearby vacant lot turns out to be owned by The XYZ Partnership. Upon checking the DBAs or Assumed Name records, you learn that one of your competitors, a large and aggressive force in the marketplace, is listed as the entity with the right to use the assumed name XYZ Partnership. This information may mean that you look for another location, or at the very least it would be taken into consideration in the decision making process.

Identifying The Parties Behind Fictitious Or Assumed Company Names

This information may be available at the county or state levels. At the county level a company may register by filing what is often called a *DBA* (Doing Business As). This will include the names of the responsible parties as well as the name of the business.

"Fictitious" and "assumed" names are basically the same thing — the language varies from state to state. There will probably be such a list at the state level and it may be accessible online. DBAs and Assumed Name filings are likely to be located in the offices handling taxation of businesses.

If time is short or the process described above is not convenient, Merlin Information Services, at www.merlindata.com may have the answer. Merlin's *National Fictitious Business Names* contains more than 10 million records from sources such as Secretaries of State Fictitious, DBA, AKA (Also Known As) and Assumed Name Filings as well as Boards of Equalization and various licensing offices, and Yellow Page listings and newspapers. More than 150,000 new businesses are added to this file each month. Some historic records go back to 1989, but the file is comprehensive from 1994.

> ▶▶ Merlin Data's *Ultimate Weapon*, shown above, allows searches across multiple databases simultaneously for fast results in several categories. ◀◀

Depending upon your business or industry, you may think of other uses for public records. Knowing how to use the information is important — knowing where to look is equally important.

"Where There Is Government, There Are Records"

From the highest to the lowest, all levels of government seem to collect records. Part of the skill involved in making use of these records is in knowing what information is collected at each of these levels, and then seeking it out. Public record vendors have done part of the work for us in this area, and have categorized the files nicely on menus or other types of lists.

Federal/Nationwide Level

Some public record databases have been created from federal government data collected in all fifty states. Both government and commercial sources may be used to retrieve records in these files. Here are some examples of federal database contents:

Stock Holdings

Searchable databases found on some commercial public record online services reflect stock-related transactions of officers, directors, and significant shareholders in publicly traded companies. For example, combining search results with data found using other tools can yield a significant amount of information regarding a company's CEO.

It is true that insider trading information can be found on the Internet, but some of those sites do not usually indicate the total number of shares held, as does KnowX at www.knowx.com.

If a company or individual owns at least 10% of the shares of another company, this information can be obtained through KnowX, at www.knowx.com. For one fee, KnowX lets you view up to 220 records in detail. Searching the Stock Holdings file reveals additional useful information that is not turned up by insider trading reports on the Internet — the names of additional companies with which a VIP's name may be connected.

Example: The typical insider trading record for John Smith of Mega Corp. might show Mr. Smith's recent or past sales of Mega Corp. stock.

Searching Mr. Smith in the type of stock transactions database described above would show the recent insider trades you have already found on the Internet, but it also would show his stock transactions with other companies where he is involved, possibly as a director. Looking at such affiliations may provide some interesting insights into Mr. Smith's business connections, true wealth, and "pet causes."

The *TFSD Ownership Database*, File 540 on Dialog, contains public corporate ownership information covering institutional holdings, 5% ownership holdings, and ownership by insiders for over 10,000 companies. This information is derived from filings made with the U.S. Securities and Exchange Commission on a quarterly or as-required basis. Records include names of specific institutions and individuals, their relationship to the company, their holdings, and their most recent trades. *Insider Trading Monitor* (File 549) would be another source to check out while looking at Dialog's offerings in this area.

Aircraft/Watercraft Ownership

These expensive items are considered assets. Identifying them can help complete a picture of a company's worth. The FAA and the Coast Guard update their files annually. Commercial sources like KnowX, ChoicePoint (www.choicepoint.com) or LexisNexis, (www.lexisnexis.com) have mounted the FAA and U.S. Coast Guard tapes and created searchable databases for this purpose. In addition, Landings.com at www.landings.com offers a data intensive website that includes a number of free searchable databases.

Canadian information of a similar nature can be found at www.tc.gc.ca/CivilAviation/databases.htm, the Transport Canada website. For other aviation-related databases, check *Bookmarks & Favorites* in Part IV of this book.

Bankruptcy

If a company has filed bankruptcy, the case file at the U.S. Courthouse is usually considered public record. The case file contains significant detail about the organization's finances, assets, etc.

A few U.S. Bankruptcy court records are currently searchable on the Internet at no cost, but, if a nationwide search is required, Merlin Information Services, mentioned previously, may be a better source. Merlin has licensed a database containing seven years worth of bankruptcy records from across the U.S.

Lawsuits/Legal Opinions

Lawsuits are filed in courts at several government levels. The list of pending or past lawsuits provides a great deal of information about a company's history, legal problems, and relationships. Several options for searching and retrieving this data are available using the Internet.

PACER (Public Access to Court Electronic Records), http://pacer.psc.uscourts.gov, provides internet access to many U.S. District, Bankruptcy, and Appellate court records. You must be a registered subscriber to gain access, and will not be able to obtain a password electronically.

PACER's U.S. Party/Case Index facilitates nationwide searching by name or Social Security Number in the bankruptcy index, name or nature of suit in the civil index, defendant name in the criminal index, and party name in the appellate index. Search results include the party name, the court where the case is filed, the case number, and the filing date. In addition, for bankruptcy searches you will receive the chapter; for civil searches you will receive the nature of suit.

U.S. Party/Case Index

All Court Types Search

Region: ALL COURTS

Case Filed date: [ ] [ ] [ ] through [ ] [ ] [ ]

Party Name: ACE WIDGET CORPORATION   **Format:** lastname, firstname

Show Case Title: ⊙ Yes ○ No

[Search] [Clear Form]

U.S. Party/Case Index - Home

Search: All Court Types | Appellate | Bankruptcy | Civil | Criminal

Reports: Court Code List | Date Range | Courts not on Index | Statistical Reports

User Options: Change Client Code | New Login | Billing History | PSC Home Page | E-Mail PSC | Logout

▸▸ The Party/Case Index can be an invaluable CI tool for determining whether a company has been sued in Federal court and where and when the suit was filed. It should be added to your list of useful sites for obtaining information on privately held companies. ◂◂

Your lawyer or legal department can interpret and explain the issues involved in the cases, and some case records may shed interesting light on a competitor company's activities, finances, problems, etc. For a nationwide search of state and federal legal opinions, Lexis, at www.lexis.com, or Westlaw, at www.westlaw.com, are the commercial online services used most frequently by the legal community.

Some Federal courts have created their own online systems that provide internet access, while others take advantage of services like RACER (Remote Access to Court Electronic Records), www.nced.uscourts.gov/racer_registration.htm. You must register to use RACER sites, but the service is free, and shrinking. There is a small fee for images of documents. Information included in database records is as follows:

- Compilation of case related information.
- Names of all parties and participants including judges and attorneys.
- Chronology of case events entered in the case record.
- A copy of all pleadings filed since September 1998 with the exception of Social Security cases, criminal cases, and cases involving minors.
- A compilation of case related information such as cause of action, nature of suit, and dollars demanded for each case.
- Judgments or case status.

Nearly every federal court offers record searching of their index at their own website. The U.S. Courts website, at www.uscourts.gov, is a good source for reaching the homepages of individual courts. Click on the Court Links tab to reach a colorful map showing the states covered by each of the U.S. Courts of Appeals, commonly written as a number followed by the word *circuit*, as in 11th Circuit.. Then click on an individual state to see a list of Federal courts within that circuit. State and county court records are discussed later in this chapter.

OSHA Filings

These filings come from the U.S. Department of Labor, Occupational Safety and Health Administration (OSHA). Searchable databases allow you to enter a business name and to retrieve records pertaining to that company or its franchises.

Depending on the industry, this can be a useful tool for locating plant sites, determining where a company has a safety problem, and more. For example, if you entered a keyword for the name of a major chemical company, you might identify a long list of plant sites where OSHA inspections had taken place. You can search OSHA files free at www.osha.gov/cgi-bin/est/est1. The information in the record would include the following:

Business Name	Union Status (union or non-union)
Address	Inspection information

LexisNexis provides access to these reports in its collection of U.S. Government Administrative Agency materials. For those with access to this service, more details may be available than are currently found on the OSHA site mentioned above. Additional OSHA databases are described in Chapter 9.

Some public record vendors offer nationwide files of various types. Read the fine print in their documentation. "Nationwide" may refer to searching the records of fifty states simultaneously, or merely those states where that vendor has access to the records. You cannot assume that every state has been checked unless that is specified in the vendor's literature or on their website.

State Level Public Records

The most frequently used state records for business applications follow on the next three pages.

Corporation/Limited Partnership Records

In electronic format, Secretary of State incorporation or limited partnership records provide varying amounts of information, depending on state law and which vendor is used.

You will usually find the corporate name, address, the names of officers and directors as well as the Corporate Charter ID or file number. This number is the key to obtaining a copy of the charter from the Secretary of State's office. These documents are not available online, but may be worth obtaining manually for the extra information they contain. In addition, you may find Taxpayer ID Number, corporate family relationships, and company assumed or fictitious business names.

Inclusion of this information varies from vendor to vendor, and availability of the information varies from state to state. The states of Hawaii and New Jersey do not sell corporation information to public records vendors, so for these states it may be necessary to use a public record retriever. One way to facilitate this process is by using the Public Record Retriever Network[2] website, www.brbpub.com/prrn, where names of retrievers can be found on a county basis.

The State of Delaware requires that online vendors use a gateway service to access corporate records. This means that searches may be submitted via the vendor's search screen, but the system then connects with the computers of the State of Delaware. There are some search limitations inherent in this process: the vendor's connectors or wildcards, for example, cannot be used. In addition, there is no full-text searching of the Delaware database, so company names must be entered using the first several words of the name, up to thirty characters.

The Delaware Secretary of State file contains active records since 1895 and inactive records since 1981 for the following:

- Corporation Filings (domestic and foreign)
- Limited Partnership Filings (domestic and foreign)
- Limited Liability Company Filings (domestic and foreign)
- Limited Liability Partnerships (domestic and foreign)
- Limited Liability Limited Partnerships
- Unincorporated Non-Profit Associations
- General Partnerships
- Business Trusts

---

[2] or PRRN, membership organization of local document retriever companies in the U.S. and N. America, 800-929-3811.

The graphic below shows a sample report from the State of Delaware Secretary of State's corporation database:

	Detail Information	
Date/Time of Results: 02-14-2001 at 11:30		
File Number: 12 12 21	**Name Type:** Delaware Company	**Stock Co Flag:**
Name: RED, WHITE & BLUE CORP.		
Kind: Corporation General	**Status:** Good Standing as of 07-04-1776	**Tax Type:** A/R Filing Required
Residency: Domestic	**State of Incorp:** DE	**Country:** U.S.
Original Country:	**Incorp/Qualify Date:** 10-13-1776	**Foreign Incorporation Date:**
Proclamation Date:	**Renewal Date:**	**Expiration Date:**
Bankruptcy Status:	**Bankruptcy Date:**	**State:**
Case No.:	**Merged To:**	**State:**
Federal ID: 999988877	**Quarterly Filing?:** Y	**Last Annual Report:** 2000
Registered Agent: 9090909 WE DO CORPORATIONS COMPANY CORPORATION CENTRAL 1 CORPORATION AVE WILMINGTON, DE 19801	**Registered Agent County:** New Castle Phone: 800-555-1212 Fax: 800-555-1234	

▶▶LexisNexis Public Records provides a gateway to the Delaware corporation records. Names of officers and directors do not appear in these records. ◀◀

In addition to corporation records, the Secretary of State's office in other states may include records for Limited Liability Companies; Assumed Name/Fictitious Name records (also available at the county level in some places); and Trademarks/Tradenames records. See *Bookmarks & Favorites* in Section 4 for a lengthy list of these sites.

Tax Records

Tax record information is available online for a few states, from commercial vendors or on a state's internet site. Various types of state tax files are searchable. Texas, for instance, provides a searchable database of corporations that pay Franchise Tax to the state, while the state of Washington provides for searching records of companies that pay Sales Tax. At least thirty-eight states will verify this information by telephone or mail. A search at Search Systems, www.searchsystems.net, provides links to individual states in the U.S., as well as U.S. Territories, Canada, and other countries across the world. Find a free similar service, listing free access to sites, at www.brbpub.com/pubrecsites.asp

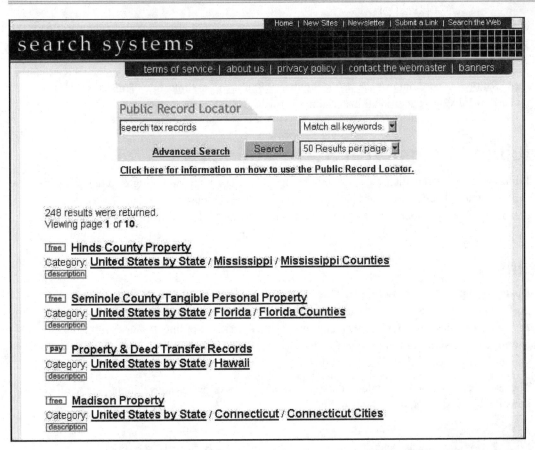

▸▸The Search Systems website provides links to nearly 16,000 searchable public record-related databases, many of which are free of charge. Descriptions are provided for each database, along with the designations "free" or "pay." ◂◂

Court Documents

Nearly every state now offers state supreme and appellate court opinions in electronic format. For example, Minnesota Supreme Court and Appeals Court opinions can be downloaded in word processing format. Twenty-two states offer access to statewide or county docket records from the State Court Administration Offices. An example is the State of Utah whose court information is online via its Xchange service, which is subscription-based. The Utah State Courts website, at www.utcourts.gov/records/xchange describes Xchange as the electronic equivalent of an information counter for all Utah courts. Search Systems, mentioned previously, offers a page of links to each state at www.searchsystems.net/index.php. This site is updated very frequently. Check individual state listings for links to databases of opinions.

Another excellent site is www.publicrecordsources.com, maintained by BRB Publications. There are links to free sites and also a commercial subscription system, called the *Public Record Research System*, which is by far and away the most detailed and advanced program of its kind in the U.S. It details how to access not only the 22 statewide court systems, but also a detailed analysis of each state's court system, and locations and access to all civil, criminal, and probate courts.

The National Center for State Courts provides a state-by-state analysis of what is available around the U.S. at www.ncsc.dni.us/ncsc/tis99/pubacs99/publicaccesslinks.htm. This list was last updated in July 2002; additional material may now be available.

Required Filings With State Agencies

Filings will vary, depending upon the industry involved. The important thing is to recognize that you can find state agency websites and look for lists of forms that must be filed, or for searchable databases. Names of agencies that regulate certain industries will vary from state to state. For instance, the agency that regulates the petroleum industry in Texas is the Railroad Commission.

Licenses

Dozens of types of businesses and professionals are required to be licensed. State agencies, professional associations, or trade associations may manage this process. Per BRB Publication's *Public Record Research System*, there are over 3,200 searchable online databases of occupational licensing in the U.S. For example, in California, a searchable database at www.cslb.ca.gov allows you to check out contractors' license status.

The list below is a good example of the types of businesses or professions that may be regulated by individual U.S. states and available online:

Accountant	Audiologist
Acupuncturist	Business Broker
Architect	Chiropractor
Asbestos Consultant	Cinerator Registration
Agent (Athletic, Talent)	Contractors - Electricians, Plumbers, etc.
Auctioneer	Counselors
Dentist	Pharmacist
Engineer Business	Physician
Funeral Director	Podiatrist
Geologist	Professional Engineer
Interior Designer	Psychologist
Land Surveyor	Real Estate
Landscape Architect	Social Worker
Naturopath	Speech & Language Pathologist
Nursing Home Administrator	State Pilot
Optometrist	Therapist
Osteopath	*and many more...*

Liens and Judgments

Lien records may be located at the state or county record levels. These would include Federal liens filed by the Internal Revenue Service. You cannot make assumptions regarding where to find Federal tax lien records, however. For example, in North Carolina, Federal tax liens on businesses are available at the state level. For individual (personal) tax liens, however, you must go to the county courthouse. Again, the best approach is to check an authoritative public records source like the *Public Record Research System*[3], and let the public records experts sort it out for you.

UCC Filings

Uniform Commercial Code filings are evidence that a loan or lease has been made. UCC databases usually can be searched using the debtor or creditor name. Searching for a company name may present valuable financial information such as where the company has banking or financial relationships. The amount of the obligation will not appear, but by obtaining a number from the online record you may request more detailed information. The majority of states make UCCs searchable at the state level. The major public record vendors provide access, but a number of states offer UCC searches at no charge.

County or Local Levels

As automated records come closer to being the norm, more and more county records are appearing on commercial public record services or free or by subscription on the Internet. The commercial services tend to seek out such records in the states or regions with the greatest population density or in what are known as the most "litigious" states – California and New York.

Obtaining public records at the county level is more complex than at other levels because you must consider at least three different sources. To make matters even more complicated, in some states, such as Vermont, you must go to the township level, not to the county seat. In certain major metropolitan areas you may find that the city controls certain records, rather than the county.

Whether using commercial or free sources, consider looking at these records:

From the County Civil Courthouse – Court Records

Court dockets, documents and images, and other lawsuit-related material from state courts may be viewed or photocopied at the local county courthouse, provided that you have the case number or cause number. To obtain the case number, you might consult a source that works like the U.S. Party/Case Index: if you know the name of the plaintiff or defendant in the suit, then you can retrieve a record that shows the name of the parties as well as the case number that you are seeking. Some jurisdictions have made court dockets available on their internet sites.

For a growing number of counties, "Defendant-Plaintiff tables" are available on commercial public record services. In large metropolitan areas such as Chicago you may have to check in several counties to locate cases. Chicagoland usually includes the counties of Cook, DeKalb, DuPage, and Will. Likewise, the Dallas-Fort Worth Metroplex in Texas is made up of four counties. To do a thorough search for

---

[3] available from BRB Publications, Inc, PO Box 27869, Tempe, AZ 85285 800-929-3811, www.brbpub.com

lawsuits in the D-FW area, it would be important to include all four counties. Some public record vendors make this task much simpler by providing a metro search.

Defendant-Plaintiff tables are important for at least three reasons:

- They generally point to *pending* as well as past lawsuits.

- They cover the lower courts that are not routinely included in online case law services like Lexis or Westlaw.

- Liens and judgments records are usually available at the county level, but as stated earlier in this chapter, it is best to determine how the various types of liens are handled in a particular state.

Probate, family court, vital records, and voter registration records are not generally available in cyberspace. The state of Kentucky, however, makes the Kentucky Vital Records Index available at http://ukcc.uky.edu/~vitalrec/, but the files are not up-to-date. Other states offer vital records files piecemeal. For example, Maine offers a searchable database of Death Records from 1960 to 1996 and a marriages database that covers the years 1892 to 1996. The availability of such records appears to be in flux. The Colorado Marriages and Divorces file, formerly available via the Internet, is no longer available online. Some divorce records for Florida and Texas are available through commercial online sources, but not from the states directly. These records would not be used on a frequent basis for CI research, but there may be occasions when it is at least useful to know where they can be located.

Again, the most extensive resource to find 7,000 county court sources and 4,260 county recorder sources of public records is the *Public Record Research System*[4]. Details include how records are indexed, access methods and requirements, how far back records are maintained, fees, etc.

From the County Criminal Courthouse - Criminal or Arrest Records

Your Human Resources Department may run routine background checks on job applicants for certain positions even if you have recruited them from the competition. A good background check includes a search of both a statewide system and a local county search. There are a number of several reputable vendors that provide criminal record checks as part of other pre-employment screening services. You might take a look at www.napbs.com to find a member of the National Association of Professional Background Screeners. While records may be ordered or retrieved online, it is important to note that criminal records ordered for employment must be in compliance with the Fair Credit Reporting Act.

Forty-five states have a state agency other than a state court administration office that offers access to a centralized database of criminal records generally assembled from court records. Sixteen states offer online access by subscription directly from a state office. An example is the Texas Dept. of Public Safety (DPS) who has established an official internet source at http://records.txdps.state.tx.us for information about criminal convictions, deferred adjudication, and sex offender registrations. This information is taken from the DPS' Computerized Criminal History (CCH) file, which is made up of records provided to DPS by courts and criminal justice agencies throughout the state.

---

[4] *Ibid.*

Although obtaining criminal history information online might sound fast and convenient, these websites are rife with warnings and disclaimers – about how to use the site correctly, the possibility of inaccurate information, and the importance of fingerprints as verification that you have the correct record.

It is important to note that there are dozens of websites offering criminal records and other types of record searches. Although many of these are mounted by reputable organizations, there are others that may not be as trustworthy or records may be incomplete or not recently updated. To avoid disappointment, it is important to know whom you are dealing with before requesting services or paying for documents.

From the County Recorder's Office – UCC Filings

UCC filings were described two pages previously. The majority of states make Uniform Commercial Code records available at the state level, but in some places UCCs may be found at the county level as well. A significant law change occurred in as of June 30, 2001, which forced many counties to stop recording UCC documents. This created a central filing location in every state. However, older records may still be viewed at the county level.

Real Property Transactions

Searching or monitoring real property transactions may provide advanced notice of a competitor's plans to expand a facility or build a new plant. The list of counties making this information available online is growing rapidly. In Maricopa County (Phoenix) Arizona, at http://recorder.maricopa.gov/recdocdata, you can view the index of real property transactions and then view a scanned image of the actual document. It is also possible to order a certified copy, if that is called for. This is very likely the wave of the future as scanning technology becomes available in more and more jurisdictions.

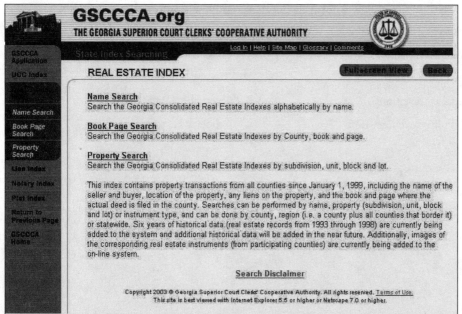

▶▶ The State of Georgia has created statewide indexes to a variety of public records. The Real Estate Index search provides several access points. Conveyances of real estate are highlighted in the search results. ◀◀

The NETRonline site, www.netronline.com, provides links to all fifty U.S. states plus Washington, DC, with a further breakdown that lists each county within each state. This site focuses on real estate and real property. Listings such as Appraisal District, Assessor/Collector, Recorder, or Clerk are examples of the entries under each county. You can quickly determine whether a county has any property-related records available online, which departments offer this service and which do not, and whether you will have to find other means of obtaining records for that county.

Search Systems and the www.publicrecordsources.com site maintained by BRB Publications, both mentioned previously in this chapter, cover the entire spectrum of public records. These sites are a good starting point when looking for county public record databases on the Internet.

Tax Office Records

At the county level, tax office records are likely to include the real property records. Searching these records may provide evidence regarding the extent of a company's holdings or tax indebtedness. You may also obtain specific details regarding individual properties. Over 2,000 counties offer online access.

How to Use County Tax Assessor Records

Many useful bits of intelligence can be located by examining tax records. The Dallas County (TX) Central Appraisal District, at www.DallasCAD.org is a prime example of an organization that has done some of the CI Sleuth's work for you, if plant information is what you need.

You might test this by entering part of a major corporation name headquartered in the Dallas area. For one such corporation, more than a dozen addresses for company facilities in Dallas County were located, of which six are labeled commercial. At least one entry involved DBA information, discussed earlier in this chapter. Several entries represented property within sports facilities. Using variations on the company name pointed to names of units of the corporation, including one for international operations.

The following categories of information are available for each property searched:

Property Location Data	Land Data
Valuation Data	Valuation Methods
Ownership Data	Taxing Jurisdictions
Legal Description	Exemption Data
Main Improvement Data	Property History

The most significant finding was listed under the following heading:

SKETCH OF THE BUILDING, INCLUDING DIMENSIONS

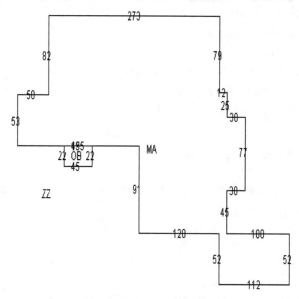

Drawing Copyright 1998, by TaxNet USA, Inc.

The inclusion of a drawing or the blueprints of the building has some interesting implications for several departments in your company. The information about plant size may be an indication of plant capacity and other manufacturing data.

Not every commercial vendor offers file types and services described here. It is important to ask vendors specific questions about their offerings to be sure the vendors provide what you are looking for. You may find it worthwhile to use the services of several different vendors in addition to "free" public record sites.

City or Local Public Records

City public records such as real estate, property, courts, and liens are now available for some cities. Nearly 1,000 cities have their own recording office, instead of recording at a county office. Most of these cities are in the New England area. A list of the websites with free record access for these cities, including Virginia Independent Cities, appears in *Public Records Online*[5].

The Chicago Contract Disclosures Database, now found at http://dmz2.ci.chi.il.us/discl/plsql/ dd_search_contract.bidder, contains affidavits provided by bidders from coffee and doughnuts shops to office equipment to $500 Million in Chicago O'Hare International General Airport Revenue Refunding Bonds. These documents provide insights on ownership of the business submitting the bid, whether large or small. Data includes the following:

---

[5] *Public Records Online*, 2004 Facts on Demand Press, BRB Publications, Tempe AZ, www.brbpub.com

Category	Type of Information Required
General Information	Exact legal name of bidder
	Address, contact information
	Project location
	Type of business entity of the proposer
	State of incorporation of proposer
	Authorization to do business in the State of Illinois
Corporations	Name and title of all officers and directors of the corporation
	Name, business address, and percentage of ownership interest of each shareholder
	Name, business address, and percentage of control of each member
Partnerships	Name, business address, and percentage of ownership interest of each therein
Limited liability companies	Names and titles of the officers
	Name, business address, and percentage of ownership interest of each (i) member and (ii) manager
For Land Trusts, Business Trusts, or Estates	Trust name (or other information identifying the trust), trustee name and business address of all trustees
	Name, business address, and percentage of ownership interest of all beneficiaries
Other Ownership Interests	Each principal's name, business address, percentage of ownership interest, and the name of the principal's agent or nominee
	Name and business address of each individual or entity possessing constructive control, the party whose interest is controlled, and the relationship between the two under which the control is or may be exercised
Other Project Information	Name and business address of each individual or legal entity currently holding legal title to the property for which City Assistance is being requested (the "Property")
	Name, business address, and percentage of ownership interest of each beneficiary if the title of the Property is held in a land trust
	Real estate tax index number(s) for the Property
	The kind, dollar amount, and due date of all water charges, sewer charges, property taxes and sales taxes, due and payable on or prior to the date hereof and concerning the Property
Additional Information	Whether the bidder or any member, partner, beneficiary or owner of the bidding entity has:
	• Ever been a defendant in any civil or criminal suits or legal actions.
	• Ever had any debts discharged, satisfied or settled under the Bankruptcy Act.
	• Ever had a judgment entered against him/her/it.
	• Ever been a party to a foreclosure, a deed in lieu of foreclosure, a loan default or a loan "workout" situation.

Certification of Environmental Compliance	Whether bidder has developed and has on file affirmative action programs pursuant to applicable federal regulations
	Whether bidder has participated in any previous contracts or subcontracts subject to the equal opportunity clause
Certification regarding Court-Ordered Child Support Compliance	Existence thereof
Equal Employment Opportunity	Whether bidder has developed and has on file affirmative action programs pursuant to applicable federal regulations
	Whether bidder has participated in any previous contracts or subcontracts subject to the equal opportunity clause
Retained Parties	Names of each and every attorney, lobbyist, accountant, consultant, subcontractor or other person retained or anticipated to be retained by the bidder with respect to or in combination with the City assistance to which this EDS pertains
Establishment of Business Relationships with City Elected Officials and Verification	Whether the bidder had a "business relationship" with any City elected officials in the 12 months prior to the date of execution of this Disclosure Affidavit
	If yes, the name(s) of such City elected official(s) and description(s) of such relationship(s)

If your business does any business in the Midwestern are of the U.S., this database could yield interesting facts about your company or its competitors. This type of information could be hard to locate in other sources if the bidders are privately held companies, partnerships, trusts, etc.

Options Abound, But Be Careful!

More and more government offices and agencies are making their databases searchable on the Internet. Most states are among those providing a variety of records, both civil and criminal. However, the greatest amount of public record information in cyberspace is provided by commercial online services of various types. When using public record vendors on the Internet, it is extremely important to choose a reputable source. Websites can come and go on a moment's notice, so it is crucial that you use a vendor that is a known entity, with a good track record.

Several years ago, before many of the current internet public record vendors had mounted websites, a search of the World Wide Web turned up a reference to a page offering public records. The "service" offered a list of record types, and made certain vague promises. They wanted a credit card number in advance, of course, and provided an email order form, but crucial information on their organization seemed to be missing. An email message was sent requesting this public record vendor's company name and location. Several days later a reply arrived:

"We don't give out that type of information."

If you are going to do business with a company, you have a right to know who they are and where they are located. This organization aroused suspicion. Several months later, the site was no longer available. The moral of this story is "Caveat vendor."

Accessing Public Record Online Services

Public record services – or public records vendors – are available both on the Internet and in traditional dial-up mode. Many long-time subscribers to these services prefer dial-up access for security reasons, while others simply resist changing to the Internet while believing that "If it is not broken, don't fix it." Still others realize that certain large internet public records services frequently seem to have one or more files "temporarily unavailable."

The major vendors have continued to support their proprietary software in addition to mounting internet sites. For heavy use, this approach is definitely recommended.

Additional Services May Be Called For

Finding a record online may not be sufficient for your needs. You may need additional services from time to time. BRB Publications at www.brbpub.com and www.publicrecordsources.com offer free lists of vendors and public record retrievers who are members of the Public Record Retrieval Network. Most vendors should be able to provide additional services that complement the public record search. Watch for these:

Document Retrieval

The online public record may provide an identifying number that points to a document that is available in full text only at the source, e.g. at a courthouse, the Tax Assessor's Office, etc. If the vendor offers document retrieval, you can request a copy of the full document, placing your order while at the vendor's website or while connected to their service via dial-up. A few additional screens must be filled in to provide instructions regarding shipping method desired, address, etc.

The vendor retains correspondents, sometimes referred to as "runners," in county seats or state capitals. When your request is received electronically, the vendor contacts the runner who is familiar with local facilities and procedures. The runner obtains the document and sends it directly to you, adhering to the your delivery instructions.

The cost for all of this work appears in your next monthly bill. You should expect to pay for three services:

- The online record search, which compensates the vendor.
- The runner's fee, which has been paid by the vendor.
- Copying fees, which are levied by the office where the documents were obtained.

Search Service

What about records that are not available online? (Most are not.) Through your vendor you may by able to order documents from jurisdictions not currently available online. You must provide as much information, or identifiers such as DOB, SSN, etc., as possible so that the correct document can be located.

Customer Service

Customer service should be available through a toll-free number. The customer service representative should be familiar with the types of public record files offered, the content of various types of records, and services offered by the vendor.

Some websites that provide products or services offer support only via email. You may not want to wait for several hours or overnight for an answer to your question. In that case, you may find it worthwhile to do business with a vendor that provides telephone support.

After noting the date of the last update to a database, you may wish to conduct a manual search at the corresponding courthouse or government office for records that may have been filed since that date. You might locate new records or updates of existing ones.

Valuable Sources — A Bit of Name Dropping

Some public record vendors, like ChoicePoint, Information America, and LexisNexis, were among the earliest vendors in the field. A sign of the times, Information America no longer exists, but its internet product, KnowX, is still available as one of ChoicePoint's brand names. ChoicePoint also owns AutoTrackXP, another formerly independent player in the public records marketplace. These services and their competitors have loaded databases of federal, state, and county files from across the country. It is from these services that you will find the greatest depth and breadth of coverage. Each of these major vendors has taken a different approach to providing access to their service via the Internet.

AutoTrackXP

Many investigators and law enforcement agencies nationwide use the AutoTrackXP service, at www.autotrackxp.com to access more than seventeen billion publicly available records. DBT makes available proprietary applications to help insurance companies and other qualified requestors gather data to solve crimes, locate people and assets, and detect and prevent fraud.

ChoicePoint Online

This services markets to insurance, government, banking, law enforcement, healthcare, and the legal industry. Their "data stores" groups together files useful for specific groups of users, including:

Address Inspector	OSHA
Business Directory	Physician Reports
Corporations & Limited Partnerships	Real Property Ownership
Death Locator	Significant Shareholder
Enhanced Creditheader	Telephone/Consumer Directory
FAA Aircraft Ownership	UCC Searches
FAA Airmen Directory	Watercraft
FEIN Financial Data	

ChoicePoint subscriptions are sold on both an individual and enterprises basis.

KnowX

KnowX, at www.knowx.com, has become one of the most popular and powerful websites for public record information on the Internet. Certain searches can be performed at no cost, with the option of paying a fee for the detailed version of the record. Since the existence of a record may be an answer in and of itself, the KnowX search service itself can be a real information bargain.

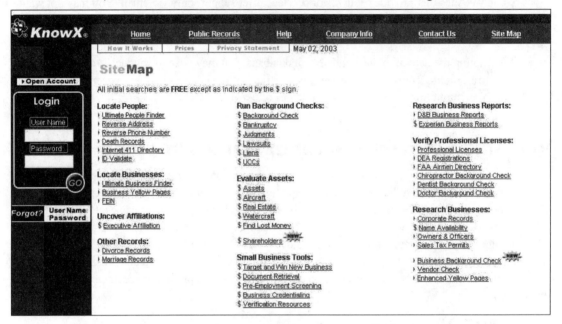

▶▶ Both "easy" and "professional" interfaces are available at KnowX,
a popular internet source for public record information. ◀◀

A real "plus" with KnowX is its approach to billing. There are no setup or registration fees. Searching is free, but to display records a fixed fee per record is incurred. Costs vary with the type of record accessed. If working on a major research project, a daily pass can be purchased, providing unlimited access for a 24-hour period for specified searches. Using pay-as-you-go or a daily pass means that you are not paying monthly subscription fees that are incurred even if you do not search during some months. In addition, you do not have the headache of dealing with monthly check writing, postage, and other administrative costs. Finally, you are dealing with a reputable source that has a long and respected track record in the business.

Lexis Public Records

LexisNexis includes its Lexis Public Records service at the www.nexis.com. Record groups with CI applications include the Asset Locator, Bankruptcy, Civil and Criminal Filings, Judgments and Liens, Jury Verdicts and Settlements categories. The list of records available should be explored, though, because with creative thinking you may uncover files that can be useful to your company.

The Jury Verdicts and Settlements file, not found on most online public record services, can be a useful source of business intelligence. Suppose, for example, that you are interested in a company that manufactures motorized equipment such as lawnmowers. A search of this database, using the company name as a search term, might indicate that the company had some problems with lawsuits involving safety issues in connection with their products. This information might not cause you to change your mind about a possible deal, but you would want to know about the lawsuits as part of your due diligence efforts, and address the subject matter during discussions with that company.

Merlin Information Services

Merlin Information Services, at www.merlindata.com, is a new force in the online public records business. Merlin offers a free search of thirty million names. Their "Ultimate Weapon" is a master index to the Merlin California Public Record and Banko National Bankruptcy databases (See picture on page 99). The *QuickInfo* selection on the homepage links to a gateway with a third-party provider that provides records of various types for 25+ states. The company's website offers free trials to interested prospects.

Merlin Information's emphasis on California records is not surprising. The State of California has been cited as the world's sixth largest economy. The huge variety of products and services produced there points to the likely possibility that, sooner or later, you will find that one or more of the competitors in your company's industry has offices or plants there.

Search Systems

www.searchsystems.net may be the largest and most comprehensive collection of links to government websites databases on the Internet. The site (see picture on page 105) boosts of providing more than 10,000 links to free or fee government record databases around the world and may occasionally be useful in business intelligence research. By comparison, the competing site at www.brbpub.com/pubrecsites.asp offers over 2000 links to free searchable public record sites.

Chapter 9

Government Databases

A Wealth of Information – Free!

Distribution methods for U.S. government information have changed radically in the past few years as more and more agencies have created sites on the World Wide Web. And CD-ROM technology has facilitated the sale of disks containing large, searchable databases. Compiled statistical data, laws and regulations, required filings, government research, and many other types of information are now available for searching and downloading.

Whether you import or export, want to sell products or services to the Federal Government, or must research laws and regulations that apply to your company, you now have easy, cost-effective or even free access to crucial data needed to survive in today's competitive environment. Government information will also help you to monitor industries or competitor companies — it is all there for the taking.

The important thing, of course, is that you take advantage of the possibilities for turning this mountain of government data in actionable intelligence. Here are some possibilities:

Finding Out Who Sells to the Government

In the U.S. it is possible to find out which of your competitors is selling goods or services to Federal Government agencies, what they are selling, how much they are selling, and for what price. Prior to January, 2002, you could find this information on the Internet at the *Commerce Business Daily*'s CBD*Net* site, http://cbdnet.access.gpo.gov/search1.html. *Commerce Business Daily (CBD)* listed notices of proposed government procurement actions, contract awards, sales of government property, and other procurement information. The printed version of *Commerce Business Daily* is no longer available, but this archive remains searchable for information posted through Dec.31, 2001.

Since January 2002, the Fed Biz Opps site, www.fedbizopps.gov, is the designated single point of universal electronic public access on the Internet for Federal procurement opportunities that exceed $25,000. Notices posted here remain active for two weeks, after which time they are moved to the Fed Biz Opps archive file, which also may be accessed from the main search screen.

Fed Biz Opps offers a full text search of the database, allowing you to limit your search by several date options. Additional options allow you to search broadly or narrowly through the following:

- Active documents
- Archive
- Synopses
- Awards
- Solicitation or Award Number
- Dates
- Place of Performance Zip Code – especially important where services are sought
- Set-aside Code – are you a small business or a *very* small business, for example?
- Procurement Classification - there are codes for both products and services
- Agency
- Office
- NAICS code

Here is an example of how the Biz Opps database can work for you. Suppose your company manufactures valves. One of your competitors is Tescom. You want to learn whether Tescom supplies valves to the Federal government, and how much these contracts are worth in dollars. Searching "Tescom" in the search box and checking the AWARDS box would retrieve the following:

Search Results

Contract Award

Archived Postings: 1/335456

March 20, 2002
Agency: Department of the Navy
Office: Naval Supply Systems Command
Location: NAVICP-Mechanicsburg
➧ Posted: March 20, 2002 **Type:** <u>Award</u> **Title:** 48---Valve,Pressure Reg
Award Number: N0010402PBF67..Sol.Nr.N00104-02-Q-BG42..NIIN.014467188

By clicking on the underlined "Award" link shown above, the award details are displayed:

48---Valve,Pressure Reg

General Information

Document Type: Award Notice
Solicitation Number:
Posted Date: Mar 20, 2002
Archive Date: Apr 09, 2002
Classification Code: 48 -- Valves

Contracting Office Address

NAVICP, 5450 CARLISLE PIKE, P.O. BOX 2020 MECHANICSBURG, PA 17055-0788

Description

Contract Award Date: Mar 25, 2002
Contract Award Number: N0010402PBF67..Sol.Nr.N00104-02-Q-BG42. NIIN.014467188
Contract Award Amount: $91,550
Contract Line Item Number: 0001
Contractor: Tescom Corp., Elk River ,MN 55330-3224

▶▶ The search results retrieved from the Fed Biz Opps database are displayed in a very readable format. Additional information includes the name of the contact person at Tescom. ◀◀

The addition of the full text search box has drawbacks for some searchers. Other than awards, there is no longer an easy way to limit search results to a particular document type. The Fed Biz Opps Customer Support line provided a tip that involves html coding. To use this method, type the following into the Full Text Search box on the search screen, exactly as it is written, but substitute another letter for x:

"x" <in> action_code_plid

Choose the appropriate letter from this list to search for a specific document type:

P = Pre-solicitation Notice   **S** = Special Notice
A = Award Notice   **F** = Foreign Government Standard
M = Modification to a Previous Notice **G** = Sale of Surplus Property
R = Sources Sought Notice   **K** = Combined Synopsis/Solicitation

Searching by additional document types can narrow search results considerably. The phrase *special notice*, for example, could appear in the full text of documents other than Document Type: Special

Notice. Searching only full text, you may have to sort through much extraneous material to get to what you are looking for. When you have successfully located documents of the type you seek, you may find a button that will allow you to sign up to receive certain notices electronically.

If using the government site seems too complicated, NEPAC, Inc. offers a subscription-based service for those who would like to automate the process of keeping up with government procurement. Located at www.cbd-net.com, *CBD/FBO Online* allows you to store one or more profiles and to search on-demand using the predetermined searches stored in your profile. A helpful human assists in creating these profiles. For an additional fee, a monitoring service is available using the categories and/or keywords in the stored profiles. You will receive a CBD/FBO email each morning containing announcements, awards, RFPs, surplus properties and special notices that meet your search criteria.

The Federal Procurement Data System - Next Generation (FPDS-NG)

To round out the study of government procurement, examining the picture for previous years may prove useful. This information can be obtained from the Federal Procurement Data System, at www.fpdc.gov/fpdc/fpdc_home.htm. Reports for the past three years may be viewed or downloaded in three parts: Total Federal View, Geographic View, and Agency Views.

Section I, the Total Federal View, provides a great deal of background information, but concludes with a table that may be useful when you have only a short time to provide the Boss with a list of the top civilian or Department of Defense contractors in areas such as research and development, construction, supplies and equipment, data processing, or architectural and engineering services.

Section II provides a geographic breakdown on a state-by-state basis. Here you can learn not only how much was spent in each state, but the names of counties where contracts were awarded; five top agencies and contracting offices in the state; type of product or service; and finally, the names of the top ten civilian and DOD contractors in each state, with contract amounts. These lists may provide useful information if you are studying a privately held company that does business with the government. SEC filings or Annual Reports will not be available to help in such cases.

Section III consists of an agency-by-agency breakdown of contract information, but may not be as useful as the first two sections for gathering business intelligence.

Procurement Information For Canada

Public Works and Government Services Canada maintains a Contracts History Database, which is searchable at http://csi.contractscanada.gc.ca/csi/prod/en/applctrl.cfm?.

Information may be retrieved here on contracts awarded by PWGSC on behalf of other federal government departments for the last three years. A directory lists contact information for managers for PWGSC purchasing organizations, together with the goods and services their divisions buy.

Learn Who Is Doing What With Government Research Dollars

The U.S. Department of Energy's (DOE) Office of Scientific and Technical Information (OSTI) provides access to a wealth of energy, science, and technology research and development (R&D) information. This agency's *Federal R&D Project Summaries* website at http://fedrnd.osti.gov provides three searchable databases:

- DOE R&D Project Summaries Database
- NIH CRISP Database - Current Awards
- NSF Awards Database

These files can be searched individually or simultaneously to retrieve detailed descriptions regarding the projects and awards, including dates; names of individuals, companies, or other organizations; funding mechanism; contract number; performance city, state, and zip; contact information; and abstract. Exact data elements vary by database, but name searching may retrieve a lengthy list of projects in which competitors are involved, names of researchers, and other details.

There are several CI applications here. By learning what other companies are already doing, you may avoid duplication of effort if your organization is considering a project that has been funded by a government grant or which is already underway. You can learn the names of researchers working for competitors or in academic environments – this may provide valuable information for your company's Human Resources Department who may be trying to recruit people with specific backgrounds, qualifications, or experience. The data found in these records may prove useful if scientists in your organization wish to obtain grants. Learning about the amounts typically awarded or "hot" topics may improve your organization's grant application.

Making the Most of SEC Filings

Publicly traded companies in the U.S. are required to file a variety of documents periodically with the U.S. Securities and Exchange Commission. Many of these documents are retrievable through the SEC's Electronic Data Gathering, Analysis, and Retrieval System (EDGAR), at www.sec.gov/index.htm.

Certain documents, such as Forms 3, 4, and 5 (security ownership and transaction reports filed by corporate insiders) and Form 144 (notice of proposed sale of securities) may be filed on EDGAR, but this is not mandatory. For example, with the exception of investment companies, a company's annual report to shareholders need not be submitted on EDGAR. Form 10-K or 10-KSB must be filed on EDGAR. As of November 4, 2002, all foreign companies and foreign governments must file their documents on EDGAR.

Of the various SEC filings that you will want to search for business intelligence, the **10-K** is one of the most important. The 10-K contains financial information not included in a company's annual report to shareholders. This filing also may mention pending litigation, related party transactions, side deals, and audit footnotes. Conversely, the Management Discussion section found in annual reports may be useful material not included in the 10-K.

Companies also are required to file a **10-Q**, which provides a continuing view of a company's financial position during the year. The filing is due 45 days after each of the first three fiscal quarters. It is not required that 10-Qs be audited, however, so always check the 10-K, which *is* audited. You never know what errors could have slipped into the un-audited 10-Q. Non-U.S. companies doing business in the U.S. must file a **20-F**, which provides a continuing view of a company's financial position during that year. The filing is due 45 days after each of the first three fiscal quarters.

EDGAR Special Purpose Searches

It is possible to search the EDGAR site by company name, and to retrieve a list that company's filings. These filing can then be displayed in full text format. As the EDGAR website has evolved, several other types of searches, described as "Special Purpose Searches," have been added. They are:

- **EDGAR CIK (Central Index Key) Lookup**
  CIK allows you to perform a more accurate search for a company's SEC filings without the confusion caused by similar-looking names. You search the EDGAR Archives using a unique identifier, (e.g. 00001111) instead of searching by company name. All companies and people who file disclosures with the SEC are given such an ID.

- **Latest Filings**
  Here you can locate a company's filings for the current official filing date including those made after the 5:30 pm deadline on the previous filing day. Available search criteria include company name, CIK, and form type. Information provided includes form number (e.g. 10-Q), formats available, description, time and date accepted by the SEC, and filing date.

- **Current Events Analysis**
  Analyze forms filed in the previous week, including 10-K (annual) and 10-Q (quarterly) reports, proxies, and others. For a given period of time, you can create a list of all companies that have made a particular type of filing.

- **Historical EDGAR Archives**
  Enter complex queries to retrieve all but the most recent day's EDGAR filings from 1993 through the present. Either simple or Internet search modes are available. The Internet mode allows you to use query language similar to that of commonly used search engines. Search results on a company may be limited by date or by the type of filing, for example, "10-K."

- **Mutual Funds Prospectus Search**
  Monitor the competition's prospectus filings now, for the past week, last two weeks, last month, or since 1994. Prospectus Search retrieves all "485" forms, such as the 485APOS, 485BPOS, and 485B24E.

- **Litigation Release or Administrative Hearings Search**
  Learn details of suits or administrative proceedings by the SEC against individuals or companies. If the SEC has sued or instituted proceedings against your competitor since 1995, there is likely to be a listing in these files. There is not a search engine here, but by using the Ctrl F command from the keyboard, your browser will locate each occurrence of a word or phrase. Releases issued before 1995 can be obtained through the agency's Public Reference Room by email at publicinfo@sec.gov.

- **Commission Opinions or Trading Suspensions Search**
  These contain more details of actions against companies or individuals. They can be search as described above.

SEC Filings May Contain a "Heads Up" for CI Practitioners

By analyzing the type and frequency of SEC filings made by one or more public companies in your industry, you may be able to make comparisons or to discern certain things that are going on within those organizations. Examine the list of filings contained in this book Appendix to see which filings contain what you are looking for and then check regularly or set up a monitoring system to watch for filings by the companies that interest you. Here are a few examples of applications:

- **Executive Compensation Test**
  Proxy Statements contain salary information for top executives. Compare executive compensation information for publicly traded companies in easy-to-read form from a proxy (DEF 14A) filing. These filings may be available in text or html. The html versions provide links for viewing the documents, including tables of contents. These point you quickly to the information you seek. Additional discussion of executive compensation is found in Chapter 7.

- **Building a List of Players in an Industry**
  The EDGAR Company Search allows searching by SIC code to retrieve a list of companies that fit the category searched. A hotlink on the search screen provides codes for easy reference.

- **Spotting patterns or trends in activities of companies or individuals**
  The Latest Filings search lets you monitor not only your U.S. competition and filings by foreign companies, but you can learn about the stock holdings of officers or directors, including the amount of their holdings after the current transaction.

The Descriptions section of the table indicates the identity of the filer by means of the following labels:

Filer – *made by and described the company named*

Subject – *describes the company named, but was made by another entity*

Filed by – *filing was made by the company named, but describes a subject company*

Reporting – *filing by an individual reporting holdings in a company*

Paper – *a paper copy is available in the SEC Public Reference Room*

If, for example, you locate a record with the *Reporting* tag, you might see something like this:

Form	Formats	Description	Filing Date
4	[html][text] 5 KB	Statement of changes in beneficial ownership of securities	2003-05-07
4/A	[html][text] 5 KB	[Amend]Statement of changes in beneficial ownership of securities	2003-05-07
4	[html][text] 4 KB	Statement of changes in beneficial ownership of securities	2003-05-07
4	[html][text] 19 KB	Statement of changes in beneficial ownership of securities	2003-05-02
4	[html][text] 19 KB	Statement of changes in beneficial ownership of securities	2003-05-01
4	[html][text] 19 KB	Statement of changes in beneficial ownership of securities	2003-04-30
4	[html][text] 19 KB	Statement of changes in beneficial ownership of securities	2003-04-29
4	[html][text] 19 KB	Statement of changes in beneficial ownership of securities	2003-04-28
4	[html][text] 17 KB	Statement of changes in beneficial ownership of securities	2003-04-25
4	[html][text] 17 KB	Statement of changes in beneficial ownership of securities	2003-04-24
4	[html][text] 17 KB	Statement of changes in beneficial ownership of securities	2003-04-24
4	[html][text] 17 KB	Statement of changes in beneficial ownership of securities	2003-04-24
4	[html][text] 17 KB	Statement of changes in beneficial ownership of securities	2003-04-21
4	[html][text] 17 KB	Statement of changes in beneficial ownership of securities	2003-04-17
4	[html][text] 17 KB	Statement of changes in beneficial ownership of securities	2003-04-17
4	[html][text] 17 KB	Statement of changes in beneficial ownership of securities	2003-04-16
4	[html][text] 17 KB	Statement of changes in beneficial ownership of securities	2003-04-16
4	[html][text] 17 KB	Statement of changes in beneficial ownership of securities	2003-04-11
4	[html][text] 17 KB	Statement of changes in beneficial ownership of securities	2003-04-10
4	[html][text] 17 KB	Statement of changes in beneficial ownership of securities	2003-04-10
4	[html][text] 17 KB	Statement of changes in beneficial ownership of securities	2003-04-08
4	[html][text] 17 KB	Statement of changes in beneficial ownership of securities	2003-04-07
4	[html][text] 17 KB	Statement of changes in beneficial ownership of securities	2003-04-04

▶▶A Director of a small California high-tech company has reduced his holdings in the company by a substantial amount during the first half of 2003, putting the proceeds into a family trust. Competitor companies studying this organization might be able to draw some interesting conclusions based on this pattern of insider stock sales. Details can be viewed by clicking on html or text. ◀◀

One additional free site for SEC or Canadian CSA filings is SEC Info, at www.secinfo.com. This site allows both general and specific access points. Homepage links provide lists of mergers and acquisitions, tender offers, IPOs, and other financial topics. Companies can be searched by name, industry, business, SIC code, area code, topic, CIK, accession number, file number, date, and ZIP. An individual company search yields a tabular list of links to compnay filings for a number of years. Filing numbers are supplemented by descriptions, dates, and numbers of documents. A nice additional feature is the email service that alerts you when a target company makes a new filing.

Subscription Services Offer Advantages

Several commercial vendors provide access to SEC filings. EDGAR Online Inc. offers both EDGAR Online, a subscription based service at www.edgar-online.com, and FreeEDGAR, at http://sec.freeedgar.com. The free service offers company searching and a few extras such as the People search, but features such as Watchlist Alerting, RTF and Excel Downloading are now available only on the subscription product. Complex fundamental, ownership, initial public offering and secondary offering datasets, and advanced search tools that were previously available only on an enterprise version of the product are now available as part of EDGAR Online Pro. Although these tools may be more useful to investment professionals than the general corporate world, the ownership information may be valuable worth the subscription cost if your organization regularly needs ownership breakdowns of publicly-held companies.

The Global Securities Information, Inc. LIVEDGAR site, www.liveedgar.com, is another vendor in this arena. EDGAR filings, SEC No-Action Letters, Non-EDGAR paper filings such as F-1s, 20-Fs, and 6-Ks, and 26,000+ Non-U.S. Registered Offerings are offered here. Links to the underlying source content are provided.

Another option would be *10-K Wizard*, at www.tenkwizard.com. The interface screen offers the predictable searches such as company name, CIK, etc. Additional search boxes contain drop-down lists that use words rather than form numbers or SIC codes. You may narrow searches by filing type or industry. The search results screen offers links as follows: Profile, Financials, Audit Letters, Filings with Exhibits.

Most commercial vendors provide additional services such as monitoring services, non-SEC offering circulars, custom research, and free annual reports.

Securities Information in Canada

Since 1997, the Canadian Securities Administrators (CSA) and the Canadian Depository for Securities (CDS) have made public securities filings and related information available online through the System for Electronic Document Analysis and Retrieval (SEDAR). Company and mutual fund profiles, SEDAR public securities filings, and news about SEDAR are all available in one convenient website at www.sedar.com.

Links on the site provide access to Securities Commissions of the various Canadian provinces, U.S. securities sites, and to stock exchanges in Canada, the U.S., London, and Tokyo. Additional pages provide links to new public company filings, new annual reports of public companies, new financial statements, press releases, prospectuses, take-over bid materials, and mutual fund filings. Designed by a former investment banker, the site offers free email alerts and one billion links within the documents and exhibits in the database.

There Is So Much More Out There...

Securities-related filings are indeed an information goldmine, but dozens of other government agencies offer searchable databases that may help you to uncover crucial business intelligence. Topics such as safety and hazards, disciplinary matters, and trade are among the wealth of available data, in addition to these examples:

Finding Out Who Gave $$$ to Whom

The Federal Election Commission

In the U.S., the FEC at www.fec.gov provides financial reports containing all receipts and disbursements that committees are required to disclose under the Federal Election Campaign Act, including contributions from individuals, party committees, PACs, and candidates regardless of amount, also loans received by committees, and other kinds of receipts. If you are interested in whether your competition is contributing to one or more congressional candidates, consider these possibilities:

- **Individual Search** - Contributions made by individuals, if the gift totals more than $200 during a year, may be searched using contributor name, city, state, zip code, principal place of business, date, and amount.

- **Committee Search** - Search for contributions received or made by a specific committee using committee name, city, state, zip code, treasurer name, party designation, committee type.

- **Candidate Search** - Search for contributions received by a specific campaign using candidate's name, state, district, party affiliation, and incumbent or challenger status.

A detailed alphabetical list of acronyms, abbreviations, initials, and common names of federal political action committees (PACs) is available on the site. This is useful for determining how companies donate to candidates' campaigns through their PACs.

Political Contributions in Canada

Elections Canada offers a searchable database on contributions and expenses reported by candidates and registered political parties. Searchable lists of contributors are available from the 1998 general election forward, though other earlier information may be downloaded.

All contributions over $100.00 and all candidates' expenses are also available. Data for political parties is drawn from their returns of election expenses and from their fiscal period returns. You can either search the data online or download the full list of contributors for each party.

The Environmental Protection Agency

The Environmental Protection Agency offers searchable databases of intelligence from filings made by companies regulated by the agency. Valuable information about a surprising number of types of businesses can be retrieved from these EPA files. Whether considering small local dry cleaning plants, major chemical companies, or municipalities – the contents of EPA records may provide details that can help your organization gain a competitive advantage over a troubled competitor. The Envirofacts Warehouse, at www.epa.gov/enviro/index_java.html, shown below, provides a single access point to more than a dozen databases, on a variety of topics. By searching all relevant files, you may compile an entire dossier on your target.

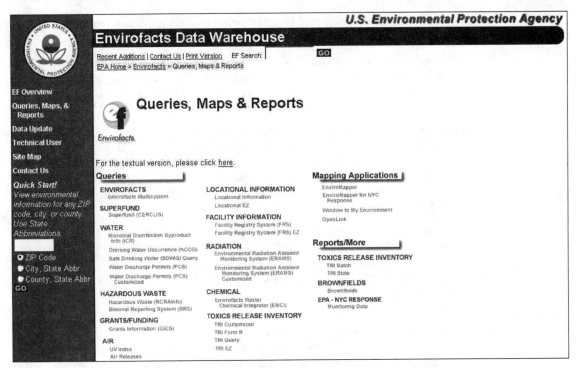

▸▸Clicking the Advanced Capabilities link on the Envirofacts homepage brings up
the detail screen shown above. ◂◂

The Envirofacts Multisystem Query

The Envirofacts Multisystem Query integrates information from six different databases, including
latitude and longitude information. Each database contains information about facilities required to
report activity to a state or federal system. You can retrieve information about hazardous waste
(including the biennial report), toxic and air releases, Superfund sites, and water discharge permits.
This query is fully integrated with EnviroMapper.

EPA links are available for searching additional specialized databases that cover these areas:

Superfund

- **Superfund Database**
  The federal government locates, investigates and cleans up the worst hazardous waste sites
  throughout the U.S., designating them "Superfund sites." This includes abandoned
  warehouses, landfills, and industrial facilities where hazardous waste was continually dumped
  into the environment before regulated. The *Superfund query form* is available for searching
  the database.

Water

- **Water Permit Compliance System**
  The Clean Water Act established pollution limits and monitoring and reporting requirements
  for wastewater dischargers and who must have a permit. The National Pollutant Discharge
  Elimination System (NPDES) permits regulate household and industrial wastes that are
  collected in sewers and treated at municipal wastewater treatment plants as well as industrial

point sources and concentrated animal feeding operations that discharge wastewater. Use the *Water Discharge Permits query form* to retrieve permit information.

- **Safe Drinking Water Information**
  The EPA collects data about how well water utilities comply with drinking water regulations and if enforcement actions were taken against utilities. Use the *Safe Drinking Water Database query form* to view a utility's violations and enforcement history for the last ten years.

- **National Drinking Water Contaminant Occurrence Information**
  The National Drinking Water Contaminant Occurrence Database (NCOD) holds information from a number of sources, including public water systems and source (ambient) water. NCOD contains regulated and unregulated contaminant data for public water systems. Use the *NCOD query form* to access information on contaminant occurrence in an individual system or by geographical area.

- **Drinking Water Microbial and Disinfection Byproduct Information**
  The Information Collection Rule (ICR) required water systems serving 100,000 people or more to collect samples and report on source water and treated water levels. Twelve months worth of these data can be searched using the *ICR query form* to view reports at the water system, state, and national levels.

Hazardous Waste

- **Resource Conservation and Recovery Information System**
  The Resource Conservation and Recovery Information System contains data provided by generators, transporters, treaters, storers, and disposers of hazardous waste. These entities provide information concerning their activities to state environmental agencies, which then provide the information to regional and national U.S. (EPA) offices. This information may be retrieved using the *Hazardous Waste Data query form*.

- **Biennial Reporting System**
  Detailed information is collected on the generation of hazardous waste from large quantity generators, and data on waste management practices from treatment, storage, and disposal facilities. The Biennial Report is compiled from this data, which is useful for trend analysis.

Grants/Funding

- **Grants Information and Control System National System**
  The Grants Information and Control System national system is used to track, award, administer, and monitor grants. Envirofacts provides the public with award information for Construction, Non-Construction, and State Revolving Funds grant programs. The *Grants Information query form* allows you to read about projects that have received grants.

Location Information

Location information for EPA-regulated facilities in Envirofacts comes from many sources, including EPA federal program systems, EPA regional offices, and the states through Supplementary Return Files. This information is stored in the Locational Reference Tables (LRT). Also available here are the applicable business rules for depicting the locations of federally regulated entities. Data elements from EPA's Facility Information database and Locational Reference database can be compiled into a tabular report or a Comma Separated Value (CSV) file for downloading by using the *EZ query form*.

Facility Information

Facility information in Envirofacts is derived from several sources, including all of the program systems in Envirofacts. The *Facility Registry System query form* or the *Facility Registry System EZ Query* can be used to view facility data.

Radiation

Environmental Radiation Ambient Monitoring System

The Environmental Radiation Ambient Monitoring System (ERAMS) is a national network of more than 200 monitoring stations that regularly sample the nation's air, precipitation, drinking water, or pasteurized milk for a variety of radionuclides and radiation types. Use the *Environmental Radiation Ambient Monitoring System query form* or the *Environmental Radiation Ambient Monitoring System Customized query form* to search this information.

Air

Aerometric Information Retrieval System /AIRS Facility Subsystem

Envirofacts contains information about stationary sources of air pollution facilities in the Aerometric Information Retrieval System (AIRS)/AIRS Facility Subsystem (AFS). Examples of facilities sources include electric power plants, steel mills, factories, and universities.

Chemicals

Envirofacts Master Chemical Integrator

The *Envirofacts Master Chemical Integrator query form* allows you to obtain the acronyms, chemical identification numbers, and chemical names reported in Envirofacts.

Toxic Releases

Toxic Release Inventory

The Toxics Release Inventory provides the public with information about potentially hazardous substances in their community. A total of 600 chemicals have been determined toxic, and some industries must report to EPA if they use or handle these chemicals. This information is added to Envirofacts and made available via several different query options:

- The *Toxic Releases Query* provides facility information and chemical reports, which include air emissions, surface water discharges, releases to land, underground injections, and transfers to off-site locations.

- *TRI State Reports* contain information by state about releases and transfers of chemicals and compounds. These reports include a list of the top five chemicals released or transferred in that state and a list of the top ten facilities that released or transferred the largest amount of chemicals.

- The *Toxics Release Inventory EZ Query* provides selective retrieval of data, offering a view of the toxic release information that interests you.

- The *TRI Customized Query Engine* allows retrieval by table name or by column heading within that table. Various sort options are available. This query is designed for advanced searchers.

- *TRI Batch Reports* provide a different look at the subject matter – retrieval is available by reporting year, release estimates, chemicals involved, geographic location, and more. These reports are run in batch mode. Requestors are notified by email when the desired report is complete.

- The *TRI Form R Query* allows you to retrieve information by facility name and to view all associated chemical and release data submitted by a facility on a Form R report.

Mapping Applications

A variety of maps may be generated by combining data from within Envirofacts and data from other sources. GIS functionality is available to examine spatial data at the county, state, and national level, to display multiple spatial layers, and to query single Envirofacts points. These mapping applications include Envirofacts, EnviroMapper, EnviroMapper for New York City Response, Window to My Environment, and OpenLink.

Brownfields

The Brownfields Initiative began in 1995. It provides up to $200,000 for two years to qualified states, cities, towns, counties, and tribes for the purpose of identifying brownfields sites and facilitating their cleanup. Since the Brownfields Initiatives program attempts to revitalize these areas economically and environmentally, it is possible that a business opportunity might be found in or near one of these areas.

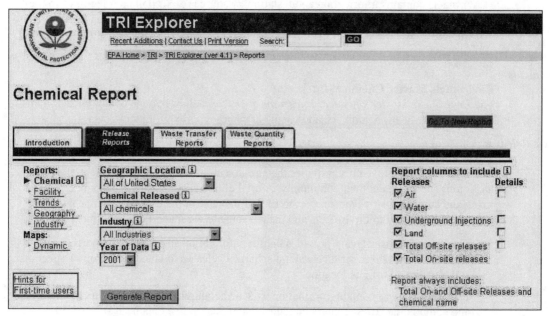

▸▸ With increasingly sophisticated technology available, Government websites have improved access to data through the use of search interfaces like the one above, which contains a variety of options for retrieval and display of information. ◂◂

Putting EPA Data to Good Use

Suppose you are interested in everything that can be located on Company X. You might perform a Facility Information search to locate plant sites. By entering all or part of the company name, you would retrieve the following, in tabular format:

Facility Name	Location Address	City Name	County Name	State	Zip	DUNS Number

To focus the search a bit, limit by geographic location (from the Zip Code to state level) or by database. The default is to search all of the databases. Another option here is to search by SIC code. This could be useful if you wished to see what companies in a certain industry sector were doing business in a particular geographic area.

Perhaps your company manufactures emissions control equipment. You might build a list of plants that are in violation, and market your technology or service to them.

If you were examining certain types of companies for merger or acquisition purposes, you would definitely want to know their track record with the EPA, otherwise, you could be acquiring more problems than you bargained for!

You also can search the Enforcement and Compliance Docket and Information Center (ECDIC), found at www.epa.gov/compliance/resources/policies/docket.html. The Civil Enforcement Docket is the EPA system for tracking civil judicial cases filed on the Agency's behalf by the Department of Justice from 1972 to the present. The Administrative Docket contains the issued administrative orders and complaints. Note that not all EPA administrative actions are included in the Docket.

To actually see where a company has been sued by the U.S. Environmental Protection Agency, go to http://cfpub.epa.gov/compliance/resources/cases/civil/. Links are provided to some of the more significant cases and settlements involving the EPA from 1998 to the present time. The actual cases are found by looking under the statute involved. Relevant press releases, fact sheet, and Consent Decree are available in PDF format. This system can be a bit cumbersome, but it provides internet access rather than the previous subscription-based CD-ROMs.

Occupational Safety and Health Administration

OSHA provides online access to information that could provide some insights into what goes on in the workplace. Here are some possible methods of gaining information on a company or industry:

- **Search for accidents** – the web page at www.osha.gov/cgi-bin/inv/inv1 allows the user to search the text of Accident Investigation Summaries (OSHA-170 form). Search keywords, by company name for a specific company, or enter an SIC code to view the types of accidents that have occurred since 1972 in that category. Beginning in 2003, NAICS codes will be collected as incidents occur, so it is likely that searching by NAICS will be available in the future.

- **Search for inspections within an industry**- at www.osha.gov/cgi-bin/sichq/sic1 users can search for OSHA enforcement inspections within a specified industry group. This page already offers NAICS searching, which may allow for a more narrow focus when searching types of businesses. Information may also be obtained for a specified inspection or inspections within a specified establishment.

- **Search for administrative review board decisions -** The Occupational Safety and Health Review Commission (OSHRC) is an independent Federal agency that decides contests of citations or penalties resulting from OSHA inspection. This commission functions as an administrative court, so if there is a review of an OSHA decision, the details will appear in these records.

- **Perform an advanced search** – Here the user may specify the types of sources used for retrieving search terms. Possibilities include Congressional testimony, the Federal Register, corporate-wide settlement agreements, and more. Results can be limited to current or archived material. It may be useful to learn where a company is mentioned, or what they have said in testimony or documents connected with occupational safety.

The Federal Deposit Insurance Corporation (FDIC)

The FDIC Bank Data Institution Directory, at www3.fdic.gov/idasp/ offers searches for institutions or bank holding companies. Data is searchable going back as far as 1992 and can be accessed by ID number, name, city, or state. The site also allows you to compare two institutions, groups, or holding companies, providing detailed data on assets and liabilities, income and expenses, and performance and financial condition ratios. Information is updated on a quarterly basis. You can create, save, and retrieve custom groups of insured institutions and bank holding companies and download up to 2.5 megabytes of information on insured institutions.

Non-financial demographic data is now updated weekly instead of monthly. You can obtain information directly on offices of insured institutions from within Institution Directory (ID), and can access information from other banking sites via links provided.

Whether financial institutions are part of your company's competition, or whether you use this information in other ways, retrieving the information in electronic format is very useful.

Intellectual Property Information

You may use the patent, trademark, or copyright laws to protect your own company's intellectual property, or you may be interested in these topics as they pertain to competitors. The material can be very complex, and may require assistance from your company attorney or legal department, or from an attorney specializing in this field. For an introduction, however, the government offices have published much useful material on the Internet:

Copyright - General information, legislation, publications, announcements, and international copyright law are among the topics addressed by the U.S. Copyright Office at the agency's site: http://lcweb.loc.gov/copyright.

Trademarks - The U.S. Patent and Trademark Office, at www.uspto.gov, produces *Basic Facts About Registering A Trademark*, which may be downloaded in word processor formats from www.uspto.gov/web/offices/tac/doc/basic. A great deal of other useful information regarding trademarks is also available at this site, including forms, which are available online in PDF format.

Reach the USPTO's free Trademark Electronic Search System (TESS) at www.uspto.gov/main/trademarks.htm and click on the SEARCH link. TESS contains more than 3 million pending, registered and dead federal trademarks. Users may choose one of four modes for searching: basic, Boolean, advanced, and index browsing.

Limitations regarding the database, database contents, database currency, and sources of more current data are published on the USPTO website. This information should be reviewed before interpreting the search results from PTO's Web Trademark Database.

You may wonder how to put this knowledge to use. Trademarks are a hot item of intellectual property. Those who have registered them guard them carefully.

EXAMPLE: Suppose your company plans to market a new type of snack food. The Advertising and Marketing Department is trying to develop a "catchy" phrase to use in advertising — something using the words "the health food that tastes good."

A quick check of the USPTO trademark database produces the news that at least twelve registered trademarks already contain the phrase "tastes good." It would now be very wise to involve the Legal Department in determining whether to go forward with the plan, or to choose new wording for this trademark. Documents in trademark disputes can now be accessed online using TTABVue, at http://ttabvue.uspto.gov. This system allows users to view images of documents relating to trademark disputes filed since January 2003. Some earlier records covering the period June 2001 to January 2003 are available.

USPTO Continues to Expand Its E-government Capacity

What if your company already has trademarks and wants to determine whether they are being violated? As is often the case, a subscription-based service has come along to offer assistance. For a fee, *TrademarkBots*, at www.trademarkbots.com, will monitor intelligence on trademarks and famous names. The service covers online sources from the visible and invisible web, including trademark databases, domain names databases, newspapers, publications, catalogs, webfeeds, Usenet groups, message boards and specialty databases. This service sends reports by email. The site describes its services as " real-time eBusiness due diligence on the brands, trademarks, and famous people that drive each private and publicly-traded business." *Trademark Intelligence Sources* identifies legitimate and illegal online competitors, while *Brand Intelligence Sources* searches seeks to discover stakeholder complaints –an indicator of potential risks – and new branding opportunities or obstacles.

Dialog, at www.dialog.com, offers 23 trademark files representing individual countries, the International Register, and the European Union, as well as records from the 50 U.S. states for a total of more than 15 million trademarks. One of the benefits of searching a subscription-based service like Dialog is the ability to search across combinations of files, including other types of intellectual property files such as internet domain name registration or patent records.

Patents - The U.S. Patent and Trademark Office site provides detailed information regarding many aspects of the patent process on a page titled *General Information Concerning Patents*, at www.uspto.gov/web/offices/pac/doc/general/index.html.

Patent information is valuable business intelligence because it has a number of applications:

- Search by Assignee Name to get a quick estimate of a company's intellectual property assets. This will provide the total number of patents assigned to that company, and a link list of the patents. Remember, however, that some of this property could have been included in the sale of part of the company, and is no longer an asset of the company searched. See Delphion, below.

- Consider intellectual property assets when looking for merger or acquisition candidates.

- Gain competitive intelligence for use in plotting your company's strategy regarding development of new products.

- Monitor industry trends by analyzing the patents of various companies in the industry.

- Discover potential markets for your products or services as they complement or impact the target company's patented products.

- Identify licensing opportunities that may solve technological problems or avoid "re-inventing the wheel."

- Make, build, or buy decisions.

- Discover inventors that might be recruited by your company.

The Build A Better Mousetrap Department

The USPTO databases mentioned above are reliable resources for many searchers, but commercial vendors who are always trying to improve their basic products may offer reliable, convenient search applications as well. Derwent Information, at www.derwent.com, has long been known in the information research business for its patent and scientific information databases.

For those who require extra features for analyzing or managing patent information, Delphion Research, at www.delphion.com, offers a subscription based database of more than 10 million patents from the following sources:

United States Patents — Applications (US)
United States Patents — Granted (US)
Derwent World Patents Index
European Patents — Applications (EP-A)
European Patents — Granted (EP-B)
INPADOC Family and Legal Status
Patent Abstracts of Japan (JP) and
Switzerland (CH)

Delphion offers a number of special features for maneuvering search results, but the outstanding items for the CI researcher might be their email alert system and the Corporate Tree feature, which allows searching by Assignee name to help avoid confusion that can occur as a result of acquisitions and mergers. An Original Assignee feature helps locate all U.S. patent records belonging to an Assignee, even if name variations have occurred. The Hierarchy feature in Delphion's system assists in locating applications and patents filed by companies that no longer exist, or whose patents have been reassigned.

My OrangeBook, at www.myorangebook.com, markets itself as a source for CI research related to Food and Drug Administration approved drugs. Subscribers can learn the following:

- Dates when key drug patents expire.

- Patent intelligence on competitors.

- How to predict when stock prices will fall.

- Drug application information and sales statistics.

- Marketing exclusivity terms and expirations.

Even if not in the pharmaceutical industry, searchers may benefit from learning some of the strategies presented by My OrangeBook and applying them to other industries.

One additional resource for business intelligence connected with patents is MIT's Technology Review 2003 Patent Scorecard, at www.technologyreview.com/scorecards. Created in conjunction with CHI Research, Inc., the Scorecard tracks the U.S. patent portfolios of 756 of the world's top technology companies, dividing them into eight high-tech sectors on the basis of each company's primary business. The Scorecard may be downloaded free from the website. Also available, for a fee, are more than 1,500 Corporate Patent Reports, which are emailed to purchasers. A sample is available on the website.

Other Government Data Resources

Like many other U.S. Government agencies, the Patent and Trademark Office provides a FOIA Reading Room, at www.uspto.gov/web/offices/com/sol/foia/readroom.htm. FOIA refers to the Freedom of Information Act, a federal law that provides access, by request, to a great deal of information collected by government.

Websites created by knowledgeable people can be a major timesaver for business researchers. In the intellectual property area, European patent attorney Ralph Beier's compilation is an excellent example. The categories listed below point to the dozens of links that Mr. Beier has gathered from all over the world:

- Intellectual Property Offices
- Intellectual Property Organizations
- Database Providers
- Official Registers and Databases
- Official Gazettes
- Official Examination Guidelines and Publications
- Courts
- Texts of Legal Regulations
- Case Law Databases
- Dictionaries

Statistical Reports

The Federal Interagency Council on Statistical Policy maintains an internet site at www.fedstats.gov that is intended to provide easy access to the full range of statistics and information produced by more than 100 U.S. government agencies. For easy access, both a hotlinked list and keyword searching are provided at the FEDSTATS site.

The FEDSTATS detailed data retrieved here may be used for a variety of different purposes. For example, suppose your company plans to market a new product aimed at a particular segment of the population. The demographic data, available down to the lot and block level, may help you to decide which neighborhoods or larger geographic areas will provide the market you seek.

If, on the other hand, income level would be the deciding factor in determining how or where to market the product, then something like Statistics of Income (SOI) – retrievable from the Internal Revenue Service at www.irs.gov/taxstats/content/0,,id=97507,00.html – might be of more use. SOI provides annual income, financial, and tax data based on individual and corporate tax returns, and returns filed by tax-exempt organizations.

Additional links to other federal and non-federal statistics sites and agency data access sites are available from the FEDSTATS homepage.

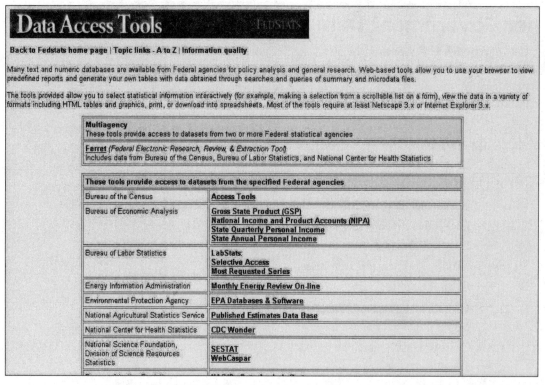

▶▶ A variety of Federal government agencies that provide statistical data can be searched individually or by using a cross-agency search tool such as *Ferret*, shown above. ◀◀

Extensive regional statistics, covering several general topics, can be obtained easily from FEDSTATS by browsing the dropdown list under the *Agencies By Subject* heading on the homepage. The following list contains a few samples:

Category	Topic	Source
Agriculture	Crops County Data	**National Agricultural Statistics Service**
	Farm Characteristics, Financial Indicators, and Top Agricultural Commodities	**Economic Research Service, USDA**
	Livestock County Data	**National Agricultural Statistics Service**
Demographic and Economic	Country Profiles	**Central Intelligence Agency**
	State and County Profiles	**Bureau of the Census**
	Demographic Indicators for Counties	**Bureau of the Census**
	State Data Centers	**Bureau of the Census**
	Science and Engineering State Profiles	**National Science Foundation**
Crime	Crime and Justice	**Bureau of Justice Statistics**
Education	Public School Student, Staff, and Graduate Counts by State	**National Center for Education Statistics**
	International Comparisons	**National Center for Education Statistics**
Energy and Environment	Commodity Minerals Data	**U.S. Geological Survey**
	Country Analysis Briefs	**Energy Information Administration**
	Environmental State and County Profiles	**Environmental Protection Agency**
	International minerals data	**U.S. Geological Survey**
	State energy data	**Energy Information Admin.**
	State minerals information	**U.S. Geological Survey**
Health	Atlas of the United States Mortality	**National Center for Health Statistics**

Category	Topic	Source
Income	Corporation tax returns	**Internal Revenue Service**
	Estate/Wealth tax returns	
	Excise taxes	
	Exempt Orgs. Bond tax returns	
	Individual tax returns	
	International or Foreign-related tax returns	
	Sole proprietorships tax returns	
Labor	Regional Information	**Bureau of Labor Statistics**
National Accounts	Personal income and gross product, by U.S. state	**Bureau of Economic Analysis**

Government statistics can be valuable in dozens of ways when studying industries, planning market strategies, importing and exporting, or various other business activities. For example, suppose you are considering building a new domestic manufacturing plant. Labor costs could be a significant expense. It would be important to compare average wages, along with other costs, when selecting the state where you plan to build. By using the detailed statistical tables available from the Bureau of Labor Statistics, state-by-state or nationwide, you can make a more informed decision. Here is a tiny sample, comparing New York and Alabama in one job category:

Comparison of 2001 State Occupational Employment & Wage Estimates: New York

SOC Code Number	Occupation Title	Employment (1)	Median Hourly	Mean Hourly	Mean Annual (2)	Mean RSE (3)
13-0000	Business and Financial Operations Occupations	335,480	$25.29	$28.27	$58,800	1.0 %
13-1011	Agents and Business Managers of Artists, Performers, and Athletes	690	$42.62	$45.97	$95,610	10.8 %
13-1021	Purchasing Agents and Buyers, Farm Products	670	$21.64	$24.06	$50,050	4.5 %
13-1022	Wholesale and Retail Buyers, Except Farm Products	9,220	$20.88	$24.98	$51,950	3.2 %
13-1023	Purchasing Agents, Except Wholesale, Retail, and Farm Products	11,290	$21.26	$22.79	$47,400	0.9 %
13-1031	Claims Adjusters, Examiners, and Investigators	14,520	$22.79	$24.41	$50,760	2.3 %
13-1032	Insurance Appraisers, Auto Damage	500	$22.49	$22.35	$46,480	2.2 %
13-1041	Compliance Officers, Except Agriculture, Construction, Health and Safety, and Transportation	10,770	$22.25	$24.62	$51,200	1.7 %
13-1051	Cost Estimators	9,780	$23.97	$25.89	$53,860	2.0 %
13-1061	Emergency Management Specialists	480	$26.61	$29.40	$61,150	4.9 %
13-1071	Employment, Recruitment, and Placement Specialists	14,120	$24.04	$28.06	$58,360	6.0 %

Alabama

SOC Code Number	Occupation Title	Employment (1)	Median Hourly	Mean Hourly	Mean Annual (2)	Mean RSE (3)
13-0000	**Business and Financial Operations Occupations**	50,570	$20.46	$22.12	$46,020	1.0 %
13-1021	Purchasing Agents and Buyers, Farm Products	130	$16.84	$19.21	$39,960	5.0 %
13-1022	Wholesale and Retail Buyers, Except Farm Products	1,220	$15.68	$17.54	$36,490	2.6 %
13-1023	Purchasing Agents, Except Wholesale, Retail, and Farm Products	3,700	$21.44	$22.20	$46,170	3.6 %
13-1031	Claims Adjusters, Examiners, and Investigators	2,100	$18.43	$20.31	$42,240	3.3 %
13-1032	Insurance Appraisers, Auto Damage	60	$18.95	$22.47	$46,740	3.3 %
13-1041	Compliance Officers, Except Agriculture, Construction, Health and Safety, and Transportation	1,380	$16.39	$18.27	$38,010	1.8 %
13-1051	Cost Estimators	2,590	$21.33	$22.04	$45,840	1.4 %
13-1061	Emergency Management Specialists	170	$14.91	$16.29	$93,870	4.6 %
13-1071	Employment, Recruitment, and Placement Specialists	1,380	$17.40	$18.28	$38,020	1.6 %

Detailed statistics regarding numbers of people employed, and hourly and annual wages for the fifty U.S. states are available for hundreds of job titles. See the Bureau of Labor Statistics site at www.bls.gov. The Bureau of Labor Statistics also provides links to statistics on a number of other areas worth searching:

Wages, Earnings, & Benefits	Wages by Area and Occupation • Earnings by Industry • Employee Benefits • Employment Costs • State and County Wages • National Compensation Data • Collective Bargaining
Productivity	Productivity and Costs • Multifactor Productivity • International Comparisons
Safety & Health	Injuries and Illnesses • Fatalities
Demographics	Demographic Characteristics of the Labor Force • Geographic Profile of Employment and Unemployment • Consumer Expenditures • Injuries, Illnesses, and Fatalities • Longitudinal Studies
Employment & Unemployment	National Employment • Employment Projections • Job Openings and Labor Turnover • Employment by Occupation • Longitudinal Studies • State and County Employment • Time Use
International	Import/Export Price Indexes • Foreign Labor Statistics • International Technical Cooperation
Industries	Industries at a Glance • Employment, Hours, and Earnings • Occupations • Injuries, Illnesses, and Fatalities • Producer Price Indexes • Employment Costs • Productivity
Business Costs	Producer Price Indexes • Employment Costs • Employee Benefits • Foreign Labor Costs • Import/Export Prices • Unit Labor Costs

Statistical data on the topics listed above can be used to determine what is happening or is likely to happen in an industry. This may impact your company's planning as well as that of competitors. The data can also be used to estimate competitors' costs in various labor-related areas.

Labor-related statistical data is also available for countries of the European Union. *Employment in Europe 2003*, found on the Internet in full text at http://europa.eu.int/comm/employment_social/news/2003/oct/eie2003_en.pdf contains a detailed statistical annex with key employment indicators and macro-economic indicators.

The Office of Labor-Management Standards

A different view of employment related data is found at The U.S. Department of Labor's Office of Labor-Management Standards, which collects reports relevant to unions. Here you can find the following:

- **Individual union reports and constitutions and bylaws**
  Reports LM-2, LM-3, and LM-4, the annual financial reports filed by unions, are each available online for the year 2000 and later. Those for 1999 and earlier may be ordered using an online order form. Note that you will need the name and number of the union. This number is often preceded by the word *Local*, as in Amalgamated Widget Makers, Local No. 789. Also available are copies of Labor Organization Information Reports (LM-1) and union constitutions and bylaws.

- **Employer and Labor Relations Consultant Reports**
  Reports LM-10 (Employer Reports), LM-20 (Agreement and Activities Reports), and LM-21 Receipts and Disbursements Reports are available online for the year 2000 and later. Older reports may be ordered, as mentioned above.

- An online database searchable by key financial data items about unions, their officers, or employees, for the year 2000 and later.

- A CD of the union report database may be purchased in the future.

OLMS data may be useful for other reasons. Perhaps your organization expects to be in negotiations in the future, or maybe you have heard that a competitor may be threatened with a strike. What is these scenarios likely to cost? In labor negotiations, the employer may hire an outside consultant to represent the company.

You probably will not find off-the-shelf studies readily available to provide data on this industry. You may not find listings in the Yellow Pages of the local telephone directory. The name, address, and amount paid to the consultant will be found on an LM-10 form filed by the employer. Searching the LM-20 files yields the records of other employment of the outside consultant for 2000, 2001, and 2002, with more detail. You can quickly determine the types of services provided, numbers of personnel involved, days of service, and charges for services. The LM-21 shows itemized receipts and disbursements by the consultant. Upon examination, it would appear that this is a lucrative field.

Finding Business Information From State Government Sources

For an easy way to locate individual U.S. State government websites, look at the National Association of State Procurement Officers (NASPO) at www.naspo.org/directory/index.cfm. Click on the United States map to reach a very useful page that contains links to procurement offices in all fifty states – information that may be very useful if you are considering doing business with individual states.

Identifying State Government Agencies Where the Competition Sells Goods and Services

Every state in the U.S. has a special office that manages the process of buying goods and services. Many of them now make a great deal of information regarding this process available on their websites. You may be able to learn several useful facts regarding your competitors or the marketplace:

- Lists of companies selling to a particular state.

- What goods and services that a given company is selling.

- Names of state agencies involved.

- Location where goods and services will be used. This information is not available for all states.

Another application for state procurement information is to add state government agencies to your own client list.

The amount and type of information available from state government varies extensively, since each state makes its own laws and creates departments or agencies at will. By searching your own state's site, you may find some headings that are more specific than those mentioned above.

Here are some typical organizations that you can seek out in your own state. Some of these may offer searchable databases.

Secretary of State

The Secretary of State's office oversees corporations licensed in the state. Various business entity filings, registrations, and reports are collected here. Much of this information is public record and is therefore made available upon request. Many states now make this information searchable via the Internet.

Florida's SUNBIZ site, at www.sunbiz.org, is a good example of the way that individual states offer access to documents filed with their Secretary of State. Searchable databases include Corporations, Trademarks, and Limited Partnerships, Federal Lien registrations, Fictitious Names, Judgment Liens, Limited Liability and General Partnerships, and UCC Information. Included in the detail of the database records are actual document image as submitted to the Division.

▸▸ Search here for detailed information about companies registered to do business in Florida. Florida offers more of this information than most states. ◂◂

Industry-Specific Regulatory Agencies

Visit your state's website and look for links to agencies such as the State Department of Environmental Affairs, Banking Department, Department of Transportation, etc. As an example, California has lists of banks, thrifts, etc. at the Department of Financial Institutions website at www.dfi.ca.gov.

State Comptroller or Comparable Office

This office handles subjects such as Licensing and Registration, Unclaimed Property, and other matters related to state finance. Databases are provided in some states, Florida and Washington for example.

Use this type of database to check the professional licensing credentials of individuals in regulated professions or businesses. Almost all license checking search sites are free.

State Securities Board

Exact names for these regulatory boards vary from state to state, but this organization administers and enforces rules and regulations connected with securities under the laws of the state.

The Pennsylvania Securities Commission, at www.psc.state.pa.us, includes lists of Cease and Desist Orders and Final Orders in regard to entities that have been charged with violation of the state's Securities laws. Click on the Enforcement Actions link from the Commission homepage. Since these lists name names and include Findings of Fact and Conclusions of Law and Order, it is possible to learn about the activities of various organizations attempting to sell securities of various types within the state.

More and more state agencies add database searching to their sites every month. A good source for links to public information is the free public records site at www.brbpub.com/pubrecsites.asp.

Useful Databases for Business Information In Canadian Provinces

The Atlantic Provinces of Canada include Nova Scotia, New Brunswick, Newfoundland, and Prince Edward Island. The Nova Scotia site for procurement information, http://198.166.215.5/finance/tour/, shown in part below, contains links to similar sites for the other provinces in the region and to other procurement sites in Canada and the U.S.

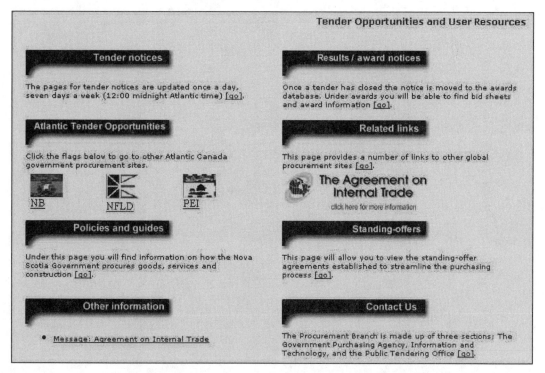

▸▸ This Province of Nova Scotia web page serves as a jumping-off place for both learning about procurement and for participating in this activity in Canada. ◂◂

Businesses in Canada can search the databases linked to this site for leads in marketing their own products as well as to learn who else is selling to the government, what they are selling, and the dollar value of the contracts.

United Kingdom Central Government Web Archive

The U.K. Central Government Web Archive, at www.pro.gov.uk/webarchive, is a selective collection of U.K. Government websites, archived from August, 2003, developed by the National Archives of the United Kingdom. The site was new at press time, but bears watching by those interested in U.K. government information.

Chapter 10

Researching Those Elusive Privately Held Companies

It Is A Different Ball Game

Previous chapters have addressed various approaches to identifying and finding information on competitor companies. By now you are convinced that almost any business organization can benefit from obtaining accurate information on competitors. Once you have identified the competition, the work is just beginning. Suppose your competitors tend to be privately held companies?

The solution to the problem is not as simple as looking at an annual report or researching filings with the SEC, because these types of public documents are not required of privately held companies. Since they do not sell shares of stock, privately held companies have fewer disclosure requirements. They may be relatively smaller in size, such as a neighborhood dry cleaner or grocery store, or they could be as large as Hallmark Cards or Cargill.

In today's global economy, a few other considerations arise. Suppose the competition includes foreign companies doing business in the U.S., or U.S. companies that are owned by parents in another part of the world?

Experience shows us that not every website that promises a database of company information will be useful. Finding and using the ones that are useful will be invaluable, especially when it is crunch time. What follows are some things to consider about private company research:

Private Company Structure

Learning the type of business entity that fits your target company may save research time. Privately held companies usually fall into one of these categories.

- **Private Corporations** - Stock is "closely held" by a group of investors or owners. These companies are regulated at the state level, so various types of records will be generated.

- **Partnerships** - Two or more persons who combine to form a business for profit without incorporating, possibly for the tax benefits to be gained. The company will be registered at the state level.

- **Limited Liability Companies** or **Limited Liability Partnerships** - These entities have the tax benefits of partnerships.

- **Sole Proprietorships** - A single individual is responsible for all the financial obligations of a company and entitled to all the profits. These companies are probably registered with the county where they do business. Available information is limited.

Making this determination will allow you to know what you may expect to find – in both quantity and quality of information.

What Is Available On Privately Held Companies?

The volume of information available, even on large privately held companies, is smaller than that of public companies. Likewise, fewer types of data can be readily obtained. Here is what you might expect to find:

- Company name and address

- Name under which the company does business – various states call these "fictitious names," "trade names," or "DBAs" (as in John J. Jones, doing business as Jones Plumbing Company).

- Names and locations of possible branches, subsidiaries, etc.

- Company's key personnel, or those who have a connection, such as law firm or accounting firm.

- Product line or services offered.

- Credit history, if searching specialized credit-related databases.

- Financial information in bits and pieces as it appears in newspapers or periodicals, or in specialized databases such as Dun & Bradstreet or Corptech.

Privately held or "closely held" companies obviously create financial reports, but they need not disclose this information publicly. If an online source contains financial information, then read the fine print carefully to be sure that the figures are not guesstimates. A Federal law, *The Sarbanes-Oxley Act of 2002*, although directed mainly at public companies, impacts those privately held companies that anticipate going public. Issues relating to corporate governance, including financial audits, also are involved. Some larger private companies will look ahead at the requirements of SOX, as the law has been nicknamed, and voluntarily enact some of the measures that the law requires of public companies.

Where To Look For Privately Held Companies

What we need are sources where all types of companies are likely to be included, then we can narrow the field to sources for privately held companies. Here are some possibilities:

Company Websites

Some researchers prefer to make a company website their first stop when researching private companies. The amount of information found there will vary greatly depending upon the size of the company and the value to be gained by mounting a sophisticated website. As a marketing tool, and assuming they have one, the company website is a useful place to brag about new products, industry awards, key personnel, etc. The site may provide clues that can be followed up using some of the other sources mentioned in this chapter. Chapter 15 discusses this topic in greater detail.

Public Records

The SEC does not regulate privately held companies, but the states where they do business require compliance with the laws of those individual states. This means that public records are generated through filings with the Secretary of State, and oftentimes at the county records offices such as the Recorder/Register or Assessor/Auditor or Tax Collector. A good source for locating the county recorder office filing locations and state agencies with public records is BRB Publication's *Sourcebook to Public Record Information*, and also their book of online public record sources, *Public Records Online[1]*. Additionally, this publisher offers a free list of 2500 free public record sites across the U.S. and Canada at www.brbpub.com.

Public records are invaluable when researching private companies, particularly those that do not make headlines. Descriptions of various types of records are included in Chapter 8 – Public Records.

If researching privately held companies across a number of states, the job can become tedious. The scene is constantly changing as various states' websites are redesigned, bookmarks become obsolete, and new files become available. What you need, ideally, is a few good websites that have done the work for you by collecting the various public record sites.

Secst.com

Secst.com, at http://secst.com, provides a well organized site with links to information regarding corporations, partnerships, limited liability companies (LLCs), businesses, and Uniform Commercial Code (UCC) records for all fifty states in the U.S. This is a subscription-based site, and the cost per year may be a bit high for infrequent users. However, there is no extra charge for more than one user in one company no matter how many locations, and multiple users in one company can access at the same time with one office password for all locations. The state of Utah may be searched free on the website to help you to see the output format and types of files available.

State and Local Government on the Net Directory

The State and Local Government on the Net Directory, at www.statelocalgov.net/index.cfm, offers one-stop access to the websites of more than 9000 state agencies and city and county governments.

Links are organized to provide access to all offices of a given state, or to sites by topic across all fifty states. Update information is available where sites have been updated recently. Additional links to Federal websites and to those of a number of national trade associations are a plus.

Chapter 8 – Public Records may also provide ideas on specific types of public records that will yield information on private companies being researched. Those companies involved in highly regulated industries obviously will generate more records than their neighbors in the industrial park. See the Bookmarks & Favorites Section, in the Appendix, for addresses of additional public records websites.

Industry Oriented Records Sites

Some websites can be especially useful because they focus on public records relevant to a specific industry, which is a timesaver for the researcher.

Construction WebLinks

A good example of this genre is Construction WebLinks, at www.constructionweblinks.com/Industry_Topics/Public_Records/public_records.html. Here you will find links to sites in all U.S. states for obtaining information on construction related businesses such as those run by architects, contractors, engineers, landscape architects, and surveyors. Most of these are privately held companies. Also covered are insurance and surety companies, some of which are privately held.

Links provide access to sites referencing licensing and registration, and to Federal and state court records. If a private company has been involved in litigation, certain records, including financials, may have been introduced as evidence. By reading the opinion, you may find data that would not have been available to you otherwise.

Portals

The-infoshop.com by Global Information, Inc. – the vertical markets research portal, at www.the-infoshop.com/cgi-bin/sse/search.cgi --offers detailed reports on privately held companies in a number of industries in the U.S. and abroad. Some examples include these:

- Windows and Doors - Private Companies
- Extruded Plastics- Private Companies Report
- Caps & Closures - Private Companies Report
- Biotechnology Pharmaceuticals - Private Companies
- Industrial Rubber Products: Private Companies Report

These reports are fairly high-priced, and some are now several years old. It is best to check dates carefully when purchasing such material and to ask questions regarding contents. More recent reports from this company focus on the telecommunications industry.

Publishers

In the relatively short life of the Internet, publishers were pioneers bringing to the electronic marketplace information or data that had been compiled for their hardcopy publications. Whether focusing on specific industries or to the business or scientific communities in general, these organizations are a boon to the CI researcher who is looking for information on private companies. The industry specialists are particularly useful because they identify companies, large or small, that are part of the industry discussed, as well as some in related industries.

CorpTech Company Profiles

This may be the exception to the warning given previously about the dearth of financial information on privately held U.S. companies. CorpTech at www.corptech.com profiles more than 50,000 public and private growth companies, approximately eighty percent of which are privately held. Searching on a privately held software company with which this author has some familiarity provided a significant amount of financial information covering three years.

Detailed searching is possible using more than 250 major technology codes and 3,000 product codes as well as SIC and NAICS codes. The following market sectors are included:

Factory Automation	Mfg. Equipment	Subassemblies and Components
Biotechnology	Advanced Materials	
Chemicals	Medical	Test and Measurement
Computer Hardware	Pharmaceuticals	Telecommunications and Internet
Defense	Photonics	
Energy	Computer Software	Transportation
Environmental		Holding Companies

Three types of profiles are available. The **Capsule** is just that – information includes address, key executives, and the opportunity to order a more complete report. One useful freebie here is the list of related companies in the corporate family. The **Standard Profile** adds more data fields and more detail. A limited amount of financial information is included. The **Extended Profile** contains much more financial detail, along with the Executive History, which can show how certain individuals have moved about on the corporate ladder, along with names that have been deleted from the history. CorpTech's corporate profiles typically consist of the following information:

Company name and address	Projected rate of employment growth
Phone and fax numbers	Key executives
Email and Internet addresses	Business description
Year formed	Products listed
Ownership	U.S. high-tech operating units
Corporate ownership identified	Start-up funding source
Company size	Government contractor status
Sales (and international sales, if any)	Female/Minority Ownership
Number of employees	Industries sold to

Several features distinguish records in the CorpTech database from those available in many of the free sources offering company profiles.

- **Key executives** – Profiles list a number of key company personnel, with titles and areas of responsibility, with contact information. A separate list shows those people *deleted* during the past few years, along with the list positions that they held.

- **Markets sold to** - This information is not commonly specified in many other sources. For competitive purposes, it is valuable.

- **Products from which bulk of company revenue is derived** – a company may produce a dozen gadgets or services, but most of the revenue may come from that one little gizmo that has caught the attention of the marketplace.

- **Historical information available** - Extended Profiles contain up to ten years of data on corporate change and executive history, and four years of performance analysis. CorpTech claims to be the only source for this type of data.

Free trial subscriptions are available as are CD-ROMs or pay-per-view searches for occasional users. Free subscribers are allowed to view unlimited capsules and up to 25 Standard and 25 Extended profiles free of charge during the lifetime of the free subscription. The Gold and Silver subscriptions offer additional features for frequent users of the Corptech database. Data can be downloaded for import into spreadsheet programs. This feature could be handy if The Boss calls from a meeting in the conference room on the Executive Floor with a request like, "The CEO wants a detailed list of privately held software producers in New England – in the next half hour! Can you help?"

Crain's New York Business

Crain's New York Business, at www.crainsny.com/businessList.cms, regularly ranks the top New York businesses in a variety of fields and sells its findings online. Lists include company addresses and contacts, employment numbers and revenue, and other information. Though there is not a lot of detail here, there are lists available for several years, making it possible to track a company's position vis-a-vis its competitors. Electronic access to individual lists can be purchased for 24-hour periods for a nominal fee. Similar business publications in other metropolitan markets around the country publish comparable lists.

Manufacturers' News Inc.

Manufacturers' News Inc., at http://manufacturersnews.com, is the nation's oldest and largest compiler and publisher of state manufacturers directories and databases, now covering all fifty U.S. states. Their site offers free corporate profiles on the Web. A lengthy list of executives, with their titles, may be included along with other types of data considered basic to this type of report.

The websites of other directory publishers such as *The Thomas Register* can also be useful. See the Bookmarks and Favorites section at the back of this book for other possibilities.

Industry Oriented Websites

Trade associations and independent companies or individuals have created hundreds of websites that focus on specific industries or related groups of industries. Useful surveys among the membership of trade groups or subscribers to an industry-related website can yield valuable information.

Take for example WardsAuto.com, at http://wdb.wardsauto.com. This website includes the annual Dealer 500 list, which is crammed with interesting financials on auto dealerships around the U.S. Dealers can compare their operation with others in the same city, in other parts of the country, or with others selling the same brands. This information can then be analyzed as part of a company or dealership's decision-making process. For manufacturers, it may be useful to compare their sales with those of the competition. For dealers, it might be a matter of deciding where to open a branch, or whether to expand the service department versus their used cars department. A dealer in a large metropolitan area might consult this website to learn the following about a competitor:

Ranking	Used Revenue
Name of Dealership	Used Units
Owner/Principals	Finance/Insurance Revenue
City	Service Revenue
State	Body Shop Revenue
New Revenue	Parts and Accessories Revenue
New Units	Total Revenue

There is no guarantee that a business has not fudged a bit on financial information contributed to a site survey like this one, but information obtained from manufacturers can serve as a crosscheck.

Journals and Newspapers

These sources are frequently mentioned as having websites that can be helpful for finding information on privately held companies. Searching newspapers and journals effectively is discussed in Chapter 6. Since many company databases update records infrequently, it is important to search newspapers and magazines directly for more recent developments on target companies.

Recruiter Websites

Personnel recruiters have taken to adding company descriptions for potential employers to their websites. This allows jobseekers to do some homework before sending off resumes to companies where they may wish to apply. A good example of this genre is WetFeet.com, at www.wetfeet.com/research/companies.asp. This site provides descriptions of a long list of U.S. public and private companies. In addition to basic contact information and data of interest to job seekers, you will find information on company revenue, one-year growth rate, number of employees, and a brief business description.

Public Company Filings

Sometimes public companies list private companies as competitors. This strategy may also yield names of officers who may be mentioned as former employees of the private company. It is also a way to determine international connections, for example a European banker as Director of a privately held U.S. financial company. Search EDGAR, www.sec.gov/edgar.shtml or one of the commercial sources for EDGAR material, and use the private company's name as a keyword rather than entering it in the company name field on the search form. Search across the text of all filings. See the Appendix A and Appendix B for descriptions of various filings and their CI applications.

Ranked Lists Created By Publishers

Lists created by publishers are mentioned in greater detail in Chapter 16. Several of them pertain specifically to privately held companies. Here are some examples:

- The Inc. 500 – *Inc. Magazine's* a listing and short description of the 500 fastest growing privately-held companies in the U.S.

- The *Forbes* 500 Largest Private Companies in the U.S. - annual listing that ranks U.S.-headquartered firms that do not have widely held common stock, and revenue over $1 billion.

- The *American Lawyer* Top 100 Law Firms - www.americanlawyer.com/amlaw100/

- *Hoover's Handbook of Private Companies* - these hardcopy publications are searchable online for subscribers of Hoover's.

- *The Lawyer* 100 - *The Lawyer's Guide* to the top 100 U.K. law firms, at www.thelawyer.com/top100

Company Oriented Online Subscription Services

OneSource   *(description on next page)*

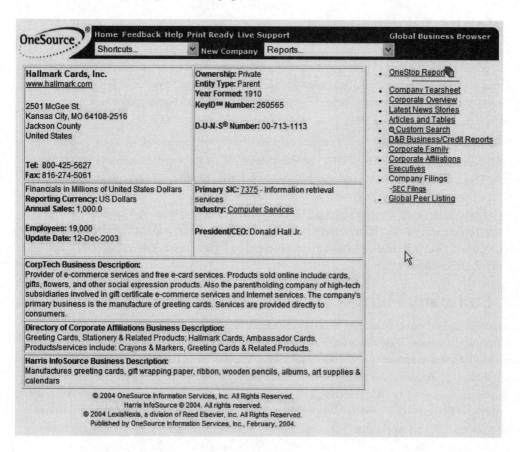

▶▶A number of links provide access to segments of a private company report retrieved using OneSource. A detailed description of a competitor company can be retrieved in seconds, as opposed to the larger amount of time required to gather the same information from individual sources. ◀◀

OneSource, at www.onesource.com, owns CorpTech, mentioned earlier in this chapter. For larger organizations where the budget allows, using OneSource offers some significant savings in time and labor when researching privately held companies. More than 35 third party data sources representing 2,500 separate information sources – including database producers, news organizations, and government sources – are combined into one report. More than 600,000 non-publicly traded companies are included in OneSource's universe of more than 1.7 million companies.

OneSource subscriptions are regionally based, with global access available as an optional addition to geographically oriented subscriptions.

SkyMinder

Skyminder, at www.skyminder.com, offers public and private company profiles, financial data for public companies, news, and market information. Site registration is required, but searching is free. Individual documents can be purchased. Those who subscribe have access to additional information concerning 46 million European, U.S., and worldwide companies and industries. Sources include Hoover's, Dun & Bradstreet, Knight Ridder, and other media.

Standard & Poor's NetAdvantage

Standard & Poor's NetAdvantage, at www.netadvantage.standardandpoors.com, is marketed to academic libraries, public libraries, and corporate libraries and information centers. NetAdvantage includes comprehensive business and investment information and online access to Standard & Poor's data, independent research, and commentary on stocks, bonds, funds, and industries. The database includes more than 85,000 companies that are not publicly traded. Searching is possible by NAICS code. Data may be downloaded into spreadsheet programs.

BVMarketData.com

BVMarketData.com™, at www.bvmarketdata.com, offers a variety of databases containing financial and transactional data relating to the sales of public and privately held companies, control premiums, minority discounts, and marketability discounts.

Although this material is frequently used by merger and acquisition professionals, including business appraisers, business brokers, investment bankers, and venture capitalists, it can be a valuable resource for price discovery if knowing the value of a privately held company would be useful to your organization. The site is the brainchild of Dr. Shannon Pratt, well-known business valuation guru and author of *Pratt's Stats* and *Shannon Pratt's Business Valuation Update* both of which are available through the website.

Dialog Company Profiles

Dialog Company Profiles, available through www.dialog.com, is one of the packaged services provided by Dialog. It combines company profiles, brand information, rankings, company histories, chronologies, news, and trade journals, and includes both private and public companies

LexisNexis Company Dossier

LexisNexis™ Company Dossier and some of the individual files in the COMPNY library contain information on privately held companies.

1Jump

World Market Watch's 1Jump, at www.1jump.com, has been widely and favorably reviewed. This subscription-based service includes important private and public companies from countries all over the world, ensuring a global focus. They strive to avoid a United States bias. Nearly half of the one million-plus companies covered are not based in the U.S.

The ability to list the companies in a particular county or city within the U.S. can be a useful feature even though not much detail may be available. Some of these businesses do not have websites and may not appear in major company databases. Reports can include up to 32 types of information, some of which are not provided in many of the online company databases. There is less of this information available for privately held companies than for those that are public. 1Jump offers 29 different data elements on which to search, and eighteen specialty directories of various industries.

Company summary	Global Peers	News	Profiles
Contact information	Industry Overview	Ownership information	Public filings
Corporate	Graphs on all company financial variables	Patents	Ratios Rivals
Detailed Directors		Peers and competitors	Stock, fund, financial information
Email	Industry Emails	Performance summary	
Employee count	Interactive 1Jump Directory	Press releases	Subsidiaries
Executive officers	Inventor information	Price/Earnings information	Trademarks and Brands
Former executive officers	Neighbor companies	Product segment data	Website

Non-U.S. Private Companies

In most countries outside of the U.S., both public and privately held companies must report detailed data to the government each year. Websites that offer foreign company profiles may obtain the information from individual countries and quickly make it available via searchable databases. Likewise, credit reports on companies outside of the U.S. may contain information that is quite current – perhaps no more than a year old. In some cases it may be easier to research a private company on a faraway continent than one in the next county.

A number of sources exist for obtaining foreign company information. The European Union has created the European Business Register, available at www.ebr.org. The Register includes eighteen million European companies from these countries:

Austria	Finland	Ireland	Spain
Belgium	France	Italy	Sweden
Denmark	Germany	Latvia	United Kingdom
Estonia	Greece	Norway	

Information is ordered through network members, each of which has access to the entire network. The information provided is official, and reasonably priced. For those who are not fluent in numerous languages, this approach offers a definite advantage over contacting countries directly, since the website is in English.

Another convenient access point for this information is EuroInfoPool, at www.euroinfopool.com/ debi/index.jsp. By setting up a temporary account you can immediately order documents, up to a fixed credit limit. Permanent accounts are accorded higher credit limits. A modest monthly subscription fee is involved.

The website of the Commercial Register Office of the Canton St. Gallen, at www.hrasg.ch/eng/welt-e.htm, provides an even longer list of links to official company registers from around the world. Researchers outside of the U.S. will find it useful because the list includes links to individual Secretary of State offices in each of the fifty U.S. states.

What If You Cannot Subscribe?

Your company may already have subscriptions in place for various database services available through the Internet. If in doubt, ask around or check with the company library to determine what is available. If nothing materializes, do not give up.

Most public and academic libraries have subscriptions to such services. It may be worth checking a nearby public library, or even traveling to a larger city with your list of privately held companies in hand. In some cases, college or university alumni association members have access to library resources at their alma mater. Also, consider using the Business & Company Resource Center, which is part of the Infotrac service available at many academic libraries.

Chapter 11

Letting "The Other Guy" Do the Work for You

Starting Points for Business Research Using the Internet

Searching for useful websites is like searching the ocean for sunken treasure from a rowboat. Web surfing may not be the most productive use of your time online – even an experienced web searcher can spend hours looking at dozens of sites without finding "the gold."

Let us consider the reality of search engines. Will your favorite search engines help identify relevant documents related to the business topic "SoHo" - the acronym for "Small Office/Home Office?" This could be very time consuming; while you may find many links that include the "SoHo" search term, some links are totally off of the subject. Soho is the name of neighborhoods in London and in New York City. It also stands for Solar and Heliospheric Observatory, a joint project of the European Space Agency and NASA. The search results will contain links to both, and most are not related to "Small Office/Home Office."

"There must be a better way to search!" you say.

Fortunately, there is help! Great websites have been compiled by knowledgeable individuals who have gathered and organized the best of the thousands of possible sites that mention your topic, and present them in a useful, readable interface, complete with site search engines and hotlinks, all for easy access.

Many such sites are the product of business schools or library science at major universities in the U.S. and abroad, reflecting the specialty, interests and/or curriculum of the institution. It is possible to determine a site's special emphasis by reading the mission statement or reviews on its main page.

This is the perfect time to introduce a specialized website, or "portal." Generally, portals let you begin by looking at broad categories, then you "drill down" by choosing narrower topics. So, searching the right portal reduces the likelihood of having to study long lists of "false hits." While you may need to explore more categories than the portal offers, remember that the material there has been screened and selected by someone with expertise on that subject. This chapter is your introduction to the best of these sites and, to decide where to start, it is best to begin by examining your question and your reason for the search.

Defining the Need Helps Define Your Search

Your questions could be broad ones, such as "What is happening in the Widget industry?" Or you may be researching a more focused questions, such as "Is the SOHO (Small Office/Home Office) market for PC's growing?" If the answer here is positive, "What is the growth rate? What is driving the growth?" For more detail about the types of company or industry reports to create and what goes into them, see the checklists provided in Chapter 17

Keeping your needs and the available online business applications in mind, in this chapter are portal sites that will help you begin your CI research. The portal sites' creators have focused on business applications, and before you visit what can be large and complex sites, answer these types of questions about your needs:

- Does the question involve a specific industry?

- Is the question related to technology? If so, what type?

- Are you researching specific companies?

- Are management issues involved?

- Should the topic be covered from a U.S. or an international perspective?

Business Sites on the WWW

The World Wide Web is filled with business sites of all kinds. The sites below are our favorites and good examples of the useful online collections of materials for business information research.

TIP — To avoid spending large amounts of time going through the multitude of material on a site, *be sure to bookmark the "gems" that you locate, or add them to your list of bookmarks or favorites!* By doing so, you will prevent a great deal of future frustration when you can not seem to remember the web address for that "great source" you saw "somewhere."

BRINT

Business Researcher's Interests (BRINT) covers an extremely broad spectrum of business, technology, and industry categories. www.brint.com touts a long list of favorable reviews from well-respected sources. The site has changed significantly over time, becoming more commercial in appearance, and more complex in content. It also has added free registration as a requirement for searching

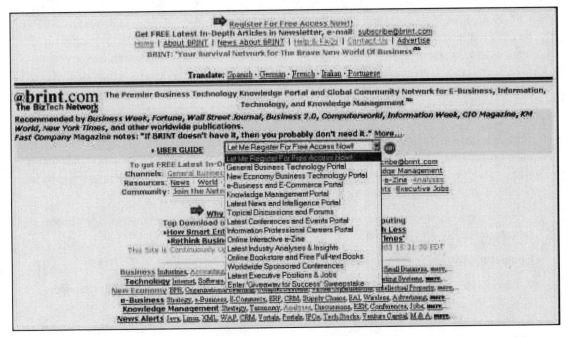

▶▶ The hotlinked categories shown above lead to pages with dozens of links to related material. ◀◀

Due to the complexity of the site, it is highly recommended that even seasoned searchers review the *Help* and *FAQ* documents at www.brint.com/help.htm

The links list for the Business and Industry category is illustrative of what can be found under the other headings:

Business and Industry

Accounting (1,365)
Advertising (3,306)
Agriculture and Forestry (10,519)
Arts and Entertainment (5,372)
Associations (14)
Business Services (7,344)
Business Software (1,207)
Business Travel (209)
Classifieds (495)
Construction and Maintenance (13,838)
Consulting (1,160)
Cooperatives (51)
Customer Service (185)
Directories (426)
E-Commerce (1,959)
Economics (1,645)

Employment (1,794)
Energy and Utilities (1,773)
Environmental and Safety (373)
Financial Services (12,751)
Food and Related Products (3,872)
History (74)
Human Resources (902)
Industries (107,762)
Insurance (2,640)
International Business and Trade (647)
Internet (0)
Investing (5,175)
Law (14,528)
Major Companies (6,309)
Management (3,027)
Manufacturing (33,581)

Marketing (2,969)
Mining and Drilling (620)
Music (705)
News and Publications (561)
Opportunities (8,485)
Printing (2,964)
Publishing (3,268)
Real Estate (1,603)
Resources (1,136)
Retail (794)
Security (2,436)
Small Business (981)
Telecommunications (2,945)
Training and Schools (728)
Transportation (6,074)
Venture Capital (1,221)

CEO Express

CEO Express, at www.ceoexpress.com, takes quite a different approach from that taken by BRINT. At CEO Express, material is categorized into types of sources, with lots of links to specific listed items such as business publications, company research, industry-specific research, government agencies relevant to business research, etc. The homepage appears less crowded than BRINT and may be easier to use.

Business.com

Business.com combines the directory approach used on other business sites with a fast and powerful business-focused search engine. Searching is simplified through the use of automatic "and" between words, automatic plurals, and word stemming. Symbols such as "+" and "-", which are used by other popular search engines, do not work here.

The directory contains more than 400,000 listings within 25,000 industry, product, and service subcategories. The site also offers industry-specific news and a jobs listing.

Competia Express

Competia is a Canadian consulting firm specializing in competitive intelligence and strategic planning. At www.competia.com/express/ is a collection of annotated industry-specific links, intended for use in developing a competitive intelligence strategy.

The Competia Express page includes links to dozens of industries:

Competia Express

We have compiled for you lists of sites that we have found to be of the most value in your industry. These lists are far from exhaustive, but they should give you a superb head start.

Featured Industries

Advertising	Food & Beverage	Space
Aerospace	Hardware	Steel
Agriculture	Insurance	Telecommunications
Aluminium	Management Consulting	Tobacco
Apparel	Manufacturing	Travel
Automotive	Mining & Mineral	Utilities
Aviation	Multimedia	Venture Capital
Banking	Oil and Gas	Wireless Telecom
Bio Technology	Packaging	
Chemical	Pharmaceuticals	

▶▶ Within each category shown above, CE lists relevant associations, company information, consultants, daily industry news, online publications, regulatory environment, and technical intelligence. ◀◀

Google

Although usually thought of as a search engine, the expanded offerings from Google include *Google Directory*, where it is possible to limit searches to only business topics using the search screen shown below, which is found at http://directory.google.com/Top/Business/. From this screen searches can be limited to the Business section of the directory or expanded to search the entire web.

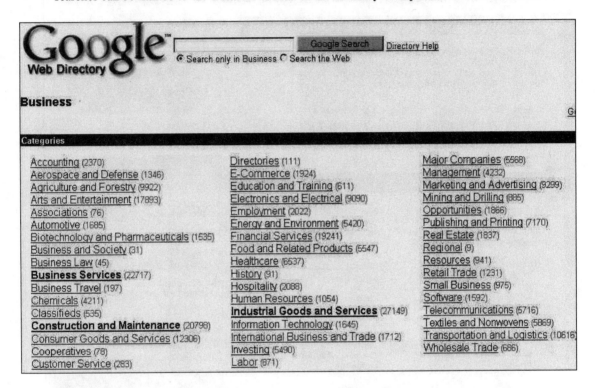

Web Guide

Web Guide, at www.business2.com/webguide/0,,,00.html is a product of *Business 2.0*, a print publication. This subscription-based Web Guide lists dozens of business-related topics under eighteen broad category headings that include Company Information, Management, Marketing, and other pertinent topics. Links within these categories point to sub-categories and related material. *Business 2.0* describes Web Guide:"our hand-picked directory of the best business links on the web."

Using International Business Resources on the WWW

The Michigan State University Broad College of Business sponsors globalEDGE, which is found at http://globaledge.msu.edu. Here there are links to data regarding the business climate, political structure, history, and statistical data for more than 190 countries. Regional and country-specific links are available in addition to a general overview of each geographic area.

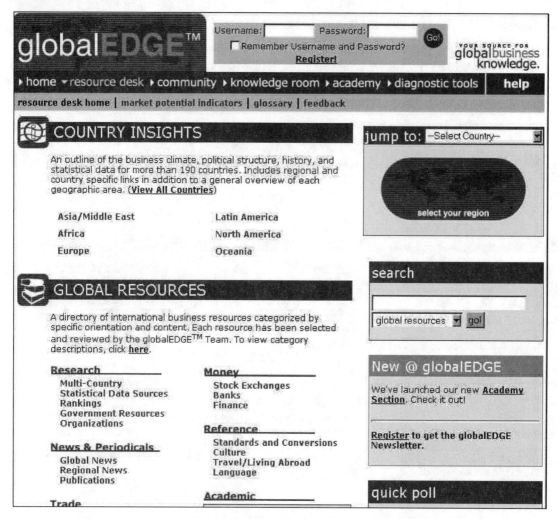

▸▸For a short course in doing business around the world,
Global Resources offers statistics and details on more than 190 countries.◂◂

Turning Free Site Information Into Useful Intelligence

All of the aforementioned are "free" sites, created by identifiable sources. How can you turn this list into useful intelligence? Suppose that your company is becoming interested in investing in Africa, one of the emerging markets of the world. On the globalEDGE portal above, the hotlink <u>Africa</u> under the heading *Country Insights*, and the subsequent link labeled *View Region Links*, would take you to a page of annotated links to government and non-government sources for African countries. Now you can follow these links to sites that provide much of the needed in-depth data and other important considerations for doing business in these countries.

Here are a few of the useful African links that are uncovered:

World Economic Forum's African Competitiveness Report

The website provides access only to the Executive Summary of *The Africa Competitiveness Report*, dated 2000-2001. The seven-page summary in PDF format identifies and measures the underlying factors that contribute to high rates of economic growth in Africa in the medium term, a time horizon of about five years. These factors are quantified and then combined into an Index of Competitiveness.

Africa: Lex Africa Business Guides

Lex Africa is a network of law firms in Africa. This site features business guides prepared by member law firms for twelve African countries. Each business guide features investment information, forms of business organizations, taxation, exchange control, tariffs, intellectual property issues, privatization issues, and more.

AFRICA: AfricaOnline

AfricaOnline, at www.africaonline.com/site/, offers current news throughout Africa with an emphasis on Côte D'Ivoire, Ghana, Kenya, Namibia, Swaziland, Tanzania, Uganda, and Zimbabwe. The site also includes country-specific information.

AFRICA: SignOn Africa

SignOn, at www.signonafrica.com, Africa is a database of trade leads representing African exporters and importers. Available leads are sorted by a long list of product categories, and a helpful product and company search feature is also available. In addition, this site provides recent supplier news. Free registration is required in order to post messages but is not necessary in order to view listed postings.

AFRICA: World Bank Africa Live Database

Africa Live Database, at www4.worldbank.org/afr/stats/ldb.cfm, is a comprehensive database of macroeconomic and sectoral indicators for the Sub-Saharan countries. The database allows viewing by country as well as by indicator, and includes rankings, charting, and benchmarking.

AFRICA: Common Market for Eastern and Southern Africa (COMESA)

COMESA is an organization of nineteen African states that promotes the development of its member nation's resources. The COMESA website, at www.comesa.int, gives an economic profile of each country and information on custom tariffs, trade databases, and legal guides for doing business in the region.

Africa: MBendi

The Mbendi website, at www.mbendi.co.za/land/af/p0005.htm, provides a country profile for most African countries, including general information, economic information, financial information, as well as detailed industry analyses and company listings.

AFRICA: MBendi - Companies of Africa

This system, at www.mbendi.co.za/coaf.htm, contains profiles of companies and parastatals (companies owned or controlled wholly or partly by the government) active in Africa. These can be viewed using an alpha-index or by using the *Organization Seeker* link at www.mbendi.co.za/a_sndmsg/org_srch.asp? to specify more selective criteria for your search.

AFRICA: MBendi - The African Trading Space

Trade listings posted at www.mbendi.co.za/a_sndmsg/trade_menu.asp?C=1 can be searched by product and offer type. Companies wishing to buy or sell items can post and update listings. There is currently no charge to use this service. A fee-based subscription is required for email notification.

AFRICA: MBendi - African Conferences and Exhibitions

The African Conferences and Exhibitions website, www.mbendi.co.za/cf.htm, contains a useful search screen to look for upcoming or past African-related events of interest.

TIP — Even though screens can be slow to appear on foreign websites, your patience may pay off in the form of useful intelligence or other opportunities.

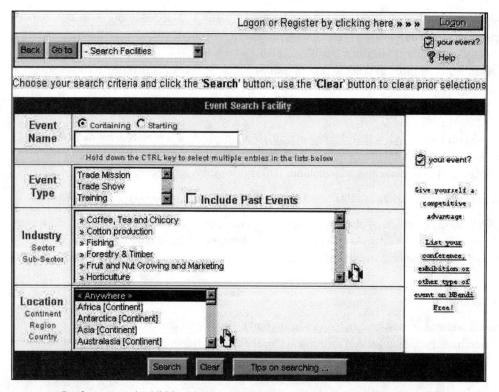

▸▸Conferences and exhibitions held on the African continent the past, present, and future can be located using the search screen shown above. Other databases cover companies, personalities, news, and more. ◂◂

More International Business Resources on the WWW

Suppose your research concerns scientific developments in Canada. An ideal source is-

ContactCanada

ContactCanada, at http://contactcanada.com, has created a database of "life-science-based" organizations across Canada. The site offers both free and subscription access to information collected directly from companies in the following industries:

- Biotechnology

- Pharma, BioPharma & Nutraceuticals

- Diagnostics - human, animal, food, environmental, plant

- Natural Health Products

- New Uses Industry - replacement of chemical products with biologically-based source materials

- Aquaculture

- Seafood processors, importers and exporters

The free service allows searching by company name, company location, product areas, industry sectors, and ownership type. Reports include company name, location, telephone number, and website. In addition, subscribers can view and print company profiles, searching by text or words, revenue levels, and staff size. Statistical summaries by provincial distribution, revenue, and numbers of employees are available for each industry.

Is your research subject connected to Latin America?

LANIC Search

The University of Texas LANIC site, at http://lanic.utexas.edu/la/region/business/ contains links to Latin American search engines from Brazil, Chile, Mexico, etc. You can search a number of country or region-specific search engines, retrieving document descriptions in either Spanish or English. There are links to other Latin American Studies sites as well.

LANIC's *What's New* section includes a detailed list of recent additions and changes to UT-LANIC, plus pointers to other pages with updates for the field of Latin American Studies and the World Wide Web in general.

lanic

site map   suggest a link
search   about lanic
english   español   portugués

Business

Business News Americas
Today's Business Headlines

Regional Resources

Country Resources

Argentina	Colombia	El Salvador	Nicaragua	Puerto Rico
Bolivia	Costa Rica	Guatemala	Panama	Trinidad & Tobago
Brazil	Cuba	Honduras	Paraguay	Uruguay
Chile	Ecuador	Mexico	Peru	Venezuela

International Business

Regional Business Resources ▲

- Business News Americas
- Caribbean Association of Industry and Commerce CAIC
- Caribbean Business Community CBCNA
- Centro de Información y Documentación Empresarial sobre Iberoamérica CIDEIBER
- Directorio de Empresas Infocomercial.com
- FT.com Financial Times - Business News Americas
- Hispanic Business Women's Alliance
- LATCO Trade Tools
- Latinbex Mercado de Valores Latinoamericanos en Euros
- Latin American Business Miami Herald
- Latin Business Chronicle

▶▶ Both Caribbean and Latin American countries are included in LANIC's coverage. ◀◀

For Asia research, a good starting portal is-

Asiaco

Asiaco has mounted portals for more than a dozen Asian countries. The Asiaco business homepage, at www.asiaco.com/business, contains links to major stock indices, Asian Business news, financial tools, jobs and careers, and the Asia Top 50 Web Sites, which include newspapers and other business oriented themes.

Asiaco's Asiawide websites provide similar pages for the following countries:

China	South Korea	Taiwan
Hong Kong (China)	Malaysia	Thailand
India	Pakistan	Vietnam
Indonesia	Philippines	
Japan	Singapore	

Many of these websites are in English, while others will require downloading character sets. Still others offer both options. Click on the Business and Economy tab. Beware of the pesky pop-up ads.

CI-Oriented Websites

A number of large consulting companies specializing in competitor/competitive intelligence have mounted complex and sophisticated websites, and, as you might expect, these commercial operations contain a wealth of useful information including upcoming seminars and speaking engagements, books by principals, and the company's products and services. See *Bookmarks & Favorites* in Part IV, under the heading "Competitive Intelligence," for further examples.

As in the case of the award-winning and favorably reviewed sites described in this chapter, these CI websites have been examined and deemed to be of value for the business intelligence function by CI consultants. You may not need to consult one of these companies today, but keep their names in your mind for future use, their web pages providing useful articles, tips, and hotlinks to sites that you will find invaluable.

The Society of Competitor Intelligence Professionals (SCIP) website at www.scip.org offers several forums on CI-related topics. To participate in discussions, registration is required. Read access is available on a guest basis. Another useful feature of this site is the searchable list of experts.

Also check this site to identify upcoming conferences or seminars where you can learn a great deal about sources and applications for online information as well as other aspects of CI. The exhibit halls at these conferences are always filled with vendors offering a variety of cyber-tools.

Fuld & Company, Inc

Fuld & Company, Inc's website at www.fuld.com is one of the best examples of sites mounted by CI consulting companies. The *New York Times* praised their Internet Intelligence Index, calling it a "good place to start a web tour of competitive-intelligence sites." The index contains more than 600 links, many that are industry-specific. The site is updated quite frequently.

TIP — Among the useful treasures located on the Fuld site is a page called *Internet Searching Tip Sheet,* located at www.fuld.com/i3/searchTips.html. Compiled by the Fuld & Company Library, this sheet is a summary of the basic commands used by many of the search engines mentioned elsewhere in this chapter. It is worth printing and placing on the bulletin board near your PC for handy reference when searching the Internet.

How About a Game of "40 Questions"?

The *Intelligence Organizer,* found at www.fuld.com/Tindex/CorpEval.html is another useful item to look at while examining the Fuld site. The questionnaire consists of a series of questions that you or your company could use to evaluate whether you use intelligence "expediently and decisively." This evaluation is designed to answer that question by examining your ability to handle and apply vital intelligence.

This site has several other links that you might investigate to find equally useful information on CI subjects.

Search Engines and Internet Directories

Search engines are an important key to searching the Internet successfully simply because search engine results let you quickly connect to a large number of available web pages. Do remember that search engines' qualities, search algorithms and coverage vary, so it is best not to depend on a single one of them when trying to do a thorough search on a topic. To reduce the possibility that important sites or items might be missed, search experts recommend using at least three search engines for important research.

Some of the search engines or locators in the lists later in this chapter may be new to you. Note that several European search engines are included. These could be especially useful for gathering intelligence using non-U.S. sites or for searching using languages other than English. Searching foreign databases and reading documents in their native languages may yield intelligence that is not apparent in translated versions. Idioms or cultural nuances may escape the translator or be misinterpreted. Machine translations may be useful for getting the "gist" of a foreign language document, but they sometimes read rather strangely. If you plan to use the document's contents for decision making, be sure to use a competent human translator who will be aware of multiple meanings for words or phrases.

Individual Search Engines

The list on the following page will assist you in identifying language availability and URLs for many popular individual search engines. Check these for "features" that would be useful in your particular type of searching. Some search engines offer features the others may not have. For example, AltaVista offers machine translation for many foreign language documents; at Wisenut, you select the browser language manually.

Individual Search Engines (General)

Language	Site Name	Web Address
English	**AlltheWeb**	www.alltheweb.com
English	**AltaVista**	www.altavista.com
English , French, Spanish, Italian, Norwegian, Danish, Portuguese, German, Dutch	**Ask Jeeves**	www.askjeeves.com
Numerous European Languages	**EuroSeek**	www.euroseek.com
English (UK, U.S., AU, NZ, Chinese, French, German, Italian, Japanese, Dutch, Spanish, Swedish	**Excite**	www.excite.com
English	**Gigablast**	www.gigablast.com
English	**Google**	www.google.com
English-French	**Google Canada**	www.google.ca
Dutch, English, Finnish, French, German, Italian, Portuguese, Spanish, Swedish	**HotBot**	www.hotbot.com
English, European Languages	**Lycos**	www.lycos.com
English (UK)	**Mirago**	www.mirago.co.uk
English	**MS Network**	http://msn.com
English	**Overture**	www.overture.com
English	**Teoma**	www.teoma.com
English	**Thunderstone**	http://dwarf.thunderstone.com/texis/websearch
English, 25 Languages	**Wisenut**	www.wisenut.com

Searching for business intelligence using a general search engine can result in huge numbers of hits, many of which are irrelevant to your topic. One way to improve your search results will be to choose carefully between the many search engines that are out there, and take advantage of features that may improve search results up front. Look for features like these:

- Combination search engine/directory sites that may include a directory category suited to the subject being searched.

- Examples or help files pertinent to that search engine. This helps you avoid making false assumptions.

- The ability to search for phrases rather than individual words, if doing so will not narrow the results too much; e.g. "steel industry" rather than steel industry without quotes. The latter would retrieve hits containing both words but not necessarily together.

- The availability of commonly used characters such as "+" and "-" to make terms mandatory or to eliminate hits containing words that you specify.

- Advanced search interfaces that may help you to narrow search results by a variety of factors. Several of the popular search engines now offer such features.

▶▶ Google's Advanced Search screen provides user-friendly assistance for constructing a meaningful search strategy through the choice of search parameters, language, and several other options that can help avoid extraneous hits. ◀◀

Meta Search Engines

Meta search engines are so called because they offer the ability to enter a search once and execute the search across multiple search engines. Some meta search engines are "smart" enough to translate your wishes into the commands expected by the individual engines, providing you with the advantage of spending less time trying to remember each search engine's individual search instructions.

Some meta sites search more than just the World Wide Web. Dogpile, a personal favorite, is a good example. It "fetches" answers from half a dozen different places in cyberspace, allowing you to do many types of searches from one "jumping off place." It may search some places you would use only occasionally, such as archived conversations that appeared in message boards several years ago.

The following is a list of other meta search engines. Depending upon the type of searching undertaken, you may find that some suit your purposes or searching style better than others. Remember: you will some find some search engines available on one meta site that are not available on another. Experimentation is a good idea. If the list below is not enough, then examine the extensive list found at http://cui.unige.ch/meta-index.html.

Meta Search Engines

Language	Site Name	Web Address
English	**Dogpile**	www.dogpile.com
English - Any Language	**EZ2Find**	http://ez2www.com
English - European Languages	**Ixquick**	http://ixquick.com/eng/
English	**Mamma**	www.mamma.com
English	**Metacrawler**	www.metacrawler.com
English	**Meteor**	www.metor.com
English	**Multimeta**	http://multimeta.com/prog/multicrawlg.cgi
English	**OpenText Query Server**	www.queryserver.com/web.htm
English	**Profusion**	www.profusion.com
English	**Surfwax**	www.surfwax.com
English - German	**Vivisimo**	http://vivisimo.com

For more search engines, see *Bookmarks & Favorites* Section 4, under "Search Engines."

Specialized Search Engines

In business, one key to success is to identify a need, and then to create and offer the product or service that meets that need. A number of websites have been created to do just that. These sites gather and organize search engine lists, usually by type. Using a specialized search engine can yield several benefits:

- Avoid wasting time wading through hundreds of sites that mention your search terms, but in the wrong context.

- Locate materials that might otherwise be elusive. With government information, for example, you may find that FirstGov, www.firstgov.gov, searches across the holdings of multiple government agencies, both state and federal. You need not first determine which agency handles the subject matter in which you are interested.

- Provide a higher confidence factor. For example, if looking for medical articles, a source like MedNets is created for healthcare professionals and may be more reliable than a search of the entire Web.

- Search only websites from a particular geographic area.

The list that follows provides some examples of the types of specialized search engines:

Specialized Search Engines

Subject	Site Name	Web Address
Agriculture	Agriculture Network Information Center	www.agnic.org
Business	Business.com	www.business.com
News	Google News	http://news.google.com
Industry – UK	Kellysearch	www.kellys.co.uk
Latin America	LANIC	http://lanic.utexas.edu/world/search/
Medicine	MedNets	www.mednets.com
Politics	Political Information	www.politicalinformation.com
South Africa	Susy Search	www.susysearch.com

➤➤ A focused search engine can often be the most efficient tool for researching a topic or for limiting search results geographically. ◀◀

Consult *Bookmarks & Favorites* in Section 4 for more URLs for search engines of various types.

Directories and Indexes

That popular internet service called Yahoo! is a classification system or directory rather than a search engine. There are Yahoo! sites in countries all over the world.

To facilitate locating business intelligence in foreign countries, use the Yahoo! list below. The advertisements, yellow pages, etc. on these sites will generally pertain to the country where the site is located, or in a group of countries identified on the home page.

Geographically Oriented Yahoo! Directories

Language	Site Name	Web Address
English	Yahoo!	www.yahoo.com
English	Yahoo! Asia	http://asia.yahoo.com
English	Yahoo! Australia & New Zealand	www.yahoo.com.au
Danish	Yahoo! Denmark	www.yahoo.dk
French	Yahoo! France	www.yahoo.fr
German	Yahoo! Germany	www.yahoo.de
Chinese-English	Yahoo! Hong Kong	www.yahoo.com.hk www.english.yahoo.com.hk

Geographically Oriented Yahoo! Directories

Language	Site Name	Web Address
Italian	Yahoo! Italy	www.yahoo.it
Japanese	Yahoo! Japan	www.yahoo.co.jp
Korean	Yahoo! Korea	www.yahoo.com.tw
Norwegian	Yahoo! Norway	www.yahoo.no
Spanish	Yahoo! Spain	www.yahoo.es
Spanish	Yahoo! Latin America	http://espanol.yahoo.com
Swedish	Yahoo! Sweden	www.yahoo.se
Chinese	Yahoo! Taiwan	www.yahoo.com.tw
English (UK)	Yahoo! U.K. and Ireland	www.yahoo.co.uk

Other Directories and Indexes

Other types of directory websites abound. Many are general in nature, covering various subject areas, while others focus narrowly. The list below provides some examples of both types.

WWW Directories

Subject	Site Name	Web Address
Multiple Subjects	**Beaucoup**	www.beaucoup.com
Business	**Brint**	www.brint.com
Multiple Subjects	**BUBL**	http://bubl.ac.uk/link/index.html
Business	**Business.com**	www.business.com
Business	**CEO Express**	www.ceoexpress.com
Computer Science	**Computer Science**	http://library.albany.edu/subject/csci.htm
Multiple Subjects	**Direct Search**	www.directsearch.com
Engineering, Mathematics, Computing	**EEVL**: Internet Guide to Engineering, Mathematics, and Computing	www.eevl.ac.uk/about.htm
Food, Business	**vFoodPortal**	www.vfoodportal.com/index.phtml
Multiple Subjects	**Google Directory**	http://directory.google.com
Multiple Subjects	**InfoGrid**	www.infogrid.com

Tools for Finding the Right Search Engine or Directory

To streamline the search for business intelligence, it is important to make good choices regarding tools. The goal of this chapter has been to provide a general description of the types of tools available, with examples of some of the better ones. Searchers who wish to keep up with advances in search tools can visit and bookmark websites like http://searchenginewatch.com. While visiting this site you can request a free subscription to *Search Engine Report Mailing List*. To read more about the various categories of search engines and for further examples, see www.searchenginewatch.com/links/.

Another good site is *Search Engine Showdown: The User's Guide to Web Searching*, at http://searchenginesshowdown.com. A useful page on this site is the *Search Engine Features Chart*, which lists and provides reviews of ten of the most popular search engines, providing comparative information on features such as Boolean searching, defaults, proximity, truncation, case, sorting, etc. Searchers who verify results by using more than one search engine often print this page and keep it handy for reference when constructing search strategies.

Search Engine Features Chart

* See also Search Engines by Search Features.
* Search engines grouped by size; all words link to more detailed reviews.

Last updated Oct. 31, 2003.
by Greg R. Notess.

Search Engines	Boolean	Default	Proximity	Truncation	Case	Fields	Limits	Stop	Sorting
Google Review	-, OR	and	Phrase	No	No	intitle, inurl, more	Language, filetype, date, domain	Varies, + searches	Relevance, site
AlltheWeb Review	and, or, andnot, (), +, -, or with ()	and	Phrase	No	No	title, URL, link, more	Language, filetype, date, domain	No if not rewritten	Relevance, site
Lycos Review	+, -	and	Phrase	No	No	title, URL, link, more	Language, domain	No	Relevance
AltaVista Simple Review	+, -, AND, OR, AND NOT, ()	and, phrase	Phrase, NEAR	Yes *	No	title, URL, link, more	Language, filetype	Yes	Relevance, site
AltaVista Adv. Review	and, or, and not, ()	phrase	Phrase, near, within, <, <~	Yes *	Yes	title, URL, link, more	Language, filetype, date	No	Relevance, if used
HotBot (Inktomi) Review	AND, OR, NOT, (), -	and	Phrase	No	Yes	title, more	Language, date	Some	Relevance, site
MSN Search Review	AND, OR, NOT, (), -	and	Phrase	No	Yes	title, link	Language, filetype, date	Some	Relevance
Teoma Review	-, OR	and	Phrase	No	No	intitle, inurl	Language, site	Yes, + searches	Relevance, metasites
WiseNut Review	- only	and	Phrase	No	No	No	Language	Yes, + searches	Relevance, site
Gigablast Review	AND, OR, AND NOT, ()	or	Phrase	No	No	title, site, ip, more	Domain, type	No	Relevance

▸▸ This copyrighted Search Engine Features Chart is reprinted with permission of Greg Notess. The chart can be found at www.searchenginesshowdown.com/features. ◂◂

Using the special features available in various search engines can produce a more focused search result. In a time crunch, this may mean that more time is available for the analysis phase of the research. For example, AltaVista might be a good choice if case-sensitive searching makes sense.

This can be extremely useful in certain searches where the same word could be both part of a company name and a generic word that can mean something totally different. Consider "apple." Capitalized, Apple becomes a proper noun and may refer to the computer company or the nickname for New York City. Written in lower case, it is most frequently used as the name of a fruit.

Research Specialists

Over the past several years, researchers have learned to depend on others out there who specialize in locating new tools and websites for information research, sharing their secrets with interested parties. One well-known example of this breed is Gary Price, who maintains a weblog and newsletter called *The Virtual Acquisition Shelf & News Desk*, and also the ResourceShelf website at http://resourceshelf.freepint.com. This website is updated daily with new articles covering search engines, the information industry, and databases. A weekly email reminder and summary service is also available.

In addition, Gary is responsible for Direct Search, at www.freepint.com/gary/direct.htm. Direct Search is a compilation of links to the search interfaces of website resources that contain data not easily or entirely searchable from the general search engines. This type of data is sometimes said to reside on the "Invisible Web." See Chapter 12 for further discussion on the Invisible Web.

Trip Wyckoff's Special Issues website, at www.specialissues.com/lol/, is now the home of *The List of Lists*, started by Gary Price in 1998. This list is a free service, as is the list of magazines from which the lists are taken. Other material at this site is subscription based.

Tara Calishain's popular Researchbuzz, at www.researchbuzz.com, provides a free weekly email newsletter as well as a more elaborate website that contains articles and archives. In an informal style, the newsletter covers new information sources in many subject areas. The website's subtitle is "Search Engine News and More Since 1998."

Chapter 12

The Invisible Web

Invisible? What Is It All About?

Since the "Invisible Web" – alternatively known as the "deep web" – crept into our vocabulary several years back, numerous books and articles have appeared telling us what it is and what it is not. For the purposes of this book, the term refers to the many documents, graphic materials, or databases not reachable by commonly used search engines, but which are potentially valuable to the CI researcher. Your favorite search engine is no doubt satisfactory for many searches, but there are times when you simply must try to locate anything and everything that can be located on a subject before analysis and decision-making can proceed. So, you turn to the Invisible Web.

The Invisible Web is thought to be much larger than the World Wide Web reached by popular search engines such as Google or even by well known meta-search engines. A study by Bright Planet, found at www.brightplanet.com/technology/deepweb.asp, describes the Invisible Web as 550 times larger than the "surface web." The Bright Planet study further states that more than 200,000 database-driven websites are affected by the invisibility problem. Chris Sherman, associate editor of Search Engine Watch at www.searchenginewatch.com, estimates that the number of quality pages in the deep web is three to four times the size of the "surface web." The actual figures may be debatable, but it is obvious that there could be a great deal of valuable intelligence hidden in some of those 200,000 database sites.

A researcher at Company A hunting for business intelligence might, for example, use the Invisible Web to locate useful material in databases that researchers at Company B did not know existed – sites that can be identified and reached only through a website that contains links to them. This fact could contribute in some way to A's gaining a competitive advantage. The key to being A, rather than B, lies in identifying and using Invisible Web sources.

Free Pint, at www.freepint.co.uk, published a feature article in its June 8, 2000 issue in which author Chris Sherman listed the following reasons search engines miss what searchers might consider valuable and important web pages:

- There are no links pointing to the relevant page, so the search engine cannot go there.

- The page is made up of data types such as graphics, CGI scripts, PDF files or other formats that search engines do not index.

- The relevant information is stored in databases reachable from a web page, but not all of the information can be described or displayed on that page — the file may be too large, for instance.

The evolution of Web technology, coupled with greater awareness of the access problem, has reduced the amount of information that is still "invisible." Webmasters have taken steps to provide links, change formats, etc., while list makers, the academic world, and entrepreneurial companies have sought to provide better access to this hard-to-reach data. No longer available are several useful finger sites mentioned in early articles on the subject, either because they were not economically viable or because the material that they referenced became accessible to search engines.

Finding Your Future Invisible Web Favorites

For the researcher wishing to locate buried treasure in the vast body of un-indexed data, it is important to understand what you are dealing with. Many popular Invisible Web sites use a subject-oriented approach that removes uncertainty about terminology. For example, while browsing a list it is easy to spot the term used by the site's creators for a machine with four wheels, an engine, and a horn. If we do not see "car" or "automobile" or "truck" or "SUV" in the list, we might notice "motor vehicles" further down the list and drill down using that subject heading.

Spelling errors and typos, the gremlins that can sabotage a search engine search, are not a problem here. All you have to do is click on a heading. In addition, seeing subjects arranged before you in a list can be a refreshing change from trying to remember the differences in spelling between British and America. It is not necessary to enter both spellings of words like labor/labour, honor/honour, etc. into the search engine in order to retrieve useful hits from across the Atlantic. You may still have to enter search terms, but at least you will not have to cull out dozens of extraneous sites that contain your search terms.

Invisible Web sites appear to fall into at least two categories:

- **Eclectic Websites** created for this purpose by researchers or librarians. As the researcher discovers material deemed to be potentially useful to others, they may categorize the sites under headings such as Business, Science and Technology, etc. Links are provided to subheadings or to individual file locations. Some of these sites may offer a search engine to identify lists of possible sites on your topic. Access is usually free.

- **Portals** created by networked or cooperative organizations such as libraries or universities, or by business entities such as publishers. Material is organized by subject. Frequently, these types of portals are further broken down into subcategories. A search engine retrieves results from various Invisible Web sources belonging to members of the group, then presents them in an organized list. These sites may provide additional services such as document delivery or inter-library loan via member organizations, so there could be some cost involved. Occasionally, search results will require subscriptions to commercial online sources or access via university password.

Eclectic Sites

The reason for researching the Invisible Web is to locate material not generally retrieved by popular search engines or indexes of the type described in Chapter 11. What could appear under a seemingly "popular" subject heading such as *Hobbies* on an eclectic list may contain important insights for an industry that manufactures or markets items related to specific hobbies. Trends, new products, or new uses for existing products may be mentioned there. This might set your company's creative minds to work considering whether they can apply that new found knowledge to dream up new products or services.

Consider the following hypothetical situation:

A scientific study by Professor Q at the University of Somewhere concludes that spending time on a particular hobby in childhood has major implications for predicting one's potential business or professional success in adulthood. It seems that this hobby trains the brain to work in certain ways that are crucial to critical analysis in later life.

The study does not get much exposure. Perhaps Professor Q delivers a paper on his or her findings at an obscure conference that does not make its proceedings available on the Internet, and the local media does not publicize the information since the U of Somewhere is located in a very small, quiet town. For these and other possible reasons, Professor Q's paper is not reachable by search engines crawling through cyberspace. However, a graduate assistant at the U of Somewhere mentions it to a librarian who adds it to an eclectic Invisible Web listing under the innocuous subject *Hobbies*.

The Sales and Marketing department at a company manufacturing items related to the hobby cited in the study is looking for a new approach to use in an upcoming advertising campaign. Sales are stagnant and holiday gift giving is months away. A business researcher is asked to do an online search that *might* provide some fresh ideas.

The searcher tries some eclectic websites like those mentioned below, finds Professor Q's paper, and sends it along to Sales and Marketing Department where the proverbial light bulb begins to glow in someone's head. Lo and behold – the theme for the new campaign is born! It will sell millions of dollars in merchandise to parents who realize that it would be wise to encourage their little Johnny or Janie to become interested in that hobby. It might make him or her rich and famous!

The sites mentioned below are eclectic. They may contain both sites that are easily located with search engines and others that are not, but they are widely cited for being high in quality.

BUBL LINK / 5:15

BUBL LINK / 5:15, at http://bubl.ac.uk/link/, is the subject-oriented version of BUBL LINK, a British website covering 11,000 internet resources in all academic subject areas. Listings have been selected, evaluated, catalogued, and described by staff members with participation from an organization called Libraries of Networked Knowledge. A minimum of five entries and a maximum of fifteen per topic is the model followed, though in some cases the rule has been stretched a bit. Users can browse a large controlled vocabulary of subjects, drilling down through a hierarchical arrangement of links to sites containing buried treasure.

Direct Search

Gary Price, whose *Resource Shelf* website is discussed further in Chapter 11, developed Direct Search, which is reachable from www.resourceshelf.com or at www.freepint.com/gary/direct.htm. Direct Search contains more than a dozen broad categories that link to detailed compilations of websites on more specific topics. The Business/Economics list is full of government, company, and industry-specific sites, many of which contain statistics and databases.

Though its search interface, the Direct Search site provides access to additional compilations, together or individually, as follows:

- Fast Facts
- Price's List of Lists
- Speech and Transcript Center
- NewsCenter
- Streaming Media: News and Public Affairs Resources
- Web Accessible Congressional Research Service Reports

Gary Price also is involved in invisible-web.net, which lists eighteen broad categories that can be broken down further for focused searching. This is the companion site to *"The Invisible Web: Uncovering Information Sources Search Engines Can't See,"* which Gary wrote with Chris Sherman. Here you can often find links directly to individual database search pages. See Appendix E for further information on this book.

Librarians' Index To The Internet

The Librarians' Index To The Internet, at www.lii.org, is an annotated, searchable index of over 11,000 resources that have been chosen and evaluated by librarians. LII.org is hosted by the University of California at Berkeley's SunSITE staff. An email newsletter alerts subscribers whenever new resources are added to the directory. A number of business categories are included here, as shown on the following page:

>> Home
>> About
>> Subscribe
>> Help
>> Suggest a Site
>> Comments
>> More Search Tools

Librarians' Index to the Internet **lii.org**
Information You Can Trust

[   ] SEARCH LII.ORG | Advanced Search

Business

General Resources

- Accounting
- Advertising
- Affirmative Action
- Agriculture
- Auctions
- Automobiles
- Banks & Banking
- Boards of Trade
- Building
- Business Education
- Business Enterprises
- Business History
- Business Law
- Business Research
- Business Taxes
- California Business
- Census
- Charities
- Clothing Trade

- Economics
- Electronic Commerce
- Entrepreneurship
- Etiquette
- Exporting
- Industrial Safety
- Industries
- Insurance
- Insurance - California
- Intelligence Service
- International Trade
- Inventions
- Investments
- Labor Statistics
- Labor Unions
- Law Firms
- Macroeconomics
- Magazines & Newspapers

- Petroleum Industry
- Product Safety
- Public Relations
- Publishing
- Rural Development
- Salt Industry
- Self-employed
- SIC Codes
- Small Business
- Standardization
- Stock Exchanges
- Sweatshops
- Taxes
- Telemarketing
- Telephone Books
- Telephone Rates
- Textile Industry
- Tobacco Industry
- Trade Shows

▶▶ From general to specific, a laundry list of topics has been indexed on the Librarians' Index
To The Internet. The business category shown above is an example. Sites are contributed by
librarians, which should add a confidence factor for users of this resource. ◀◀

Portals

U.S. Based Portals

Portals are proliferating as improved technology makes it easier to build and populate them. The
term "portal" is used to describe both individual websites and software products used on intranets to
provide access to internet sites. The portals mentioned here are websites within the description
mentioned on the second page of this chapter.

IncyWincy: The Invisible Web Search Engine

In addition to crawling the millions of pages found in the Open Directory Project, IncyWincy, at
www.incywincy.com, uses its "Universal Search Engine" to dig into the one million web search
portals of the Invisible Web. Both simple and advanced searches are available. The advanced search
allows for limiting search results to the contents of one of more than a dozen broad categories. The

advanced search also removes duplicates and provides other optional limitations that narrow or focus search results.

INFOMINE

INFOMINE, at http://infomine.ucr.edu, is a virtual library of internet resources relevant to faculty, students, and research staff at the university level. Compilers include librarians from the University of California, Wake Forest University, California State University, the University of Detroit - Mercy, and other academic institutions. Included in INFOMINE are databases, electronic journals, electronic books, bulletin boards, mailing lists, online library catalogs, articles, directories of researchers, and many other types of information. Subject areas covered include these:

- Biological, Agricultural and Medical Sciences
- Business and Economics
- Cultural Diversity and Ethnic Resources
- Electronic Journals
- Government Information
- Maps and GIS
- Physical Sciences, Engineering, Computing and Math
- Social Sciences and Humanities
- Visual and Performing Arts
- Books and monographs

Both searching and browsing options are available for accessing the more than 115,000 resources available at INFOMINE. A very descriptive page of search tips is included at http://infomine.ucr.edu/?view=help/index.html.

Medbioworld

With 25,000 links, Medbioworld, at www.medbioworld.com/index.html, claims to be the largest medical reference site available. It includes all medical journals and medical associations, and similar resources in the biological sciences. Links are provided to 6,000 medical journals in 80 subspecialties, and to the home pages of 4,000 medical associations. Also available at this site are tools such as medical glossaries, disease databases, clinical trials and guidelines, and medical journals offering full-text articles.

Profusion

Profusion, at www.profusion.com, was originally called invisibleweb.com. It looks like many similar sites, offering a listing of subject oriented links and providing either basic or advance search interfaces. However, the Profusion site offers some nice additions to the typical portal search:

- Search groups can be organized to match the searcher's research needs.
- A detailed breakdown and analysis of search results is provided.
- Alerts are available – on demand or in regularly scheduled delivery.
- Results are sorted by date.
- Search terms are highlighted in results.

Free registration is required, and details about the service are not available until the searcher has registered and signed in.

Portals For Invisible European Information

Resource Discovery Network

The RDN, at www.rdn.ac.uk, is a collaboration of over seventy British educational and research organizations, which select, index, and describe the sites chosen for inclusion. The cooperative network consists of the Resource Discovery NetworkCentre (RDNC) and eight independent service providers called hubs. These hubs divide the subject matter as follows:

- ALTIS — Hospitality, Leisure, Sport and Tourism
- Artifact — Arts and Creative Industries
- BIOME — Health and Life Sciences
- EEVL — Engineering, Mathematics and Computing
- GEsource — Geography and Environment
- Humbul — Humanities
- PSIgate — Physical Sciences
- SOSIG — Social Sciences, Business and Law

Some of the services above may have restricted access. The relevant hub will provide details where that occurs. A document entitled Working With the RDN, found at www.rdn.ac.uk/publications/ workingwithrdn, provides technical details regarding interacting with RDN.

FIZ CHEMIE Berlin

Germany's FIZ CHEMIE Berlin, at www.chemistry.de, provides free searching of three subject-specific search engines that claim to access more than 7000 servers with more than 15 million web pages not located by search engines.

- ChemGuide — chemistry
- MedPharmGuide — medicine and pharmacology
- PublishersGuide — scientific publishers

These are reached by clicking on the Databases link of the homepage. The company now offers "These free-to-use search engines access more than 7,000 servers with more than 15 million web pages," many of which are not accessed by regular search engines. Information from universities and research institutes constitutes much of this material.

Although the search is free, documents must be ordered from the site's document delivery facility. An alert service is available by subscription.

Vascoda

Vascoda, at www.vascoda.de, went online in August, 2003. It is an integrated network comprised more than twenty virtual libraries and four scientific information networks involving major libraries and information providers in Germany and their international partners. The site is available in

English. Coverage includes the humanities, economics, social science, life sciences, engineering, and the physical sciences. A variety of media are available here, including the following:

- Full text access to journal articles, working papers, etc.
- Subject gateways that point to subject-specific websites containing scientific and other high-standard resources.
- Document delivery from several sources.
- Print media, including books and journals, microfilms etc., listed in library Online Public Access Catalogs (OPACs), some of which may be obtained via document delivery systems.
- Other types of information resources such as calendars, statistical data, or videotapes.

Either searching or browsing is offered in the various individual subject categories.

Complete Planet

Complete Planet, at http://completeplanet.com, uses BrightPlanet technology to provide access to 103,000 databases and specialty search engines using a 7000-category directory structure. Business intelligence topics covered here include:

- Competitive Intelligence
- Product Research (R&D)
- Market Research
- Brand Monitoring
- Compliance/Legal Monitoring
- News Monitoring

A lengthy but well organized tutorial in PDF format is available at www.brightplanet.com/deepcontent/bp_searchtutorial.pdf. This tutorial provides detailed instruction on searching Complete Planet, but experienced searchers may skip to the section on Specialty Searches, found later in the document. Here you will find headings for Product Searches, Competitor Intelligence, and Market Research.

An enterprise approach to using this technology is provided through BrightPlanet's *Deep Query Manager (DQM2)*, which searches multiple search engines and deep web databases.

Chapter 13

Staying on Top of the Subject

The ongoing business of gathering data and analyzing the competitive situation in your industry, or any industry — or within your own market sector — can be extremely labor intensive and time consuming. Timeliness is crucial — certain news could require an immediate response or reaction, and in certain circumstances, skipping even one day's CI research could put your company at a disadvantage.

Therefore, it is necessary to keep up with competitors' announcements, press coverage, products, personnel, and more. Keeping up to date means having a tracking mechanism in place and, for that purpose, there are several types of cyberspace tools that make the job easier. These tools allow you to use a proactive rather than reactive approach to minding other companies' business.

Custom News Services — Tracking Companies, Industries, and Trends

Commercial online vendors have offered current awareness services for years. With the advent of the Internet, however, a new class of products entered the marketplace. Custom news services are used to put news, stock quotes, and other timely information on desktops across Corporate America.

Researchers now have access to at least three categories of products or services:

- PUSH Technology
- Alert Services
- Vertical Market Products

Each of these types of services fills a need in the information gathering process. Many companies use all three options, either on a regular basis or as needed.

PUSH Technology

Using the combined resources of multiple vendors, PUSH services bring information right to your computer desktop in the form of a direct feed, email, or as an icon that runs your searches on demand. In general, PUSH services allow you to customize your news by choosing from a list of topics. The list of subjects varies from service to service, as do the features. Some even highlight the keywords you are looking for within the articles.

Some PUSH services are sold as enterprise packages, making them available to your organization on a company-wide basis. Other alert services may be available at no charge, but are advertising supported. Although material from some sources may be free, you may be asked to pay for other articles if you want them in full text. In general, the more costly services are the ones that offer more features, greater customization, and fewer, if any, additional costs.

The variety of choices means that even the smallest companies, or those with small budgets for information tracking, can still take advantage of automated company or industry tracking.

In the fickle world of internet tools, the popularity of PUSH technology waxes and wanes. An article by Steve Smith in the July, 2003 edition of *eContent* magazine discusses this topic, indicating that in 2002 media sites such as *CNN* and *USA Today* had mounted PUSH news sites. At press time, this article is still available on the Web at http://econtentmag.com/?ArticleID=4639. Mr. Smith mentions eight websites offering PUSH services. Yet, only two months later, half of the URLs listed, mainly the ones from the media sites, were unreachable, unavailable, or "under construction." The sites for PUSH technology vendors were still available, though.

To learn about the possibilities, see the following:

- Serence   www.serence.com

- QPass   www.qpass.com

- RocketInfo   www.rocketinfo.com

Popular services from only a few years ago, such as Pointcast, are now long gone from the scene. All is not lost as newer, more-advanced products and services have entered the marketplace.

Nexcerpt

Nexcerpt, at www.nexcerpt.com, bills itself as "a sophisticated briefing service. In the April, 2003 issue of *Searcher Magazine*, well-known and respected editor Barbara Quint called Nexcerpt a "killer product." The full text of this editorial/review is available at www.infotoday.com/searcher/apr03/voice.shtml.

Nexcerpt monitors a universe of web-based sources, isolates material that matches the user's defined interests, extracts the most relevant excerpts, and then delivers the excerpts, their written context, and links to the original web sources. Sources included are newspapers, news groups, press releases, business sources, and magazines. The material can then be PUSHed, if desired, to your colleagues, clients, contacts, etc. at will.

Alert Services

Constantly monitoring your company's competitors, industry, or topics of interest, is a major undertaking. To do this efficiently, you need an electronic helper that will monitor particular sources for any references to items of interest, even if you are on vacation, taking a "sick day," or are just too busy to take the time to do so yourself.

All of the large commercial online vendors offer their web or direct-access subscribers current awareness or alert services in one form or another. In some environments the phrase "selective dissemination of information" – SDI – is used to describe the process.

Let us say your Sales and Marketing Department wants to keep abreast of the market strategies of a dozen companies in the U.S. and abroad. Think how much time and labor could be saved if you automate the process. Rather than try to read and clip dozens of newspapers, trade publications, newswires and other sources, let the online vendor's computer do the work for you.

If you opt to receive the articles by email, you will have relatively timely information. Of course, *how* timely depends upon the frequency with which the vendor updates and reloads the database. You may find that Vendor A reloads a certain database more frequently than Vendor B. If talking with vendors about their services, be sure to ask about their frequency of updates. This and other questions are discussed in Chapter 5.

The vendor's staff should be able to help you choose the best sources and construct optimal search strategies. They can also advise you concerning additional files that were recently added to their service, which may yield new and valuable intelligence.

Dialog and LexisNexis are popular sources for this type of alert service. A third player, Factiva, offers two variations on this theme in the forms of its Factiva Tracker and Factiva Alerts services. Dozens of other vendors, many of which focus on specific industries, geographic areas, or other limiting factors, also offer such services. To keep things convenient, many venders let you set up these alert services by completing forms available on their websites.

Here is how the system works, assuming that you are a subscriber:

- You follow instructions on the vendor's website, contact your designated representative or call the vendor's Customer Support Department.

- You construct one or more searches that the system runs automatically every time a database is reloaded — daily, weekly, or annually.

- Using email, fax, or whatever alerting method has been agreed upon, the vendor sends you relevant documents or articles that have been added to the system since the last reload.

- You are charged a modest fee for storage of your query on the vendor's computer, plus a fee for each item retrieved.

Using alert services from large vendors that license many files has its advantages. For one, you can receive records from multiple files of your choice in a single set of results, with duplicates automatically removed. Also, you can also specify precisely when you want the results delivered. In addition, these vendors often create subject-oriented groups of files that can be searched simultaneously. This reduces or eliminates the need to study long lists of publications to sort out those regarding a particular industry. It also means that the files you select can be searched simultaneously, with ease.

Other Players in the Monitoring Marketplace

Not all monitoring and clipping services are part of the major online services described above. Services like Burrelle's, featured in Chapter 6, and CyberAlert are specialists in monitoring a wide range of publications for a variety of clients.

CyberAlert

CyberAlert, at www.cyberalert.com, offers automated press clipping, broadcast monitoring, and web clipping for clients involved in public relations, marketing, brand management, market research, competitive intelligence, and other types of business research. Message boards and Usenet groups are included among the more than 13,000 publications and sources monitored in 17 languages. CyberAlert uses flat fee pricing, offers next morning email delivery plus electronic clip searching and storage.

AccuClip Express, an additional service of CyberAlert, offers a more human touch. After the automated search is run, professionally-trained editors filter the retrieved clips, removing inappropriate clips and deleting extraneous copy and graphics. The goal here is to provide clients with only so-called "good clips."

▶▶ CyberAlert is among a new generation of monitoring services that take advantage of improved technology to search thousands of sources and deliver results in convenient email mode. ◀◀

These services are good for monitoring a broad range of topics; what if you wish to focus on business-related information, or a specific culture?

Business Journals

Business Journals publishes business newspapers in 40+ major U.S. cities using the name *[City name] Business Journal*. The company's website, at www.businessjournals.com, contains a searchable archive of a half-million local business articles from across the nation. The site is generous with free alert services:

- Daily city-specific business news updates by email.

- Industry-specific updates by email (one per industry level per week)

- The ability to set up your own Industry Journal, with over 45 industries to choose from.

- Name tracking of customers, prospects, and competitors, with email alerts when they appear in one of the various Business Journals.

NewsNow

NewsNow, www.newsnow.co.uk, automatically searches more than 13,000 news sources every five minutes. Subscribers receive 24/7 coverage of key online, national, regional, and international publications. Email alerts regarding the appearance of a specified keyword or keywords in an article can be delivered within minutes of an article's publication. A nice feature of this U.K.-based service is its search engine locates more than just keywords. Coverage is available in more than fifteen languages, which is helpful for organizations in the international business arena. NewsNow maintains a searchable thirty-day archive.

Minority-related Information Services

A minorities-oriented product lines have developed in the electronic clipping business, focusing on the African-American and Hispanic information communities. These services may be especially useful if your company is seeking to expand its marketing activity to these population segments. If you are already actively competing in these markets, these services should definitely be considered for addition to your list of CI sources.

LatinClips

LatinClips, a sister company of Hispanic PR Wire, is found at www.latinclips.com. LatinClips offers monitoring services in the U.S. Hispanic, Latin American, and Caribbean markets. Sources include wire services, newspapers, magazines, trade publications, Hispanic radio and television, and general market dailies in the top twenty Hispanic markets. Special features include instant translation from Spanish or Portuguese at no charge, targeted searching by region or country, or types of media outlets, and availability of Boolean search language for construction of search strategies.

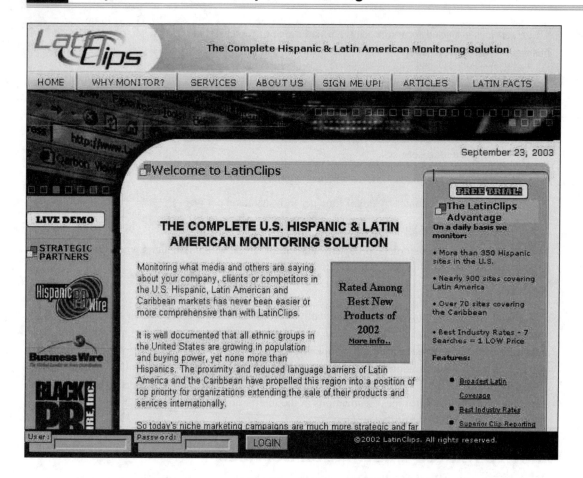

▸▸ *The Measurement Standard*, an industry newsletter, rated The LatinClips website, shown above, among the best new products of 2002. ◂◂

During the second half of 2003, LatinClips introduced *Black Sources*, an online monitoring product for African-American media, to augment its partnership with Black PR Wire, mentioned below. Black Sources is part of a line of multicultural-related tracking services called Diversity Solutions.

The Black Sources package covers online news sources for the U.S. African American market either as a stand-alone service or in combination with other offerings of LatinClips or Black PR Wire. Clients can access their online clips daily via a password-protected database. The print clips from publications monitored by Black PR Wire's Clipping Service staff are mailed out on a weekly basis. A per-month charge for service applies, as do per-clip fees, and the services can be bundled.

Black PR Wire

Black PR Wire, at www.blackprwire.com, offers clippings on a statewide, regional, and national basis from the top 60 African-American newspapers in the U.S. Articles can be provided electronically or in hard copy. This service is available on a stand-alone basis or in conjunction with its partner LatinClips, mentioned above.

PUSH Technology as an Alerting Service

In addition to the purpose-built alert services discussed earlier in this chapter, consider PUSH technology for alerting purposes as well. The PUSH technology method is to feed news and other stories on your previously selected topics or industries to your desktop, automatically. Remember, though: PUSH services may not search all those sources that you consider important.

TIP — You may need a combination of several alerting tools to feel confident that you are monitoring *all possible outlets* for business intelligence.

Vertical Market Products

Vertical market online services focus on providing products and services that meet the information needs of specific markets or industries.

Reuters

Reuters is a good example of such a supplier in the news area because of the variety of subject matter in their vertical offerings, which may be obtained directly, or through the Internet. Reuters specialty services run the gamut from geographically-oriented collections to entertainment, technology, sports, or similar specialty topics. Details can be found on the Reuters website at http://about.reuters.com/media/productlist.aspx, as shown below:

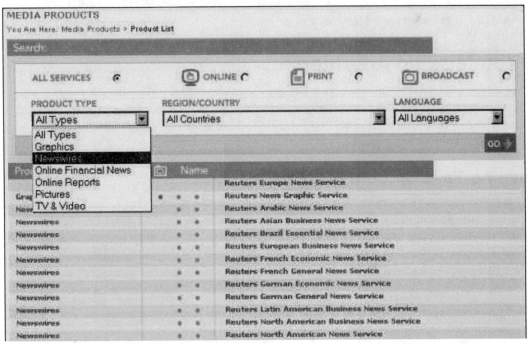

Although Reuters services are marketed chiefly to the media, the rapid access to information inherent in a service like this has attracted many large corporations who consider it a worthwhile investment. Special services have been developed for the insurance, advertising, and transportation industries as well as health and other corporate and professional sectors. These services may be very useful for keeping in touch with what is happening in faraway places where you and your company have a significant investment in material or personnel.

ABIX

ABIX, at www.abix.com.au, offers smartBIX, a personalized alert service covering more than 150 publications from Australia and Australasia. Alerts are in you mailbox by 7:30 a.m. Australian time. Access to the ABIX database of twenty years' worth of business and finance data comes with the subscription, allowing you to gather historic data on clients, prospects, or competitors in this market.

Computerwire

Another example of vertical market information products is Computerwire, at www.computerwire.com. ComputerWire provides integrated news, opinion, research, and analysis from London, New York, San Francisco, Sydney, and Paris information sources 24 hours a day.

Nerac

If your business intelligence needs relate to science or technology, then consider Nerac, at www.nerac.com. Nerac offers much more than the typical alerting service; for subscribers who want the interaction of a human helper, their assigned Nerac representative will keep a "tech track" running behind the scenes on specified companies, words, or phrases. As new information comes into their system it is turned around and sent to the client automatically by either email, hard copy, or posted to a password protected website.

Are You Missing Anything?

Not all stories of potential interest to your company are picked up on vertical market wires. They may be important to you, but may not be categorized as "industry specific." You may find that you need to search general sources as well, on a regular basis, to avoid missing such items. General sources are discussed in Chapter 11.

Keeping Tabs on Competitors' Websites

In today's business environment, monitoring competitors' web pages is a useful, if not crucial, activity for most companies. Because of improvements in technology, the Internet has become a key marketing tool in many industries, and companies are anxious to update their websites as soon as new products or services are released. Suppose that you would like to monitor the sites of several companies or organizations. This could mean investing significant time in visiting each website, looking at key areas, or perhaps browsing the entire site, looking for new items such as these:

- **Press releases** – A company is likely to include all of its press releases on its own site, whereas newspapers or trade publications may not pick them all up.

- **Promotions** – You may want to match or better a competitor's offer, or at least have your reply prepared if a customer mentions that deal over at the XYZ website.

- **Partnerships/Alliances** – It is crucial to know about these "connections." Deals involving competitors allows your own organization to know if it needs to react – offensively or defensively.

- **Product Announcements** – As with press releases, these do not all make the headlines, but they could be important information for someone within your company. Product announcements may also contain evidence that a company is *repositioning* itself in the market. For example, a software developer might have chosen to stop marketing certain products. They may now use new language such as "interactive system" in the section of their site that formerly touted the features of the individual products. This may be of great interest if you are trying to determine competitors' marketing strategies.

- **Price Changes** - The trend toward selling everything over the Web from automobiles to zoo tickets means that you can more easily gather pricing information, and that you can easily track changes in prices as your competitor responds to market factors that influence pricing.

- **Employment Opportunities** - This could alert you to someone's departure, or perhaps give you an idea about a new direction the company intends to take in product development, R&D, etc. Sometimes the mere fact that they are hiring or not hiring is useful information.

- **Issues Statements/White Papers** – These documents may provide insight into a company's stand on important issues that impact the company, the industry, or the world. Having this information may be useful if dealing with or competing against that company.

How do you keep up with all of this information without tearing out your hair? Choose a monitoring or alert service, specify your search targets, and let automation do the work for you. You can setup an alert that tells you when certain pages change on a website, or set your alert service to watch for specific keywords, or make other requests. These alert services vary from vendor to vendor.

This strategy can help track government information as well. By monitoring pertinent regulatory sections on government websites, you will be made aware of new or changed regulations and adjust your activities accordingly. Your Legal Department may or may not have noted this, but as always, when it comes to compliance, it is better to be safe than sorry.

Government sites may also contain calendar information. If a competitor has a meeting on the Food & Drug Administration's calendar, there is a reason. For example, if you are in a competition to gain approval on drugs for treating a disease, it is very important to know everything possible about the progress and status of your competitor's product.

Free Services For Monitoring Websites

Free monitoring services such as *Netmind*, *Mindit*, and *Spyonit* have disappeared from the Internet, having either been bought up by large companies seeking to market enterprise products, or for other undetermined reasons. Several new names are currently being marketed to fill this void.

ChangeDetect, at www.changedetect.com, offers some of the same features that made the earlier monitoring products attractive to the CI sleuth. At no charge, ChangeDetect provides automatic checking of up to five Web pages, email notification regarding changes to target pages, minimizing of false positives and notification about insignificant changes, and guaranteed privacy protection. A number of advanced features are available for ChangeDetect Pro members. For a small monthly fee, additional pages can be monitored. A graduated fee schedule allows coverage for up to 5000 pages.

WatchThat Page, at www.watchthatpage.com, is a free monitoring service that provides several delivery options. Users may choose to receive one comprehensive email covering several websites or pages, or to separate topics into individual alerts. You may choose to track all changes or only those that contain selected keywords. Updates are available daily or on selected days of the week. If desired, delivery can consist simply of a list of pages that have changed, leaving you to visit the pages when time allows. WatchThatPage will also notify you if pages become unreachable.

TrackEngine, at www.trackengine.com/servlets/com.nexlabs.trackengine.ui.Login is free to individuals or available to businesses for a fee. With TrackEngine you may track a competitor's banner ads, note every time they are mentioned on industry-specific websites, or see whether your company or those you watch are being watched by monitoring websites such as those mentioned in Chapter 7.

Fee-based Web Monitors

Infominder is the product of iMorph Inc. Located at www.infominder.com, Infominder offers a list of services that are similar to those mentioned above, plus a few additional features to justify a small annual subscription fee. Features include the following:

- Ability to track up to 100 web pages
- Email received in digest format arranged by categories
- IE Assistant to allow tracking of a page while browsing
- Daily notification
- Ability to filter changes by multiple keywords or number of changes on a page
- Ability to import bookmarks/favorites from Netscape or Internet Explorer

Watch360 is iMorph's upscale product in this category.
Value-added advanced features include these:

- Setup Wizards for speed and ease in getting started in a monitoring activity.
- Extensive and searchable company databases that have been categorized into industry, letting you watch companies in a particular industry. This may point out competitors you did not know existed.
- Tracking by categories to retrieve the type of information you want. These include Products and Services, Press Releases, News and Events, Management, Financial, and Partners.

Tracerlock, at www.tracerlock.com, describes itself as " your personal early warning system and assistant." Each day, this service scans articles published on news sites, online trade journals, e-zines, search engines, and newsgroups for clients' specified information requests.

In addition, Tracerlock subscribers can provide a list of websites to monitor for changes. Email alerts are sent within as little as fifteen minutes of publication on the Internet, according to Tracerlock's website. Subscriptions begin at a low monthly rate and a 30-day free trial is available.

TIP — Using one of the services described above, test the service by using their keywords tracking to track *your company name* on appropriate news site pages. When a news site mentions your company, the service should alert you. This can also provide an indication of which of your company press releases are being picked up, and where.

IdExec, at www.idexec.com, offers a database that contains contact information and executives' titles and job responsibilities for almost 400,000 business decision-makers from over 60,000 of the world's largest public, private, government, and nonprofit organizations. idEXEC tracks U.S. organizations reporting revenues of more than $30 million, also international organizations reporting over $50 million in revenue, or asset-based firms with over $200 million. Company executives are categorized by forty different functional responsibility types.

Some interesting features here include EXECAlert, a custom-produced file of idEXEC adds, changes, and deletes of executive decision-maker information, pushed out to the client via a weekly email. Contact data can be downloaded in customized formats directly from the Internet. Although this service is intended to provide contact information for sales and marketing applications, the information can, of course, be used for many other applications such as to identify "fast trackers" within a competitor's organization.

IdEXEC's "FIRMAlerts" service is intended as a sales and research activity trigger. Important changes within specified companies or geographic sales territories automatically trigger notification.

A free trial is available, but first you will have to complete a detailed form and wait for a sales person to contact you by telephone. Both pay-per-view and flat-rate subscriptions are available.

Monitoring Your Competitor's Advertising

Competitors' ads and publicity can provide valuable competitive intelligence for business-to-business companies. Billing themselves as "much more than a clipping service," **Ad Facts**, at www.adfacts.com, has added electronic media to the print sources it monitors for clients. In addition to email or PDF copies of the ads themselves, Ad Facts provides analytical studies. Think about how useful it could be to know:

- Where a competitor has advertised.

- The amount of money they spent.

- The amount of editorial coverage they received, measured in column inches.

- How their products were positioned.

Though it is not a monitoring service, another useful website for checking competitors' ads might be www.adflip.com, which bills itself as "The world's largest archive of classic print ads." For a modest fee, an archive dating from 1940 to 2001 can be searched, either by year or by product name. This site does not offer monitoring, but is a useful reference tool.

Watching the Commercials

Video Monitoring Service, at www.vidmon.com, offers some of the same services as the monitoring companies mentioned above, but they have a unique specialty. The majority of Video Monitoring Service's clients are public relations firms, advertising agencies, and marketing departments that are interested in their library of 1.5 million pieces of creative advertising dating back to the 1960s.

Each day hundreds of television advertisements are added to the database of over 1 million television commercials from 90 markets, along with commercials airing on more than 100 major market radio stations. A search of these might be useful to your company's Marketing Department in comparing the strategies used by competitors in various markets. In addition, print ads are gathered in connection with Burrelle's, with same-day access to ads from select publications. More than 2,700 websites are monitored for possible additions to a banner ad library. Last but not least, consider the ubiquitous billboards – eight markets are monitored and a library of 2500+ items has been created. More than 100 billboard ads are captured each month.

Looking At the Big Picture

Yes, there is a value to monitoring the websites of other companies. Presumably you or others in your organization may take some sort of action from time to time as changes are detected. But consider whether there might be some value to be gained from being able to predict a competitor's next move based on word searching across a batch of stored html files containing Company X's web pages over a period of time. This might really impress the Boss!

One way to making this happen is an inexpensive browser add-on called **SurfSaver Pro,** which is found at www.surfsaver.com. SurfSaver captures web pages directly from your browser then stores them in searchable folders. With some creative organizing and word searching, over time it could be possible to track changes in one company's New Products web page, or to group companies into industry folders and compare the New Products pages of several companies with one search.

Another product of this type is **WebSite-Watcher,** at http://aignes.com/index.htm, which can downloaded free or purchased on CD if you prefer. WebSite-Watcher monitors designated sites for updates and changes. When changes are detected, the last two versions are saved to your hard disk and all text changes are highlighted.

Monitoring Reloads of Your Favorite Government Site

As discussed earlier, in Chapter 9, there is a wealth of information on government websites. Many industries are affected by government regulations. Since agencies and departments publish new or changed regulations on their websites, you can keep current by using the monitoring or alert services discussed previously.

Another strategy might be to add a competitor's name as keywords to a government agency's public calendar page. This may make you aware of meetings between that company and regulatory agencies such as the Food & Drug Administration.

Monitoring Facts and Figures

Suppose that your company needs to answer questions like these:

- Is this a good time to borrow money?
- Should we make a particular capital investment?
- Should we expand the business?

The company's corporate planning department or comptroller might use government figures as part of their effort to make decisions that are in the company's best interests. The planners would, of course, want the latest information. They also would want to monitor trends or changes in these figures over time. This information is now easily retrieved from a Government Printing Office website at www.gpoaccess.gov/indicators/browse.html.

The Council of Economic Advisers prepares and publishes *Economic Indicators* monthly for the Joint Economic Committee of the U.S. Senate. Links are available here to the past three years' reports. To give you an idea of the type of data that is available here in PDF or text format, some of the headings found in the January, 2004 monthly report are summarized below:

ECONOMIC INDICATORS – JANUARY 2004

Total output, income, and spending

Gross Domestic Product
Real Gross Domestic Product
Implicit Price Deflators for Gross Domestic Product
Gross Domestic Product & Related Price Measures: Indexes and Percent Changes
Nonfinancial Corporate Business— Output, Costs, and Profits
National Income
Real Personal Consumption Expenditures
Sources of Personal Income
Disposition of Personal Income
Farm Income.
Corporate Profits
Real Gross Private Domestic Investment
Real Private Fixed Investment by Type
Business Investment

Employment, Unemployment & Wages

Status of the Labor Force
Selected Unemployment Rates
Selected Measures of Unemployment and Unemployment Insurance Programs
Nonagricultural Employment
Average Weekly Hours, Hourly Earnings, and Weekly Earnings—Private Nonagricultural Industries
Employment Cost Index—Private Industry
Productivity & Related Data, Business Sector

Production and Business Activity

Industrial Production & Capacity Utilization
Industrial Production—Major Market Groups & Selected Manufactures
New Construction
New Private Housing & Vacancy Rates.
Business Sales & Inventories—Manufacturing & Trade.
Manufacturers' Shipments, Inventories, & Orders.

Prices

> Producer Prices
> Consumer Prices—All Urban Consumers.
> Changes in Producer Prices for Finished Goods.
> Changes in Consumer Prices—All Urban Consumers.
> Prices Received & Paid by Farmers

Money, Credit, and Security Markets

> Money Stock & Debt Measures
> Money Stock & Debt Measures
> Aggregate Reserves & Monetary Base.
> Bank Credit at All Commercial Banks
> Sources & Uses of Funds, Nonfarm Nonfinancial Corporate Business
> Consumer Credit
> Interest Rates & Bond Yields
> Common Stock Prices & Yields

Federal Finance

> Federal Receipts, Outlays, & Debt
> Federal Receipts by Source & Outlays by Function.
> Federal Sector, National Income Accounts Basis.

International Statistics

> Industrial Production & Consumer Prices — Major Industrial Countries.
> U.S. International Trade in Goods & Services.
> U.S. International Transactions.

By monitoring this site, you will receive an email when each succeeding month's figures have been added. A similar strategy might be wise for the MANUFACTURERS' SHIPMENTS, INVENTORIES, AND ORDERS "M3" report that is issued periodically by the U.S. Census Bureau at www.census.gov/indicator/www/m3/.

The Office of Scientific and Technical Information (OSTI) developed **SC Alerts**, at http://scalerts.science.energy.gov, for the Office of Science. This alert service combines three areas discussed in this chapter – 1. It offers an alert service; 2. …from a government website; 3. …focusing on a vertical market.

Users create one or more personal interest profiles, which OSTI's **E-print Network** then uses as it searches for keywords contained in "Preprints." These are delivered weekly via email. "Preprints" are unpublished manuscripts being circulated for comment within the scientific community. Since the material is so new, Preprints may or may not have been reviewed, submitted, or accepted for publication, but they are intended for publication or presentation at a conference.

SC Alerts claims to be the first alerting service that retrieves its search results from the Invisible Web, which is discussed further in Chapter 12. The SC Alerts service is free, as is most of the full text information retrieved.

E-print Network, at www.osti.gov/eprints/, is a gateway to over 12,000 websites and databases worldwide covering basic and applied sciences. Though focused primarily on physics, the network also covers chemistry, biology and life sciences, materials science, nuclear sciences and engineering, energy research, computer and information technologies, and other disciplines of interest to the Department of Energy.

Researching the Competition Anonymously

If your company maintains a website, your computer services department may monitor the site to see who visits. Frequent visitors may be the competition. Just as you visit competitors' sites, they visit yours, and they problably know when you visit theirs. You may wish to visit them anonymously, and there are ways you can avoid being an obvious visitor.

Suppose that you are interested in what a competitor is saying about a particular topic on their website. You may not care if they know you visited, but you do not want them to know exactly which pages interest you. An anonymous visit is what is called for.

Perhaps you are considering electronic commerce – online ordering and purchasing at your website. You visit internet sites offering this service because you will soon be their competitor. You want to see what is being offered, and how matters such as accepting credit cards, placing orders, etc. are handled. If you can make it easier, more secure, or otherwise more attractive for internet shoppers to do business at your site, your site will likely be "a winner." If, however, the competition can see that it was *you* who has visited so many times recently, they may guess what you are planning and speed up plans to revamp their own sites. You could lose that competitive advantage! Again, an anonymous visit may be called for.

The Anonymizer, at www.anonymizer.com, allows you to make such visits. The free product of a few years ago has been replaced by Anonymizer Private Surfing 2.1, a subscription-based service that includes a toolbar for turning anonymity on and off, along with other features for handling cookies, ads, and other privacy-related issues.

A free product called **The Cloak** can be found at www.the-cloak.com/anonymous-surfing-home.html. The Cloak is an http and https anonymizing proxy. It provides an encrypted connection and remote handling of cookies, which may be deleted at the end of each search session. It also provides a user configurable content filtration for removal of unwanted scripts.

The WebVeil site, at http://webveil.com/matrix.html, offers a chart describing and comparing several other products of this type. Webveil also offers a portal service for those wishing to search the Web by proxy.

Taking the Proactive Approach -
Monitoring Your Own Company

The concept of searching for business intelligence on your own company was discussed in previous chapters as a means of determining the types of data available and the best sources for finding it, that information then being applied to gathering intelligence on competitors or other companies.

There is another side to this intelligence gathering activity. Most successful organizations already know the importance of gathering market intelligence on *their own* products or services in an effort to grow their business, anticipate trends in consumer preference, increase their competitive advantage, etc. The creation of a cutting-edge comprehensive business intelligence package is crucial to decision making in all departments.

The components of such a package appear in a number of different places, in a variety of formats. An interesting statistic – widely attributed to Merrill Lynch – says that 85% percent of all business data currently exists as unstructured data.

The challenge becomes one of determining how to synthesize these disparate pieces into one useful, comprehensible bundle so that analysts and decision makers can do what they are supposed to do, rather than spending time on the compilation side of the project. This has opened the window of opportunity for technology companies to address the problem, and there now is at least one useful product for the task.

Intelliseek

Intelliseek's products take unstructured data of various types and package it for clients into a desktop analytical tool. A description of these products is available online at www.intelliseek.com/marketingi.asp.

The Intelliseek product that may be of greatest interest to internet researchers is **BrandPulse Internet**, which collects and analyzes content from public online databases and discussion boards. Related products synthesize in-house material from published documents, video and audio files, PDFs and other unrelated media forms, or combine the internet material with the in-house material.

Here are a few examples of the questions that can be answered using a program like BrandPulse Internet:

- What is being said out there about my product or service? Is the volume growing or shrinking?
- Is my advertising message getting across?
- Where on the Internet are our products/services and those of our competitors discussed?
- What new products/services or improvements should be made?
- What jargon is being used on the Internet in connection with our products and services?
- How does the Internet influence consumer purchase decisions and brand loyalty?

BrandPulse Internet is a high-end type of product, but using it could save untold hours of human effort at retrieving, converting, and organizing data.

Biz360, at www.biz360.com, an award-winning name in this field, offers Market 360 and Market360 Analyst. These products offer media analytics, point-of-view sentiment data, message tracking, issue tracking, and a global languages option among their offerings intended to help customers drive better business performance. Tailored Industry Solutions focus on at least nine major industries.

As time goes on, other internet technology companies likely will offer these services.

Chapter 14

Examining an Industry

Looking at the Big Picture

Competitor/competitive intelligence involves much more than looking at individual companies in a given market or comparing one company's market share with that of another. It is important to examine the industry you are in, and to study other industries, for several purposes:

- **Keeping up with developments or trends in your industry.**
  To compete successfully within your own industry, your company must aim for competitive advantage in one area or another. In order to make the right moves, it is necessary to know what has happened in the past, what is currently happening, and to be able to forecast the future.

- **Watching developments or trends in another industry.**
  These may have a direct impact on your company. Those involved in strategy or planning may use this information to decide the direction in which your company will move. It is also of interest to those in the sales and marketing area.

- **Moving into a new industry.**
  To keep a company viable over time, it is often decided to move into new product areas, which possibly will make you a player in a totally different industry. Before making that decision, it is important to have researched the "new" industry carefully.

- **Considering an acquisition or merger.**
  Mergers or acquisitions are not undertaken lightly. Considerable research goes into the big decision. A thorough understanding of both the present and the future of one or more industries is crucial in the due diligence process that accompanies this type of undertaking.

Hard Facts and Figures Abound Online and Elsewhere

For most industry categories, it is not difficult to gather statistics. The challenge lies in whether the analysts and strategists in your company can use the data to create knowledge. Industry information will come from several sources: government agencies, editorial pages, cyber listening posts, commercial vendors, industry forecasts. These are examined in this chapter.

Government Agencies

Government sources are an invaluable resource in this undertaking, since they collect data so extensively. Much of the important statistical data from dozens of agencies is now available on the Internet. In many cases it can be downloaded and loaded into your company's software for further analysis.

For starters, the U.S. Bureau of the Census provides detailed data that can be viewed or downloaded in PDF format at its Current Industrial Reports site, www.census.gov/cir/www. This site's format and frequency of update varies by industry.

One of the more traditional government data sources is the Census' *Statistical Abstract of the United States*, at www.census.gov/statab/www. By choosing the *USA Statistics in Brief* link on this site, you can quickly focus on topics that may include relevant industry data:

Population - Sex, Age, Region	Transportation	Income
Population by Race	Social Welfare	Prices
Vital Statistics, Health	Government	Business
Households, Housing	Agriculture	Finance
Education	Energy	Foreign Companies
Law Enforcement	Employment	Communications

Statistics abound on social and economic conditions in the United States, and you will find state rankings and selected international data. The *Statistical Abstract* site also points you to additional data from the U.S. Census Bureau, from other Federal agencies, and from private organizations. The website links to chapters in PDF format. The *Abstract* also contains ordering information for the CD-ROM version. A number of other useful government statistics sites can be located in the *Bookmarks & Favorites* section of Part IV under "Statistics."

An indirect access point for Federal government information on an industry is political campaign contribution lists. The Center For Responsive Politics site at www.opensecrets.org compiles industry reports in addition to its tallying of political contributions by organizations and individuals. Here it is possible to look at the political contributions of an industry by broad sector (e.g. communications and electronics); by industry within a sector (e.g. TV/movies/music); and by categories within an industry (e.g. cable TV). The data is available for at least a ten-year period, making it possible to analyze industry contributions and to discern patterns or effects of such contributions on Federal legislation.

Of major interest on the Center For Responsive Politics site is the periodic reports from special interest groups that discuss industry topics. For instance, a report titled *The Biotech Boom* should shed light on the biotech industry. As always is true, when reading material from special interest groups, it should be expected that the material might not be totally unbiased. The amount of data available, however, and the search engine and well-organized compilation of retrieved data make the CRP site a useful tool for looking at the way in which a given industry attempts to influence legislation.

Finding the "Softer" Information

Soft information about an industry is generally considered to be non-statistical intelligence. Soft information is gleaned from untraditional sources and is usually found in print or electronic format, so much of this soft intelligence can be found using cyber-tools.

Consider the value of "softer" information. Softer information may reveal a lot about changes in "public sentiment." Changes in public sentiment may have a dramatic impact on an industry. This could mean, therefore, that the statistical trends observed during the past five years are *not* a true picture of where an industry is going, or that forecasts for the industry are impacted by certain unforeseen events and, therefore, those forecasts turn out to be incorrect.

The tobacco industry is an example. Prognosticators pointed out that statistics indicated profitable days were ahead, but health-related lawsuits against this industry then became big news for several years. At one point, rumors began to circulate in print regarding the sell-off of their tobacco units by some large companies involved in both the tobacco and food industries. "Letters-to-the-Editor" from corporate watchdog groups called for boycotts of these companies. If you had been correctly monitoring the major U.S. newspapers, then you would have been informed of all of these developments affecting "public sentiment" toward the tobacco industry.

Trends and forecasts in the tobacco industry prior to the filing of these lawsuits did not take into consideration the changes in public opinion that were ahead. Industry analysts or others creating such prognostications could not look into a "crystal ball" – they were unable to predict the saga that would unfold.

For challenging research such as this it may be necessary to look at the subject from a slightly different perspective. Sharp Market Intelligence, at www.sharpmarket.com, discusses this in case studies and other material on its website. A free newsletter is also available. Their Case Studies page is sub-titled "Not the X-files, but just as fascinating."

Searching Editorial Pages

Searching for an industry topic and the words "op-ed" or "letters" in commercial vendors' newspaper files is a good research strategy. Visiting websites of various newspapers and searching archives also works well, and is less costly. A number of individual newspapers websites are included in *Bookmarks & Favorites* Section 4, under the heading "Newspapers."

A search of the *San Francisco Chronicle*, at www.sfgate.com/search, is an example:

> *Search strategy:* tobacco and op-ed
> *Results:* 38 articles in one year, including Letters to the Editor and other material.
> The searchable archives go back to 1995.

Usenets, Groups, & Listservs: Cyber Listening Posts

The internet's Usenets and newsgroups cannot be overlooked as places to find soft information and "take the pulse of the nation." Trends toward or away from certain types of products may begin right here. It is not unusual that someone initiates a topic online and expresses an opinion, then others join in, the media becomes interested, and the headlines begin to appear.

Consider, too, Usenets and newsgroups as sources for "leaked" or insider information. There are times in the corporate world where a "leak" regarding a pending deal can cost a company and its stockholders millions or even billions of dollars. Insiders carefully guard the information, and CEOs may even contract information research outside of the organization as a security measure. A rumor picked up through an internet chat room or group could be disastrous to the deal, and might have industry-wide ramifications. And, this may give you an advantage.

Google Groups

In 2001, Google purchased the archive of DejaNews, one of the early sources for learning what was on the minds of participants in these online groups. The resulting service is Google Groups. Here hundreds of internet discussion groups can be searched individually or simultaneously, helping you to determine public opinion on a topic.

The `biz.` category may be broken down into a number of sub-groups. Some of the groups are now moderated, which is, no doubt, a benefit to serious searchers. Unfortunately, some of these groups appear to have been attacked by spammers, as the subject lines will attest. Other groups that initially sound promising for CI purposes, such as *biz.newprod*, contain the warning that they are no longer being archived. For some CI researchers, other categories such as `misc.`, `comp.`, or `rec.` might yield more useful information, depending upon the industry in question.

Yahoo!

The various chat rooms available through Yahoo! at www.yahoo.com and similar sites provide another access point for this type of search. Here you will find industry or company-specific groups where employees with loose lips or gripes air their opinions. Internet groups are of growing interest to corporate security departments.

Employment-Oriented Websites

Another cyber source to consider is employment-oriented websites.

The Vault

An interesting example from the business intelligence perspective is The Vault, at www.vault.com, which archives messages put up by jobseekers. As with Yahoo!, searching The Vault is possible by company or industry. The Vault may turn out to contain the type of CI "gold" that your company wants if you are researching competitors or comparing your organization to the rest of the industry. At the least, The Vault site may provide some tips such as areas to research further.

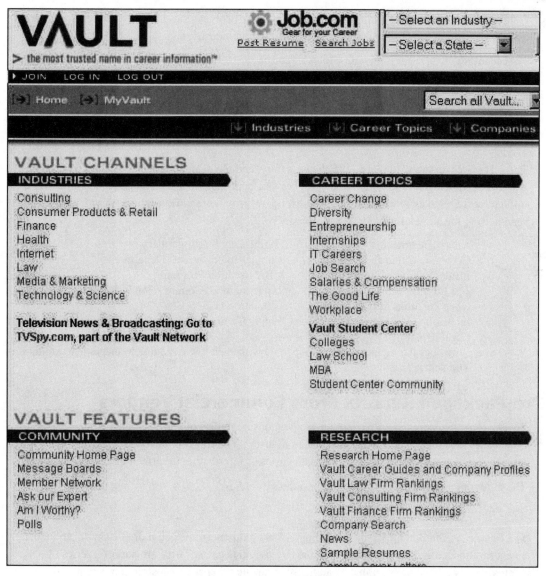

▶▶ A section of the site map at the Vault's website provides a snapshot view of the many topics covered here. Though marketed to jobseekers, there is an abundance of business intelligence to be found by the business intelligence researcher. ◀◀

Access is free to messages posted within the past sixty days. The rest of The Vault is accessible only to subscribers. Basic membership is free. This is useful for jobseekers, allowing them to post messages and read messages posted during the past sixty days.

The Gold Membership, which can cost less than $5.00 per month, is useful for CI purposes. Gold Members have access to company snapshots like none you will find on typical company profile databases. Chapter headings here include The Scoop, Getting Hired, Our Survey Says, Benefits,

Getting In, and Moving Up and Staying In. Four types of surveys submitted by site registrants are available for more than 1400 companies in the following industries:

Accounting	Health Biotech Pharma	Non-Profit
Advertising &PR	Investment Banking	Real Estate
Consulting	Investment Management	Technology
Entertainment	Law	TV News (TVSPY.COM)
Fashion	Media & Marketing	Venture Capital
Government		

The surveys cover the workplace, interviews, salary, and the business outlook – in the opinion of employees. Employees and potential employees also contribute to a searchable database of over one million messages available on the site. The list below provides an idea of the topics retrieved from a search using the name of a major U.S. corporation:

Salary Treatment	Engineering Starting Salary
Corporate Culture	Summer Internship at [Department]
Insider Stock Holdings	MBA Rotation Program
The Environment	Pay Increase & Compression Raise
Open Positions in [Location]?	Generation Gap
Internships	Supply Chain Structure
Legal department	

Why does [Company name] hire people with such low Graduate Management Admission Test scores?

Pre-Packaged Reports From Commercial Vendors

Several reputable commercial vendors package industry studies of various types. It may be cost-effective to take this route toward studying an industry. You might choose to supplement what is learned from a packaged study, using the categories of information described in the next chapter.

The following is a sampling of sources for industry studies.

The Financial Times

The Financial Times, at http://surveys.ft.com, offers industry studies on more than a dozen industry categories, most of which are dated from the two previous years. These are part of a series of approximately 240 surveys published annually by the newspaper. A subscription is required.

Dialog

Dialog, at www.dialog.com, is a good source for databases on specific industries, as well as those that cover many industries.

FINDEX - Dialog File 196, FINDEX, is a database of industry and market research reports and studies, consumer studies, major multi-client studies, surveys and polls, audits, and industry or company reports issued by investment brokerage firms. Using FINDEX, you could receive comprehensive analyses of markets, industries, products, and companies. Ordering information is included, for both U.S. and non-U.S. sources. When searching for industry reports in a broad database such as FINDEX, include the word "industry" as part of your search string to "zero in" on the industry studies and avoid other types of reports.

Valuation Resources

Another source that covers various industries is ValuationResources.com, at www.valuationresources.com. This website offers Industry Resources Reports listing resources available from trade associations, industry publications, and research firms that address subjects such as industry overview, issues, trends, and outlook, financial benchmarking, compensation surveys, and valuation resources. Reports are available for more than 220 industries. This site is discussed further in Chapter 10, which discusses finding information on privately held companies.

Frost & Sullivan

Other sources may focus on industry segments from the U.S. and abroad. *Frost & Sullivan Market Intelligence* - Dialog File 765, contains in-depth analyses and forecasts of *technical market* trends. Reports contain five-year forecasts of market size by product category and end-user application. Marketing and distribution strategies are discussed, and assessments of the competitive and legislative environment are also provided. European, U.S., and worldwide studies are organized by geographic region. Reports include the following elements:

Executive Summary	Competitor Market Shares and Profiles
Introduction	5-Year and Interim Forecast by Major National Market
Scope and Methodology	Product Group and End-user/Application
Technical Review	Trends and Opportunities
Current Product Characteristics	Company names and addresses.
End-user/Application Analysis	

The technical market, as covered by Frost & Sullivan, covers a wide segment of industries, which include these:

Aerospace and Defense	Food and Beverages
Automotive	Industrial Automation
Biotechnology	Instruments and Controls
Data and Telecommunications	Medical Devices
Data Processing and Office Automation	Paper and Packaging
Diagnostic Equipment and Reagents	Pharmaceuticals
Energy	Plants and Machinery
Electro-medical Instrumentation	Plastics
Environmental Controls	Security and Access Control
Fast-moving Consumer Goods	Textiles

EIU Industry Forecasts

In 2003 the Economist Intelligence Unit launched *Industry Forecasts*, a series of 108 reports covering eight industries in 60 countries. This covers more than 95% of world trade and output. Included are five-year forecasts for each industry in each country, along with data and analysis on key industry players, market segmentation, a risk overview, and five-year historical trends in consumption and production.

Industries covered are as follows:

Automotive	Food, Beverages and Tobacco
Consumer Goods and Retailing	Healthcare and Pharmaceuticals
Energy and Electricity	Telecoms and Technology
Financial Services	Travel and Tourism

Reports may be purchased at www.store.eiu.com. IndustryWire, a related product, is updated daily.

Hoover's

Hoover's, at www.hoovers.com, has established itself as a favorite research site for many searchers. Over time the site has been enriched with the addition of increased industry information. The main Industry Directory is a listing of more than 600 industry classifications, with links to descriptions of each industry, and the Hoover's-covered companies within each industry.

Hoover's has added some unique features to its industry search. The industry keyword search retrieves all industries, no matter how diverse, that contain the word as part of their vocabulary. Another search called "Find Similar Companies," locates companies with attributes in common such as location, key numbers, and other criteria. As is true of other parts of Hoover's, some information is available free, while the remainder is subscription based.

Tip –If a prepackaged study or online report is not in the budget, if you are researching an unusual industry, or if you just want the fun of a "do it yourself" project, read Chapter 18 carefully. You will learn what to look at and where to start looking.

Sites That Lead You To Others

A number of good websites have been created for the purpose of leading searchers to other useful sites on a topic. When it comes to locating industry information, the librarians at the Cole Library of Rensselaer at Hartford, an affiliate of Rensselaer Polytechnic Institute, have put together a winner at www.rh.edu/dept/library/industry/industry.htm. For each of the 23 broad industry categories covered, SIC and NAICS codes are listed and explained. Lists of sources, links to useful websites, and references to onsite databases are available on the following topics:

Industry Profiles	Trade and Industry Associations
Industry Financials and Statistics	Trade and Industry Publications
Industry Forecasts	Government and Regulatory Agencies
Industry News	Company Links
Current Issues	

For finding companies in industries not listed on this site, a link to Locating a Company on the World Wide Web, at www.rh.edu/dept/library/research/coweb.htm, is provided. Although intended for the RH student and faculty communities, CI researchers will find that this well-organized site can serve as a good starting place when researching a particular industry. While references are made to online services available only to those with passwords, some of these services, such as LexisNexis for example, are available on the Internet using both subscription and credit card access.

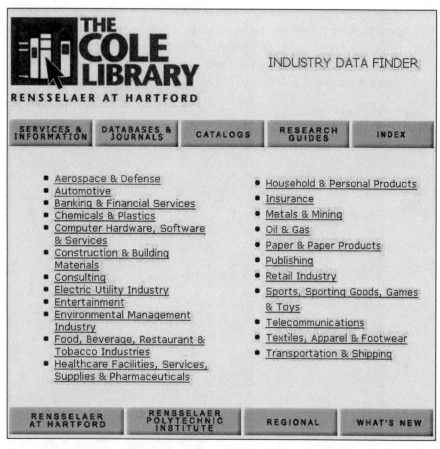

▸▸ The Cole Library's well-organized pages behind the links above aid the CI researcher in identifying key sources of information for each industry category. ◂◂

Dozens of other public and academic library sites around the world have put together similar web pages on topics related to – or of interest to – researchers in the areas of business and industry. Another site to remember for this type of list is Competia Express, mentioned in Chapter 11.

IndustryLink, at www.industrylink.com, takes a slightly different approach. Its homepage contains a list of industry categories. Behind each of these, however, the listed sites include not only companies in that industry, but also companies that service that industry. These are categorized using terms such as Market Place Site, Manufacturing Site, Resource Site, Distribution Site, etc.

Industry-Specific Websites

The Internet contains hundreds of industry-specific sites. Some were created as marketing tools, while others try to compile links to useful material regarding the industry. Farms.com, at www.cybercrop.com, and SteelVillage.com, at www.steelvillage.com, are examples of the latter. In general, those created by trade associations or academic institutions are less likely to flood your monitor screen with pop-up ads and similar irritating items. Some sites may require registration, although they are free. See *Bookmarks & Favorites* at the back of this book for addresses for helpful sites in a number of industries.

Chapter 15

Mining Company Web Pages

Information Gold Versus Fool's Gold

One of the first thoughts that comes to mind these days when searching for factual information on a company is to check the company website to see if the answers are there. This is often the first and best route to finding what you want to know, especially when researching privately held companies.

Internet sites are designed to present a company in the best possible light. Since it is *their* site, they can brag -- if they choose to -- about products, services, accomplishments, and so on. Keep that thought in mind as you read what they are presenting, but reputable companies usually present accurate information, generally choosing to ignore topics that they consider negative. You will have to find *that* material elsewhere.

The Major Benefits of Searching Company Websites

Company websites can be an extremely useful and convenient research tool. If you need to gather intelligence on a particular company, or even a small group of companies, then a search of the company sites offers several advantages over other methods of information retrieval. This is why:

- **You may find the hard-to-find.**
  Suppose that you are trying to create a list of the countries where a multi-national competitor operates. You may find that their website provides not only a numeric answer, for example, "*We operate in 75 countries,*" but it may also include world maps that show where the corporation does business. This information is probably updated as they move into additional countries.

- **There is probably no cost involved.**
  If what you seek is basic information about products, services, ordering and directories, then using company sites can save you money since that information is gathered at no cost. For in-

depth data such as financials, however, you may still need to supplement this basic information with additional details that are likely to be obtained by searching a commercial source.

- **It is convenient.**
  It may be a simple matter to copy and paste the data you find, adding it to a report created in a word processing program or attaching it to an email message.

- **The material is likely to be up-to-date.**
  You will probably find that the information on the company website is timelier than that obtained from certain other sources such as printed directories.

Most directory publishers update their records annually, or perhaps less frequently. The company's webmaster, on the other hand, is probably charged with keeping the site up-to-date, making changes as frequently as daily. Daily updates are often the case on websites that include news coverage on their homepages.

How to Use What You Find on a Company Website

Touring a number of company internet sites can provide insights into the types of information that is often included on other sites in that same genre. Larger companies may spend more money on website projects than smaller companies. Larger companies tend to use sophisticated, eye-catching graphics, and make available archives of company publications or educational material aimed at teachers and students. On some company sites, the page count may number in the hundreds. These sites may attract thousands of online visitors daily.

You will find that the types and amount of information found on company websites vary greatly. A certain amount of "copy cat" behavior occurs, however, so it may be worth checking competitors' sites frequently to see what is new there.

Consider Who Needs This Information

Seeing what others do on their websites can help your own company take proactive steps to improve its image on the Web, but more importantly, various people in your organization can make use of the information found there. Here are some examples:

- **Marketing Managers** can keep abreast of the market strategies of competing companies. They may devise special promotions to equal or better the deal being offered at a competitor's website.

- **Public Relations Personnel** can prepare and get approval of official responses in anticipation of calls from the media when a major competitor makes big news and brags about it, or comments on an *incident* on their website. (Note: Incident is a euphemism used in industry to describe an unpleasant or unfortunate occurrence.)

- **The Public Affairs Department** may be interested in what Competitor X is saying on an important industry issue.

- **Product Managers** can keep up with news of updates to specific products that your organization competes with. They can spot and download any new white papers that are posted regarding products.

- **Sales Managers** might monitor websites for leads or prospects, to create new initiatives that might help your company sell more products.

- **Business Development Personnel** can learn more about your company's partners to promote better relationships between the organizations.

- **The Legal Department** may be interested in competitor websites in their ongoing efforts to protect your company's patents and trademarks from infringement. In addition, they may use information from websites to support arguments connected with ongoing litigation.

The Alpha List of What to Look For

The alphabetical list that follows will give you an idea of additional types of information that you may find on company websites, and some hints about how the information can be useful. Remember: if you do not want them to know that you are visiting, you can research anonymously, as described at the end of Chapter 13.

Community/Charitable Activities

Looking at a company's charitable activities may give a "tip-off" about their corporate philosophy toward such activities. The site may actually list groups or organizations that the company supports. Your strategists may take this into consideration when entering a marketplace in which a competitor is already active. Seeing what a competitor is doing in this area may provide ideas about projects that your company might undertake in its own Community Relations efforts

Company History

Company history is often useful in assessing an organization's corporate culture. If you are familiar with the company's history, you may be able to predict corporate behavior.

If a company has existed for decades or longer, its management or Board of Directors may be very aware of what the company founder would have done or said in certain situations. They may make decisions that reflect that knowledge or follow that precedent.

On the other hand, high-tech start-up companies founded within the past twenty years may reflect a totally different culture, which may be much easier to discover. For example, the company founder may have been interviewed extensively in newspapers or the trade press, and, as examined in Chapter 13, you can readily find this information.

Whichever best describes your target company, knowing their history can prove useful, and their website may be a good starting point for obtaining that information.

Company Magazines

Most companies publish magazines or newsletters for stockholders and employees. To the extent that the company considers them to be useful public relations or marketing tools, you may find these publications in an archive that is available from their website.

These publications may contain photographs of work sites and equipment, descriptions of projects, or other useful intelligence information. Usually, the content is carefully screened during the editorial process, so it is not likely that you will find the company's strategic marketing plan for the next five years. Still, you will find a lot of information about people, places, and things.

Corporate Philosophy/Beliefs

Words like "environment" and "diligence" appear frequently on the sites of companies in certain industries. We assume that they will say "politically correct" things, so you will not find a statement like "We don't care..." Determining what they have said may help your company to market products or services to them.

While a company's "Position Statement" on important issues may be useful for reaching conclusions about their strategy, that information may also be useful as you plan your own company's position statements, and as you consider whether or not it is to your advantage to concur with the competition's positions on issues.

Customer Endorsements

Any endorsements or success stories included on a company's website are bound to be favorable, but reading them may not be the waste of your time you may think it is. Looking at these endorsements can provide insights into areas where the competitor is strong; i.e., satisfied customers rave about customer support, a money-back guarantee or other replacement policies. Endorsements can provide insights into their customer or client base, particularly if the happy customer's age, gender, profession, employer, or similar information is included.

Employment Opportunities

The amount and types of employment opportunity information on corporate websites runs the gamut from very general to the extremely detailed.

Some companies state that there are openings for recent graduates with degrees in (*fill in the blank*). The site may include a hotlink to their Human Resources Department's page, which may accept emailed resumes, which, if not read directly, may be scanned electronically and pre-screened automatically. Other companies may provide lists containing details such as job title, skills required, and location of the opening. These, of course, provide the greatest amount of business intelligence as they point out which people the company is seeking.

Executive Speeches

Some company websites contain the text of a selected speeches by company executives. These may vary in value in terms of competitive intelligence, yet you cannot judge their value until you read them.

Honors, Awards, Achievements

If a company has received prestigious honors or awards, then they are likely to mention them somewhere on the company website. Important industry awards generally receive significant coverage in the trade press, and the programs or activities that helped garner the honor may be described in detail. Local newspapers should also be searched for this type of story.

Investor Information

Facts and figures intended to provide information to shareholders also provides information to competitors! Among the items that you might expect to find in this area of a company website are the Annual Report to Shareholders, stock prices, dividend information, links to the SEC, and that ubiquitous internet phenomenon, "frequently asked questions" (FAQs).

Miscellaneous Publications

A "miscellaneous" category may include many different publications, such as reports on the company's operations in another part of the world, topic-oriented position papers, or brochures. Checking these items carefully can yield tidbits of intelligence that may be of interest to you, their competitor.

News/Media Coverage

Hopefully, you have one or more monitoring mechanisms in place; see Chapter 13. Still, a periodic run through of your competitors' websites could provide links to articles that you had not seen previously. Articles on that website may have come from a location or source not covered in your monitoring activity. You may then wish to revise or add to that list of sources to be monitored.

At the company website you may even find a few press releases that never made it into print. The Business Editor at the newspaper may have passed these up, but company's web version may provide you with valuable intelligence, such as the name of the new Vice President, or a new product roll-out.

Operations Locations

A competition's website may provide numbers on, or better still, lists of plant locations and other facilities. These should not be considered complete, however, and more research may be called for if you need a list that includes all company facility locations. However, lists found on the website can be used for validating or augmenting existing information.

Product Manuals and Documentation

The company has probably put product manuals and other documentation online as a service to their customers. These publications can provide detailed product descriptions or diagrams that could be of interest to your company's R&D or engineering departments. Often, you may have to be a registered owner of a specific product to gain access to this data. At other company websites, you may not.

Products/Services

A company's listing of products and services on their website gives an indication of the way they position those products or services. This information can be quite useful when considering how to position your own products, or when developing new ones, or evaluating what the competition is offering.

Research and Development Activity

While it is highly unlikely that a company website will provide information about products still in development, some sites offer lists of general areas where the company is engaged in research and development. These lists can be used to guide you in further research about such activity.

SEC Filings (Publicly-traded Companies)

Company websites of publicly-traded companies often contain hotlinks to the full texts of Annual Reports to Shareholders or SEC filings such as 10-K Reports. Some sites also list additional filings of various types. It is not unusual to find hotlinks to the U.S. government's EDGAR site where a more comprehensive search can be run. Refer to Appendix A for a detailed list of these filings, including descriptions of their contents.

The filings listed on a company website may represent only a portion of those actually available online. If you are interested in all filings for a publicly-held company, to obtain them consider going directly to the SEC's EDGAR site or using commercial online sources.

Subsidiaries/Affiliated Companies

A company website may include references to or lists of related companies. These may be useful references, but should not be trusted as a comprehensive listing of all divisions, subsidiaries, affiliates, or other members of the corporate family. It is recommended that additional resources be used to create such a list, and that you cross-check what you have found.

Trademarks/Trade Names

Some websites contain extensive lists of a company's trademarks or trade names. There is often a warning, however, that such lists may not be complete. More research may be called for if you require a comprehensive list of such intellectual property. The company's website list can be used for cross-checking or validating information located previously.

Finding Subsidiary, Division, or Affiliate Websites

Finding all internet sites connected with a competitor can be a bit of a challenge. Some corporate websites provide links to related sites, but that list may be incomplete. It may be necessary to try several different approaches to locating those elusive sites. Include these approaches:

- **Search the company name using your favorite search engine.** This can be very problematic, however, because some company names contain familiar words that have been used across corporate America. For example, the word "sun" appears in the names of hundreds of companies, large and small, across the country. Locating "all" websites for "Sun Microsystems" using one of the popular web search engines could become a time-consuming task, requiring that the searcher dig through a long list of results. Also, there is no guarantee that the list is complete.

  In addition, Sun Microsystems could be responsible for some sites that do not use the word "sun" as part of the web address. These sites would be more difficult to identify.

- If dealing with a public company, **obtain an electronic copy of the company's Annual Report** and search it for subsidiary information that may have been included. If you discover a subsidiary not previously identified, use its name to search for its website.

- **Consult one of the internet services that identify websites connected with a company.** There are several sources on the Web that offer free or subscription services to handle this task. These services come in varying degrees of sophistication. A description of one of these tools follows. For others, see *Bookmarks & Favorites* in Part IV of this book.

Whois Source

Whois Source, at www.whois.sc, takes the traditional Whois search further – and provides information that may lead you to a company's sites that you might otherwise have missed. Whois Source supports four types of searches:

- Internet Protocol Address, or IP address, searching (www.whois.sc/66.218.71.198)
- Partial word(s) searching ("xxxx", where xxxx is a company or personal name)
- Full domain ("xxxx.com" goes directly to whois)
- Reverse IP lookup

To use IP lookup you simply enter an IP address and learn the identity of the IP. A report full of technical information is included.

The partial word search allows you to enter a name and retrieve a list of domains that contain that word. This means that you may retrieve not only a company's own sites, for example, but *any* sites that contain the word. This could turn up negative websites such as "ANTIXXXX", at www.antixxxx.com. In the case of franchises such as service stations, you might locate all of the XXXX franchises that have websites if they use the company name in their domain name.

The full domain search, www.xxxx.com, retrieves what can be a lengthy report connected with this

particular domain, including a link that will allow you to monitor the site. Here is an example for XXXX Company:

XXXX.COM

Website Title: XXXX is the parent of AAA, BBB, and LLL companies all over the world.
Meta Description:

Meta Keywords: (Open Directory Project subject heading)

Server Type: Microsoft-IIS/5.0

DMOZ: (Number of listings in Open Directory Project)

Website Statue: Active

Reverse IP: (Web server hosts [number] websites; Reverse IP tool requires free login)

IP Address: nnn.nn.nn.nn.nnn

IP Location: United States – Nebraska – Omaha – XXXX

Whois History: (Number of records stored)

Record Type: Domain Name

Monitor: Monitor this Domain (hot linked for setting up list of sites to monitor)

Wildcard search: (possible spelling variations to consider)

Other TLDs: .com .net .org .info .biz .us

Name Server: (Name of server as designated within XXXX)

ICANN Registrar:

Created: (date)

Expires: (date)

Status: ACTIVE, LOCK, etc.

Detailed contact information for the organization, administrator, and technical personnel may be given, as well as names and IP addresses of XXXX company's servers.

Whois Source's Reverse IP lookup can be very useful in business intelligence research. Enter a domain name and retrieve the IP address for that site, along with a list of the other domains hosted by that provider. In the case of a large organization, you may find that the company hosts its sites on an in-house server. This should provide an accurate list of the company's public websites. Some of the sites listed may not contain words that include the company name as part of their domain name – you may find a name that makes no logical sense, so you probably would not have found it by guessing.

To avoid looking at irrelevant material, the Whois Source search screen allows you to control what is retrieved. Search results may be restricted to a particular category from those listed below, or to left or right anchoring of the search term, or in a particular order.

For each list of search results, Whois Source uses a color-coding system to indicate the status of each domain name using the following criteria:

- Registered and Active website
- Registered and Parked or Redirected
- Registered and No website
- On-Hold (Generic) [Accessible to registered members only – free]
- On-Hold (Redemption Period) [Accessible to registered members only – free]
- On-Hold (Pending Delete)
- Deleted and Available again
- Never registered before

Other services, such as Internet statistics and a Domain News Archive are also available at the Whois site. Free membership is available. Subscriptions are available for those needing additional detail.

Domain Names

Dialog and SnapNames.com Inc. have created the Domain Names database, File 225 on the Dialog system at www.dialog.com. Both current registration (WhoIs) records and historic ownership (WhoWas) records may be searched by registrant name, domain name, email address, phone number, ZIP Code, and numerous other fields. Historic data is available from 1997 forward.

DomainWatch

DomainWatch, at www.domainwatch.com, is another option for obtaining this type of information. Using the free service you can determine who, if anybody, has an internet presence with any given name, as well as whether the Server organization is gaining or losing market share. A subscription service offers daily facts and figures as well as other intelligence and details that would be useful to companies in internet-related businesses.

For more on website identification, visit SearchEngineWatch.com or retrieve Danny Sullivan's article *Domain Name Search Engines*, at www.searchenginewatch.com/links/article.php/2156131.

Searching Historical Websites

Thanks to sites or tools described in this chapter, or using others that you have used in the past, you have now compiled a list of the domain names used by a particular organization. Now you can learn the "who, what, when, where," and maybe even the "why" regarding their business. But what were they saying or doing six months ago, or a year ago, or even five years ago? You may find out using the *Wayback Machine*, available at www.archive.org/web/web.php.

A service of Internet Archive and Alexa Internet, the Wayback Machine allows searchers to access and use archived versions of stored websites. By entering a URL and selecting a date, you will be able to look for the types of material described earlier in this chapter *as they existed on the website on the date you select*. You might find facts relating to the following:

- People – who, for example, was Vice President, Sales & Marketing for XXX Company in 1999? Could changes noted in a competitor's marketing efforts or product line be attributed to a change in the power structure? Will this change affect your company or the industry?

- XXX's product line – has it changed? Stayed the same? Have they discarded something that your company is currently considering? Can you determine why?

- Issues - Have they "changed their tune" on critical issues?

Analyzing changes that have appeared on a company's website over time may help various departments in your own organization to deduce what is going on over there. By creating a timeline scenario and plugging in the changes that have been noted on various pages of that site may be helpful in predicting future actions or stances on issues critical to your industry or to related industries.

Chapter 16

Using the Internet to Locate Information About People

The CI Perspective

Scoping Out a Competitor's Personnel

The World Wide Web is used constantly by being used to find information on individuals, for a variety of reasons, and there exists a variety of cyber tools available to the CI professional for personal and professional information searching. The same approaches that we use to find information on companies and industries can also be applied to locate important business intelligence on a competitor's key personnel. Consider the advantage in knowing the CEO's career experience, politics, family background, favorite "causes" or charities, likes and dislikes, hobbies, personality quirks, etc. when doing business with that person or in predicting the direction in which he or she will take the company.

The CEO may be an easy research target, but what about other important players in an organization? Do you know the names of Company X's key players in their sister companies, branch offices or subsidiaries in far-flung parts of the world? Print directories cannot keep up with recent changes in personnel, but a good search strategy, combined with broad coverage, may help identify those changes. Indeed, recent personnel changes may indicate that certain things are "going on" in that company's camp, and this data can be analyzed for its possible potential impact on a company or even on an industry.

A website like NewsNow, at www.newsnow.co.uk, described in Chapter 13, is a good tool for identifying personnel within international companies. This source monitors over 13,000 sources worldwide. Using NewsNow or a similar online product, you may find stories in local publications from other continents that mention the company, a spokesperson, or a quote from an executive, for examples. The content of a story may have only local interest, but the name and title could be an addition or update to your file of names for that company and its various offices. As discussed in Chapter 6, information such as career experience, political preference, family background, and favorite causes or charities can turn up in local newspapers as part of the social page, articles on local charity events, or other non-business stories.

Such detail may not always be your search goal. If you are planning to market products or services to another company, then it may be a list of names and job titles that you need. Directing a mailing to "Occupant" or "Vice President of Sales" would be an obvious waste of postage. Obtaining "Occupant's" name may be possible with a telephone call, but suppose you are compiling a list of a hundred companies to contact? Under these circumstances, the telephone approach would be expensive and time-consuming.

Whether it is compiling a dossier on the competitor's CEO or generating a list of their personnel, online information sources can help. The secret to finding this information lies in knowing where to begin looking, and in not giving up if you do not find much initially. You simply dig wider and deeper — all in publicly available sources, of course — no engaging in unethical behavior!

Here are some places to look:

SEC Filings Point to Affiliations and Holdings

Although the Securities & Exchange Commission — SEC — had made public company filings available via the Internet, it is the private sector that has made it possible to search document filings related to company personnel. _EDGAR Online_ offers a people search feature at www.edgar-online.com/people. The EDGAR database allows you to search an individual's name and see a list of the companies with which he or she is connected as an officer or director. The EDGAR Online search also allows you to create a list of all people associated with a specific company name. The EDGAR site hotlinks allow you to get further data on filings, company information, or to perform searches using additional hotlinked research tools. The site compiles data from SEC Form 144, which must be filed by certain "insiders" prior to their intended sale of restricted stock. Form 144 is filed by the seller at the SEC. EDGAR Online adds all of the current day's Form 144 paper filings to their database as each business day ends.

The Top "This & That" Lists

Several popular business magazines offer lists that track successful people. Whether it is wealth, power, or gender, these lists can provide some insights into the positions of these people within their companies, along with indirect clues about other corporate matters.

The Rich – Famous or Not

At the Forbes.com website, at http://forbes.com/lists/, a tab titled Lists links to a screen that contains a variety of lists compiled by the magazine. Those that contain information on people include these:

- 100 Top Celebrities – judged on money and media hits

- Executive Pay – described in Chapter 7
- Forbes 400 – the 400 wealthiest Americans
- World's Richest People – billionaires from all over the globe
- Overworked Corporate Directors – those serving on multiple Boards of Directors
- Midas – successful venture capitalists

The Forbes.com People Tracker, at www.forbes.com/cms/template/peopletracker/index.jhtml, is discussed in Chapter 7 as a means of locating executive compensation information. It is also an excellent tool for obtaining reports on these people as they relate to their companies. Another approach is to enter the stock symbol for publicly held companies; this retrieves a list of top executives and directors, as seen in the example below:

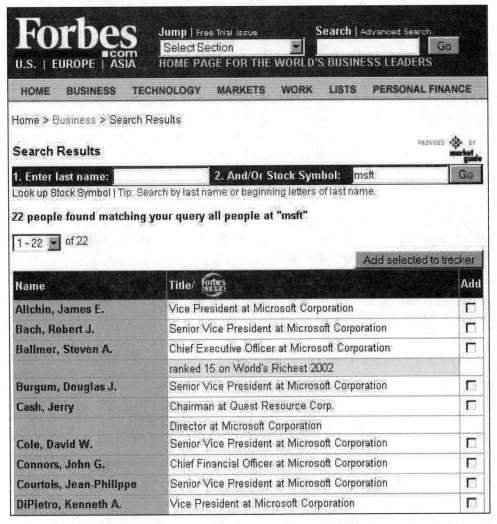

▸▸ Individuals selected from the list above may be added to a tracking list by simply checking off their names. Names are hotlinked, letting you retrieve detailed reports that include job histories, directorships on other companies' boards, presence on select lists, and more. ◂◂

See Chapter 10, Privately Held Companies, for more Forbes lists that apply to publicly and privately held companies.

Fortune has long been noted for *The Fortune 500* list of companies, but other lists on the magazine's website can be useful for locating information on people. Some of these are publicly available on the Internet, while others are restricted for viewing by subscribers to the magazine:

- 40 Under 40 - Young Americans "rising from nothing and nowhere to achieve wealth and power."
- 25 most powerful business leaders outside the U.S.
- 50 Most Powerful Black Executives in America
- The Power 50 – The most powerful women in American business
- The International Power 50 – The most powerful women in business internationally
- Highest Paid - The highest paid women executives at S&P 500 companies
- Women to Watch - Five businesswomen to keep an eye on

Stars That Shine in Their Companies or Industries

Value added resellers have become an important segment of the business community. Their numbers are significant enough to provide plenty of competitors for the VARBusiness 500 Awards, found at www.varbusiness.com/sections/main/2003vb500.asp. This site not only lists the award winners, but allows the searcher to determine where each current winner stood on the list during the period 1995-2003. Links connect with the home pages that covered the awards for each of these years, providing additional detail. A related article, The Top 100 Solution Providers, at www.varbusiness.com/sections/research/research.asp?articleid=42627, gives credit to the people who made their companies successful enough to make the list. Names, job titles, and a brief job history are available for each of these individuals.

Recruiter Magazine Online offers The Top 100 Most Influential People in the Recruiting Industry at www.recruiter.com/magazineonline/top100intro.cfm. Entries provide detailed descriptions, with photos, of these individuals and their careers.

Taking the Easy Way Out

A good search engine and a search strategy such as "top 100" will locate more lists like those mentioned above, but to save time, consult Gary Price's special section on executives in his *List of Lists*, at www.specialissues.com/lol/dispLOL.cfm?Subject_ID=EXECUTI003. This list contains some of the lists mentioned in this chapter, plus lots more.

Another source where someone else does the work for you is the University of Central Florida Library, at http://library.ucf.edu/Line/BusinessRef/ListofLists.htm.

Names Behind the Names

Companies that formerly published print directories now operate websites with searchable databases that generate lists of all kinds. Competition within an industry provides a field day for these entrepreneurial listmakers. Wanting to be among the "Top Ten Whatevers" or "Top 100 Widget Dealers in the Country," etc., businesses are willing to provide details that will place their companies' names in the public eye. This also puts them on the computer screen of the business intelligence researcher. This data may contain the names of owners or principals.

Business information from lists is especially useful when considering privately held companies, where such information may not be readily available.

See also Chapter 12 Privately Held Companies, and Chapter 8 Public Records, for further detail on this topic.

Players in the Scientific/Nonprofit Communities

The Center for Science in the Public Interest has launched the Integrity in Science Internet Database at www.cspinet.org/integrity/database.html. This database provides information about the corporate ties of scientists, academics, and non-profit organizations in the fields of nutrition, environment, toxicology, and medicine. The database is described as "an effort to encourage transparency in the conduct, oversight, and reporting of science," but the CI researcher will find it valuable as a tool for discovering connections between people and organizations. The file can be used to answer interesting questions such as:

- What companies have supported Professor X's research on YYY?
- What foreign governments have done likewise? Who is researching ozone?
- Who is on the list of individuals whose research is supported by Company Z?
- What types of research projects are going on at the University of Arizona?

Also available from the Integrity In Science Database site is a lengthy PDF file titled Professional Associations, Charities, and Industry Front Groups.

"Who's Who" Publications

The Internet abounds with sites that contain member directories or searchable directories of people that meet some type of criterion — they are in a particular industry, live in a certain place, etc. While some of these sites initially sound promising, rather than providing some sort of authoritative list you may find that in reality they are commercial websites that want businesses to register with them.

Others may be an electronic version of a recognized hardcopy publication. Canadian Who's Who on the World Wide Web, at www.utpress.utoronto.ca/cgi-bin/cw2w3.cgi, is an example of a publication presented online. Here you can search the Canadian Who's Who database compiled by the University of Toronto Press. The database contains the biographies of more than 15,000 prominent Canadians by name, date of birth, city, or full text. Chances are that you will find more than a few corporate CEOs among the listings. The 1997 version can be searched for no charge. Newer versions on CD-ROM or a searchable web-based database are available by subscription.

Who's Who European Business and Industry, at www.who-database.com, is available in English, German, French, and Spanish. This site offers several approaches to searching:

Top manager search by profession	Manager search by initial letter
Company search by branch	Company search by country

This is a fee-based service but the reports contain a good amount of detail as well as the promise of an email message when data on a search subject changes or is added. This file is also available on LexisNexis.

Trade Publications

The trade press is also a good place to identify and track the careers of executives. It may be possible to follow their employment path as they move up the corporate ladder or from one company to another. This information may be useful to your organization's recruiters, in both identifying promising candidates for a position they wish to fill and for verification purposes.

The names and other data found in industry-specific newspapers or magazines supplies crucial intelligence that is needed to build or complete your "picture" of a competitor's organization or of its staffing. Thousands of these publications are searchable in databases throughout the ranks of commercial online services such as Dialog, LexisNexis, or Factiva.

Specialized reference services exist in many industries. Some of the most important can be found on the Internet. In the broadly defined high tech industry, for instance, the Corptech Directory's Advanced Search, at www.corptech.com/search/forms/extended.php, allows searchers to specify the job title in the *Executive* category on the search form. This information is available to subscribers only, however.

A geographic search may be useful if your quest for business intelligence related to people focuses on specific parts of the world. For many years, DataStar at www.datastar.com has been a basic source for databases covering European topics, which would include people, companies, and industries. For Australia and Asia, ABIX at www.abix.com.au hosts a twenty-plus year database of business information from over 150 key Australasian publications, covering a large cross section of industry types. In addition, the other major online services often contain geographically focused files of trade publications among their offerings. See Chapter 13 for references to some tools that may help you to continually track high-profile individuals.

Industry Directories

Directories like the *Thomas Register of American Manufacturers* or the various Dun & Bradstreet databases, mentioned elsewhere in this book, frequently list job titles as well as the names of the people filling those positions. At the very least, these sources provide you with a starting place when contacting individuals within a company. The job title can be especially useful if the person filling the position has been reassigned.

Watch the officers and directors and other personnel listings in records found in company directories. You may occasionally notice that one or two individuals appear to carry several titles. You may interpret this fact in various ways, but it usually means that a small group of people is in charge.

Commercial Vendors' Websites

Commercial sources are another valuable resource for locating information on people. Here is a sampling, by vendor, that should give you some ideas about places to search as you begin to build your company's knowledge base regarding competitors' personnel:

DIALOG

The Dialog service, at www.dialogweb.com, contains many science and technology files that can be searched for biographical articles. For the strictly biographical approach, Dialog offers these files, among others:

Bowker Biographical Directory – File 236 – A collection of biographical directories that includes American Men & Women of Science. AMWS covers leading U.S. and Canadian scientists and engineers in the physical, biological, and related sciences.

European Research & Development Database - File 113 - Separate profiles are available for professionals currently engaged in research. Detailed biographies give information on the career history of over 85,000 heads of organizations, senior researchers, research directors, and managers.

Marquis Who's Who - File 234. Marquis Who's Who contains detailed biographical information on "outstanding achievers worldwide in a wide variety of professions and virtually every important field of endeavor." The file contains over 790,000 profiles drawn from the entire 19-volume Marquis Who's Who library since 1985.

Standard & Poor's Register - Biographical - File 526 contains extensive personal and professional data on approximately 70,000 key business executives. Most officers and directors in the file are affiliated with public or private, U.S. or non-U.S. companies with sales of $1 million or more.

To accommodate the needs of users with varying degrees of search skills, Dialog offers several variations on its DialogWeb product, including Dialog1, DialogPRO, DialogClassic and DialogSelect. The files mentioned above are also available using these services.

DataStar

DataStar, at www.datastarweb.com, is a sister company to Dialog. Its 350+ files cover subject matter similar to that of Dialog, but emphasis is on non-U.S. databases. For example:

Agence France-Presse Newswires: Documentary - ADOC's international coverage includes biographies as well as lists of governments and key economic data on countries and regions. French language.

In general, Datastar's emphasis is on European company information; news; mergers and acquisitions; and biomedical, pharmaceutical and health care information.

LexisNexis

LexisNexis, at www.lexisnexis.com, offers several approaches to locating information on people. Its People, Business, and Asset Locators are part of its public record offerings, while the Directories area offers dozens of searchable databases that are perhaps even more useful for CI purposes.

This extensive list of sources may prove fruitful when searching for corporate executives and employees. Even the elusive personnel connected with privately held companies may appear if they made the Duns Decision Makers list, which is included in the list below:

Almanac of American Politics	Judicial Staff Directory
The Almanac of the Unelected	Judicial Yellow Book
American Medical Information	Kaleidoscope
American Men and Women of Science	Marquis Who's Who Biographies
The Associated Press Candidate Biographies	Martindale-Hubbell Law Directory Practice Profiles
Civil Servants (UK)	The Official American Board of Medical Specialists
Congressional Member Profile	Member of European Parliament and Candidates
Congressional Yellow Book	Nat. Directory of Law Enforcement Administrators
Directory of Bankruptcy Attorneys	*New York Times* Government Biographical Stories
Directory of Hospital Personnel	Obituary Information
Dun's Decision Makers	Standard & Poor's Register of Corps, Directors & Execs
European Research & Development Database	State Legislative Directory
Executive Changes, Promotions, Appts, Resigns	Washington Post Biographical Stories
Federal Staff Directory	Who's Who in American Art
Federal Yellow Book	Who's Who in American Politics
Financial Post Directory of Directors	Who's Who in European Business & Industry
Gale Biographies	Who's Who in Russia & the Commonwealth of Independent States
Peers & Members of House of Lords	

Alacra's *Corporate Connections*

A new offering to watch for will be Alacra's Corporate Connections, from www.alacra.com. Although Alacra could not provide specifics at press time, the company has indicated that this product was developed in response to librarians and researchers who expressed their need for sources that identify executives of companies. *Connections* will be marketed as an adjunct to their new *Alacra Credit Research* product, which provides a single point of access to credit research and reports from the three major credit ratings agencies – Moody's, Standard & Poor's (S&P), and Fitch Ratings. New Alacra book applications have also been released, including *Alacra Book for MS Word*; *Alacra Book for Industries*; and *Alacra Book for Countries*

Internet Email Address Books

There are various "people finder" services available on the Internet. You can enter a name and possibly retrieve an address or email address. These services will not likely yield addresses of VIPs at major companies. These people generally do not register for this type of service. Their Security Departments may frown on distribution of such information.

One problem with internet address books is that they can be badly out of date. Some of them are built by allowing people to register themselves. Since many individuals change internet service providers (ISPs) frequently, the email address that you locate for them simply will not work. Do not try to reach this author using the CompuServe address shown on one of the internet address books. It has not been active for several years!

It is useful to know that these free people finder services are there – for occasional use – and they can help locate businesses. See *Bookmarks & Favorites* section in Part IV for a current selection.

Focused Databases and Websites

IdEXEC

As mentioned earlier in Chapter 13, IdEXEC, at www.idexec.com, provides automatic email notification when changes occur on a targeted website. This service is useful for tracking targeted executives or other important changes within companies, or specified geographic sales territories. This type of service could be a major timesaver if you maintain lists of company executives.

EComp

Ecomp, at www.ecomponline.com, offers executive compensation data on move than 12,000 U.S. public companies and 50,000 senior executives as well as Board of Director reports, Executive Title Reports, and similar material, some of which is industry-specific. Although the reports must be purchased, some data is available free. Registration is required.

The Corporate Library

The Corporate Library at www.thecorporatelibrary.com offers company and CEO databases containing comprehensive reports. Free searches area available for S&P 500 companies. Corporate Library subscribers have access to full profiles on over 1700 U.S. and 260 international companies and CEOs. The Director database containing full profiles on more than 21,000 directorships including 18,000 unduplicated individuals. The file can be searched on a variety of data elements. The same rules apply for the databases mentioned here.

Also...

Subscribers to Hoover's Pro, at www.hoovers.com, can take advantage of its Build Executive List feature. This is a tool that allows you to search for executives by name, keyword, job function, salary, company location, company information, or industry. This is a good tool for comparing companies as to location, corporate structure, salary schedule, and more. Using a tailored list created here, your Recruiting Department could build a list of candidates for an executive position or learn additional information about candidates they plan to interview.

Executive Paywatch, at www.paywatch.org, described further in Chapter 7, is an additional source for salary information.

Part III

Organizing Your Research

Chapter 17

Organizing Your Competitive Intelligence Research

What Is In A Company Report On A Competitor Company?

The answer depends upon the task at hand. The content of a Company Report reflects the requirements of the requestor. If your work involves a specific function within the company, you may have a more or less standard template that is used to gather information on competitors. If you field questions from many directions, or address a new subject, then the assignment becomes much more complex. You could spend hours creating something that lacks a crucial "ingredient" rather like simmering a pot of soup all day, but forgetting to season it.

The templates provided in this chapter are intended, therefore, to help you know what to look for when you try to examine a company from a particular perspective. Some examples of electronic sources are provided, but many more may be found by consulting Bookmarks & Favorites and the Resource List in Part IV at the back of this book. Vendor contact information is also available there. In some cases no specific source has been recommended. Certain information may be confidential, or just not the type of thing that gets published. This information may be obtained through interviews, observation, or other legal and ethical methods, however, so it remains in the template to serve as a reminder.

The Company Profile Report

The quality of company "profiles" varies widely, depending upon the source. The accuracy and timeliness of the data and the amount of detail included are important considerations. Some Internet sites that promise free company profiles provide only sketchy data, while others are excellent resources. In some cases, online sources provide a brief company profile at no charge, but if you are willing to subscribe, or to take out your credit card, you may save a good deal of time.

The list below provides a means of getting a good look at what a company is all about. You may access several sources to locate all of the required information. Also, you might combine this report with one of those that follow, since they address specific aspects of the competitor's operations. See the Resource List at the back of this book for descriptions of online and other sources.

Company Profile

Data Elements	Types of Information Sources	Online Information Sources
BASIC DETAILS		
Company Name	Company Profiles-	Dun & Bradstreet
Company Address		Hoover's
Description of Business		**Bookmarks & Favorites:** COMPANY PROFILES
Public or Privately Held? Y N		
Ownership, Percent (if Privately Held) _____%		
Year established, or Year Acquired, Headquarters state of incorporation	Public Records - Secretary of State	**Database Files:** ChoicePoint KnowX LexisNexis Public Records
Technological Developments / Intellectual Property	Patents Databases-	Derwent Inpadoc (Dialog, STN) www.uspto.gov
MANAGEMENT ISSUES		
Management - Quality, Style	Business Management Files-	ABI Inform BAMP
Community Involvement, Reputation	Local, Regional Newspapers-	**Bookmarks & Favorites:** NEWS SITES
Company Competitors	Directory-	Hoover's
Bill Payment History	Credit Reports- Credit Bureau Websites-	Dun & Bradstreet Equifax Experian Trans Union
PERSONNEL		
Key Personnel Changes	Newspapers- Trade Publications-	Dialog Factiva NEXIS

Data Elements	Types of Information Sources	Online Information Sources
Where They Went	Newspapers- Trade Publications-	**Bookmarks & Favorites:** NEWS SITES
Sales Force: Size, Organization, Compensation:		
VIPs: Track Records, Stock Transactions	Newspapers- Trade Publications-	**Bookmarks & Favorites:** NEWS SITES

INDUSTRY-RELATED DATA

Data Elements	Types of Information Sources	Online Information Sources
Impact of Industry Mergers/Joint Ventures	Trade Publications	Dialog Alacra
Other companies in industry	Directories-	Hoover's
Other firms entering the industry	Newspapers- Trade Publications-	**Bookmarks & Favorites:** NEWS SITES
Social Concerns or Similar Issues		**DATABASE FILES:** MARS
Trends affecting industry	Business Databases Government Data- Trade Publications-	**DATABASE FILES:** Dialog: Globalbase PROMT Trade & Industry TableBase
	Trade Associations-	**Bookmarks & Favorites:** ASSOCIATIONS
Laws and regulations that affect the industry	State & Federal Laws & Regulations State & Federal Agencies	**Bookmarks & Favorites:** Legal Information - Misc. Individual State websites Individual Agency websites
	Trade Associations-	**Bookmarks & Favorites**: ASSOCIATIONS
Significant events in recent history: major developments	Newspapers- Trade Publications-	**Bookmarks & Favorites:** NEWS SITES

SALES & MARKETING

Data Elements	Types of Information Sources	Online Information Sources
Major Products/Services	Trade Publications	**Bookmarks & Favorites:** INDUSTRIES & PROFESSIONS - ADVERTISING
	Newspapers	**Bookmarks & Favorites:** NEWS SITES
Customers/Clients:		
Market Share	Business Databases-	**DATABASE FILES:** Dialog Business & Industry TableBase
	Trade Publications-	Datamonitor Market Research

Data Elements	Types of Information Sources	Online Information Sources
Threats of substitutes:	↘	
Market Inroads By Foreign Competitors	↘	
Dependence on Suppliers	↘	
Dependence On Other Products	↘	
Media Used in Promotions (Past & Present)	Advertising Trade Publications-	**DATABASE FILES:** Advertiser and Agency Red Books
Advertising & Marketing Spending	↘	
Ad Campaigns	↘	
Marketing & Promotion Practices Used In This Industry	Business Databases- Trade Publications-	**DATABASE FILES:** ABI Inform Trade & Industry MARS
New Distribution Channels In Use	↘	
Price Structures, Margins and Mark-ups, Past & Present	↘	
Pricing Changes	Business Databases-	**DATABASE FILES:** BCC Datamonitor Euromonitor New Products Plus PROMT TableBase
Comparison With Competitors: Age, Size, Sales/Income, Products/Services	↘	

TECHNOLOGY ISSUES

Data Elements	Types of Information Sources	Online Information Sources
New technologies: Do They License or Develop	Newspapers- Trade Publications-	**DATABASE FILES:** Dialog Factiva NEXIS
Cost Structure: Production, Distribution, Overhead	↘	
New Patent/Trademarks Registrations	Patents Databases-	**DATABASE FILES:** Derwent Inpadoc (Dialog , STN) www.uspto.gov
New Technologies In Use	Newspapers- Trade Publications-	Varies By Industry

Data Elements	Types of Information Sources	Online Information Sources
Downsizing/Re-engineering Taking Place	↘	
Impact On Rivals' Strategies	↘	
Special Expertise Required	↘	
Age of Technology or Equipment	↘	

Mergers and Acquisitions

Before considering any sort of merger, acquisition, or joint venture, you no doubt check out a target company carefully. The information referenced below, if gathered and analyzed, will give you a good picture of that company's structure, history, and current activity. This will help determine whether there is a good "fit" between your company and theirs.

Company Mergers and Acquisitions Checklist

Data Elements	Types of Information Sources	Online Information Sources
CORPORATE STRUCTURE		
Divisions, Subsidiaries	Company Profiles- Directories-	Dun & Bradstreet **DATABASE FILES:** SDC Dialog (File 551)
Branch locations	↘	
Public or Privately Held	↘	
OWNERSHIP		
Ownership Structure	↘	
Other Companies Held By Owner	Public Records-	**DATABASE FILES:** ChoicePoint KnowX LexisNexis Public Records
POSSIBLE ADVERSE ITEMS		
Hazardous Waste Issues, If Any	Environmental Protection Agency (EPA) - State Environmental Agency-	**Bookmarks & Favorites:** ENVIRONMENT **Bookmarks & Favorites:** GOVERNMENT SITES US
Labor Problems or Issues	Newspapers- Trade Publications-	**Bookmarks & Favorites:** NEWS SITES

Data Elements	Types of Information Sources	Online Information Sources
Company Lawsuits, Past and Pending	Public Records-	**DATABASE FILES:** ChoicePoint
		Bookmarks & Favorites: PUBLIC RECORDS
		KnowX
		LEXIS Public Records
	Case Law -	LexisNexis Universe
		WESTLAW
Lawsuits, Past/Pending – Company Officers	Public Records	
Negative Media Coverage	Newspapers, Radio, TV-	**Bookmarks & Favorites:** NEWS SITES
		Burrelles
		www.vidmon.com

SALES & MARKETING

Data Elements	Types of Information Sources	Online Information Sources
Annual Sales	Company Profiles-	**DATABASE FILES:** Dun & Bradstreet
	Trade Publications-	Hoover's
Current Products/Services		**DATABASE FILES:** Hoover's
		New Product Announcements/Plus
Former Products/Services		**Bookmarks & Favorites:** COMPANY PROFILES
Product Market - Industrial/Consumer	Business Databases-	BUSINESS & INDUSTRY
	Trade Publications-	MARS
		PROMT
Customers	↘	
Relationship With Customers	↘	
Reputation in Industry	↘	
Strategic Physical Location, If Relevant	Industry Directories	
	Trade Publications	
Regulated By - State	State Laws & Regulations	**Bookmarks & Favorites:** LEGAL INFORMATION - MISC.
	State Agencies-	Individual States' Websites
Regulated By - Federal	Federal Laws & Regulations-	**Bookmarks & Favorites:** Legal Information - Misc
	Federal Agencies-	Individual Agency Websites

Data Elements	Types of Information Sources	Online Information Sources
MISCELLANEOUS		
Management - Quality, Style	Business Management Files-	ABI Inform BAMP
Community Involvement, Reputation	Local, Regional Newspapers-	**Bookmarks & Favorites:** NEWS SITES
Company Competitors	Directory-	Hoover's
Bill Payment History	Credit Reports- Credit Bureau Websites-	Dun & Bradstreet Equifax Experian TransUnion
Key personnel Changes	Newspapers, Trade Publications-	Dialog Factiva NEXIS
Where They Went	Newspapers- Trade Publications-	**Bookmarks & Favorites:** NEWS SITES
TECHNOLOGY ISSUES		
Special Expertise Required to Operate	Trade Publications-	Online availability varies by industry
Age of Technology or Equipment	Trade Publications-	Online availability varies by industry
New technologies: Licensed/Developed	↘	
Cost Structure: Production, Distribution, Overhead	↘	
New Patent/Trademarks Registrations	↘	
New Technologies In Use	↘	
Downsizing/Reengineering Taking Place	↘	
Impact on Rivals' Strategies	↘	

Useful Labor-Related Information

Retrieving labor information from cyberspace regarding a competitor company may be more challenging than simply checking a few routing sources such as directories.

Company Labor Information Checklist

Data Elements	Types of Information Sources	Online Information Sources
State-sponsored retraining programs	Business Databases-	**DATABASE FILES:** ABI Inform
	Newspapers- Trade Publications-	**Bookmarks & Favorites:** NEWS SITES
Wages in relation to other regions and competitors	↘	
Number of hourly employees by job classification	↘	
Number of unionized employees	↘	
Wages by job category	↘	
Wage trends	↘	
Benefit packages	↘	
Retirement	↘	
Insurance	↘	
Incentive	↘	
Stock options	↘	
Longevity of employees	↘	
Hiring and layoff history	↘	
Union contracts, past and current history	↘	
Organization and structure of middle management	↘	
Track record of management	↘	
Numbers of:	↘	
Management	↘	
Professional	↘	
Technical	↘	
Support	↘	
Salaries of management	Proxy Statements	
Management's benefit packages	↘	
Internal or external promotion to upper management	Newspapers- Trade Publications-	**Bookmarks & Favorites:** NEWS SITES

More Company Reports

The issues mentioned in the Company Strategy Report below are topics that must be considered as a company develops its strategy in various areas. By gathering information on what is going on within the industry, or by researching and/or deducing competitors' strategies, it may be possible to develop strategies that will out-perform competitors, or at least allow you to gain competitive advantage.

Note that not all of the blanks have been filled in on this and the additional company reports in this chapter. This allows them to be used as templates. The sources described in other forms in this chapter (and the next) should provide you with good ideas for choosing the types of sources to search.

Company Strategy Report

Company's Strategy	Content	Online Information Sources
Markets/Marketing Issues		
Has anyone in the industry tried a new distribution channel; results?		**Trade Publications** Business & Industry (Dialog File 9) IAC Trade & Industry Index (Dialog File 148)
Are foreign competitors moving into the domestic market?		**Trade Publications Newspapers**
Advertising and promotion spending by competitors.		
Changes in ads or marketing strategies of competitors?		**Advertising Media** MARS (Dialog File 570)
Infrastructure supports of marketing staff?		
Pricing Issues		
Competitor prices - are any changes anticipated?		
Competitors' cost structure: production, distribution, overhead?		
Technology Issues		
How are new technologies being used by others in industry?		**Trade Publications**
Are new technologies being acquired or developed?		

Company's Strategy	Content	Online Information Sources
New patents and trademarks registrations, pending expirations?		Current Awareness Services

Customers

Competitors' main clients or customers?		

Personnel Matters

Competitors' top executives and their track records?		Company Profiles Trade Publications
Staffing cuts, downswing, or re-engineering strategies?		Newspapers Trade Publications
Sales force size; how are they organized?		
Industry compensation; how do they compare?		Industry Directories
Competitors, firm and industry large stock transactions?		Newspapers Trade Publications

Miscellaneous

Product or service share being purchased?		
Mergers or joint ventures in the industry?		Newspapers Trade Publications
Impact on rivals' strategies?		

Company Report - Products & Services

Company Products and Services	Content	Online Information Source

Description of Products or Services

Description of the major products and services		**Directory Record** CorpTech Thomas Register
Description of minor product lines		
List of products and services		Company website
Scope and limitation of products and services		
Additional product distinctions; key features		
Full product range vs. Limited product range		
Advanced technology vs. Basic (low) technology		
Product and services differentiation		
Product and services key innovation		
Product and services performances		
Product and services features		

Sales of Products or Services

Dollar sales of all products and services	
Sales dollars by products and services	
Unit sales of all products and services	
Sales of key products and services	
Sales by company, by product line	
Sales of units by products and services	

Company Products and Services	Content	Online Information Source
Retail prices for products and services		
Prices for key products and services		
High price vs. Low price		

Market/Marketing Issues

Market Position of Products and Services by Industry		
High quality vs. Low quality perception of products		
Perceptions in marketplace of product and services		
Market position of key products and services		

Miscellaneous

Services and maintenance provided to support the products		
Training requirements of products and services		
Quality ratings of products and services		

Company Report - Finances

Company Finances	Content	Online Information Sources
Company Name		**Company Profiles** **Industry Directories** Hoover's Dun & Bradstreet

Sales/Revenues

Sales of company or division	
Sales of individual business unit	
Trends: historical, future outlook	
Total company revenues	

Costs

Direct costs	
Indirect costs	
Cost relevant to success	

Earnings/Profits

General profitability of company	
Profits by branch, division or business units	
Assessment of overall profitability	
Dividends paid	

Growth

Revenue growth / past three years	
Revenue growth / past five years	
Major factors affecting revenue growth	
Asset data on company/industry	
Factors affecting growth	
Liability information	

Alacra, at www.alacra.com, provides a number of specialized databases that could be useful in compiling the data needed for this report.

Company Report - Plant Site Locations

The list below specifies the data needed to create a detailed analysis of plant sites. Not all of this information can be expected to be found in online sources, but with diligent searching, and monitoring the media for references to the company or to a specific plant, a great deal of intelligence can be compiled over time. This information gathering process can be supplemented with telephone interviews, visits to local government offices, and other manual or onsite research.

Identity of Plant Sites	Content	Online Information Sources
List of all facilities		**Online Directories:** American Business Dir. (Dialog File 531) Duns Market Identifiers (Dialog File 516)
Function served by each facility		**Online Industry Directories:** Examine descriptions of listed plants.
Location of all facilities		**Online Directories:** American Business Dir. (Dialog File 531) Duns Market Identifiers (Dialog File 516)
Description of Plant Sites		**Tax Assessor's Office Online** (Many now include drawings)
Equipment used		
Number of shifts		
Production capacity		
Products manufactured		**Local, Regional Business Directories**
Manufacturing equipment		**Equipment Manufacturers' homepages** (Check for lists of customers)
Region served by facility		**Thomas Register**
Number of production lines		
Square footage of facility		Duns Market Identifiers (Dialog File 516)
Production utilization rate		
List of parts purchased from suppliers		
Major Distribution Facilities of Company		**Industry Directories**

Proximity to suppliers	_____	
Description of facilities	_____	
Flexibility for product production	_____	
Distribution facilities located at:	_____	
Geographic region served by facilities	_____	
Sophistication, safety and efficiency of plant	_____	**OSHA** www.osha.gov/oshstats

Sample Report –

PC Industry Analysis Report

This industry report on the PC Industry contains brief information of the type needed to "fill in the blanks" in the Industry Report form. A list of citations to articles (the "Ref #'s") is at chapter end.

Industry Analysis Report - The PC Industry

Data Category	Content	Source	Ref #
Status of the Industry — Relative size and scope of the industry - growing, stable, or declining?	1. Industry growing, per shipment information below. 2. China PC industry growing rapidly, may soon out-do Japan.	Economic Daily News	13
History of Industry	Detailed series of articles, one year at a time, chronicling events in the industry during that year.	Electronic Engineering Times	15
Trends in Industry	1. Moving from PC's for Internet access to use of "information appliance" 2. More low-cost PC's being made/sold 3. Shipments up, revenues down.	Financial Times	2
Forecasts regarding size of the industry	Personal Computers Shipments Yr. 1998: 12,800,000 1999: 14,850,000 2002: 23,050,000 2003: 26,900,000 2004: 31,000,000 CONFLICTING INFORMATION[1]	Tablebase	1

---

[1] It will be necessary to study both information sources carefully, and to possibly seek out other sources to determine which of two seemingly conflicting numbers is accurate.

Data Category	Content	Source	Ref #
	U.S. figures for 1998 : 35,200,000, up 16% from 1997	Computer Reseller News	8
SIC or NAICS Codes	SIC=3571; NAICS=334111	www.census.gov/ep cd/www/naics.html	

Customers For Products or Services

Data Category	Content	Source	Ref #
Customers	Home market expected to grow slightly faster than business sector. Buyers will be lower-income households and two-PC households.	Newsbytes News Network	14
Size of Market	Computer and office equipment shipments for Feb. 1999 = $11,225,000	www.census.gov /ftp/pub/indicator /www/m3/index. htm	9
Potential New Buyers	Customers for PC-based control systems used in industrial control.	Process Engineering	4
Directions in the Market	"There is a big move toward growth," concurs John Mariotti, IW columnist and president of The Enterprise Group, a manufacturing consulting business, "mainly because people feel that they have wrung everything they can out of downsizing.	Industry Week	23
Import Penetration	Hewlett-Packard offering its HP Pavilion PC in the Philippines. To gain market penetration in the home PCs segment, HP will address operational excellence, customer and channels satisfaction, and integrated product/technology offering.	Newsbytes News Network	
Forecasts for Market	China PC sales to grow 35%	Singapore Business Times	10
Distribution Methods	1. Wholesale Distributors are growing faster than the PC industry. Attributed in part to growth of Small Business, partly to value-added services offered.	Computer Reseller News	8
	2. Dell Computer called an anomaly; other vendors moving away from selling direct.		

Market/Marketing Issues

Data Category	Content	Source	Ref #
Scope of Products	1. Home/business PCs	Financial Times Surveys Edition	9
	2. More emphasis on servers, to centralize IT operations and build systems such as intranets and websites.		
	3. Supercomputers		
Brand Loyalty	1. According to the Ziff-Davis 1998 Technology User Profile, 3 out of 4 people who purchased a Gateway computer in 1997 were repeat purchasers.	Des Moines Register	18
	2. Apple computer users said they would consider another brand only if the price	USA Today	17

Data Category	Content	Source	Ref #
	were at least $606 less.		
	3. Brand loyalty might be the major reason notebook leaders Toshiba America Information Systems Inc., The IBM PC Co. and Compaq Computer Corp. have held on to market share despite across-the-board shortages last year, analysts said.	Computer Reseller News	19
Product Leader description	Compaq and IBM dominate nearly all major markets except Japan.	Nikkei Weekly	5
Product Differentiation	Becoming harder for manufacturers to come up with a leap in performance to justify upgrading hardware. Consumers less willing to upgrade.	Wall Street Journal	7
Alternate Products/Services	Moving from PC's for Internet access to use of "information appliance"	Financial Times	2
Complementary Products	Palm computer market grew 60% in 1998, compared with 15% for PC's.	Globe & Mail	3
Quality Continuum	Concern about Y2K issues may slow sales, study shows.	Computer Reseller News	12
Marketing Media Used	N/A		
Price Structure	Compaq, H-P, IBM cut prices, offered monitor promotions in 1998 to clear excess inventory and affect market share.	Computer Reseller News	8
Price Margins	Shrinking, with demand for low-cost PC's	Computer Reseller News	8

Manufacturing Goods Issues

Technology in Use	N/A		
Technological Trends	CD-ROM vs. DVD-ROM transition will be slower than originally projected.	Electronic Buyers News	6
Industry Innovations	N/A		
Emerging Technologies	Intel Corp.'s 100 MHz system bus and 440BX core-logic chip. PC-100 memory spec. may be a concern.	Computer Reseller News	

Service Business Issues

Scope of Services	N/A		
Level of Services	N/A		

Fiscal Matters

Changes that may impact supplier prices	N/A		

Data Category	Content	Source	Ref #
Legislation/Regulations	FTC, Intel to square off over interpretation of law (Intel, computer chip firm, facing FTC antitrust charges for abusing 80% market share to harm 3 computer companies)	USA Today	20
Availability of raw materials	N/A		
Other Sales by Major Product Type	Servers: $10.5bn in 1997; projected to be $21bn in 2001	Financial Times Survey Edition	9

Productivity-Related Matters

Manufacturing Rates	N/A		
Efficiency Levels	N/A		
Product Innovation	...the launch of the world's first flat monitor will help the company in maintaining the premier position in terms of product innovation and market share.	BusinessLine	21
	(Apple Computer interim CEO Steven Jobs introduces fastest Mac ever, powered by IBM PowerPC microprocessor using copper-metalization)	Newsbytes News	22

Industry Analysis: References to Articles

1. U.S. shipments of business appliances in units for 1998 and forecast for 1999, with shipments breakdown by each of 18 alphabetically-listed appliances
Journal: **Appliance** , v 56 , n 1 , p 52 Publication Date: January 1999 Document Type: Journal; Time Series ISSN: 0003-6781(United States)

2. INSIDE TRACK: Battle to bridge the information gap: IT VIEWPOINT STEVE FRANCE: The PC will be soon be challenged as a way to access the internet by information appliances', bringing two industry sectors into direct conflict. (It is predicted that there will be 200 mil Internet connections worldwide by 2002, with 60 mil online households in the U.S.)
Financial Times London Edition , p 16 March 30, 1999

3. BOOM IN PALM COMPUTER NOT LIKELY TO SUBSIDE (According to Dataquest Inc, the market for palm computers grew by more than 60% **Globe & Mail** , p R5   February 26, 1999

4. PC -based control set for growth (By 2004 the European market for PC -based control systems will be valued at more than UKPd80

mil; potentially lucrative opportunities exist in the food and beverage industry)
Process Engineering , v 79 , n 6 , p 9   6/1998

5. Industry sees Windows of opportunity (Personal computer makers expect growth in market with introduction of Windows 98 in July)
Nikkei Weekly , v 36 , n 1,824 , p 4 May 11, 1998

6. PC makers delay move to DVD-ROM (Industry watchers and suppliers rethink transition from DC to DVD and readjust forecasts for sales to 5 mil units this year)
Electronic Buyers News , p 1 November 30, 1998

7. Upgrade Fatigue Threatens PC Profits (Unwillingness to upgrade PCs looms a big issue for the industry)
Wall Street Journal , v CCXXXI , n 94 , p B1+ May 14, 1998

8. Distributors Outrun Industry In Growth (Distributors continue to grow faster than PC industry , thanks to increasing number of vendors and products selling through

two-tier channels)
Computer Reseller News , p 71 May 04, 1998

9. **Financial Times Surveys Edition** , p 05 March 04, 1998
Document Type: Business Newspaper; Industry Overview ISSN: 0307-1766 (United Kingdom)

10. **Newsbytes News Network** , p N/A January 26, 1998 Document Type: Journal; Ranking ISSN: 0983-1592 (United States)

11. China PC sales to grow 35% (China Ministry of Information Industry forecasts 35% increase in PC market to Yuan50 bil in 1999)
Singapore Business Times , p 9
January 25, 1999

12. Vendors, VARs React To Study Findings (Some personal computer vendors are expecting some slowdown in the industry because customers might hesitate to upgrade systems not affected by the year 2000 bug)
Computer Reseller News , p 115
November 30, 1998 , Document Type: Journal; Survey ISSN: 0893-8377 (United States)

13. Mainland China's PC Industry Explodes. (Mainland China's personal computer production will reach 7.6 mil/yr by the year 2000)
Economic Daily News , p N/A June 01, 1998
Document Type: Newspaper (Taiwan) Language: Chinese Record Type: Abstract

14. PC Shipments Up, Revenue Growth Down - Dataquest Forecast (A new study by Gartner Group division Dataquest says worldwide PC shipments will be up 15.6 percent in 1998 but industry revenues will be up only 6.4 percent)
Newsbytes News Network , p N/A April 20, 1998. Document Type: Journal ISSN: 0983-1592

15. Dialog(R)File 148:IAC Trade & Industry Database (c) 1999 Info Access Co. All rts. reserv. 1996. (a history of the electronics industry)(EE Times Chronicles: 1972-1997) (Industry Trend or Event) Rostky, George
Electronic Engineering Times, n978, p244(1)

16. HP Pavilion PCs Enter Philippines Market (Hewlett-Packard is now offering its HP Pavilion PC in the Philippines)
Newsbytes News Network, p N/A
February 26, 1999
Document Type: Journal ISSN: 0983-1592 (United States)

17. Computer users display brand loyalty (Apple computer owners express greater brand loyalty then IBM users in a survey of 1,600 home and office computer users)
USA Today, v 13, n 40, p B1, Nov. 9, 1994
Document Type: National Newspaper; Survey ISSN: 0161-7389 (United States)

18. Gateway muffling its (sacred) cow. Is abandoning folksy, Midwestern image in hopes of continuing growth and carving out bigger slice of the corporate computer mkt
Ridgeway, Michael **Des Moines Register (IA)** Sept 14, 1998 p. B4

19. Resellers enter 'notebook zone': Logical Solutions finds what works for desktops does not always work for notebooks
Bliss, Jeff
Computer Reseller News Feb 10, 1997 p. 81 ISSN: 0893-8377

20. FTC, Intel to square off over interpretation of law (Intel, computer chip firm, facing FTC antitrust charges for abusing 80% market share to harm 3 computer companies)
USA Today, v 17, n 121, p 1B+, 3/ 05, 1999
Document Type: National Newspaper; Cover Story ISSN: 0161-7389 (United States)

21. India: 100 pc flat monitor from LG Electronics (LG Electronics is debuting the zero deflection 15-inch TFT LCD monitor and the 17-inch Flatron monitor in India)
Business Line , p N/A June 15, 1998
Document Type: Journal ISSN: 0971-7528 (India)

22. Apple Products At Seybold (Apple Computer interim CEO Steven Jobs introduces fastest Mac ever, powered by IBM metalization)
Newsbytes News Network, p N/A
March 17, 1998
Document Type: Journal ISSN: 0983-1592 (USA) States)

23. GOING FOR GROWTH
(IBM, a computer giant, hired 26,000+ employees in 1996 to propel growth; firm had reduced its staff to 225,000 employees in 1995)
Industry Week, v 246, n 11, p 32+ 6/9/1997
Document Type: Journal; Geographic Profile ISSN: 0039-0895 (United States)

Chapter 18

Industry Studies, Revisited

~~~~~~

The "Do-It-Yourself" Approach

~~~~~~

To accurately size up an industry it is should be examined from a number of different perspectives. To determine where the answers might be found for your industry, consider the broad topics and suggested sources presented in this chapter. The sources are intended as guides, to get your research started, and you will find that some sources will be more useful than others. You will notice that certain key business databases appear over and over because they cover many industries or are considered basic tools for this type of research.

Online research may be only one of the tools needed to find the information included in the Industry Study Template at the end of this chapter. To learn more about other means for gathering this business intelligence, consult the articles and books mentioned in Appendix E of Part IV.

The question to be addressed is: Is the industry growing, stable, or declining? To make this determination, look at the following:

History of the Industry

The depth and amount of information available will vary according to the specific industry under consideration. For high tech industries, this material will be available in electronic format. For long-established industries such as meatpacking, oil, or automobiles, it may be possible to locate printed histories that provide the necessary background. Economics-oriented sources could also be useful.

~~~~~~

Hot Tip - As you begin to identify key sources for an industry, study the vendor's documentation or click on the Search Tips button on a website. You can usually narrow or focus the research easily by taking advantage of suggestions provided there. Most expert searchers have a few "tried and true" favorite sources that are used over and over.

General Industry History Sources

Trade publications

Search industry-specific publications. To identify key publications, consult *Fulltext Sources Online*, in the archives of business oriented publishers, or explore websites such as Free Trade Magazine Source at www.freetrademagazinesource.com/index.aspx.

Trade associations

Identify relevant trade associations using the *Bookmarks & Favorites* Section in Part IV and search their websites.

Specific Industry History Sources

Industry-specific databases

Consult commercial vendor documentation or the *Bookmarks & Favorites* Section in Part IV under headings for Database Vendors or for specific industries.

Resources List

See sources listed under "Industry History" in the *Data Elements List* in Part IV.

Trends in the Industry

What has been happening in an industry may help your company's planners and strategists to make crucial decisions regarding new products, new markets or, possibly, what company to acquire. In some cases the decision might even be made that it is best to be acquired! Decisions of this magnitude involve the investment of money and resources, so it is important to research developments in the field and "educate" the decision makers.

General Sources for Trends

Trade publications

Search industry-specific publications. To identify key publications, consult *Fulltext Sources Online* or in the archives of business oriented publishers.

Trade associations

Identify relevant trade associations using the *Bookmarks & Favorites* Section in Part IV and search their websites.

Specific Sources for Trends

Industry-specific databases

Consult commercial vendor documentation or *Bookmarks & Favorites* Section in Part IV.

Other Sources

Resources List - See sources listed under "Industry Trends" in the *Data Elements List* in Part IV. Also, check Industry Insider at www.investext.com.

Forecasts Regarding Size of the Industry

Government sources provide data regarding the size of many industries. Trade associations also collect this information. By examining this type of data for a period of years, it is possible to make observations about growth patterns or the lack thereof.

General Industry Forecast Sources

Trade publications

Search industry-specific publications. To identify key publications, consult *Fulltext Sources Online* or *Net.Journal.*

Trade associations

Identify relevant trade associations using the *Bookmarks & Favorites* Section in Part IV and search their websites.

Specific Industry Forecast Sources

Industry Insider

www.investext.com

Bookmarks & Favorites

Look in "Industry & Research" under the subheading "Forecasts" in Part IV.

Industry-specific databases

Consult commercial vendor documentation or the *Database Coverage of Industries* section in the Resources List of Part IV.

Customers for Products or Services

The customer base for products or services provides crucial intelligence needed to understand the industry. Gather the data below to examine customer issues:

Size of Market

Knowing the size of the market will help you to determine where your company stands in relation to the rest of the companies in the industry, and to make crucial decisions regarding bringing new products or services to market.

General Sources of Customer Information

Trade publications

Search industry-specific publications. To identify key publications, consult *Fulltext Sources Online* or *Net.Journal.*

Trade associations

Identify relevant trade associations using the *Bookmarks & Favorites* Section in Part IV and search their websites.

Government Statistical Sources

Market research reports and analyst reports

Specific Sources of Customer Information

Resources List

See sources listed under "Market Size" in the *Data Elements List* of Part IV.

Bookmarks & Favorites

Look at site listed under heading "Statistics" in Part IV.

Potential New Customers

Learning about possible new customers for an industry's products is crucial to increasing sales. Your company's Sales & Marketing Department is always looking for this type of information.

General Sources of New Customer Information

Trade publications

Search industry-specific publications. To identify key publications, consult *Fulltext Sources Online* or *Net.Journal* in the *Data Elements List* of Part IV.

Specific Sources of New Customer Information

Resources List

See sources listed under "Consumer Trends" and "Emerging Markets" in Part IV.

Changes that Affect the Market

Activity in the market is affected by a number of factors. Here are some ideas for examining several things that can impact the market *for and industry products.*

Import Penetration

Have foreign imports affected the market for an industry's products in your country? Is the trend expected to continue? What effects can be expected?

General Sources for Import Information

Trade publications

Search industry-specific publications. To identify key publications, consult *Fulltext Sources Online* or *Net.Journal.*

Government Statistics

Search the *Bookmarks & Favorites* Section in Part IV under heading "Industry Research."

Industry-specific Databases

Consult vendor's documentation for appropriate files. Search using terms like "market" and "penetration" and "imports." Also see *Database File Coverage of Industries* in the Resource List, Part IV.

Specific Sources of Import Information

Resources List
See sources listed in the *Data Elements List* under the heading "Market Penetration." Within the database files listed in Part IV, search using terms like "market" and "penetration" and "imports." Add name of industry.

Market Forecasts

General Sources of Market Forecast

Trade Associations
Identify relevant trade associations using the *Bookmarks & Favorites* Section in Part IV and search their websites.

Specific Sources of Market Forecasts

Bookmarks & Favorites
In Part IV, look in "Industry Research" under the subheading "Forecasts" for both government and non-government sources. Look specifically for market forecasts.

Resources List
See sources listed in the *Data Elements List* under the heading "Forecasts" and "Product Forecasts" in Part IV. Within the referenced database files, search on keywords like "market" and "forecasts" with name of a specific industry. Also consider sources listed under "Market Research."

Distribution Methods

Changes or innovation in distribution methods within an industry can result in new leadership among the companies vying for success when it comes to the bottom line. Locating examples of success stories may provide your organization with the inspiration for similar undertakings.

General Sources of Distribution Information

Trade Publications
Include "distribution" in keywords searched. You may not want to limit your search to one industry, however. Look at examples in other industries that might work in your own. Consider using words like "innovative" to narrow search results.

Specific Sources of Distribution Information

Industry-specific Databases
Consult vendor's documentation for appropriate files. Search using terms like "distribution." See also *Database File Coverage* of Industries in the Resources List Section of Part IV.

Resources List
See sources listed under "Distribution Methods" under the *Data Elements List* in Part IV.

Market & Marketing Issues

Markets and marketing issues cover a wide span of topics, as evidenced in the list below. Market Forecasts, because they affect the market, are discussed in the previous section.

Scope of Products

The scope of products in the industry in question may be broader than expected. Likewise, it could contain some surprises. It is crucial, from the CI perspective, to know what is being offered by those in the industry.

General Sources of Product Information

Newswires
Product announcements generally are made using a press release. Search by company or type of product.

Company websites
Search company websites under hotlinks like "Products" to gain insight into the types of products offered by companies in an industry.

Specific Sources of Product Information

Industry-specific Databases
Searching in these focused files using keywords like "products" yields good results. Searching for "product line" in article titles can work well, too.

Resources List
See sources listed under "Product Introductions" and "Product Forecasts" in the *Data Elements List* within the Resources List Section of Part IV.

Brand Loyalty

Brand loyalty means continuing business from returning customers. It can vary from industry to industry and from market to market.

General Sources of Brand Loyalty Information

Trade publications
Search industry-specific publications. To identify key publications, consult *Fulltext Sources Online* or *Net.Journal*.

Specific Sources of Brand Loyalty Information

Resources List
See sources listed under "Brand Share" and "Brand Loyalty" in the *Data Elements List*. Use those terms as keywords when searching the databases.

Product Leaders

Who is leading the way, where and why? These distinctions - product differentiating - will, of course, vary by geography and by market segment.

General Sources for Information on Product Leaders

Trade Publications

Having identified the key publications in the industry, try searching for words like "product or brand" in titles, along with "leader or leading."

Specific Sources for Information on Product Leaders

Resource List

See sources listed under the heading "Market Share" in *Data Elements List* in Part IV. Combine the keywords "market share" with the name of a product, such as "coffee."

Product Differentiation

Differentiating its products from "the rest of the pack," whether because of quality, features, or other means, may be crucial to the growth of an industry.

General Sources of Product Differentiation Information

Trade Publications

Search for words like "product" near "differentiation."

Specific Sources of Product Differentiation Information

Resource List

See sources listed under the heading "Product Differentiation" in the *Data Elements List* in Part IV.

AdWeek
www.adweek.com

BrandWeek
www.brandweek.com

Substitute or Complementary Products or Services

These products or services may co-exist with products or services already available and, over time, may supplant them due to changes in consumer preferences or other factors.

General Sources of Alternative Product Information

Trade Publications

Identify the industry's key publications and search using terms like "alternate" or "substitute" with the name of a product or service.

Specific Sources of Alternative Product Information

Resource List

See sources listed in the *Data Elements List* under the heading "Product Differentiation" or similar topics.

Quality Continuum

Quality Continuum – what is being done to improve, enhance, or invigorate a product?

General Sources of Quality Continuum Data

Trade Publications

Identify the industry's key publications and search using terms like "quality" with the name of a product or service.

Marketing Media Used

The media used to market an industry's products varies greatly from industry to industry. Consumer products are aimed at a much different market than raw materials or industrial products.

General Sources of Marketing Media News

Trade Publications

Search by industry name with additional keywords like "marketing" and "media."

Specific Sources of Marketing Media News

Resource List

See sources listed in *Data Elements List* in Part IV under headings that start with the word "marketing."

AdWeek	**BrandWeek**	**Advertising Age**
www.adweek.com	www.brandweek.com	www.adage.com

Price Structure

Learning about the price structure in an industry will aid your organization in both pricing its products competitively, and in developing alternative pricing strategies.

General Sources of Price Structure Data

Trade Publications

Search by industry name with additional keywords like "price" or "pricing."

Specific Sources of Price Structure Data

Resource List

See sources listed under headings in *Data Elements List* in Part IV that start with the word "price," or under "product pricing."

Price Margins

General Sources for Price Margin Information

Trade Publications

Search by industry name with additional keywords like "price" or "pricing."

Trade associations

Identify relevant trade associations using the *Bookmarks & Favorites* Section in Part IV and search their websites.

Specific Sources for Price Margin Information

Industry Insider   www.investext.com

Resource List

See sources listed in *Data Elements List* in Part IV under headings that start with the word "price trends."

Manufactured Goods Issues

Examine the various subtopics listed below to help build the company's knowledge base regarding manufacturing industries.

Technology in Use

The technology in use may be high-tech or low-tech, and at worst, antiquated. These factors affect the bottom line of the companies in the industry, or the vitality of the industry itself.

General Sources of Technology Information

Trade publications

Search industry-specific publications. To identify key publications, consult *Fulltext Sources Online* or *Net.Journal*.

Trade associations

Identify relevant trade associations using the *Bookmarks & Favorites* Section in Part IV and search their websites.

Specific Sources of Technology Information

Industry-Specific Databases

Consult vendor's documentation for list of databases or click on a hotlink like sources on a website. Look for a subject-oriented list of sources. See also *Database File Coverage* in the Resources List of Part IV.

Bookmarks & Favorites Section in Part IV

Examine sites bookmarked under the heading "Industries & Professions," subheading "Manufacturing."

Resources List in Part IV

See sources listed under "Manufacturing" in *Data Elements List* in Part IV.

Industry Insider

www.investext.com

Technological Trends

General Sources of Technology Trends

Trade publications

Search industry-specific publications. To identify key publications, consult *Fulltext Sources Online*.

Trade associations

Identify relevant trade associations using the *Bookmarks & Favorites* Section in Part IV and search their websites.

Specific Sources of Technology Trends

Industry-Specific Sources databases

Consult commercial vendor documentation or the *Bookmarks & Favorites* Section in Part IV.

Resources List

See sources listed in *Data Elements List* under "Industry Trends" in Part IV.

Industry Insider
Thomson Financial

Industry Innovations

General Sources for Industry Innovations

Trade publications

Search industry-specific publications. To identify key publications, consult *Fulltext Sources Online*.

Trade associations

Identify relevant trade associations using the *Bookmarks & Favorites* Section in Part IV and search their websites. Trade associations monitor what is going on in the industry, and which companies are moving forward with innovation.

Specific Sources for Industry Innovations

Industry-Specific Databases

Consult commercial vendor documentation or the *Bookmarks & Favorites* section in Part IV.

Industry Insider
Thomson Financial

Emerging Technologies

General Sources on Emerging Technologies

Trade publications

Search Industry-specific publications. To identify key publications, consult *Fulltext Sources Online*.

Specific Sources on Emerging Technologies

Resources List
See sources listed in *Data Elements List* under "Emerging Technologies or Patents."

Knowledge Express
This web-based commercial online service specializes in new technologies. Explore it at www.KnowledgeExpress.com.

Service Business Issues

Service business issues are often quite different from those which must be addressed in the manufacturing or product-oriented environment. Measurement and evaluation are much more subjective than in product-oriented industries, and an industry may be more dependent on feedback from its customers.

Scope & Level of Services

Consider these as "quality" and "quantity" questions. What types of services are being offered in various types of service industries? What level of service is provided? Is the industry responding to the wants and needs of its market?

General Sources of Services Information

Trade Publications
Search industry-specific publications. Use *Fulltext Sources Online* to identify titles.

Trade Associations
Identify relevant associations using *Bookmarks & Favorites* in Part IV and search their websites.

Specific Sources of Services Information

Resources List
See sources listed in the *Data Elements List* under the headings such as "Service Industries" or "Service Introductions" in Part IV.

Fiscal Matters

In one way or another, money drives most industries. As a matter of fact, it *is* an industry, if you consider banking and related industries. At the same time, fiscal matters can involve that which is impacted by the presence or absence of money. A variety of sources are available for obtaining this information.

General Sources of Fiscal Information

Business Newspapers/Trade Publications
Search industry-specific publications. Use *Fulltext Sources Online* to identify titles.

Trade Associations

Identify relevant trade associations using the *Bookmarks & Favorites* section in Part IV and search their websites.

Specific Sources of Fiscal Information

Factiva

This commercial online service is noted for coverage of financial business matters of all sorts: www.factiva.com

The Census Bureau

Manufacturers' Shipments, Inventories, and Orders - www.census.gov/prod/2003pubs/m3-02.pdf

Bookmarks & Favorites section in Part IV

Choose from the wide variety of financial sites listed under "Financial Information Sites" and "Financial Media." Also look at government sites included under "Economics/Economic Data" and under "Statistics."

Resource List in Part IV

Search the databases reference under "Financial Information" in the *Data Elements List* in Part IV.

Impact of New Laws or Regulations

It is important to determine which level of government regulates the industry in question. Industries such as finance, telecommunications, and transportation are subject to both federal and state regulation, while education, finance, franchising, health, insurance, and professional services are regulated by the states.

Certain industries are not subject to such regulation, which is, in itself, an important fact. Since there is so much variation in state laws, if there is any question regarding this matter, it is best to check with your company's legal department as to whether a particular industry is regulated by your state.

General Sources for New Laws & Regulations

Newspapers & Trade Press

Search industry-specific publications. Use *Fulltext Sources Online* to identify titles. The issues of interest to the industry will be covered in depth. Search on name of bill or law, or on name of a regulating agency, as well as by keywords that identify the industry, such as "telecommunications."

Trade Associations

These organizations can provide the industry's perspective on the laws and regulations that govern the industries that they represent. Seek out websites for an industry and then look for appropriate hotlinks.

Case Law

In some cases, the legality of laws or regulations governing an industry has been tested in federal or state courts. Search the industry name in case law databases like Lexis or Westlaw. (Remember that credit card access is available for non-subscribers.)

Specific Sources for New Laws & Regulations

Bookmarks & Favorites

Examine the links under the heading "Activist/Interest Groups" in Part IV. These organizations often provide copies of laws or regulations, as well as position papers and other explanatory materials. Try to find sites that are non-partisan. At other sites, remember the "bias factor" as you explore the material or hotlinks provided.

Also consult *Bookmarks & Favorites* under the heading "Legal Information" in Part IV. In some cases, Specific Sources:headings like "Government/Legal/Regulatory" are provided for industries included under "Industries & Professions." The telecommunications industry is an example.

Availability of Raw Materials

General Sources of Raw Material Information

Trade Publications

Search industry-specific publications. Use *Fulltext Sources Online* to identify titles.

Business Newspapers

If raw materials come from foreign countries, check that country's media.

Specific Sources of Raw Material Information

Bookmarks & Favorites

Examine *Bookmarks & Favorites* under heading "Economics/Economic Data" or "Statistics" in Part IV. Government sites are a good source.

Resource List

Search databases listed in the *Data Elements List* in Part IV under "Raw Materials (Availability)."

Sales By Major Product Type

General Sources for Major Product Sales

Trade Publications

Search industry-specific publications. Use *Fulltext Sources Online* to identify titles.

Trade Associations

Identify relevant associations using *Bookmarks & Favorites* in Part IV and search their websites.

Market Research Reports

Choose among many databases available on major commercial online services. Search by product or industry and keyword "sales."

Specific Sources for Major Product Sales

Resource List

Search the database sources listed in the *Data Elements List* in Part IV under headings "Sales By Product" and "Sales Volume."

Bookmarks & Favorites section in Part IV
Look for government sites whose agencies deal with this information e.g. the Bureau of Economic Analysis, www.bea.doc.gov. See the heading "Government Sites" in Part IV.

Productivity-Related Matters

Is this industry productive? Is it vegetating or adjusting to the times? By examining productivity-related matters, and combining your findings with other material in your organization's knowledge base, you may reach a more clear understanding of the industry's productivity level.

Manufacturing Rates

General Sources for Manufacturing Rates

Trade Publications
Search industry-specific publications. Use *Fulltext Sources Online* to identify titles.

Trade Associations
Identify relevant trade associations using the *Bookmarks & Favorites* Section in Part IV and search their websites.

Specific Sources for Manufacturing Rates

Resource List
Search the database sources listed in the *Data Elements List* in Part IV under "Manufacturing Industries"

Efficiency Levels

General Sources for Efficiency Information

Trade Publications
Search industry-specific publications. Use *Fulltext Sources Online* to identify titles.

Specific Sources for Efficiency Information

Resource List
Search the database sources listed in Part IV under headings "Efficiency Levels."

Product Innovation

General Sources for Product Innovation Information

Trade Publications
Search industry-specific publications. Use *Fulltext Sources Online* to identify titles.

Trade Associations

Identify relevant trade associations using the *Bookmarks & Favorites* Section in Part IV and search their websites.

Specific Sources for Product Innovation Information

Resource List

See headings in the *Data Elements List* beginning with "Product" and search the resources listed there, using keywords "product" and "innovation."

Bookmarks & Favorites section in Part IV

See the website entitled Business Research Reports at www.saibooks.com.

What About Other Topics?

For other topics, use the Industry Study template shown below:

Industry Study Template

STATUS OF THE INDUSTRY

Relative size and scope of the industry - growing, stable, or declining? _____

History of industry _____

Trends in industry _____

Forecasts regarding size of the industry _____

SIC or NAICS Codes _____

CUSTOMERS FOR PRODUCTS OR SERVICES

Customers _____

Size of market _____

Potential new buyers _____

Directions in the market _____

Import penetration _____

Forecasts for market _____

Distribution methods _____

MARKET/MARKETING ISSUES

Scope of products

Brand loyalty

Product leader description

Product differentiation

Alternate products/services

Complementary products

Quality continuum

Marketing media used

Price structure

Price margins

MANUFACTURED GOODS ISSUES

Technology in use

Technological trends

Industry innovations

Emerging technologies

SERVICE BUSINESS ISSUES

Scope of services

Level of services

FISCAL MATTERS

Changes that may impact supplier prices

Legislation/Regulations

Availability of raw materials

Other Sales by major product type

PRODUCTIVITY-RELATED MATTERS

Manufacturing rates

Efficiency levels

Product innovation

Part IV

References & Appendices

Bookmarks & Favorites

The CI Sleuth's Guide to the Universe

Do It Like a Pro

Nearly every week the Internet listservs frequented by professional searchers contain several "Does anybody have a good site for (fill in the blank)" questions. Essentially, the searcher has been asked for something on an unfamiliar topic or has "struck out" searching the usual sources, so he or she has posted a message asking for assistance.

Invariably several colleagues quickly reply, providing one or more hot-links to sources on the topic. How do they do this so quickly? The answer, of course, is obvious:

BOOKMARKS (Also Known As FAVORITES)

The pros know that they will need certain material repeatedly or that particular sites may be useful again. Thus, with one or two fast mouse clicks, they perform the equivalent of the following:

- Writing down a name and web address (the URL)

- Going to the supply cabinet and taking out a manila folder

- Labeling the folder appropriately

- Tossing in the slip of paper containing the valuable information

- Walking to the file cabinet, opening a drawer, and placing the folder carefully in its place alphabetically.

Because they have stored important Internet sites as bookmarks/favorites, they can easily take a minute to make suggestions to a colleague, even on a busy day. All they do is open their browser, examine their bookmarks list, and use the copy and paste features to add the sites' Internet addresses (URLs) to an outgoing email message.

On the commercial online side, the process may be a bit more complex, since the reference may be to a source that requires a subscription.

Once inside of a vendor's site, you must know which of the many files available should be searched for the intelligence that is needed. The next search may take you back to the same vendor's site, but to a different file or group of files, containing material relevant to the project or question in hand. Frequent searchers can develop and save mental or written lists consisting of points like these:

- What files are available on my topic?

- Which vendors offer the file for searching?

- Where can I get the best price and/or greatest efficiency?

- Do I have a subscription to the necessary service?

- If not, is there an Internet source that offers that the database on a pay-as-you-go basis?

If bookmarks or the list above does not provide answers, we are back to the top of this section — the pros ask their colleagues to check their bookmarks.

Managing Your Bookmarks/Favorites File

Your bookmarks files may be varied or highly focused, depending upon your job. Librarians, for example, will collect bookmarks for a wide variety of subjects, while others in the company may concentrate on information sources suited to their department's activities.

The remainder of this chapter consists of bookmarks chosen over several years, but checked and re-evaluated frequently. The intent is to provide a skeleton framework to get you started, and to provide some examples for categorizing what could become hundreds or thousands of individual bookmarks. The categorizing provides greater efficiency and prevents overlooking a "great site" because its name is not a clear indicator of its contents.

When you find a useful site for business intelligence, or even a particular page buried somewhere on a larger site, remember to BOOKMARK IT IMMEDIATELY, preferably in a folder with a meaningful heading. Otherwise, you may not easily find it again.

Examine the name of a site when you bookmark it, and edit if necessary, using language that will give a clear indication of the site's contents. For more effective alphabetizing of your bookmarks, delete words before the name of the site, like "Welcome to…"

Web pages disappear and relocate frequently. Run your browser's program for checking bookmarks monthly and try to visit those that are marked unavailable when the check was performed. The server may merely have been busy. If the site has moved, a new address may be available for a limited period of time. Follow the link to the new site, create a bookmark and save it in the appropriate folder within your bookmark file. If you receive a "404" message, delete the bookmark from your list.

The Usual Disclaimer...

These Internet addresses were last updated in May, 2004 and were current at that time. Sites containing searchable databases were preferred. For the most part, personal pages or sites of particular companies within an industry are not included. The list is not comprehensive — creating such a list would be an impossible task. This list is a starting point. To help with the thought process, notes about applying certain information when performing CI have been included. Many of the sites included here can serve as "jumping off places" to further research a topic. A number of award-winning or favorably reviewed Internet sites offer collections of links to dozens of other valuable sites, a fact which is made clear by the name used so frequently to describe this key part of the Internet: the World Wide Web. To locate additional bookmarks and other useful material, visit the Burwell Enterprises website at www.burwellinc.com.

Bookmarks Are Arranged by These Categories...

Activist / Interest Groups	European Union	People Locators
Associations	Executive Compensation	Political Risk
Bookstores	Experts – Locating	Products
Broadcast Monitors	Financial Information Sites	Public Records
Business Sites – Compilations/Reviews	Geographic Searching Sites	Publishers
Business Sites – General	Government Sites – U.S.	Push Technologies
Classification Systems – Business	Industries and Professions	Reference Tools
Company Information	Industry Research	Sales Leads
Competitive Intelligence Sites	Information Brokers	Science/Technology
Conferences/Trade Shows	International Organizations	Search Engines/Internet Directories
County/World Sites	Internet Tools	Software
Database Vendors	Legal Information	Statistics
Demographics	Libraries	Standards and Specifications
Directories	Maps	Telephone Information
Economics/Economic Data	Market Research	Trade
Employment/Want Ads	News Sites	Travel
Environment	Newspapers	Usenet/Listservs
	Nonprofits and Charities	
	Patents/Trademarks	

Activist / Interest Groups

Some of these groups may have an impact on your company or industry, so it is important to know who they are and what they are up to. They also may be valuable sources of information —providing documents, copies of laws or proposed legislation, hotlinks on their websites, names and addresses or other useful intelligence. It is important to remember that although they have an opinion, or an "axe to grind," they do a great deal of research that can save you time and may be useful to your company if you keep in mind their potential bias.

Advocacy Groups (Canada)
www.canajun.com/canada/politics/advocacy.htm

America's Union Movement
www.aflcio.org

Center for Responsive Politics
www.opensecrets.org

Center For Science In The Public Interest
www.cspinet.org/integrity/database.html

Common Cause - Soft Money Laundromat
www.commoncause.org/laundromat/

Consumers Guide: Advocacy Groups
www.caslon.com.au/consumersguide4.htm

CorpWatch.org
www.corpwatch.org

CSRwire.com -- Corporate Social Responsibility Newswire
http://csrwire.com/search.cgi

EFFweb - The Electronic Frontier Foundation
www.eff.org

Environmental Background Information Center
www.ebic.org

Environmental Working Group | Public Interest Watchdog
www.ewg.org

Executive PayWatch
www.aflcio.org/corporateamerica/paywatch

FACSNET: Reporter's Cardfile
www.facsnet.org/sources/newssources

Facts @ Your Fingertips - Internet Research Manual for AFSCME Activists - Index
www.afscme.org/wrkplace/ftipstc.htm

Follow The Money
www.followthemoney.org

Friends of the Earth
www.foe.org

Greenpeace USA
www.greenpeaceusa.org

Links to the world - special interest groups
www.leg.state.mn.us/lrl/links/special.asp

Marin Institute Alcohol Industry & Policy Database
www.marininstitute.org

Multinational Monitor Online
http://multinationalmonitor.org

OMB Watch - Home
www.ombwatch.org

Political Advocacy Groups
www.csuchico.edu/~kcfount

PoliticalMoneyLine
www.tray.com/fecinfo/

Political Science Resources: United States Politics
www.lib.umich.edu/govdocs/psref.html

Right-To-Know Network
www.rtk.net

RTK NET Environmental Databases
www.rtk.net/docketsearch.html

Scorecard
www.scorecard.org

United For A Fair Economy
www.ufenet.org/press/2003/EE2003_pr.html

Associations

Trade associations may provide a wealth of material on the industry they represent.
Searching some of the sites below may point to associations that you may not have identified.

Associations Canada
www.mmltd.com/Directories/Associations.htm

AcqWeb's Directory of Associations & Organizations
www.library.vanderbilt.edu:80/law/acqs/assn.html

AeroWorldNet - Aviation & Aerospace Associations
www.aeroworldnet.com/indass.htm

American Petroleum Institute
www.api.org

American Society for Testing and Materials (ASTM)
www.astm.org

American Society of Assn Executives Database
http://info.asaenet.org/gateway/OnlineAssocSlist.html

ASMENET: American Society of Mechanical Engineers
www.asme.org

Associationcentral.com
www.associationcentral.com

Association of Advertising Agencies
www.aaaa.org/inside/roster/default.asp

Association of Private Pension and Welfare Plans (APPWP)
www.appwp.org

Auto-Links TRADE PAGE - Associations
www.findlinks.com/autolinks.html#asns

Bevier Engineering Library: Associations, Societies & Organizations
www.library.pitt.edu/subject_guides/engineering/#assoc

Canopedia
www.canadopedia.com/english-canada/society/associations

Clay.net Professional Associations
www.clay.net/profass.html

Directory of Associations
www.marketingsource.com/associations/

International Organization / NGO Websites
www.uia.org/website.htm

Internet Public Library: Associations on the Net (AON)
www.ipl.org/div/aon

MedBioWorld - Medical journals and associations and biology resources
www.sciencekomm.at/

PhRMA (Pharmaceutical Research & Mfr. of America)
www.phrma.org

Yahoo! Business & Economy: Organizations: Professional
www.yahoo.com/economy/organizations/professional

Yahoo! Business & Economy: Organizations: Trade Associations
http://dir.yahoo.com/Business_and_Economy/Organizations/

Bookstores

Search these sites to identify books written about your industry or your competitors. You can also use their search engines to identify the newest CI books.

Amazon.com
www.amazon.com

Barnesandnoble.com
www.barnesandnoble.com

Powell's Bookstore-used, new, and out of print books
www.powells.com

Broadcast Monitors

Track new products, competitors' ad campaigns or coverage of media companies, or obtain transcripts of specific broadcasts.

Burrelle's Transcritps and Tapes
www.burrellesluce.com/tt/ttothers.html

CBS Main Menu: Transcripts
www.burrelles.com/transcripts/cbs/cbs.htm

Elibrary
www.eLibrary.com

NewsLibrary- News Wires Search
http://nl.newsbank.com/nlsite/region_pgs/newswire.htm

Transcription Company
www.transcripts.net

Vanderbilt Television News Archive
http://tvnews.vanderbilt.edu

Video Monitoring Services of America LP (VMS)
www.vidmon.com

Business Classification Systems

Use these systems to identify competitors by searching for companies that are classified under the same number that your company uses to describe what it does. NAICS is the newer of the two system, and is more specific. The first bookmark on this list cross references the two systems.

1987 SIC Correspondence Tables
www.census.gov/epcd/www/naicstab.htm

Download NAICS and SIC tables
www.census.gov/epcd/www/naicstab.htm#download

NAICS Association
www.naics.com

NAICS 2002
www.census.gov/epcd/naics02/naicod02.htm

NAICS 2007
www.census.gov/epcd/naics07/index.html

North American Industry Classification System (NAICS)
www.census.gov/epcd/www/naics.html

OSHA: Standard Industrial Classification Search
www.osha.gov/oshstats/sicser.html

Business Sites

Government Bids

Government contracts can be a lucrative source of revenue for your company. The sites mentioned below may be useful in learning about the process or in actually helping to obtain contracts.

B2G Market: Gateway to Government Business
www.bidmain.com

Government & Contract Bids from BidNet
www.bidnet.com

GovernmentBids.com
www.governmentbids.com

Top 100 Federal Prime Contractors -- 2003
www.washingtontechnology.com/top-100/2003

Compilations & Reviews

Use these sites to identify other sites of interest in your research.

BRINT - Business Research, Management Research & Information Technology Research
www.brint.com/interest.html

BUBL LINK: Browse by Subject
www.bubl.ac.uk/link/subjects

Business.com - Business Search Engine and Business Directory for Business
www.business.com/index.asp?partner=FT

Direct Search: Search Tools & Directories
www.freepint.com/gary/direct.htm

ENTERWeb The Enterprise Development Website
www.enterweb.org

Global Business Centre
www.euromktg.com/gbc

Hieros Gamos: The Comprehensive Law & Government Site
www.hg.org/guides.html

The Biz
www.thebiz.co.uk

Virtual International Business & Economic Sources (VIBES)
http://library.uncc.edu/display/?dept=reference&format=open&page=68

Web Guide
www.business2.com/webguide/0,,,00.html

Business Sites - General

These general business sites will provide you with an overview of what is out there and how it is generally categorized. non-U.S. sites are included. Some of these sites are updated frequently, and are worth repeat visits to keep on top of what new sites are out there.

BUBL LINK: Business
http://link.bubl.ac.uk/business

BusinessGateway (Canada)
http://businessgateway.gc.ca/en/hi/

Business in Latin America - LANIC
http://lanic.utexas.edu/la/region/business

Canada Business Service Centres - Centres de services aux entreprises du Canada - Bie
www.cbsc.org

CEOExpress_ Business portal for executives created by a CEO
www.ceoexpress.com/default.asp

Economist Intelligence Unit
www.eiu.com

EuroInfoPool - Welcome
www.euroinfopool.com/debi/index.jsp

Global Business Centre
www.euromktg.com/gbc

Hoover's Online - The Business Information Authority
http://hoovers.com/free

International Business Guide: Worldclass Supersite
http://web.idirect.com/~tiger/supersit.htm

International Business Resources on the WWW
http://ciber.bus.msu.edu/busres.htm

Prices's List of Lists
www.specialissues.com/lol/

Strategis - Canada's Business and Consumer Site
http://strategis.ic.gc.ca/cgi-bin/allsites/motd/motDspl.pl?lang=e&link=/engdoc/main.html

Valuation Information
www.valuationinformation.com

ValuationResources.Com - Business Valuation Resources
www.valuationresources.com

Webliography: A Guide to Internet Resources
www.lib.lsu.edu/weblio.html#Business

Yahoo! Business and Economy; Business to Business; Government
http://dir.yahoo.com/Business_and_Economy/Business_to_Business/Government/

Company Information

How-To Sites

Researching an Industry or Specific Company
www.virtualpet.com/industry/howto/search.htm

Researching Companies on the Internet - A Tutorial
www.learnwebskills.com/company/index.html

Industry-specific - Worldwide

Keep up with the players in worldwide markets by looking for sites like these. Many of the sites contain searchable databases or company profiles that may be especially useful for finding and learning about privately held companies. If your competition happens to be a multi-national corporation, locate addresses of foreign offices using some of the country-specific files.

Altis (Hospitality, Leisure, Sport and Tourism)
www.altis.ac.uk

AeroWorldNet (Aerospace Companies)
www.aeroworldnet.com/companie.htm

Banks in China
www.reserve-bank.com/cnbank.htm

Biotech Companies in Germany
www.i-s-b.net/firmen/sme.htm

CorpTech Database of 50,000 U.S. Technology Companies
www.corptech.com

Directory of Swiss Banks
www.swconsult.ch/cgi-bin/banklist.pl

Germany – Energy Companies
http://dir.yahoo.com/Regional/Countries/Germany/Business_and_Ec
onomy/Business_to_Business/Energy/

Industry Medicinal Chemistry Company Sites
www.phc.vcu.edu/CoolSites/link/industrylinks.html

NewsOnJapan.com – Banks
http://newsonjapan.com/html/linkbase/Business/Financial/Banks/i
ndex.shtml

List of Banks in Nigeria
www.wabao.org/waba/print/pr_bank_nigeria.html

Maurice Railroad Equipment Industry List (MREIL)
http://mercurio.iet.unipi.it/misc/industry.htm

PharmWeb Yellow Pages
www.pharmweb.net/pwmirror/pwb/detail/pharmwebb_pc.html

PR Mania #01 (Advertising Organizations and Agencies Worldwide)
www.geocities.com/MadisonAvenue/1020/adworld.htm

Solar Electric Power Association
www.solarelectricpower.org/about/pv_industry.cfm

Virtual Library: Pharmacy Page
www.pharmacy.org/company.html

Tennessee High Tech Company Database
www.state.tn.us/ecd/hightech.htm

Who Makes Machinery in Germany
www.vdma.com/vdma_root/www_vdma_com

Non-U.S. Public Company Filings

Filings made by public companies are available in some countries. These provide valuable intelligence, but the amount will vary from country to country.

ABR Public
http://abr.business.gov.au/

Advice For Investors (Canada)
www.fin-info.com

Australian Securities & Investments Commission
www.asic.gov.au

Canada – New Public Company Filings
www.sedar.com/new_docs/new_en.htm

Carlson Online Services Inc (Canada)
www.fin-info.com/index.html#basicsearch

Cerved S.p.A. - Italian Companies (In Italian)
www.cerved.com/xportal/home-eng.jsp

Companies House (UK)
http://ws2info.companieshouse.gov.uk/info/

Companies Registration Office (Ireland)
www.cro.ie/

Corporate Direct (Japan)
www.c-direct.ne.jp/english/de/de-index.asp

Global Register: New Zealand Companies
www.globalregister.co.nz/nzcomp.htm

Companies and Public Record Office – South Africa
www.cipro.co.za/Home/

Non-U.S. Public / Private

These sites may refer to public or privately held companies outside the U.S. Many can be searched by company name. Also consider the venture capital information websites, listed under the Financial Information heading below.

AFRICA

MBendi Profile - Companies of Africa - Index
www.mbendi.co.za/coaf.htm

Africa and The Middle East Company Profiles
www.dialog1.com/business_intelligence/forms/company_africa_mideast.shtml

ASIA/PACIFIC

ABIX (Australian Industries, Companies, News)
www.abix.com.au

Indian Company Research
www.indiainfoline.com/comp

Indonesia Net Exchange
www.indoexchange.com

InfoCamere (In Italian)
www.infocamere.it

Irasia.com (Asia Pacific, UK)
www.irasia.com/listco/

Japan Company Records
http://japanfinancials.com

Orient Business Express (ASIA)
www.accessasia.com/cgi-win/imagemap.exe/newmap?152,212

EUROPE

BizEurope.com (Germany)
www.bizeurope.com/bsr/country/germany.htm

CAROL (UK)
www.carolworld.com/creditReports.htm

Companies in Bulgaria
www.eunet.bg/catalog/index.html

Corporate Reports Ltd (UK)
www.corpreports.co.uk

European Business Register - EBR
www.ebr.org

FreePint UK Company Research Gateway
www.freepint.com/icc

French Companies - DAFSA (In French)
www.dafsa.fr/

Hemscott - UK & European companies
www.hemscott.net

Hoover's Online UK
www.hoovers.com/global/uk/

Hoppenstedt (Germany)
www.hoppenstedt.com

H u g i n Online (Press releases on European companies)
www.huginonline.com

Kobmanstanden (Denmark)
www.kob.dk/english

Kompass Ireland - Company Register
www.kompass.ie

Kompass
http://www3.kompass.com/kinl/index.html

Liquidations Search, Insolvency (UK)
www.insolvency.co.uk/liq/liqfind.htm

Malta Registry of Companies
http://registry.mfsc.com.mt/

Perfect Information (UK)
www.perfectinfo.com

RUSTOCKS.com_Home
www.rustocks.com

SKATE: Online Company Data (Russia)
www.rustocks.com/index.phtml/rcg/

Yell.com Online business directory from Yellow Pages in the UK
http://search.yell.com/search/DoSearch

NORTH AMERICA

Canadian Corporate Information
www.corporateinformation.com/ctryind.asp?ctry_cod=124

Canada's Power Book
www.globeinvestor.com/series/top1000/

Canadian Company Capabilities
http://strategis.ic.gc.ca/sc_coinf/ccc/engdoc/homepage.html

Company Directories - The Strategis Guide to Canadian and Intl. Companies
http://strategis.ic.gc.ca/sc_coinf/engdoc/homepage.html?categor
ies=e_com

Competition Bureau - Canada
http://strategis.ic.gc.ca/SSG/cp01120e.html

Corporations Canada
http://strategis.ic.gc.ca/cgi-
bin/sc_mrksv/corpdir/dataOnline/corpns_se?h_lang=e

Federal Corporation Search – Canada
http://strategis.ic.gc.ca/epic/internet/incd-
dgc.nsf/en/h_cs01424e.html

FPInfomart.ca (Canada)
www.infomart.ca

Mexican Corporate Information (Choose from country list)
www.corporateinformation.com

Teikoku Databank America Inc
www.teikoku.com

Top 300 Private Companies (Canada)
www.globeinvestor.com/series/top1000/tables/private/2003/?ga

WORLDWIDE

1Jump® - The Ultimate Company Research & Business Information Tool
www.1jump.com/whatpeoples.html

2003 Forbes International 500
www.forbes.com/2003/07/07/internationaland.html

CorporateInformation.com (search by country)
www.corporateinformation.com

Scannery
www.thescannery.com

Thomas Global Register - Welcome to the Thomas Global Register
www.aernet.com

Worldscope [OCLC]
www.oclc.org/support/documentation/firstsearch/databases/dbdetails/details/Worldscope.htm

Wright Research Center: Country List Page (Multiple Countries)
www.wisi.com/ramainnew.htm

U.S. Company Profiles - Public/Private

These sites have been identified as containing searchable databases or lists of company profiles. The quality and quantity of information will vary from site to site, so it will be important to obtain several profiles on the companies that are searched, and to compare their contents. Some sites are updated more frequently than are others. Be sure to read the fine print regarding the source of the information, as well.

Bizresearch
www.bizresearch.com/company-research.htm

Corporate Financials Online
www.cfonews.com

Corporate Information
www.corporateinformation.com

Corporate Library
thecorporatelibrary.com

Dun & Bradstreet Small Business Solutions
http://smallbusiness.dnb.com/

Dun & Bradstreet Reports
www.dnb.com

Fortune 500 Official Websites
http://officialsearch.com/cgi-bin/cat.cgi?qs=f500

Hoover's Company Capsules
www.nytimes.com/partners/quote/hoovers.html

Hoover's Online
www.hoovers.com

NASDAQ-100 Index
    www.nasdaq.com/asp/nasdaq100_activity.stm

National Association of Investors Corporation
    http://store.yahoo.com/betterinvesting/23303.html

Individual.com NewsPage - Companies: Company Lookup
    http://companies.newspage.com/selectCompanies.php

OneSource Information Services
    www.onesource.com

Platt's on the Internet
    www.platts.com

Quicken Brokerage - Profile
    www.quicken.com/investments/snapshot/?symbol

Standard & Poor's Compustat
    www.compustat.com/www/db/na_descr.html

TechWeb Finance - Quotes & Data
    www.techweb.com/wire/finance/quotes

The PRS Group
    www.prsgroup.com

SharkRepellent.net - Home
    www.sharkrepellent.net

Thomas Register of American Manufacturers
    www.thomasregister.com/index.html

VaultReports.Com
    www.vaultreports.com

U.S. Private Companies

These are the most difficult types of companies to research. In addition to sites like those listed below, remember to search public records and local or regional newspapers by company name. One of the best spots in cyberspace for collective sources of information on private companies is the Corporation Information site. The Venture Capital sites, listed under financial information sites, also cover private companies.

Denver Business Journal - Private Companies
    www.amcity.com/denver/stories/041398/list.html

Forbes: The 500 Top Private Companies, 2003
    www.forbes.com/maserati/privates2003/privateland.html

Greater Washington: Top Private Companies
    www.washingtonpost.com/wp-dyn/business/localbusiness/top200/2003/topprivate/

Los Angeles Business Journal – Private Companies
    www.toplist.com/bol2000/LAX/index.asp?pg=list&category_id=29&list_id=64

New York City Top Private Companies
    www.newsday.com/business/local/longisland/ny-biz-nytop100private,0,4776564.story

Top Triad Private Companies
www.greensboro.com/97top50/private.htm

U.S. COMPANIES – TOP COMPANIES LISTS

Forbes.com - 200 Best Small Companies
www.forbes.com/lists/2003/10/08/200bestland.html

Forbes.com Lists
www.forbes.com/lists/

Forbes.com - America's Best Big Companies
www.forbes.com/platinum400/

Fortune 500
www.fortune.com/fortune/fortune500/1,16741,,00.html

Fortune.com - All Fortune Lists
www.fortune.com/fortune/alllists

Fortune.com - Best Companies to Work For
www.fortune.com/fortune/bestcompanies/

Fortune.com - Most Admired
www.fortune.com/fortune/mostadmired/

Global 500: 2003 List
http://pathfinder.com/fortune/global500/index.html

Globe 100 Top Technology Companies (Boston)
www.boston.com/globe/business/packages/globe_100/2003/charts/tech.htm

Inc 500
www.inc.com/500

NCB Co-op 100 – Top Co-ops in the U.S.
www.co-op100.coop/coop100/index.htm

Newsday.com - Long Island Top 100 Public Companies 2003
www.newsday.com/ny-biz-litop100public,0,1074779.story

Newsday.com - New York City Top Public Companies 2003
www.newsday.com/ny-biz-nytop100public,0,1720955.story

Republic 100 database (Arizona Companies)
www.azcentral.com/business/rep100/1005aboutthedb.html

Software Magazine - 2003 Software 500
www.softwaremag.com/L.cfm?Doc=2003-12/2003-12software500

Technology Fast 500 - Fast 50
www.public.deloitte.com/fast500/default.asp?type=home

The Top500 of All Countries of Europe
www.top500.de

VARBusiness 500 Awards
www.varbusiness.com/sections/main/2003vb500.asp

U.S. Public Companies - Company Filings

Even though everyone says that public companies are the "easy ones" to research, it's nice to have a handy collection of sites for filings by public companies. Both government and commercial sources are included here. To collect annual reports on competitors without ordering directly, consider one or more of the Annual Report services listed below. Remember that not all filings are required to be made electronically, so checking EDGAR alone may not be sufficient when researching company filings.

Annual Reports

Annual Report Gallery
www.reportgallery.com/index.htm

Annual Reports Library
www.zpub.com/sf/arl

Annual Reports & Accounts from Corporate Reports
www.corpreports.co.uk/

Barron's Annual Report Service
http://barronsonline.ar.wilink.com/asp/BAR5_search_ENG.asp

Free Online Annual Reports - AnnualReportService.com
www.annualreportservice.com

Historic Corporate Annual Reports
http://oldsite.library.upenn.edu/etext/collections/lippincott/

Public Register's Annual Report Service (PRARS) - NASDAQ, NYSE, AMEX, OTC
www.prars.com

Vcall - A Service of PrecisionIR
http://vcall.ar.wilink.com/asp/A502_search_ENG.asp?mkt_code=goo
gadword

Wall Street Journal: Annual Reports Service
http://info.wsj.com/products/dswsjars.html

W I Link
www.wilink.com/wil/our_services/order_reports.stm

Miscellaneous Reports

10-K Wizard
www.10kwizard.com

aRMadillo Company Database
www.rmonline.com/pr2.htm

Bureau van Dijk Electronic Publishing
www.bvdep.com

Company Annual Reports Online (CAROL) - UK
www.carol.co.uk

Directory of OTC Bulletin Board Companies
www.otcbb.com/asp/SP_Search.asp

Standard & Poor's Market Access Company Sponsored Descriptions
www.proinvestor.com/pub/maccess/index.html

EDGAR
www.sec.gov/edgar.shtml

EdgarIQ_ New SEC Research Tool
www.edgariq.com

EdgarScan
http://edgarscan.pwcglobal.com/recruit/other.html

EDGAR Online
www.sec.gov/edgar.shtml

EDGAR-Online the Source for Today's SEC Filings
www.edgar-online.com/bin/esearch

FreeEDGAR.com: Companies - Today's filings (free registration required)
www.freeedgar.com/search/TodaysFilings.asp?

Global Securities Information
www.gsionline.com

McGregor BFA (South Africa Companies)
www.mcgbfa.com

Moody's Investors Service
www.moodys.com

SEC EDGAR Historical Archives
www.sec.gov/cgi-bin/srch-edgar

SEC Info - EDGAR online database
www.secinfo.com

U.S. Regional Sites

Some regional sites also are included under other headings in this list.

Chicago Fact Book: Business
www.ci.chi.il.us/PlanAndDevelop/ChgoFacts/Business.html

D-FW Top 200
www.dallasnews.com/cgi-bin/2003/dfwtop200.cgi

Globe 100 Top Technology Companies (Boston)
www.boston.com/globe/business/packages/globe_100/2003/charts/tech.htm

Long Island Top 100 Private Companies 2003
www.newsday.com/business/local/longisland/ny-biz-litop100private,0,4130388.story

New Jersey Insider
www.njinsider.com/largestemployers01.htm

Oregon Business Magazine
www.mediamerica.net/obm_100_best_companies.php

Thomas Regional Directory
www.thomasregional.com

Top 100 Most Influential People in the Recruiting Industry
www.recruiter.com/magazineonline/top100intro.cfm

The Top500 of All Countries of Europe
www.top500.de

US Corporate Information: (choose individual states in U.S.)
www.corporateinformation.com

Washington Top 100 Companies
www.washingtontechnology.com/top-100/2003/

Competitive Intelligence Sites

These sites are a combination of web pages of CI consulting companies and sites that address the concept of CI. There is overlap, so they have been combined into one list. At the Fuld site, pay particular attention to the Internet Intelligence Index.

Brain Mass Professional
www.brainmasspro.com/research.php

Cipher Systems
www.cipher-sys.com

Competia - Library
www.competia.com/library/index.html

Competitive Intelligence Handbook
www.combsinc.com/handbook.htm

Links Competitive Intelligence
www.synectservices.com/links_competitive_intelligence.htm

Competitive Intelligence Resource Index
www.bidigital.com/ci/Companies/Information/Information_Services

Competitive Intelligence Sources On the Internet
http://web.syr.edu/~jryan/infopro/intell.html

Fuld & Company Inc: Competitive Intelligence Guide
www.fuld.com

Second Sight Internet Intelligence LLC
www.2s2i.com

Society of Competitive Intelligence Professionals (SCIP)
www.scip.org

Sun Tzu & the Art of Business
www.suntzu1.com

The Benchmarking Exchange (TBE)
www.benchmarking.org

Conferences/Trade Shows

LOCATING/IDENTIFYING

Conferences and trade shows can be useful sources of business intelligence for different reasons, depending upon your company's interests. As mentioned in earlier chapters, these sources are useful for finding experts, identifying topics of competitors' speakers, or learning about competitors' new products.

All Conferences.com
www.allconferences.com

Center for Business Intelligence
www.cbinet.com

EventSeeker The World Events Calendar
http://w3.eventseeker.com

Export.gov
www.export.gov/tradeevents.html

InterDok – Meetings
www.interdok.com/mind/

Mbendi – African Conferences and Exhibitions
www.mbendi.co.za/a_sndmsg/event_srch.asp?P=0&C=1

TechWeb Tech Calendar
www.techweb.com/calendar/

Trade Shows and Special Events
www.funindustries.com/trade-shows.htm

Trade Show News Network (TSNN)
www.tsnn.com

PROCEEDINGS

*Conference proceedings are acknowledged by top researchers to be an excellent source for learning what's going on in the scientific and business communities. Here people deliver papers about what they've been doing, thinking about, or testing back at their shop. Within conference proceedings you may unearth the earliest hints about a competitor's new products or possible plans, though a bit of analysis and interpretation may be required. For example, **your** scientists might be the best people in the organization to understand what **their** scientists are talking about. The same holds true for sales and marketing, personnel, or other areas of the organization. Several of the large online vendors offer files dedicated to this material, but these websites may also be of interest.*

Conference Papers Index
www.csa.com/csa/ids/ids-main.shtml

Inside Conferences - Inside Web
www.bl.uk/services/current/inside.html

InterDok – Proceedings
www.interdok.com/html/dopp.cfm

Country/World Regional Sites

Search these websites when interested in business intelligence outside of the U.S.
Many of them contain links to various general topics, such as finance, laws, industries, etc.
in the specific country or region. Government sources have been included.

AFRICA

Centre for Research into Economics and Finance in Southern Africa
www.finanz-adressen.de/afrika/ZA-adr-lse.html

COMESA
www.comesa.int/

Country Business Intelligence Reports
http://worldofinformation.safeshopper.com/10/cat10.htm?547

Mbendi: Information for Africa
http://mbendi.co.za

South African Resources
www.undp.org.za/misc/resources.html

ASIA

Asia
www.meatnpotatoes.com/asia.html

Asia Inc Online
www.asia-inc.com

Asia Internet Resources
www.d230.org/stagg/LiskaLinks/asia.htm

Asia Pacific Chambers of Commerce
www.cacci.org.tw/

Asian Business Watch
www.asianbusinesswatch.com/LINKS.html

Asian Sources Online
www.asiansources.com

Asian Studies WWW VL
http://coombs.anu.edu.au/WWWVL-AsianStudies.html

Asia-Pacific Information
http://sunsite.sut.ac.jp/asia

Companies Office
www.companies.govt.nz/pls/web/dbssiten.main

Companies Registry
www.info.gov.hk/cr/

Indobiz.com (Indonesia)
www.indobiz.com/

Ministry of Commerce, Cambodia
www.moc.gov.kh/

Ministry of Domestic Trade and Consumer Affairs - Malaysia
www.kpdnhq.gov.my/homepage/english/mainE.html

Sources for Asia-Pacific business research
www.asia-pacific.com/links.htm#links

Southeast Asian Studies WWW Virtual Library
www.iias.nl/wwwvl/southeast.html

Thailand Page.com
www.thailandpage.com

CHINA

China Council For The Promotion of International Trade
www.ccpit.org/servlet/org.servlet.en.OrgWebEn?actionType=Home&OrgId=1

China Information
http://sunsite.sut.ac.jp/asia/china

ChinaBig Yellow Pages
www.chinabig.com/en/srch/

ChinaOnline
www.chinaonline.com

Finding News About China
http://chinanews.bfn.org

JAPAN

Bridge to Japan
www.daiwa-foundation.org.uk

Business In Japan - General Information
www.gpb.org/peachstar/irasshai/culwww/bs1.htm

Japan - General Information
http://SunSITE.sut.ac.jp/asia/japan/general

Japan in Figures 2004
www.stat.go.jp/english/data/figures/

Japan Information - Government Sites
http://SunSITE.sut.ac.jp/asia/japan/gov

Japanese Public Opinion
www.ropercenter.uconn.edu/JPOLL/home.html

EUROPE

Business Czech.cz
www.czech.cz

CCTA Government Information Service UK)
www.open.gov.uk

Company Registrations Around the World
www.hrasg.ch/eng/welt-e.htm

Europe – Russia and Caucasus
www.meatnpotatoes.com/europe.html

Lursoft (Latvia)
www.lursoft.lv/

Registro Mercantil Central – Spain
www.rmc.es/

RUSSIA

American Chamber of Commerce in Russia
www.amcham.ru

Governments on the WWW: Russian Federation
www.gksoft.com/govt/en/ru.html

Investment Guide to Russia
www.fipc.ru/fipc

Russian Internet
www.neystadt.org/russia

Russian Legal Server
www.friends-partners.org/partners/fplegal/main.html

The List of Russian Web Servers – Weblist
http://weblist.ru

LATIN AMERICA

Anguilla Online
www.anguillafsc.com/indexm.html

Business in Latin America - LANIC
http://lanic.utexas.edu/la/region/business

Central American Report
www.inforpressca.com/CAR/

Inter-American Understanding
http://interamerican-understanding.freewebspace.com

Orientation Latin America & the Carribean
www.meatnpotatoes.com/southamerica.html

WWW Virtual Library: Latin American Studies
http://lanic.utexas.edu/las.html

MIDDLE EAST

ArabNet - The Resource for the Arab World in the Middle East and North Africa
www.arab.net

Association for International Business (AIB): Middle Eastern Links
http://earthone.com/middleast.html

Middle East Studies Resources
www.columbia.edu/cu/libraries/indiv/area/MiddleEast

MULTI-COUNTRY

2003 World Factbook
www.odci.gov/cia/publications/factbook/index.html

Africa and Offshore Islands
www.meatnpotatoes.com/africa.html

Australia and Pacific Islands
www.meatnpotatoes.com/australia.html

Australian Department of Foreign Affairs & Trade
www.dfat.gov.au

BIOME: Health and Life Sciences
http://biome.ac.uk/

Economist Intelligence Unit
www.eiu.com

Foreign & Commonwealth Office (Britain)
www.fco.gov.uk

Library of Congress / Federal Research Div. / Country Studies / Area Handbook Series
http://lcweb2.loc.gov/frd/cs/cshome.html

North America and Carribbean
www.meatnpotatoes.com/northamerica.html

Pan-American Health Organization
www.paho.org/default.htm

Travel Health Online: Destination Information
https://www.tripprep.com

US State Department - Services - Background Notes
www.state.gov/r/pa/ei/bgn/

USPTO Upcoming Opportunities - Information Technology
www.uspto.gov/web/offices/ac/comp/proc/upopp.htm

CANADA

Agriculture & Agri-Food Canada's Electronic Information Service (ACEIS)
www.agr.ca

BC OnLine - Access to Government Information
www.bconline.gov.bc.ca

Canadian Council of Ministers of the Environment
www.ccme.ca/

Canadian Industry Statistics
http://strategis.ic.gc.ca/sc_ecnmy/sio/homepage.html

Canadopedia _ Directory Search Engine of Canada
www.canadopedia.com/

CANUTEC – The Canadian Transport Emergency Centre
www.tc.gc.ca/canutec

Corporations Database Online (Canada)
http://strategis.ic.gc.ca/cgi-
bin/sc_mrksv/corpdir/dataOnline/corpns_se

Current Economic Conditions
http://strategis.ic.gc.ca/sc_ecnmy/engdoc/homepage.html?categor
ies=e_eco

Departments and Agencies
http://canada.gc.ca/depts/major/depind_e.html

Environment Canada's Green Lane
www.ec.gc.ca/envhome.html

National Energy Board
www.neb.gc.ca

Natural Resources Canada
www.nrcan-rncan.gc.ca/inter/index.html

Nova Scotia (Canada) Procurement Site
http://198.166.215.5/finance/tour

Public Works and Government Services Canada
http://csi.contractscanada.gc.ca/csi/prod/en/applctrl.cfm?.

Strategis - Canada's Business Information Site
http://strategis.ic.gc.ca/engdoc/main.html

Technical Standards & Safety Authority
www.tssa.org

Database Vendors

*Error! Bookmark not defined.The major commercial online vendors' websites have been
collected here, along with some more recent entries into this field. If you don't subscribe to a
commercial service, look for access through a vendor in the "Pay By Credit Card" section.
Also check to see if the subscription-based vendors have added credit card access recently.*

PAY BY CREDIT CARD
BizAdvantage
www.bizadvantage.com

CorpTech Database of 45,000 U.S. Technology Companies
www.corptech.com

Dialog
www.dialog.com

Environmental Data Resources
www.edrnet.com

Factiva
www.factiva.com

HGLexis
www.hg.org/hglexis.html

IDS home page
www.csa.com/csa/ids/ids-main.shtml

KnowX | Home
www.knowx.com

Multex: Institutional Investment Research, Earnings and Equity Reports
www.multex.com

SkyMinder - Worldwide Business Information
www.skyminder.com

WestDoc
http://creditcard.westlaw.com

SUBSCRIPTION-BASED

Alacra
www.alacra.com/alacra/index.htm

Asia Pulse
www.asiapulse.com

Companies House
www.companieshouse.gov.uk/

DataStar
www.datastarweb.com

Delphion
www.delphion.com

Dialog
www.dialog.com

Equifax
www.equifax.com

Factiva
www.factiva.com

GEM (EINS)
www.eins.org

Experian Uniform Commercial Code sample report
www.experian.com/product/pubrec/uccsample.html

H.W. Wilson Co.
www.hwwilson.com

Harris Info Online
www.HARRISinfoonline.com

Knowledge Express
www.knowledgeexpress.com

LEXISNEXIS
www.nexis.com/research

Manning & Napier
www.mnis.com

Nerac
www.nerac.com

NTIS Online Subscriptions
www.ntis.gov

Questel-Orbit
www.questel.orbit.com

Teikoku Databank America Inc
www.teikoku.com

Thomson/Gale
www.gale.com

Thomson Research
http://research.thomsonib.com

Thomson & Thomson
www.thomson-thomson.com

Westlaw
www.westlaw.com

Demographics

Data contained in some of these sites can be invaluable to your company's Sales and Marketing department. For new businesses, this data will be needed in the company's business plan. There is some duplication of information among the sites, but some of them are often quite busy. If that is the case, try another URL.

Census Data – Canada
http://www12.statcan.ca/english/census01/datafinder/update.cfm

Census Data – India
www.censusindia.net/cendat/

Census Online: Links to Online Census Records (Canada, U.K., U.S.)
www.census-online.com/links/

CPS – Current Population Study
www.bls.census.gov/cps/cpsmain.htm

Demographic Profiles
http://censtats.census.gov/pub/Profiles.shtml

Population Index
http://popindex.princeton.edu

State & County QuickFacts
http://quickfacts.census.gov/qfd/

U.S. Census Bureau
www.census.gov

U.S. Census Bureau: County Business Patterns
www.census.gov/epcd/cbp/view/cbpview.html

U.S. Census Bureau Subjects Index
www.census.gov/main/www/subjects.html

U.S. Demography
www.ciesin.org/datasets/us-demog/us-demog-home.html

Directories

Some of these links point to membership lists for certain organizations. Search those to identify directories in an industry or topic of interest. Still others list companies or organizations that can be contacted directly.

American Economic Association
www.eco.utexas.edu/AEA/

American Hospital Directory (AHD) Guest Services
www.ahd.com

American Institute of Architects (AIA)
http://dir.yahoo.com/Arts/Design_Arts/Architecture/Organization
s/Professional/American_Institute_of_Architects__AIA_/

ASAE Gaateway to Associations Online
http://info.asaenet.org/gateway/OnlineAssocSlist.html

Askalix - online business directory (Europe)
www.askalix.com/uk/

Australian Business Directory
www.aus-biz.com.au/

Business Directories and Search Engines
www.laisha.com/business.html

Canadian Business Map - Home Page
http://commercecan.ic.gc.ca/scdt/bizmap/interface2.nsf/engdocBa
sic/0.html

CanadaOne
www.canadaone.com/business

CorpTech Database of 50,000 U.S. Technology Companies
www.corptech.com

Direct Search: Search Tools & Directories
www.freepint.com/gary/direct.htm

Directory of Agents and Brokers on the Internet
www.iiin.com/iiinagents.html

Directory of Professional and Trade Associations and Non-Profit Organizations
www.marketingsource.com/associations/

Europages, European business directory yellow pages
www.europages.com/home-en.html

Find: Financial Information Net Directory
www.find.co.uk

Gebbie Press PR Media Directory - Newspapers Radio TV Magazines PR, faxes, email
www.gebbieinc.com/dailyint.htm

Online Directory of Translation and Interpreting Services
www.americantranslators.org/tsd_listings/

Public Relations Resources
www.business.com/search/rslt_default.asp?r4=t&query=public+rela
tions+resourc

RICH'S Directories
www.norcalcompanies.com

ThomWeb
www.infospace.com/uk.thomw/

Who's Who Sutter's International Red Series
www.whoswho-sutter.com

Economics/Economic Data

These links points to a wide variety of resources for gathering statistical economic data needed to make good business decisions. Some sites contain files for downloading into spreadsheets or other software for further manipulation or analysis. Government sites are included. Cost of living websites have been grouped under a separate heading for convenience.

2002 Economic Census Report
www.census.gov/econ/census02/

BUBL LINK: Economics
http://link.bubl.ac.uk/economics

Business Monitor International (BMI)
www.businessmonitor.com/about_bmi.htm

Census Bureau - Economic Clock
www.census.gov/econ/www/

Census Bureau - Economic Census
www.census.gov/econ/census02/

Economagic.com: Economic Time Series Page
www.economagic.com

Economic Indicators_ 2004
www.gpoaccess.gov/indicators/browse.html

Economic Report of the President, Statistical Tables
www.gpoaccess.gov/usbudget/fy01/erp.html

Economic Statistics Briefing Room (US)
www.whitehouse.gov/fsbr/esbr.html

Economics Gateway – SOSIG (UK)
www.sosig.ac.uk/economics/

Economy.com
www.economy.com/research/default.asp

Fed in Print – Index to Federal Reserve Economic Research
www.frbsf.org/publications/fedinprint/

Federal Reserve Bank of Atlanta
www.frbatlanta.org/econre.cfm

Federal Reserve Bank of Boston
www.bos.frb.org/economic/index.htm

Federal Reserve Bank of Cleveland
www.clevelandfed.org/Research/index.htm

Federal Reserve Bank of Kansas City
www.kc.frb.org/home/subwebs.cfm?subWeb=5

Federal Reserve Bank of Minneapolis
http://woodrow.mpls.frb.fed.us/research/data/

Federal Reserve Bank of New York
www.newyorkfed.org/research/index.html

Federal Reserve Bank of Philadelphia
www.phil.frb.org/econ/index.html

Federal Reserve Bank of Richmond
www.rich.frb.org/research/

Federal Reserve Bank of San Francisco: Pacific Basin Center
www.frbsf.org/economics/index.html

Federal Reserve Bank of St. Louis
http://research.stlouisfed.org/fred2/

Federal Reserve Head Office Search
http://132.200.33.161/nicSearch/servlet/NICServlet?REQ=MERGEDOU
T&MODE=SEARCH

FRB: Beige Book (Current Economic Conditions)
www.federalreserve.gov/fomc/beigebook/2003/default.htm

FRED: Federal Reserve Economic Data
www.stls.frb.org/fred

GDSourcing – Canadian Government Data
www.gdsourcing.ca/gds7.htm

Geospatial & Statistical Data Center
http://fisher.lib.virginia.edu/

Latin America Research Group - Atlanta Federal Reserve Bank
www.frbatlanta.org/econ_rd/larg/larg_index.cfm

National Bureau of Economic Research (NBER)
www.nber.org

Office of Trade & Economic Analysis
www.ita.doc.gov/tradestats

Regional Indicators: Asia Pacific Economic Cooperation
www.eia.doe.gov/emeu/cabs/apec.html

Sovereign Data
www.csfbdna.com/sov_index.html

STAT-USA
www.stat-usa.gov

Strategis: Canada's Business and Consumer Site
`http://strategis.ic.gc.ca/sc_ecnmy/engdoc/homepage.html?categor`
`ies=e_eco`

US Census Bureau Economic Programs
`www.census.gov/ftp/pub/econ/www`

WebEc - WWW Resources in Economics
`www.helsinki.fi/WebEc`

WWW Virtual Library: Economics
`www.hkkk.fi/EconVLib.html`

COST OF LIVING

ACCRA
`www.accra.org`

Bankrate.com
`www.bankrate.com/brm/movecalc.asp`

Canadian Relocation Systems
`www.relocatecanada.com`

Consumer Price Indexes
`www.bls.gov/cpi/home.htm`

National Compensation Survey
`www.bls.gov/ncs/home.htm`

Regional economics, Demographics & Statistics: The Dismal Scientist
`www.economy.com/dismal/`

Statistical Resources on the Web/Cost of Living
`www.lib.umich.edu/govdocs/steccpi.html`

The International Salary Calculator: Relocation, Cost of Living, Real Estate
`http://www2.homefair.com/calc/salcalc.html`

Employment/Recruitment/Want Ads

Search sites like these for job openings and job descriptions that may indicate a competitor's plans or for legal notices published in compliance with state or federal law. They also point to a company's planned actions.

AdQuest Classifieds - Currently Updating Ads
`www.adquest.com/sorry.asp`

BioSpace: Biotechnology and Pharmaceutical News, Jobs, Companies, Stocks
`www.biospace.com`

Canada WorkinfoNET
`www.workinfonet.ca/cwn/english/index.cfm?cat=`

CareerBuilder
`www.careerbuilder.com`

Career Resources @ JobBank USA
`www.jobbankusa.com`

CareerCast Job & Resume Search
www.careercast.com

TrueCareers
www.careercity.com

CareerMosaic
www.careermosaic.com

CareerPath.com
www.careerpath.com/res/owa/home.display_rblogin?

Employment In Europe 2003
http://europa.eu.int/comm/employment_social/news/2003/oct/eie2003_en.pdf

International Foundation of Employee Benefit Plans
www.ifebp.org

Internet Career Connection
http://iccweb.com

Materials Edge - Science, Engineering & Technology Recruitment, Jobs & News
www.materials-edge.net/html/index.php

Monster.com
www.monster.com

Monster.com
www.occ.com

Search Engines: Beaucoup! (Employment)
www.beaucoup.com/1empeng.html

Sherion
www.spherion.com/corporate/careercenter/home.jsp

Wanted Technologies, Inc.
www.wantedtechnologies.com

WetFeet.com ; Companies
www.wetfeet.com/research/companies.asp

Yahoo! Classifieds
http://classifieds.yahoo.com

Environment

Some of these sites, such as the EPA's Envirofacts, may be searched for competitors' names. Learn about "incidents" involving their companies. Environmental impact statements can be located using the Northwestern University's Transportation Library site.

BUBL LINK: Environment & Economics of Land & Energy
http://link.bubl.ac.uk/environment

Eldis - Electronic Development and Environment Information System
http://nt1.ids.ac.uk/eldis/eldwhat.htm

Enforcement and Compliance Docket
www.epa.gov/compliance/resources/policies/docket.html

ENDS Environment Daily - European environmental news
www.ends.co.uk/

Envirofacts Query Form
www.epa.gov/enviro/html/multisystem.html

Environmental Data Resources Inc.
www.edrnet.com

Environmental Reporting Clearinghouse - Corporate Environmental Reports by Sector
http://cei.sund.ac.uk/envrep/corprepS.htm

EPA Lawsuits Against Companies
http://cfpub.epa.gov/compliance/resources/cases/civil/.

EPA _ Science Inventory - Science Inventory
http://cfpub.epa.gov/si/

EPA Enforcement and Compliance History Online
www.epa.gov/echo/

National Environmental Data Index
www.nedi.gov

National Oceanic & Atmospheric Administration: Environmental Information Services
www.eis.noaa.gov

NUL Transportation Library Environmental Impact Statement Collection
www.library.northwestern.edu/transportation/searcheis.html

RTK NET Environmental Databases
www.rtknet.org/rtkdata.html

Scorecard Home
www.scorecard.org:9005/env-releases/

U.S. Environmental Protection Agency (EPA)
www.epa.gov

European Union

If your company is multi-national, you need to be familiar with the EU. These sites will get you started.

Chambers of Commerce of the EU Members in the U.S.
www.eurunion.org/infores/business/chambers.htm

Essential List of UK and World Government Related Sites
www.tagish.co.uk/links/

Euro Links
www.euro-sceptic.org

Europa
http://europa.eu.int

European Union Information Resources
www.eurunion.org/infores/home.htm

    Exeter Subject Tree - European Information
      www.ex.ac.uk/library/internet/eurostudies.html

Executive Compensation

Executive compensation may be of interest to those researching the CEO of a competitor company, or by your own Human Resources department to determine competitive compensation for a particular job title. This list contains both general and industry-specific websites.

    Big Bosses and Paychecks
      www.forbes.com/home/2002/04/25/ceos.html

    CEO Pay Slows, But Still Grows
      www.findarticles.com/cf_dls/m4070/2001_Dec/81114070/p1/article.jhtml

    eComp
      www.ecomponline.com

    Executive Compensation Guide For Investors
      www.sec.gov/investor/pubs/execomp0803.htm

    ExecutiveInsight
      www.equilar.com/executive.html

    Executive PayWatch □ The Ceo and You
      www.aflcio.org/corporateamerica/paywatch/

    Forbes.com_ What The Boss Makes
      www.forbes.com/2003/04/23/ceoland.html

    Startribune.com
      www.startribune.com/pay/

    Executive Excess Report
      www.ufenet.org/press/2003/EE2003_pr.html

    Top Five Data Services
      www.top5.com

    WSJ/Mercer CEO Compensation Survey
      www.mercerhr.com/summary.jhtml?idContent=1089750

Experts – Locating

    FACSNET: News Sources
      www.facsnet.org/sources/newssources/

    KnowThis.com
      www.knowthis.com/research/other/experts.htm

    NRC Expertise Database
      www.nrc.ca/expertise

    U.S. Census Bureau Contacts by Subjects: 2004
      www.census.gov/contacts/www/contacts.html

Financial Information Sites

The financial sites have been subdivided for convenience. Locate profiles, track competitors, etc. among foreign companies by visiting stock exchange sites.

GENERAL SITES

ADRs (American depositary receipts), global shares and foreign shares from J.P. Morgan
www.adr.com

Advisor Insight (S & P)
www.advisorinsight.com/ai/preview/index.htm

Fisher College of Business Financial Data Finder
http://fisher.osu.edu/fin/fdf/osudata.htm

Qualisteam Banking & Finance Portal
www.qualisteam.com/eng/catal.html

Moody's Investors Service
www.moodys.com/cust/default.asp

OSU Virtual Finance Library
www.cob.ohio-state.edu/dept/fin/overview.htm

Reuters Investor - Financial Research and Information
www.investor.reuters.com/Home.aspx

Reuters - Latest Financial News - Full News Coverage
www.reuters.com

Standard & Poor's Ratings Services
www.online.sp.co.gg/ratingsfinder/index.cfm

Worldwide Directory: The Best & Banking Resources on the 'Net
www.qualisteam.com/eng/catal.shtml

Yahoo! Finance
http://finance.yahoo.com

FINANCIAL MARKETS - WORLDWIDE

Amex: The American Stock Exchange
www.amex.com

Australian Stock Information
www.asx.com.au/

Bolsa - Madrid Stock Exchange
www.bolsamadrid.es

Bonds in the World
www.qualisteam.com/eng/obl.html

Bourse de Paris
www.bourse-de-paris.fr

CBS MarketWatch - Global Markets
http://cbs.marketwatch.com/news/default.asp?siteid=mktw

Center for Latin American Capital Markets: Exchanges
http://users.netrus.net/gmorles/

Chicago Board of Trade
www.cbot.com

Chicago Mercantile Exchange
www.cme.com

Informa Global Markets
www.informagm.com/gml/

London Stock Exchange
www.londonstockexchange.com

NASDAQ
www.nasdaq.com

New York Stock Exchange
www.nyse.com

RUSTOCKS.com
www.rustocks.com

Stock Exchanges Worldwide links
www.tdd.lt/slnews/Stock_Exchanges/Stock.Exchanges.htm

Tokyo Stock Exchange
www.tse.or.jp/english/index.shtml

WCSU Libraries: Finance and Investment
www.wcsu.edu/library/b_finance_investment.html#Stock

Yahoo! Finance - FTSE 100, Share Prices, Charts, News and more...
http://uk.finance.yahoo.com

IPOs

Be sure to search these sites to see if a company is planning to do an Initial Public Offering. Keep abreast of rumors and new developments by visiting them. IPOs can also be identified through S&P files and Investext; both are on several systems. Dialog and LexisNexis offer EdgarPlus Prospectus files Dialog offers the SDC Initial Public Offerings File and IPO Maven.

EDGAR Online IPO Express
www.edgar-online.com/ipoexpress

Hoover's Edgar Online: IPO Central
www.ipocentral.com

Initial Public Offerings
http://edgarscan.pwcglobal.com/EdgarScan/ipos.html

IPO Maven
www.investools.com/cgi-bin/Library/mavn.pl

IPO Data Systems Inc
www.ipodata.com

IPO Intelligence Online - Rennaisance Capital
www.ipo-fund.com/default.asp

INSIDER TRADING

InsiderScoop Home
www.insiderscoop.com/home/

MSN Money: Insider Trading Monitor
http://moneycentral.msn.com/investor/invsub/insider/trans.asp

MERGERS & ACQUISITIONS

Corporate Affiliations
www.corporateaffiliations.com/Executable/cn_mergers.asp

Merger Info (Canada)
http://competition.ic.gc.ca/epic/internet/incb-bc.nsf/en/h_ct01255e.html

Mergers & Acquisitions Report
www.mareport.com/mar/news_updates.cfm

Mergerstat
www.mergerstat.com

UK Business Park
www.ukbusinesspark.co.uk/bpmerg.htm

Yahoo Finance
http://biz.yahoo.com/me/

NON-U.S. FINANCIAL INFORMATION

Thanks to the World Wide Web, you can research financial topics and financial markets for most parts of the world. Here are a few places to get started.

Electronic Share Information Ltd
www.martech-intl.com/best2/esi.htm

Financial.de
www.financial.de/

Find: Financial Information Net Directory
www.find.co.uk

Investment Trusts & Offshore Funds
www.trustnet.co.uk/general/trust00.html

Japan
http://japanfinancials.com

U.S. FINANCIAL INFORMATION

Some of these sites are also listed under Economics / Economic Data, since there is some overlap between the two categories of information. This list will point you to the major U.S. government and non-government sites for such financial matters as the markets, mutual funds, and that bastion of financial news, Dow Jones. Search using competitors' names or analyze the industry using these tools.

10-K Wizard
www.tenkwizard.com

ABI World (Bankruptcy Information on the Web)
www.abiworld.org

BankruptcyData.Com - Experts in Bankruptcy Research
www.bankruptcydata.com

Cleveland Federal Reserve Bank Research Department: Economic Research
www.clevelandfed.org/Research/index.htm

Core Data
www.coredatagroup.com

DailyStocks
www.dailystocks.com

DBC Financial Links
www.dbc.com/cgi-bin/htx.exe/core/dbc/links.html

DJIA (Downloadable to Spreadsheet)
www.djindexes.com/jsp/industrialAverages.jsp?sideMenu=true.html

Fast Quote - Quote.com
http://fast.quote.com/fq/excite/quote

Federal Reserve Bank of New York: Links to Federal Reserve Banks
www.newyorkfed.org/research/index.html

Federal Reserve Bank of St. Louis
http://research.stlouisfed.org/fred2/

Finance News for IT Managers
http://stocks.internetnews.com

Financial Statistics: Canada
www.bankofcanada.ca/en/rates.htm

Futures & Options at the Chicago Mercantile Exchange
www.cme.com

InsiderTrading
www.stocksmart.com/pls/ri/sm.p?pn=insdr

Internet Bankruptcy Library - Distressed Securities
http://bankrupt.com/

List of Defaulted Borrowers
http://defaulteddocs.dhhs.gov/cgi-bin/ddocs_counter.pl

Microsoft Investor
http://investor.msn.com/home.asp?newguid=1&

Money Online
www.cnnmoney.com

Morningstar.Net
www.morningstar.com

New York Stock Exchange
www.nyse.com

OneSource Information Services
www.onesource.com

Quote.com – Quotes, News, Investment Research & More
`www.quote.com`

StockMaster Stocks By Name
`www.stockmaster.com/sm/stocks/C.html`

US Securities & Exchange Commission
`www.sec.gov`

***USA Today* Mutual Funds**
`www.usatoday.com/money/stocks/mutual/mutdex/dmut000.htm`

Yahoo! Finance
`http://biz.yahoo.com`

Zacks Investment Research, Inc.
`www.ultra.zacks.com`

VENTURE CAPITAL

Learn where privately-held competitor companies get their funding by searching these venture capital sites. Note that some regional and non-U.S. sites are included.

American Venture Capital Exchange & M&A Service
`www.avce.com`

European Private Equity & Venture Capital Association (EVCA)
`www.evca.com`

PricewaterhouseCoopers: Global: Insights & Solutions: MoneyTree Survey
`www.pwcmoneytree.com/moneytree/index.jsp`

Venture Capital Resource Directory - VC database of Venture Capital Firms
`www.vfinance.com/home.asp?Toolpage=vencaentire.asp`

Geographic Searching Sites

Once you have identified a competitor's plant sites and other business locations, these Websites may help to find them on the map - and to learn more about the communities where they are located. This intelligence may be plugged in to your analysis of a competitor's labor force, potential for expansion, etc.

American Community Network
`www.acn.net`

International Chamber of Commerce & City-State-Province Directory
`www.chamber-of-commerce.com`

Government Sites – U.S.

The amount of information here is unbelievable! Finding what you want is sometimes confusing, because the name of the agency is not a clear indication of the scope of the information it may provide. Some data can be downloaded into spreadsheets and databases for further analysis.

A tour of these sites may be in order, with the question "How can our company use this data?" clearly in mind as you drill down through it all. Note also that government sites have been included under general subject headings elsewhere in this list of bookmarks and favorites.

MISCELLANEOUS U.S. GOVERNMENT SITES

This is a collection of assorted useful federal government sites - you could find some surprising intelligence sources here.

Committee on Government Reform & Oversight: Policy & Supporting Positions (Plum Book)
www.access.gpo.gov/plumbook/toc.html

Federal Aviation Administration Search
www.faa.gov/search.html

Federal Deposit Insurance Corporation Bank Data Institution Directory
http://www3.fdic.gov/idasp/

Federal Information Center
http://fic.info.gov

Federal Procurement Data System
www.fpdc.gov/fpdc/fpdc_home.htm

Federal Web Locator
www.infoctr.edu/fwl/

FedWorld Information Network
www.fedworld.gov

FirstGov: The U.S. Government's Official Web Portal
http://firstgov.gov

Engine.com - Federal, State & Local Government and Court Resources
www.govengine.com/

Government Information from UT Library Online
www.lib.utexas.edu/Libs/PCL/Government.html

GPO Access
www.gpoaccess.gov

Investigators Guide to Sources of Information
www.gao.gov/special.pubs/soi/contents.htm

Material Safety Data Sheet Searches
www.epa.gov/superfund/sites/index.htm

NASA Acquisition Internet Service
http://prod.nais.nasa.gov/cgi-bin/nais/index.cgi

SBA - PRO-Net - What is PRO-Net? (Procurement Search Engine)
http://pro-net.sba.gov/index2.html

Search Engines : Beaucoup! (Politics/Government/Law)
www.beaucoup.com/1poleng.html

State & Local Government on the 'Net
www.statelocalgov.net/index.cfm

State and Local Governments (Library of Congress
http://lcweb.loc.gov/global/state/stategov.html#meta

US Department of Agriculture
www.usda.gov

US Securities & Exchange Commission
www.sec.gov

World Factbook
www.odci.gov/cia/publications/factbook/index.html

CENSUS BUREAU

Check out the offerings at the Censtats site in addition to the free sites listed below. Your Sales and Marketing department may be very interested in the M3 report as they engage in strategic planning regarding market-related issues.

American FactFinder
http://factfinder.census.gov/java_prod/dads.ui.homePage.HomePage

M3 Report - Shipments, Inventories, Orders
www.census.gov/ftp/pub/indicator/www/m3/index.htm

US Census Bureau
www.census.gov/index.html

US Census Bureau - FERRET Login Form
http://ferret.bls.census.gov/cgi-bin/ferret

US Census Bureau - New Retail/Wholesale Page
www.census.gov/econ/www/retmenu.html#WHOL

US Census Bureau – CENSUS 2000
www.census.gov/main/www/cen2000.html

US Census Bureau: Metropolitan and Micropolitan Statistical Areas
www.census.gov/population/www/estimates/metrodef.html

CONGRESS

Here are several sites for the U.S. Congress or which cover Congress. The University of Michigan has a searchable database for locating hearing transcripts. This material can be searched by competitor company or individual's name to locate their testimony.

C-SPAN - Capitol Spotlight
www.c-span.org/capitolspotlight/

Congress: THOMAS: U.S. Congress on the Internet
http://thomas.loc.gov

Congressional Hearings on the Web
www.lib.umich.edu/govdocs/hearings.html

House of Representatives
www.house.gov

House of Representatives - Search
www.house.gov/house/searchall.htm

Index of Congressional Research Service Reports
www.house.gov/markgreen/crs.htm

Senate
www.senate.gov

US Congress (GPO Access)
www.access.gpo.gov/congress/index.html

DEPARTMENT OF COMMERCE

Included here are trade or commerce related sites. You may find that a subscription with Stat-USA is a very good investment because of its customer support feature which allows you to discuss questions with a staff member familiar with government information sources.

GovCon - Commerce Business Daily, FACNET, Government Regulations & Databases
www.govcon.com

Office of Trade & Economic Analysis
www.ita.doc.gov/tradestats

STAT-USA/Internet Site Economic, Trade, Business Information
www.stat-usa.gov

DEPARTMENT OF ENERGY

Information Bridge
www.osti.gov/bridge/

International Energy Annual
www.eia.doe.gov/iea/

OpenNet
www.osti.gov/opennet/

US Department of Energy National Laboratories & Programs
www.energy.gov/engine/content.do?BT_CODE=OF_NLTC

US Department of Energy Homepage
www.energy.gov

DEPARTMENT OF LABOR

Many business decisions require the kind of data that may be retrieved from these sites.

Occupational Employment & Wage Data (US)
http://stats.bls.gov/oes/oes_data.htm

Bureau of Labor Statistics
http://stats.bls.gov

Bureau of Labor Statistics: Economy At A Glance
www.bls.gov/eag/eag.us.htm

Davis-Bacon Wage Determination Database
http://davisbacon.fedworld.gov

ILAB - Foreign Labor Trends Reports
www.dol.gov/ILAB/media/reports/flt/main.htm

National Industry-Specific Occupational Employment and Wage Estimates
www.bls.gov/oes/2002/oessrci.htm

DEPARTMENT OF STATE

The Department of State offers pages covering contract opportunities, country commercial guides and economic and trade policy pages among the sites listed below. The page offering links to related foreign affairs sites may also prove useful if your country does business outside of the U.S..

US State Department - Index
www.state.gov/www/ind.html

US State Department - Official Website
www.state.gov

US State Department – Commercial and Business Affairs
www.state.gov/e/eb/cba/

US State Department - Related Foreign Affairs Sites
www.state.gov/www/websites.html

US State Department - Services - Contracting Opportunities & Related Information
www.state.gov/www/services_admin.html

US State Department - Services - Country Commercial Guides Index
www.state.gov/e/eb/rls/rpts/ccg

ENVIRONMENTAL PROTECTION AGENCY

See the general heading Environment above for additional environment-related sites. Also look at the Public Records category for U.S. government databases.

Superfund Search
www.epa.gov/superfund/sites/index.htm

US Environmental Protection Agency
www.epa.gov

US Environmental Protection Agency: Business Opportunities
www.epa.gov/epaho

Water Quality Standards Database
www.epa.gov/wqsdatabase/

FEDERAL AVIATION ADMINISTRATION

The FAA's Corporate Search Facility may turn up a variety of interesting intelligence if your business intelligence quest involves aviation or aerospace matters.

FAA: Federal Aviation Administration
www.faa.gov

FEDERAL COMMUNICATIONS COMMISSION

FCC ID Search Form
www.fcc.gov/oet/fccid

FCC Home Page
www.fcc.gov

FEDERAL ELECTION COMMISSION

*The FEC's Direct Access Program means that you can download and search files of
contributions data to learn about your competitors' donations to political campaigns.
You might also look under the Public Records heading in this bookmark list for a FECInfo,
a non-government source for this information.*

FEC Disclosure Reports
http://herndon1.sdrdc.com/info.html

FEC Homepage
www.fec.gov

EC Image/Query System
www.fec.gov/finance_reports.html

FECInfo
www.tray.com/fecinfo

PoliticalMoneyLine
www.tray.com/fecinfo/

FOOD & DRUG ADMINISTRATION

*Be sure to use the SEARCH facility and examine ARCHIVES to calendars at the FDA to find
out the who/what/when/where information regarding competitors' activities with this agency.
The see the agency's FOIA reading room or consider a FOIA request for further information.*

FDA Public Calendar
www.fda.gov/opacom/calendar.html

Food & Drug Administration (FDA)
www.fda.gov

RegSource Regulatory Page - Regulatory affairs, FDA information
http://regsource.com

US Food and Drug Administration Archives
www.fda.gov/opacom/hpnews.html

US Food and Drug Administration FDA Search Page
www.fda.gov/search.html

GOVERNMENT PRINTING OFFICE

*Use these links to locate government publications on almost any topic.
The A-Z list might provide some tip-offs to material that hadn't known about previously.*

GPO Access - Search Online Databases
www.access.gpo.gov

GPO Access – A-Z Resource List
www.gpoaccess.gov/databases.html

U.S. Government Online Bookstore
http://bookstore.gpo.gov

LIBRARY OF CONGRESS

Library of Congress
http://lcweb.loc.gov

OCCUPATIONAL SAFETY & HEALTH ADMINISTRATION

Occupational safety and health issues, as they pertain to your competitors, could be of great interest within your own company. These records may also provide the addresses of plants or other company facilities.

Occupational Safety & Health Administration - OSHA
www.osha.gov

OSHA Statistics & Data - Searchable
www.osha.gov/oshstats

Search For Accidents
www.osha.gov/cgi-bin/inv/inv1

Search For Inspections Within An Industry
www.osha.gov/cgi-bin/sichq/sic1

POSTAL SERVICE

USPS ZIP+4 Code Lookup
www.usps.gov/ncsc/lookups/lookup_zip+4.html

SOCIAL SECURITY ADMINISTRATION

Social Security Online
www.ssa.gov

HUMAN RESOURCES

Benefits - Human Resources Net Links
http://humanresources.miningco.com/msub2.htm

U.S. Department of Health & Human Services
www.os.dhhs.gov

Industries & Professions

These bookmarks are a "tip of the iceberg" list, with a few government sites included for regulated industries such as banking. To see a more comprehensive collection, see the Internet Intelligence Index at the Fuld.com site listed under Competitive Intelligence. The Fuld page contains links to a list of individual industries. The Industry Data Finder from Rensselaer at Hartford, mentioned below, is another excellent source.

MULTIPLE INDUSTRY LINKS SITES

Business Communications Company
http://ecnext.imrmall.com/bcc/

CEIR Industry Research
www.c-e-i-r.com/C_industry.html

Competia - Express
www.competia.com/express/index.html

Competitive Intelligence Guide - Fuld & Company Inc
www.fuld.com/i3/index.html

Dun & Bradstreet Industry reports by SIC code - Free
www.zapdata.com/zapmarkets/

FT.com Industry Surveys
http://surveys.ft.com/

Hoover's Industry Snapshots
http://hoovers.com/free/ind/dir.xhtml

Industry Data Finder
www.rh.edu/library/industry/industry.htm

IndustryLink - your manufacturing and industrial career resource
www.industrylink.com/

Industry Portals
www.virtualpet.com/industry/mfg/mfg.htm

Industry Reports -by U.S. Business Reporter
www.activemedia-guide.com/industry_profile_cp.htm

Industry Resources Reports
www.valuationresources.com/IndustryReport.htm

Manufacturers' News, Inc. - About MNI Information
http://manufacturersnews.com/about.asp

Open Secrets: Industry Profiles
www.opensecrets.org/industries/index.asp

TerraFly (Flyover + local details)
http://terrafly.com

ACCOUNTING

CPA Links
www.aicpa.org/yellow/index.htm

Tax and Acccounting Sites Directory
www.taxsites.com/associations2.html

ADVERTISING

100 Leading National Advertisers Index
www.adage.com/page.cms?pageId=597

Ad Council
www.adcouncil.org

Ad Age Data Center
www.adage.com/datacenter.cms

Ad Facts Inc.
www.adfacts.com/

Ad Track
www.usatoday.com/money/index/ad001.htm

Adflip.com: Ads archive, greeting cards of automobile, celebrity, audio magazines advertising
www.adflip.com/

Advertiser & Agency Red Books
www.redbooks.com/cd.htm.

Advertising Research Foundation
www.arfsite.org

***Adweek* Online**
www.adweek.com

American Advertising Federation
www.aaf.org

AEROSPACE/AVIATION International Advertising Association
www.iaaglobal.org

ELODA (Television advertising)
http://eloda.com/en/

Evaliant
www.evaliant.net

AVIATION/AEROSPACE

Aerospace & Defense Industry Data Finder
www.rh.edu/library/industry/aero.htm

Aerospace Technology
www.aerospace-technology.com/

Aircraft Performance
www.risingup.com/planespecs

Aircraft Registration (Canada)
www.tc.gc.ca/aviation/activepages/ccarcs/en/default_e.asp?x_lang=e

Aviation Accident Database Query
www.ntsb.gov/ntsb/query.asp

Bermuda Department of Civil Aviation - Register of Aircraft & Flight Crew
www.dca.gov.bm

Canada Aircraft Registration and Leasing
www.tc.gc.ca/CivilAviation/gen

Irish Aviation Website - Irish Register
www.irishaviation.net/

Landings: Aviation Search Engines
http://www1.drive.net/evird.acgi$pass*8099593!mtd*7!map*_landings/images/landings-strip.map?51,40

Landings: Search for Certified Pilots
www.landings.com/evird.acgi$pass*62142018!_h-www.landings.com/_landings/pages/search/certs-pilot.html

New Zealand Civil Aviation Aircraft Register Query
www.caa.govt.nz/Scripts/Air_Reg_Query.asp

Planenews Aviation Portal
http://planenews.com/index.php

Scramble on the Web
www.scramble.nl/civ/ph/nedreg_main.htm

Singapore Changi Airport
www.changi.airport.com.sg

Spotters' Nest: Italian Aviation Database
www.spotters.it/en/database.htm

APPAREL

ApparelSearch
www.apparelsearch.com

Canadian Apparel Federation
www.apparel.ca

Fibre 2 Fashion
www.fibre2fashion.com

Indian Apparel Portal
http://apparel.indiamart.com

Industry Data Finder
www.rh.edu/library/industry/textile.htm

ARCHITECTURE

Architect Directory
http://rebuz.com/Directory/architectdirectory.htm

Architects On Line
www.architectsonline.it/

ProFile on the Web
www.cmdg.com/profile

AUTOMOTIVE

Industry Data Finder: Automotive
www.rh.edu/library/industry/auto.htm

Kelley Blue Book New Car Pricing and Bluebook Values
www.kbb.com

Office of Automotive Affairs
www.ita.doc.gov/td/auto/

Ward's Directory of Suppliers & Product Guides
http://wardsauto.com/suppliers/index.htm

World Wide Web Virtual Library: Autos
www.cyberauto.com/index.php/vehicles.htm

BANKING

Bank for International Settlements
www.bis.org

Banking on the WWW: Guides
www.gwdg.de/~ifbg/bank_1.html

Banks and Financial Institutions by Country
www.internationalist.com/business/finance.html

Banks of the Carribbean
www.escapeartist.com/banks31/banks31.htm

Central Banks of the World: Central Banking Resource Center
http://patriot.net/~bernkopf

Directory of All Swiss Banks
www.swconsult.ch/chbanks/cantons.htm

Federal Deposit Insurance Corporation (FDIC)
www.fdic.gov

FFIEC Home Page
www.ffiec.gov/default.htm

Global Banking Law Database
www.gbld.org

Industry Data Finder: Banking & Financial Services
www.rh.edu/library/industry/finserv.htm

Internet Banking: Directory of Banks on the Web
www.qualisteam.com/eng/conf.shtml

National Information Center (NIC)
www.ffiec.gov/nic/general_information.htm

OCC Weekly Bulletins
www.occ.treas.gov/occ_current.htm

Online Banking Report_ Internet Strategies for Financial Institutions. RESOURCES
www.onlinebankingreport.com/resources/100.html

World Bank Group
www.worldbank.org

World Banks by Country
www.aaadir.com/banks/f_left_top.html

Worldwide banking guide
www.qualisteam.com/Banks/

BIOTECHNOLOGY

Bio.com
www.bio.com

Biological Data Transport Biotech Registry

www.data-transport.com/ochnl.asp?keywords=biotechnology&t=b&chnl=1&submit=Search

BioSpace.com: ... for Biotechnology & Pharmaceutical News, Jobs, Companies, Stocks
www.biospace.com

Biotech East
www.biotecheast.com

BUBL LINK: Biotechnology
http://link.bubl.ac.uk/biotechnology

Knowledge Express
www.knowledgeexpress.com

PJB Publications Ltd
www.pjbpubs.com

Recombinant Capital (ReCap)
www.recap.com

Registry of Biomedical Companies
www.hum-molgen.de/companies/profile.php3/125

CHEMICALS

ChemConnect
www.chemconnect.com

ChemIndustry.com
www.chemindustry.com

Chemical Search Engine
www.chemindustry.com

Industry Data Finder: Chemicals & Plastics
www.rh.edu/library/industry/chem.htm

Just for plastics.com - quotes for plastics products and services
www.justforplastics.com/

Plastics Network
www.plasticsnet.com

Swain Chemistry & Chemical Engineering Library Web Guides
http://www-sul.stanford.edu/depts/swain/colres/coll/metaindexes.html

COMPUTER TECHNOLOGY

Compinfo.ws
www.compinfo.co.uk/index.htm

Hardware Central
http://systems.webopedia.com/TERM/C/computer.html

Industry Data Finder
www.rh.edu/library/industry/comput.htm

Yahoo! Business & Economy: Companies: Computers
http://dir.yahoo.com/Business_and_Economy/Business_to_Business/Computers/

CONSTRUCTION

Building Online
www.buildingonline.com

Construction Market Data Inc
www.cmdonl.com

Construction Resources Online
www.copywriter.com/constr.htm

Construction WebLinks
www.constructionweblinks.com

The Construction Site - Construction's Best Directory
www.constr.com/tcs.htm

Industry Data Finder
www.rh.edu/library/industry/build.htm

DEFENSE

Defense-I
www.defense-i.com

Jane's FastTrack to Defence Industry
http://fasttrack.janes.com

Jane's Information Group
www.janes.com

ELECTRONICS

Electronic Industries Alliance
www.eia.org

Electronics Web
www.electronicsweb.com

Semiconductor Online
www.semiconductoronline.com

ENERGY

Chronology of World Oil Market Events 1970 - 2000
www.eia.doe.gov/cabs/chron.html

Country Analysis Briefs - No Frames Version
www.eia.doe.gov/emeu/cabs/contents.html

ElectricNet: Digital Marketplace
www.electricnet.com/

Energy Information Administration_ Annual Energy Review 2002
www.eia.doe.gov/emeu/aer/contents.html

EnergyFiles
www.osti.gov/energyfiles/

Energysearch: Search
www.energysearch.com

Electric Power Research Institute (EPRI)
www.epri.com

Gov.Research-Center: Energy Science and Technology Database
http://grc.ntis.gov/energy.htm

IHS Energy Group
www.ihsenergy.com

Industry Data Finder: Oil & Gas
www.rh.edu/library/industry/oil.htm

International Energy Agency
www.iea.org

Landmen Net's Oil Links
www.landmen.net/links.html

Nigerian Oil & Gas Online
www.nigerianoil-gas.com/

Offshore Technology
www.offshore-technology.com/

Oil Industry Websites
http://freespace.virgin.net/alan.foum/index.htm

Petroleum Place
www.petroleumplace.com

Platt's on the Internet
www.platts.com

PolySearch - Energy
http://www2.hawaii.edu/~jacso/extra/egyeb/poly-energy.htm

Power Online
www.poweronline.com

Power Technology
www.power-technology.com

Propane Gas Association of Canada Inc
www.propanegas.ca

State Electricity Profiles
www.eia.doe.gov/cneaf/electricity/st_profiles/e_profiles_sum.html

ENGINEERING

Edinburgh Engineering Virtual Library (EEVL)
www.eevl.ac.uk

Engineering Resources
www.n-e-x-u-s.com/engineering/index.html

University Research: Engineering
www.princeton.edu/Siteware/ResearchEngrg.shtml

Virtual Library: Engineering
http://dart.stanford.edu/vlme/

Yahoo! Science:Engineering
www.yahoo.com/Science/Engineering

FARMING/AGRICULTURE

Farms.com
www.cybercrop.com

FOOD & BEVERAGE

Industry Data Finder: Food, Beverage, Restaurant & Tobacco Industry
www.rh.edu/library/industry/food.htm

Thomas Food & Beverage Market Place
www.tfir.com/thomasfood/index.asp

QSR Magazine - Drive-Thru Time Study
www.qsrmagazine.com/drive-thru/2003/charts/final.html

WWW Virtual Library: Beer & Brewing
www.beerinfo.com/vlib/index.html

HEALTHCARE

Clinical Trials

Cancer Clinical Trials Homepage
www.cancertrials.org.uk/

CenterWatch Clinical Trials Listing Service Home Page
www.centerwatch.com

Clinical Investigator Inspection Results
www.regsourceplus.com/Description.cfm?sid=87445811

Clinical Trial Posting!
www.clinicaltrials.com

ClinicalTrials.gov - Clinical Trials and Human Research Studies
www.clinicaltrials.gov

Clinical Trials Resource Center: Breast Cancer
www.centerwatch.com/demo/breastcancerfund/ctrc.html

CenterWatch Clinical Trials Resource Center
www.centerwatch.com/demo/imf/ctrc.html

Consumer Health

Consumer Health
www.ahcpr.gov/consumer

Healthfinder - a gateway consumer health and human services information website from the United States government
www.healthfinder.gov

Health Information Resource Database
www.health.gov/nhic/NewSrch.htm

Health Related Search Engines

MedWatch: The FDA Medical Products Reporting Program
www.fda.gov/medwatch

Search Engines - Beaucoup! (Science/Nature/Technology)
www.beaucoup.com/1scieng.html

Hospitals

American Hospital Directory
www.ahd.com

Best Hospitals 2003
www.usnews.com/usnews/health/hosptl/tophosp.htm

Hospitals
http://web.mel.org/viewtopic.jsp?id=277&pathid=3367

Insurance

Industry Data Finder: Insurance
www.rh.edu/library/industry/ins.htm

Insurance Companies on the Internet
www.iiin.com/iiincompanies.html

Insurance Industry Internet Network
www.iiin.com

Insurancetimes.co.uk
www.insurancetimes.co.uk/

International Insurance Factbook
www.internationalinsurance.org

Lloyd's
www.lloyds.com/index.asp

Risk Management Insurance Safety - Description of Services rmis.com
www.rmlibrary.com/offer.htm

Miscellaneous Healthcare

Academy for International Health Studies: International Resources
www.aihs.com/resources.html

Achoo Healthcare Online
www.achoo.com

Industry Professionals Resources
www.centerwatch.com/professional/index.html

Additions/Deletions for Prescription and OTC Drug Product Lists
www.fda.gov/cder/rxotcdpl/pdplarchive.htm

American Cancer Society
www.cancer.org

BioMedNet
www.bmn.com

Cancer.gov
www.cancer.gov/cancerinfo

Center for Devices and Radiological Health MDR Data Files
www.fda.gov/cdrh/mdrfile.html

Contact Canada® - Comprehensive Life Science Industry
www.contactcanada.com/

CPSNet
http://pmd@cpsnet.com

Espicom Business Intelligence – Devices and Pharmaceuticals
www.espicom.com

EMEA - The European Agency for the Evaluation of Medicinal Products
www.eudra.org

Frost & Sullivan - Healthcare Market Engineering
www.frost.com/healthcare

Hardin MD - Hardin Meta Directory of Internet Health Sources
www.lib.uiowa.edu/hardin/md/index.html

Health On the 'Net Foundation
www.hon.ch

Healthtouch: Online for better health
www.healthtouch.com

HealthWeb
www.healthweb.org

Manufacturer and User Facility Device Experience Database - (MAUDE)
www.accessdata.fda.gov/scripts/cdrh/cfdocs/cfMAUDE/search.cfm

Medical Dictionary Online
www.online-medical-dictionary.org/

Medical Equipment and Hospital Equipment Classified Ads - Medmatrix!
www.medmatrix.com

Medical Matrix
www.medmatrix.org/reg/login.asp

Medicine on the 'Net
www.corhealth.com

MEDLINE: PubMed & Internet Grateful Med (Free)
http://shop.store.yahoo.com/allheart/pubmedmedline.html

MDChoice
www.mdchoice.com

MedWatch: The FDA Medical Products Reporting Program
www.fda.gov/medwatch

MGH Neurology - Neurology Web-Forum
http://neuro-www.mgh.harvard.edu/forum

National Cancer Institute: Cancer.gov
http://cancer.gov/cancerinformation

National Center for Biotechnology Information
www.ncbi.nlm.nih.gov

New Drug Application (NDA) 1996 and Older
www.fda.gov/cder/foi/nda/index96.htm

Online Medical Dictionary
http://cancerweb.ncl.ac.uk/omd/

Organizing Medical Networked Information (OMNI)
http://omni.ac.uk

PSL Group
www.pslgroup.com

Search the Studies
http://clinicalstudies.info.nih.gov

TeleSCAN: Telematics Services in Cancer
http://telescan.nki.nl/index.html

The Virtual Hospital: Information for Healthcare Providers
www.vh.org

US Medicine Information Central
www.usmedicine.com

Regulatory Resources

FDA Dockets Management
www.fda.gov/ohrms/dockets/default.htm

LAW ENFORCEMENT

Officer.com
www.officer.com

MANUFACTURING

Appliance Manufacturer Online
www.ammagazine.com

Industry Data Finder
www.rh.edu/library/industry/paper.htm

Manufacturing.net
www.manufacturing.net/magazine/rd/rd100/
100award.htm

Manufacturing - Manufacturing Extension Partnership
www.mep.nist.gov

Manufacturing Extension Partnership
www.mep.nist.gov

Pneumatics Online
www.pneumaticsonline.com

Process Industry Practices Home Page
www.pip.org

RAM Database – (Recent Advances in Manufacturing)
www.eevl.ac.uk/ram/

SteelVillage.com - Steel for the 21st Century
http://steelvillage.com

TGR Europe, Thomas Global Register Europe
www.tipcoeurope.com

Thomas Regional Directory
www.thomasregional.com

Thomas Register Europe Home Page
www.tipcoeurope.com

Thomas Register of American Manufacturers
www.thomasregister.com

MARITIME

Current Vessel Search
http://cgmix.uscg.mil/psix/psix2/

PHARMACEUTICALS

BioSpace.com - The Hub Site for Biotechnology
www.biospace.com

CDER Drug Application Process
www.fda.gov/cder/regulatory/applications/ind_page_1.htm

CDER New and Generic Drug Approvals: 1998-2004
www.fda.gov/cder/approval/index.htm

Competitive intelligence on FDA-approved drugs - Drug Patent Expiration Dates
www.myorangebook.com

Espicom Business Intelligence
www.espicom.com

New Drug Application (NDA) – 1996 and Older
www.fda.gov/cder/foi/nda/index96.htm

PUBLIC RELATIONS

O'Dwyer's Inside News of PR
www.odwyerpr.com

PR Central
www.prcentral.com

Public Relations Society of America (PRSA)
www.prsa.org

RETAIL / WHOLESALE

Grocery Retail Online
www.groceryretailonline.com

Industry Data Group
www.rh.edu/library/industry/retail.htm

Mintel Group
http://reports.mintel.com

U.S. Census Bureau: Retail & Wholesale Trade
www.census.gov/econ/www/retmenu.html#WHOL

TELECOMMUNICATIONS

Company Websites

Espicom Business Intelligence
www.espicom.com

Ericsson
www.ericsson.se

InterDigital
www.interdigital.com

Electronic Commerce

Advisory Commission on Electronic Commerce
www.ecommercecommission.org

Center for Research in Electronic Commerce
http://cism.bus.utexas.edu

Global Information Infrastructure Commission (GIIC)
www.giic.org

Government / Regulatory Sites

Federal Communications Commission (FCC)
www.fcc.gov

Federal Standard 1037C: Glossary of Telecommunications Terms
www.its.bldrdoc.gov/fs-1037

International Telecommunication Union (ITU) Home Page
www.itu.ch

National Telecommunications & Information Administration
www.ntia.doc.gov

Miscellaneous

Glossary of Telecommunications Industry Terms
www.its.bldrdoc.gov/fs-1037/

Industry Data Finder
www.rh.edu/library/industry/telecom.htm

Telecom Web: Daily Telecommunications New and Analysis
www.telecomweb.com/

TELECOM Digest & Archives
http://mirror.lcs.mit.edu/telecom-archives/

Telecommunications Magazine
www.telecommagazine.com

Telecoms Virtual Library
www.analysys.com/vlib

Telephony Online
www.internettelephony.com

TRANSPORTATION

Bureau of Transportation Statistics
www.bts.gov/smart/links/transportation.html

Industry Data Finder – Transportation and Shipping
www.rh.edu/library/industry/trans.htm

Logistics World
www.logisticsworld.com/

National Transportation Library
http://ntl.bts.gov/

SafeStat Online
http://ai.volpe.dot.gov/mcspa.asp

Transport Research
http://www2.dlr.de/vl/TransWWW.HTM

Transporation Related Organizations: Government and Quasi-Public
http://members.aol.com/qcscdas/ldragon.htm

Tansportation Resources
http://ntl.bts.gov

State Transportation Profiles
www.bts.gov/publications/transportation_profiles/

UTILITIES

Energy Online
www.energyonline.com/

Industry Data Finder: Electric Utilities Industry
www.rh.edu/library/industry/elecutil.htm

Profiles and Rankings of Shareholder-Owned Electric Companies - April 2004
www.eei.org/products_and_services/descriptions_and_access/profi
les_ranking.htm

Industry Research

One of the key items in industry research is forecasts for an industry for the next few years. This information is needed for crucial decision making.

FORECASTS

2004 Industrial Forecasts
www.industrialinfo.com

Business Monitor International (BMI)
www.businessmonitor.com/about_bmi.htm

BusinessWeek online: Industry Outlook 2004
www.businessweek.com/magazine/toc/04_02/B38650402indout.htm

Corporate Wireless Contracts & Procurement Practices, Trends & Forecast
www.instat.com/r/nrep/2004/IN0401661MBM.htm

Department of Interior Forecast of Fiscal Year Acquisitions
http://ideasec.nbc.gov/forecast

Department of State Forecast of Contract Opportunities
www.state.gov/m/a/sdbu/pubs/c6447.htm

Department of Transportation Contracting and Procurement Opportunities

http://osdbuweb.dot.gov/business/procurement/forecast.html

EPA Acquisition Forecast
http://yosemite1.epa.gov/oarm/oam/forecastdatabase.nsf

Farm and Foreign Agriculture Services FY 2004 Procurement Forecast
www.usda.gov/da/smallbus/20fsa.htm

Federal Aviation Administration Procurement Forecast
www.faa.gov/Newsroom/FY04-15AerospaceForecasts.cfm

Fiscal Year 2004 Forecast of Contract Opportunities
www.ustreas.gov/offices/management/dcfo/osdbu/marketing-
publications/forecast.html

InfoTech Trends (Formerly Computer Industry Forecasts)
www.infotechtrends.com

Kennedy Space Center
http://apps.ksc.nasa.gov/forecast/index.cfm

MobileInfo Market Outlook
www.mobileinfo.com/Market/market_outlook.htm

Naval Air Warfare Center Training Systems Division - Business Forecast
www.ntsc.navy.mil/EBusiness/BusOps/Forecast/Index.cfm

Nuclear Regulatory Commission Forecast of Contracting Opportunities for FY 2004
www.nrc.gov/who-we-are/forecast.html

HUD Fiscal Year 2004 Forecast of Contracting Opportunities
www.hud.gov/cts/cts4cast.html

Small & Disadvantaged Business Utilization Program
www.acq.osd.mil/sadbu/

Small Business Forecast - National Institutes of Health
www.hhs.gov/osdbu/publications/04nih.html

Treasury Bureau - Forecast of Contract Opportunities
www.treas.gov/sba/getsic.html

U.S. Department of CommerceForecast of Contract Opportunities
www.osec.doc.gov/osdbu/ForecastFY04_FY05.htm

USAID Forecast Reports - Procurement
www.usaid.gov/procurement_bus_opp/procurement/forecast/wforecast.htm

MISCELLANEOUS INDUSTRY RESEARCH SITES

Current Industrial Reports - Production, Inventories, & Orders
www.census.gov/pub/cir/www/

Industry Information: Hoover's Industry Snapshots
www.hoovers.com/free/ind/dir.xhtml

Industry Research Desk
www.virtualpet.com/industry

Industry Research Desk: Industry Home Pages
www.virtualpet.com/industry/mfg/mfg.htm

Information Brokers

Information brokers are information professionals or information research consultants worldwide, who perform online searching, library research, competitor intelligence, and similar services for business, industry, government, academia and the scientific communities. The companies listed on the sites below subscribe to codes of ethics of professional associations such as the Society for Competitive Intelligence Professionals or the Association of Independent Information Professionals.

Association of Independent Information Professionals
www.aiip.org

International Organizations

This is a brief list of such organizations.
See links on sites below for locating additional organizations.

North American Free Trade Agreement
www.sice.oas.org/trade/nafta/naftatce.asp

Organization of American States
http://oas.org

Union of International Associations
www.uia.org/extlinks/pub.php

United Nations
www.un.org

United Nations System
www.unsystem.org

US Department of State: Organization of American States
www.state.gov/p/wha/rt/oas/

The World Bank Group
www.worldbank.org

Internet Tools

A wide variety of useful tools is represented in this group of bookmarks. Several of them are described earlier in this book.

A4Mark (formerly Show URL) – Manages Bookmarks
www.faico.net/a4mark/

Alexa Internet
www.alexa.com

Anonymizer Inc
www.anonymizer.com

DomainWatch
www.domainwatch.com

Free online network utilities
http://centralops.net/co/

Internet Archive
www.archive.org

InterNIC
www.internic.net

Network-tools.com
http://network-tools.com

Nymserver
www.nymserver.com/Download-PC-Games/download-pc-games.php

Open Directory Project
http://home.netscape.com/bookmark/4_76/dmoz.html

Search, reserve, register domain names from checkdomain.com
www.checkdomain.com

The-cloak – Free Anonymous Web Surfing
www.the-cloak.com/anonymous-surfing-home.html

TracerLock. Monitor the Web. Lock, stock and barrel
www.tracerlock.com

Whois Source - Domain Whois Search Lookup!
www.whois.sc/

Monitoring/Alerting Services

It is important to distinguish between the two types of monitoring services included in this list. Those shown below are intended for determining when a website changes. For example, a competitor may add recent press releases, announce new products, offer promotions, etc. which are of interest to those in your organization.

A second type of monitoring service is listed later, under the heading News Sites. This type of service monitors the media and provides customers with search results based on selected criteria.

ChangeDetect
www.changedetect.com

ChangeDetection.com
www.changedetection.com/monitor.html

Dot.com Monitor
www.dotcom-monitor.com/web-site-monitoring.asp

Ewatch
www.ewatch.com

InfoMinder - The coolest way to track web pages
www.infominder.com/webminder/index.jsp

TrademarkBots®
www.trademarkbots.com

TrackEngine
www.trackengine.com

WatchThatPage
www.watchthatpage.com

WebSite-Watcher - internet monitoring software
http://aignes.com/

WebVeil
http://webveil.com/matrix.html

Journals/Magazines (full text)

British Library Net: Journals
www.britishlibrary.net/journals.html

Business Journals
www.businessjournals.com

Free Medical Journals: PubMed Search
www.lib.uiowa.edu/hardin/md/ej.html

Fulltext Sources Online
www.fso-online.com

Loden-Daniel Library
www.fhu2.net/library/onlinejournals.htm

MagPortal.com - Magazine Article Search Engine, Directory, and Data Feeds
www.magportal.com

MedBioWorld_ Bioscience Journals
www.medbioworld.com/bio/journals/bio-journals.html

Science Direct
www.sciencedirect.com

USC Law: General Law Reviews
http://lawweb.usc.edu/library/resources/journals.html

Legal Information

Use these bookmarks to locate laws and regulations of the U.S. and other countries around the world.

MISCELLANEOUS

AALLNET WEB: American Association of Law Libraries
www.aallnet.org

BusinessLaw.gov
www.businesslaw.gov

Center for Information Law & Policy: The Federal Web Locator
www.infoctr.edu/fwl/

Federal Court Locator
http://vls.law.vill.edu/Locator/fedcourt.html

FindLaw - Law, Lawyer, Lawyers, Attorney, Attorneys and Legal Resources
www.findlaw.com

FindLaw California Case Law Supreme Court and Appellate Court Opinions
www.findlaw.com/cacases/

GSU College of Law -- Meta-Index for U.S. Legal Research
http://gsulaw.gsu.edu/metaindex/

Hiieros Gamos: Law Library
www.hg.org/lawlibrary.html

Internet Legal Research Compass
http://vls.law.vill.edu/compass/

Lawcentral.com
www.lawcentral.com

Loislaw, The Electronic Law Library
www.pita.com

LRRX.com
www.llrx.com/international_law.html

Stanford Securities Class Action Clearinghouse
http://securities.stanford.edu/index.html

Supreme Court of the United States
www.supremecourtus.gov

Verdict Search
www.verdictsearch.com

VersusLaw
www.versuslaw.com

USC Law: General Law Reviews
http://lawweb.usc.edu/library/resources/journals.html

CASE LAW

EurLex
http://europa.eu.int/eur-lex/en/search/search_case.html

FindLaw Cases and Codes
www.findlaw.com/casecode/

Legal Information Institute – Court Opinions
www.law.cornell.edu

Lexisone: The Resource for Small Law Firms
www.lexisone.com/caselaw/freecaselaw

LexisNexis
http://web.lexis-nexis.com/ln.universe/page/content

VersusLaw
www.versuslaw.com

westlaw.com
www.westlaw.com

CRIMINAL LAW-RELATED

Criminal Justice Links
www.criminology.fsu.edu/cjlinks/other.html

Criminal Law
www.findlaw.com/01topics/09criminal/

HierosGamos: Criminal Law
www.hg.org/crime.html

NYU Law Library: Foreign and International Criminal Law
www.law.nyu.edu/library/foreign_intl/criminal.html

NON U.S. / INTERNATIONAL LAW

Foreign & International Law
www.washlaw.edu/forint/forintmain.html

International Law Guides
www.llrx.com/international_law.html

NYU Law Library: Guide to Foreign and International Legal Databases
www.law.nyu.edu/library/foreign_intl/

U.S. LAW / REGULATIONS

Center for New York City Law at New York Law School
www.citylaw.org

Court Websites
www.ncsconline.org/D_KIS/info_court_web_sites.html

FedLaw
www.thecre.com/fedlaw/default.htm

FindLaw: Supreme Court Opinions
www.findlaw.com/casecode/supreme.html

GPO Access at PALNI (Search Federal Register)
www.palni.edu/gpo

Internet Law Library - U.S. Code (Searchable)
www.lawguru.com/ilawlib/

NARA: Code of Federal Regulations
www.gpoaccess.gov/cfr/index.html

US Code Table of Popular Names
www.law.cornell.edu/uscode/topn

US Federal Courts Finder
www.LAW.emory.edu/FEDCTS

U.S. STATE LEGAL SITES

Alalinc: Alabama's Legal Information Network
www.alalinc.net

AllLaw.com: State Law Search
www.alllaw.com/state_law_search/

California Law
www.leginfo.ca.gov/calaw.html

Full-text state statutes and legislation on the Internet
www.prairienet.org/~scruffy/f.htm

USA States: Prosecuting Attorneys, District Attorneys, Attorneys General & U.S. Attorneys
www.co.eaton.mi.us/ecpa/PA-South.htm#TX

Libraries

These are a few of the many library sites on the Internet. Most major universities have excellent sites, as do some public and special libraries.

Internet Public Library
www.ipl.org

Libdex – Index to 18,000 Libraries
www.libdex.com

Research-It! - Your one-stop reference desk
www.iTools.COM/research-it

University of Michigan: Documents Center
www.lib.umich.edu/govdocs/

Maps

Many of these map sites will be useful in pinpointing the location of competitors' business operations. Your Sales and Marketing department may find them useful for reaching your clients' sites.

CheapTickets (Street Maps)
www.cheaptickets.com/trs/cheaptickets/content/maps_driving/street_map_search_by_address.xsl

Map Collections: 1597-1988
http://lcweb2.loc.gov/ammem/gmdhtml/gmdhome.html

MapBlast! BlastOff
www.mapblast.com

MapQuest!
www.mapquest.com

Maps On Us: A Map, Route and Yellow Pages Service
www.mapsonus.com

Microsoft Expedia Maps - Place Finder
www.expedia.com/pub/agent.dll?qscr=mmfn

Market Research/Market Intelligence

These websites supplement the many market research sources available on commercial vendors' sites.

B2bsalesand marketing
www.imarketinc.com

Biz360 Market Intelligence driving Business Performance
www.biz360.com

Euromonitor.com
www.euromonitor.com/results_country.asp?country=US

FIND/ SVP: Business Research
www.find.com

Freedonia Group - Market Research - Chemical Research
http://freedoniagroup.com/chemical.html

Frost & Sullivan - Industrial Market Engineering
www.frost.com/industrial

IBISWorld USA - Market Research Industry Reports and Information
www.ibisworld.com

Intelliseek
www.intelliseek.com/marketingi.asp

Marketing Research and Marketing Plan Data from Bizminer
www.bizminer.com/market_research.asp?aid=78

MarketResearch.com
www.marketresearch.com

Mintel
www.mintel.com

New York AMA GreenBook - Greenbook Search
www.greenbook.org

Nielsen Media Research Local Universe Estimates
www.nielsenmedia.com/DMAs.html

OPINAMOS.COM – Market Research for Latin America
http://opinamos.com

Sharp Market Intelligence - Case Studies
www.sharpmarket.com/cases/index.html#

What ever happened to...
www.weht.net

News Sites

News sites contain links to multiple news information sources from around the world Individual newspapers' sites are listed further down this list. Newswires and other news sources are included here as well. Some of these sites allow searching many sources simultaneously, which can facilitate retrieving business intelligence.

GEOGRAPHICALLY-ORIENTED NEW SITES

ASIA

Kiudon Media Link
www.kidon.com/media-link/index.shtml

China's Newspapers
www.chinapages.com/news/newspp.html

News Central Asia
www.newscentralasia.com

EUROPE

Central Europe Online
www.centraleurope.com

Financial Media on the 'Net
www.qualisteam.com/eng/docu.html

Mario's Cyberspace Station: News & Information
http://mprofaca.cro.net/search2.html

NORTH AMERICA

AJR NewsLink
www.newslink.org/biz.html

Bourque NewsWatch Canada
www.bourque.org

Business Week Online
www.businessweek.com

Business Wire
www.businesswire.com

Canada NewsWire
www.newswire.ca

CNN
www.cnn.com

CNBC
www.cnbc.com

CNNmoney
http://money.cnn.com

CRAYON.net - News Links
http://crayon.net/using/links.html

DowJones Newswires
www.djnewswires.com

Forbes
http://forbes.com

Fortune
www.fortune.com/fortune

Google News
http://news.google.com

Internet Public Library: Newspapers
www.ipl.org/div/news/

Wired News
www.wired.com/news

Library of Congress: Lists of Newspapers, Periodicals & News Resources
http://lcweb.loc.gov/rr/news/lists.html

Library of Congress: Newspaper Indexes
http://lcweb.loc.gov/rr/news/oltitles.html

MediaFinder from Oxbridge Communications, Inc.
www.mediafinder.com

MSNBC
www.msnbc.com/news/default.asp

NewsCentral: North America
www.all-links.com/newscentral/northamerica

News Is Free - Provides Daily Current News Headlines, Search and Alert Services
www.newsisfree.com

NewsLibrary.com
www.newslibrary.com

NewsLibrary - News Wires Search
http://nl.newsbank.com/nlsite/region_pgs/newswire.htm

NewsNow - Canada
www.newsnow.co.uk/newsfeed/?name=Canada

NewsVoyager
www.newspaperlinks.com/voyager.cfm

NPR Online
http://iris.npr.org

PR Newswire
www.prnewswire.com

Search Engines - Beaucoup! (Media)
www.beaucoup.com/1medeng.html

Time Warner's Pathfinder!
www.pathfinder.com/welcome/?navbar

US News Archives on the Web (Special Libraries Associations)
www.ibiblio.org/slanews/internet/archives.html

Yahoo-News and Media
www.yahoo.com/News_and_Media/Newspapers

UNITED KINGDOM

BBC News
http://news.bbc.co.uk

NewsNow - The UK's #1 News Portal
www.newsnow.co.uk/

WORLDWIDE NEWS SITES

Computerwire
www.computerwire.com

Electronic News
www.reed-electronics.com/electronicnews/

ISI Emerging Markets
www.securities.com

NewsCom
www.newscom.com

NewsDirectory.com
www.newsdirectory.com

NewsLink
http://newslink.org

NewsTrawler
www.newstrawler.com/nt/nt_home.html

Reuters News
www.reuters.com/news/index.html

Thousands of newspapers on the Net

www.onlinenewspapers.com

MEDIA MONITORING

The sites listed below are examples of services that monitor print and online publications upon request, using search criteria specified by their clients. Some organizations may offer this type of service in-house on their intranets under contract with providers. (In addition, most of the major online services also offer such services.)

Industries, Companies, News
www.abix.com.au

Black PR Wire
www.blackprwire.com

Cyberalert
www.cyberalert.com

LatinClips
www.latinclips.com/?trackcode=bizcom

Nexcerpt
www.nexcerpt.com

SmartBrief - Various Industries
www.smartbrief.com/signup

WPS: Russian Media Monitoring Agency
www.wps.ru:8101/e_index.html

Xtreme Information - Home Page
www.bmcnews.com

Newspapers

Individual newspapers' sites have been collected here. You will want to add bookmarks for newspapers in cities where you or your company's competitors do business. Some of them may not be included in the group files offered by News Sites, above, or by commercial online vendors' collections.

African News Sources

Africa News Online.
www.africanews.org

Africa Online.
www.africaonline.com

Africa Press International
http://home.global.co.za/~boervolk/index2.htm

Business Day
www.bday.co.za

Daily Graphic.
www.ghana.com/republic/graphic/index.html

Financial Mail.
www.fm.co.za

Journal of African Business.
www.utoledo.edu/~jab/

Post
www.zamnet.zm/zamnet/post/post.htm

Science in Africa
www.scienceinafrica.co.za/

Times of Zambia.
www.times.co.zm/

Asia News Sources

Asahi Shimbun.
www.asahi.com/english/english.htm

AsiaOne.
www.asia1.com.sg/

Asia-Pacific Law & Policy Journal.
www.hawaii.edu/aplpj/

Asia Times Online - News media with an Asian perspective
www.atimes.com

Australian Financial Review
www.afr.com.au

Bangkok Post
www.bangkokpost.net

Beijing Daily Online
www.beijingdaily.com.cn/

Central Asia Caucasus Analyst
www.cacianalyst.org

China: Adsale
www.adsalepub.com.hk/

China Daily
www.china.org.cn

China News Services
www.chinanews.com

China News Digest
http://my.cnd.org/modules/news/index.php?&sel_lang=english&storytopic=2

Comparative Connections--East Asian Bilateral Relations E-Journal
www.csis.org/pacfor/ccejournal.html

Hong Kong Standard
www.csis.org/pacfor/ccejournal.html

India: The Hindu
www.hindu.com

Indonesia Net Exchange
www.indoexchange.com

Inside China Today
www.insidechina.com

Japan Today
www.japantoday.com

Korea Herald
www.koreaherald.co.kr

Kyodo News
http://home.kyodo.co.jp

Malaysia
www.jaring.my

Malaysia: The Star
http://thestar.com.my

Nikkei BP Asia BizTech
http://thestar.com.my

People's Daily
www.peopledaily.com.cn

Pakistan TV
www.ptv.com.pk

Philippines: BusinessWorld Online
www.ptv.com.pk

Shanghai Daily
http://china-window.com/shanghai/sstr/sst.html

Straits Times Interactive
http://straitstimes.asia1.com

South China Morning Post
www.scmp.com/news

Economic Times
www.economictimes.com

Sunday Leader
www.thesundayleader.lk/20030504/home.htm

The Times of India
www.timesofindia.com

Vladivostok News
www.vladnews.ru/

Xinhua News Agency
www.xinhua.org

Europe – News Sources

Albania News
www.albanianews.com

Allnews.ru
http://allnews.ru/

The Baltics Worldwide
www.balticsww.com

Beta News Agency
www.beta.co.yu/

Bulgaria: PARI
www.pari.bg/doc/ENG/PARI/

Central Europe Automotive Report
www.autoindustry.com/employme.htm

Central Europe Business Journal
www.ceebiz.com

Central Europe Online
www.centraleurope.com

Central Europe Review
www.ce-review.org

Central European Business Daily
www.cebd.com

Concise Business to Business Information
www.conciseb2b.com

Croatian News Agency (HINA)
www.hina.hr

Czech Happenings
www.ceskenoviny.cz/news/

Dnevnik
www.dnevnik.si

Economist
www.economist.com

Estonian News Agency
http://eta.www.ee

EurasiaNews
http://eurasianews.com/erc/homepage.htm

Financial Times
http://news.ft.com/home/europe

IHT (International Herald Tribune)
www.iht.com/ihtsearch.php

Interfax
www.interfax.ru/eng/

Kyiv Post
www.thepost.kiev.ua

Latvian News Agency (LETA)
www.leta.lv/english/

Magyar Hirlap
www.mhirlap.hu

Mediafax
www.mediafax.ro/

Moscow Times
www.moscowtimes.ru

Nine O'Clock
www.nineoclock.ro/

Postimees
www.postimees.ee

Prague Daily Report
www.hazardous.com/tng/praguereport/

Prague Tribune
www.prague-tribune.cz/

Radio Prague
www.radio.cz

Russia On-Line
www.online.ru

Russia Today
www.russiatoday.com

Russian Information Agency: RIA Novosti
www.rian.ru

Russian National News Service
www.nns.ru/engind.html

Russian Story
www.russianstory.com

St. Petersburg Times
www.sptimes.ru

Symsite
www.symsite.sk/

Warsaw Voice
www.warsawvoice.com.pl

Yugoslavia: Alternative Information Network
www.aimpress.ch/

Latin America

Buenos Aires Herald
www.buenosairesherald.com

Business News Americas
www.bnamericas.com

Chile Information Project
www.chip.cl/

Clarin (Argentina - In Spanish)
www.clarin.com/diario/hoy/index_diario.html

El Comercio Peru
www.elcomercio.com

El Diario de Monterrey
www.milenwww.milenio.com/monterrey/io.com/monterrey/

El Economista
www.economista.com.mx/

El Espectador.
www.elespectador.com

El Mercurio.
http://diario.elmercurio.com/2004/03/20/_portada/index.htm

El Norte
www.elnorte.com

El Panama America.
www.espasa.www.espasa.com

El Siglo
www.elsiglo.com

El Tiempo
www.eltiempo.com

El Universal (Mexico)
www.el-universal.com.mx

El Universal (Venezuela)
www.el-universal.com

Estrategia
www.estrategia.cl

Folha de Sao Paulo
www.uol.com.br/fsp

Gazeta Mercantil
www.gazeta.com.br

InfoBrazil
www.infobrazil.com

Jornal do Brasil
www.jb.com.br

La Jornada
http://serpiente.dgsca.unam.mx/jornada/index.html

La Nacion
www.lanacion.com.ar

La Republica
http://ekeko.rcp.net.pe/LaRepublica

LANIC Newsroom
http://lanic.utexas.edu/info/newsroom/

O Globo
www.oglobo.com.br

Venezuela Online
www.venezuelaonline.com

Middle East

Al Anwar
www.dm.net.lb/alanwar

Al Ayam (Arabic and English)
www.alayam.com

Al Ittihad
www.alittihad.co.ae

Bahrain Tribune
www.bahraintribune.com

Egypt Daily
www.egyptdaily.com

Globes
www.globes.co.il/

Gulf Times
www.gulf-times.com

Iran Daily
www.iran-daily.com

Iran Press Service.
www.iran-press-service.com

Iran: Neda Net
www.neda.net

Iraq Daily
www.iraqdaily.com

IRNA. Iraq Daily
www.iraqdaily.com

Jerusalem Post
www.jpost.co.il

Middle East Economic Digest
www.meed.com

MidEast Business Weekly Update
www.infoprod.co.il/MEB/meb1.htm#s

Turkish Business World
www.turkishbusinessworld.com

Turkish Daily News
www.turkishdailynews.co

Zaman Daily
www.zaman.com.tr

United States of America

American City Business Journals
http://amcity.com

Kansas City Star
www.kansascity.com

New York Times on the Web
www.nytimes.com

San Francisco Chronicle
www.sfgate.com/search

Wall Street Journal Interactive Edition
www.wsj.com

The Washington Post
www.washingtonpost.com/wp-srv/searches/mainsrch.htm

Nonprofits and Charities

These sites can be quite useful. Identifying VIP's on a charity's Board of Directors, for example, may provide more background details on a competitor's CEO. It also is possible to determine what charities exist in a geographic area and the identity of their major benefactors. Some of the sites below provide IRS Form 990's for the organizations in their database.

Better Business Bureau Business Wise Giving Alliance
www.give.org/reports/index.asp

The Center on Philanthropy At Indiana University
www.philanthropy.iupui.edu

Chronicle of Philanthropy
http://philanthropy.com

Exempt Organizations Search - IRS
www.irs.gov/charities/index.html

Foundation Center: Finding Funders
http://fdncenter.org/funders/grantmaker/gws_pubch/pubch1.html

GuideStar - The Donor's Guide to Charities & Nonprofits
www.guidestar.org

Idealist Home
www.idealist.org

Internet Nonprofit Center
www.nonprofits.org

National Center for Charitable Statistics at The Urban Institute
http://nccsdataweb.urban.org

NonProfit Times
www.nptimes.com

PJ Online: Philanthropy Links : Meta Index of Non-Profit Sites
www.charitablegift.org/resource/links/phil.shtml

Private Foundations on the Internet
http://fdncenter.org/funders/grantmaker/gws_priv/priv1.html

The Foundation Center
http://fdncenter.org

The Foundation Center's Foundation Finder
http://lnp.fdncenter.org/finder.html

The Rich List
www.richlist.com/jewish.htm

Search for Charities, Online Version of Publication 78
www.irs.gov/charities/page/0,,id=15053,00.html

Patents / Trademarks/Intellectual Property

A variety of U.S. and non-U.S. sources have been collected here. Some of these offer services such as data analysis in addition to patent searches. The USPTO website warns that theirs is the only OFFICIAL site.

Copyrights

CIPO - Copyrights Database
http://strategis.gc.ca/cipo/copyrights/jsp/search.jsp

Copyright Office Records Search
www.loc.gov/copyright/rb.html

Thomson & Thomson
www.thomson-thomson.com

Miscellaneous IP Sites

Intellectual Property Links compiled by Patent Attorney Ralph Beier
www.ip-links.de/

IP Australia
www.ipaustralia.gov.au/

IPONZ Search (New Zealand)
www.iponz.govt.nz

Manning & Napier
www.mnis.com

PIPACS (Hungary)
http://pipacsweb.hpo.hu/

USPTO FOIA Reading Room
www.uspto.gov/web/offices/com/sol/foia/readroom.htm

USPTO Official Gazette Notices
www.uspto.gov/web/offices/com/sol/og/index.html

USPTO Official Website
http://patents.uspto.gov

World Intellectual Property Organization
www.wipo.org/eng/dgtext.htm

Patents

Canadian Intellectual Property Office - Canadian Patent Database
http://Patents1.ic.gc.ca/intro-e.html

Collections by Type--Patents
http://www-sul.stanford.edu/collect/patents.html

Delphion
www.delphion.com

European Patent Office
www.european-patent-office.org

Global Patent Search Engine
http://patentsearch.patentcafe.com

Intellectual Property Digital Library
www.wipo.int/ipdl/en/index.jsp

Japan Patent Office Home Page
www.jpo.go.jp/

MicroPatent
www.micropat.com

PRH -- National Board of Patents and Registration of Finland
www.prh.fi/en.html

PRV – Swedish Patent & Registration Office
www.prv.se/

QPAT-US
www.qpat.com

STO's Internet Patent Search System
www.ibiblio.org/patents/intropat.html

Technology Review 2003 Patent Scorecard (MIT)
www.technologyreview.com/scorecards

Thomson Derwent Scientific and Patent Information
www.derwent.com

Thomson Patent Store
www.ipr-village.info/derwent/index_ipr.html

UK Patent Office
www.patent.gov.uk/

United States Patent and Trademark Office
www.uspto.gov

Trademarks

ATMOSS - Australian Trade Mark Online Search System
http://pericles.ipaustralia.gov.au/atmoss/falcon.application_start

Basic Facts About Registering a Trademark
www.uspto.gov/web/offices/tac/doc/basic

CIPO - Canadian Trade-marks Database
http://strategis.ic.gc.ca/cipo/trademarks/search/tmSearch.do

Final Decisions - Trademark Trial & Appeal Board
www.uspto.gov/web/offices/com/sol/foia/ttab/ttab.htm

OAMI-ONLINE - Trade Mark Consultation Service
http://oami.eu.int/search/trademark/la/en_tm_search.cfm

Researching Trademarks
www.info-law.com/tmsearch.html

Thomson & Thomson
www.thomson-thomson.com

Trade mark links
www.bl.uk/services/information/patents/tmlinks.html#leg

Trademark Electronic Search System (Tess)
http://tess2.uspto.gov/bin/gate.exe?f=tess&state=coi8rn.1.1

TTABVUE – Trademark Dispute Documents
http://ttabvue.uspto.gov

UK Patent Office - Trade marks - Database Search
www.patent.gov.uk/tm/dbase/index.htm

People Locators

These sites may be useful in gathering biographical information about a competitor's personnel or those formerly connected with the company. They should, of course be supplemented by the use of newspapers and magazines and other types of sources mentioned earlier in this book.

AMA Physician Select
www.AMA-ASSN.ORG/aps/amahg.htm

BellSouth Real Pages
www.whitepages.com/10340?from=NBK

Bigfoot
www.bigfoot.com

Canadian Who's Who 2004
www.utpress.utoronto.ca/cgi-bin/cw2w3.cgi

Congressional Biographical Directory
http://bioguide.congress.gov/biosearch/biosearch.asp

Dictionary of Canadian Biography Online
www.biographi.ca/index2.html

Disqualified Directors Search - UK
http://ws3.companies-house.gov.uk/ddir/index.shtml

EDGAR Online: People
http://people.edgar-online.com/people

E-Mail Directory
www.worldemail.com

Forbes.com_ World's Richest People
www.forbes.com/2003/02/26/billionaireland.html

Fortune.com - 40 Under 40 Richest
www.fortune.com/fortune/40under40/richest/0,18384,,00.html

Fortune: The Most Powerful People in Business
www.fortune.com/fortune/mostpowerful

Fortune.com - Most Powerful Women
www.fortune.com/fortune/powerwomen

GTE SuperPages
http://superpages.gte.com

Idexec
www.idexec.com

InfoSpace.Com
www.infospace.com

Landings: Search for Certified Pilots
www.landings.com/evird.acgi$pass*62286838!_h-www.landings.co
m/_landings/pages/search.html

LexisNexis
www.nexis.com

Martindale-Hubbell Lawyer Locator
www.martindale.com

MetaEmail Search Agent (MESA)
http://mesa.rrzn.uni-hannover.de

Netscape White Pages
http://wp.netscape.com/netcenter/whitepages.html

People Lookup - Find Street Address and Telephone Number
www.peoplelookup.com

SearchBug - The Most Useful Searches
www.searchbug.com

Tele-Info OnLine (German)
www.teleinfo.de

The Noble Group: Internet Directories
www.experts.com

The Ultimates
www.theultimates.com

Who's Who European Business and Industry - Database
www.who-database.com

Yahoo! People Search
www.yahoo.com/search/people/email.html

Political Risk

These sites provide a great deal of intelligence for companies doing business in other countries. In addition to advising on the stability of the business environment in these countries, they provide detailed country reports and data on licensing and related business issues.

International Credit Reports, Collection Svcs & Marketing
www.kreller.com

The Economist Intelligence Unit
www.eiu.com

The PRS Group
www.prsgroup.com

Procurement

Many of these sites have been included elsewhere in this list.
For convenience, they have been gathered together here.

Corporate Wireless Contracts & Procurement Practices, Trends & Forecast
www.instat.com/r/nrep/2004/IN0401661MBM.htm

Department of Transportation Contracting and Procurement Opportunities
http://osdbuweb.dot.gov/business/procurement/forecast.html

Federal Aviation Administration Procurement Forecast
www.faa.gov/Newsroom/FY04-15AerospaceForecasts.cfm

Federal Procurement Data System
www.fpdc.gov/fpdc/fpdc_home.htm

National Association of State Procurement Officers (NASPO) Search for State Websites
www.naspo.org/directory/index.cfm

Nova Scotia (Canada) Procurement Site
http://198.166.215.5/finance/tour

SBA - PRO-Net - What is PRO-Net? (Procurement Search Engine)
http://pro-net.sba.gov/index2.html

USAID Forecast Reports - Procurement
www.usaid.gov/procurement_bus_opp/procurement/forecast/wforecast.htm

Products

Your Sales and Marketing or Research and Development departments are always interested in what your competition is doing regarding product development. They may also be interested in what competitors types of manuals competitors are providing for customers and what customers think about products. Here are some sites that may be useful in their quest.

Ad Age Marketing Intelligence
www.adage.com/MarketingIntel/

ConsumerReview.com
www.consumerreview.com/

Intelliseek
www.intelliseek.com/marketingi.asp

LiveManuals
www.livemanuals.com/help/h1.cfm#1

MegaBrands Index
www.adage.com/page.cms?pageId=598

Planet Feedback
www.planetfeedback.com/homepage/0,2585,,00.html

PNN - Product News Network
http://productnews.com

Productscan
www.productscan.com

SurfSaver Pro
www.surfsaver.com

Public Records

This large collection of public record sites on the Internet has been subdivided for more efficient use. The initial group contains both commercial and free sites, containing various types of information.

ASSORTED SITES & VENDORS

Access Gateway to All 50 Secretary of State Websites
www.secst.com

ADP Select Online
https://ox.avert.com/apps/Login.jsp

American University's Campaign Finance Website
http://www1.soc.american.edu/campfin/index.cfm

Assessor Offices Cybersites
http://recenter.tamu.edu/links/clappd.html

Assessor webs
www.ci.mil.wi.us/citygov/assessor/otherassessorwebs.htm

Campaign Finance
http://campaignfinance.org/states.html

ChoicePoint Public Records Group
www.choicepointonline.com/cdb/

City-County Directory (Yahoo!)
http://local.yahoo.com/bin/get_local

County Information Address Locator
www.genealogy.com/00000229.html?Welcome=1081864295

Dataquick Real Estate Information
http://products.dataquick.com/consumer

Experian Credit & Real Estate Information
www.experian.com

Experian: Uniform Commercial Code Sample Report
www.experian.com/product/pubrec/uccsample.html

Family Tree Maker's Genealogy Site: Resources by County
www.familytreemaker.com/00000229.html

Federal Reserve Press Releases - Enforcement Actions
www.federalreserve.gov/boarddocs/press/enforcement

How to Obtain Birth, Death, Marriage & Divorce Certificates
www.cdc.gov/nchswww/howto/w2w/w2welcom.htm

Incorporation
www.afscme.org/wrkplace/incorp.htm

Informus (Employment screening)
www.informus.com/

Investment Adviser Public Disclosure
www.adviserinfo.sec.gov/IAPD/Content/IapdMain/iapd_SiteMap.asp

KnowX | Home
www.knowx.com

Landings: Aviation Search Engines: FARs, N-Numbers, NTSBs, SDRs, ADs, AMEs, Pilots, Medical Examiners, Regulations
www.landings.com/evird.acgi$pass*63314412!_h-www.landin
gs.com/_landings/pages/search.html

Merlin Information Services
www.merlindata.com

Militarycity.com
www.militarycity.com

National Association of Professional Background Screeners
www.napbs.com

NASD-R Public Disclosure Program [Broker Search]
http://pdpi6.nasdr.com/pdpi/Req_Type_Frame.asp

National Public Records Research Association (NPRRA)
www.nprra.org

Netroline – Real Estate and Real Property
www.netronline.com

New Generation Research (Bankruptcy Publications)
www.turnarounds.com

Opensecrets.org: Lobbyists
www.opensecrets.org/lobbyists/index.asp

Opensecrets.org: Political Action Committees
www.opensecrets.org/pacs/index.asp

PoliticalMoneyLine
www.tray.com/fecinfo/

Privacy Act
http://foia.state.gov/privacy.asp

Public Records Online
www.netronline.com/public_records.htm

PublicRecordSources.Com
www.publicrecordsources.com

Social Security Administration & Genealogy FAQ
http://members.aol.com/rechtman/ssafaq.html#11

Social Security Death Index
www.ancestry.com/ssdi/advanced.htm

State Bar of California Member Records Online
www.calsb.org/MM/SBMBRSHP.HTM

State Privacy Laws
www.epic.org:80/privacy/consumer/states.html

USDatalink
www.usdatalink.com

UCC Direct Services
www.uccdirect.com

Vital Records
www.publicrecordfinder.com/vitalrecrds.html

COURTS

Courts.net
www.courts.net

Public Access to Court Electronic Records
http://pacer.psc.uscourts.gov

State Court Locator
http://vls.law.vill.edu/Locator/statecourt/

U.S. Courts Website
www.uscourts.gov

CREDIT RECORDS

Business Credit USA
www.businesscreditusa.com

Credit Information Reports from Business Credit Management UK
www.creditman.co.uk

Delos Creditinfo Ltd. – Cyprus, Iceland, Lithuania, Malta
www.creditinfo.ro/

Dun & Bradstreet Reports
www.dnb.com

Equifax Iberica (Spain)
www.asnefequifax.es/equifaxnet/servlet/com.efx.equifaxnet.servl
ets.SEntrada

Equifax Italy
www.equifax.it/

National Credit Information Network
www.WDIA.com

Online Canadian Credit Report and Credit History Information Equifax Canada
www.equifax.com/EFX_Canada/

Online Credit Reports and Credit Reporting from a Leading Credit Agency Equifax
www.equifax.co.uk/

FOIA REQUESTS

Department of Justice: Other Agencies' FOIA Websites
www.usdoj.gov/foia/other_age.htm

Freedom of Information Act (FOIA)
http://foia.state.gov/foia.htm

Freedom of Information Act Group Inc.
www.foia.com

National Freedom of Information Coalition
www.nfoic.org

SPJ: FOI Resource Center
www.spj.org/foia.asp

US Department of State Electronic: Reading Room: Reference
http://foia.state.gov/refer.htm

INDIVIDUAL STATES/COUNTY FILES - FREE

A large and current collection of public record sites on the Internet is available online at
www.brbpub.com/pubrecsites.asp. You may search for free federal, state, county and
other public record sites. Varying by state, you may find websites for searching *Assessors,
Corporations, County Court Records, Court Opinions, Deaths, Fictitious Business Names,
Incarceration Records, Legislator Lookups, Liens, Marriages, Missing Persons Pages, Most
Wanted Lists, Non-Profit Organizations, Sex Offenders, State Archives, Statewide Criminal and
Statewide Court Records, Supreme and Appellate Court Decisions, Tax Sales Lists, Trade
Names, Trademarks, Treasurer, UCCs, Unclaimed Property.* Even obscure information as *dog
tag lookups* and *restaurant inspections* can be found online for some U.S. counties.

NON-U.S. PUBLIC RECORD SITES

aRMadillo
www.rmonline.com/pr2.htm

BC OnLine - Access to Government Information
www.bconline.gov.bc.ca

Canada Public Records – via Search Systems
www.searchsystems.net/list.php?nid=68

Canada - Search for Public Company Documents
www.sedar.com

Companies Houst (UK)
www.companieshouse.gov.uk/

Industry Canada Corporations Database
http://strategis.ic.gc.ca/cio/search-recherche/site.do?language=eng

Japan Company Records
http://japanfinancials.com

Liquidations Search, Insolvency (UK)
www.insolvency.co.uk/liq/liqfind.htm

Outside USA Public Records
www.publicrecordfinder.com/outside_usa.html

Office of the Superintendent of Bankruptcy Canada - Insolvency Name Search
https://strategis.ic.gc.ca/sc_mrksv/bankruptcy/bankruptcySearch/engdoc/

Public Record Office _ UK Central Government Web Archive
www.pro.gov.uk/webarchive/

Register of Charities – UK
www.charity-commission.gov.uk/registeredcharities/first.asp

Teikoku Databank America Inc
www.teikoku.com

UK Data Ltd (UK Company Information)
www.ukdata.com

UK Trade Marks
www.patent.gov.uk/tm/dbase/index.htm

JUMPING OFF PLACES FOR OTHER PUBLIC RECORD SITES

BRB Publications, Inc.
www.brbpub.com/pubrecsites.asp

Consumer Business DB Link Page
www.security-online.com/info/baddebt.html

National Assn. Of Licensed Investigators Investigative Links
www.nalionline.org/region.html#Virginia

Search Systems Free Public Records Directory
www.searchsystems.net

SUBSCRIPTION OR FEE REQUIRED

ADP Screening and Selection Services
https://ox.avert.com/apps/Login.jsp

ChoicePoint
www.choicepointonline.com/cdb/

DCS Information Systems
www.dnis.com

Experian Credit and Real Estate Information
www.experian.com

KnowX
www.knowx.com

LexisNexis
www.nexis.com/research

Merlin Information Services
www.merlindata.com

Superior Information Services
www.superiorinfo.com

UNCLAIMED PROPERTY

This is a combination of commercial and government sites. Although usefulness as business intelligence is limited, unclaimed property generates public records that could contain names and addresses, which is why they have been retained in this list.

FindCash.Com - UNCLAIMED MONEY Database
www.findcash.com

Foundmoney.com
www.foundmoney.com

National Unclaimed Property Database
www.nupd.com/FAQ.htm

Nevada County California Unclaimed Property
http://treas-tax.co.nevada.ca.us

Rhode Island Unclaimed Property
www.state.ri.us/treas/treas.htm

U.S. GOVERNMENT SEARCHABLE PUBLIC RECORD SITES

A number of U.S. government databases have been made available for searching on the Internet. Competitors' names may appear on any of these, and you may therefore add this data to your knowledge base.

Employer Sanctions Database
www.cis.org/sanctions/

Envirofacts Query Form
www.epa.gov/enviro/html/multisystem.html

Exempt Organizations Search - IRS
www.irs.gov/charities/page/0,,id=15053,00.html

Fannie Mae - Search
www.mortgagecontent.net/reoSearchApplication/fanniemae/reoSearch.jsp

OSHA DATA Regulatory Compliance History Information Service
www.oshadata.com

OSHA Statistics & Data
www.osha.gov/oshstats

US Department of Education: Grant Award Action Database 2000
http://web99.ed.gov/grant/grtawd00.nsf

Publishers

Dozens of publishers maintain homepages on the Internet. This short list includes publishers whose materials facilitate successful online searching, and therefore more successful competitor intelligence gathering.

BRB Publications Inc
www.brbpub.com

Information Today Inc
www.infotoday.com

Push Technologies

This technology may be useful for gathering business intelligence as it becomes news. The Intranet Content Management site contains a survey of current PUSH products, with pricing information.

Inquisit
www.inquisit.com

Intranet content management and push products
www.intranetjournal.com/tools-km.shtml

NewsEdge
www.dialog.com/newsedge/

Serence
www.serence.com

QPass
www.qpass.com

RocketInfo
www.rocketinfo.com

Reference Tools

These sites contain a variety of information that may be useful in many types of research, not strictly limited to business intelligence.

Aardvark: Asian Resources for Librarians
www.aardvarknet.info/user/subject26/index.cfm?all=All

Acronym Finder
www.acronymfinder.com

All Yellow Pages
www.wtn-de.com/tradedi/wwyellow.html

The American Secular Holidays Calendar
www.smart.net/~mmontes/ushols.html

AltaVista's Babel Fish Translation Service
http://babelfish.altavista.com/

Biographical Dictionary Search Page
www.s9.com/biography/search.html

CCFINDER (Credit Cards)
www.ccfinder.com

City-County Directory (Yahoo!)
http://local.yahoo.com/bin/get_local

Digital Librarian_ a librarian's choice of the best of the Web
www.digital-librarian.com

Embassy & Consulate Directory of Embassy & Consulate Addresses & Websites
www.embassyworld.com

Encyclopedia Brittanica
www.britannica.com

FaganFinder
www.faganfinder.com/translate

FedEx | Tracking
www.fedex.com/us/tracking/

Free Dictionary.com
http://encyclopedia.thefreedictionary.com

The Inflation Calculator
www.westegg.com/inflation

Information Please Home Page
www.infoplease.com

Medline Plus Medical Dictionary
www.nlm.nih.gov/medlineplus/mplusdictionary.html

The National Address Server
www.cedar.buffalo.edu/adserv.html

National Virtual Translation Center
www.nvtc.gov/aboutus.php

NewsEngin Inc.
http://newsengin.com/newsengin.nsf

NewsEngin's Cost-of-Living Calculator
http://newsengin.com/nefreetools.nsf/cpicalc

OANDA Currency Converter, Historical Charts, Current Exchange Rates, and Forex Forecast
www.oanda.com

Online Dictionaries and Translators
http://dictionary.reference.com/translate/text.html

Online Medical Dictionary
http://cancerweb.ncl.ac.uk/omd/

POSTINFO : World-Address postal information service
http://postinfo.net

Prices's List of Lists
www.specialissues.com/lol/

Refdesk.com
www.refdesk.com/

ReferenceDesk.org -- The Internet's Best Reference Source!
www.referencedesk.org

ResourceShelf
http://resourceshelf.freepint.com

The Quotations Page
www.starlingtech.com/quotes/index.html

University of Central Florida
http://library.ucf.edu/Line/BusinessRef/ListofLists.htm

UPS Package Tracking
www.ups.com/tracking/tracking.html

USPS ZIP+4 Code Lookup
www.usps.gov/ncsc/lookups/lookup_zip+4.html

Virtual Gumshoe-Investigative Resources on the Web-Government Directories
www.virtualgumshoe.com/gator80.htm

Sales Leads

B2b Sales and Marketing
www.imarketinc.com

Harris InfoSource
www.harrisinfo.com/servlet/HIServlet?moduleName=session&methodName=getHomePage

Science/Technology

Although there is a great deal of material available on the Internet that falls under the heading "science and technology," these sites may have some application in the process of determining what is happening in an industry of interest where science or technology is a key component. See also bookmarks for the biotechnology industry listed previously in the Industry category.

BIOSCIENCE

MedBioWorld - Bioscience Journals
www.medbioworld.com/bio/journals/bio-journals.html

BIOTECHNOLOGY

BUBL LINK: Biotechnology
http://link.bubl.ac.uk/biotechnology

CHEMISTRY

American Chemical Society Publications Essential Resources / Chemical Sciences
http://pubs.acs.org

SciFinder
http://info.cas.org/SCIFINDER/scicover2.html

World Wide Web Virtual Library: Chemistry
www.chem.ucla.edu/chempointers.html

DOCUMENTS / REPORTS

Canada Institute For Scientific and Technical Information (CISTI)
http://cisti-icist.nrc-cnrc.gc.ca/cisti_e.shtml

Canadian Federal Government Research Agencies
www.dfait-maeci.gc.ca/can-am/menu-
en.asp?act=v&did=1176&mid=11&cat=481&typ=1

CSA – Internet Data Service
www.csa.com/csa/ids/ids-main.shtml

Defense Technical Information Center
www.dtic.mil/dtic/prodsrvc/stinet.html

DOE Reports Bibliographic Database
www.osti.gov/bridge/

Economist Intelligence Unit
www.store.eiu.com

Environmental Data Resources
www.edrnet.com

Federal R&D Project Summaries
http://fedrnd.osti.gov

Gov.Research-Center: NTIS Database
http://grc.ntis.gov/energy.htm

NASA Technical Report Server (NTRS)
http://ntrs.nasa.gov

National Center for Manufacturing Sciences
www.ncms.org

National Patterns of Research & Development Resources
www.nsf.gov/sbe/srs/nprdr/start.htm

Networked Computer Science Technical Reports Library
http://sunsite.berkeley.edu/ncstrl

OpenNet
www.osti.gov/opennet/

Science & Technology Documents & Subscription Information
http://clinton1.nara.gov/White_House/EOP/OSTP/html/pub-
plain.html

The Scientist - Hot Papers Archives
www.the-scientist.com/hotpapersarchive.htm

STINET: Scientific & Technical Reports Collection
www.dtic.mil/dtic/prodsrvc/stinet.html

UCSD Engineering Library - Technical Reports
http://scilib.ucsd.edu/howto/guides/techrepts.html

US Government Laboratories
www.re-quest.net/g2g/govt/federal/labs/

Yahoo! Science: Computer Science: Technical Reports
http://dir.yahoo.com/Science/computer_science/technical_reports/

MISCELLANEOUS SCIENCE/TECHNOLOGY SITES

Community Research and Development Information Service (CORDIS)
www.cordis.lu

Federal Laboratory Consortium (FLC): Resource Directory Search
www.federallabs.org/servlet/FLCLabIndexServlet

IDRIS - Inter-Agency Development Research Information System
http://idrinfo.idrc.ca/scripts/minisa.dll/144/IDRIS?DIRECTSEARCH

In-cites
www.in-cites.com/index.html

Isis Innovation - University of Oxford Innovation and Technology Transfer
www.isis-innovation.com

National Research Council Canada
www.nrc.ca

NIST Tech Beat - September 26, 2003
www.nist.gov/public_affairs/techbeat/tb2003_0926.htm#free

Science and Engineering Indicators: 2002
www.nsf.gov/sbe/srs/seind02/start.htm

ScienceDirect - Home
www.sciencedirect.com

ViFaPhys - The Physics Virtual Library
http://vifaphys.tib.uni-hannover.de/

Web of Science: Thomson
www.isinet.com/products/citation/wos/

Search Engines & Internet Directories

These tools are often considered the backbone of the Internet. The list below includes both meta search engines, that search multiple search engines at one time, and the more traditional search engines. The Beaucoup sites are a favorite of this author because they gather so many specialized search engines together on one page. This is a great way to manage an organized search across many search engines since the links on the list change color after you've accessed them. Some links to search engines are included under specific subjects elsewhere in this Bookmarks list.

INVISIBLE WEBSITES

*The Invisible Web is a new concept since the first edition of this book. The sites listed below and others like them provide access to thousands of databases that are **not included in the searches run by typical search engines**. They are frequently found as links on portals or other websites that collect such resources. The Invisible Web may provide access to intelligence that could otherwise be overlooked. Smart searchers will include searches here if trying to locate comprehensive information on a topic.*

BUBL LINK / 5:15 Catalogue of Selected Internet Resources
http://bubl.ac.uk/link/

Complete Planet
http://aip.completeplanet.com/

Deep Web Search
www.mach9design.com/deep/deep1.html

Direct search
www.freepint.com/gary/direct.htm

The GrayLIT Network
www.osti.gov/graylit/

IncyWincy: The Invisible Web Search Engine
www.incywincy.com

INFOMINE
http://infomine.ucr.edu/cgi-bin/search

Invisible-Web.Net
www.invisible-web.net

Librarians' Index to the Internet
http://lii.org

ProFusion
www.profusion.com

Resource Discovery Network
www.rdn.ac.uk/

Search Adobe PDF
http://searchpdf.adobe.com

Searchlight ALL homepage
http://searchlight.cdlib.org/cgi-bin/searchlight

Special search engines
www.leidenuniv.nl/ub/biv/specials.htm#Par62

Those Dark Hiding Places
http://library.rider.edu/scholarly/rlackie/Invisible/Inv_Web_Main.html

Vascoda (Germany)
www.vascoda.de

What is the Invisible Web?
http://websearch.about.com/library/weekly/aa061203a.htm

META SEARCH ENGINES

Ask Jeeves
www.askjeeves.com

Copernic Agent
www.copernic.com/en/index.html

Debriefing
www.debriefing.com

DMOZ Open Directory Project
http://dmoz.org

Dogpile, the Friendly Multi-Engine Search Tool
www.dogpile.com

EZ2Find
http://ez2www.com

Fazzle Search
www.fazzle.com/log.jsp

HotBot
www.hotbot.com/Default.asp

Internet Sleuth
www.isleuth.com

Ixquick
www.ixquick.com

LookSmart
http://search.looksmart.com

MAMMA
www.mamma.com

MetaCrawler
www.metacrawler.com

Metasearch
http://metasearch.com

Mirago
www.mirago.co.uk

Multimeta
www.multimeta.com

One Search
www.onesearch.com

OpenText Query Server
www.queryserver.com/web.htm

ProFusion
www.profusion.com

Search.com
www.search.com

Surfwax
www.surfwax.com

Vivisimo
www.vivissimo.com

MISCELLANEOUS INTERNET SEARCH TOOLS

About
http://home.miningco.com

All-in-One Search Page
www.allonesearch.com/all1srch.html

AllSearchEngines.com - search engine index, search engine directory
www.allsearchengines.com

AlltheWeb
www.alltheweb.com/advanced

AltaVista
www.altavista.com

Beaucoup! (Main Menu)
www.beaucoup.com

BUBL LINK: Browse by Subject
www.bubl.ac.uk/link/subjects

Business.com
www.business.com

EuroSeek
www.euroseek.com

Excite
www.excite.com

FinderSeeker_ The Search Engine for Search Engines
www.finderseeker.com

Galaxy Search Engine & Directory
www.first-search.com

Google
www.google.com

Google Canada
www.google.ca

Inference Find!
www.shindale.com/metasearch.html

Internet Searching Center
www.clearinghouse.net/searching/index.html

Internet Sleuth (iSleuth.com)
www.isleuth.com

Kellysearch
www.kellys.co.uk

Mirago - The UK Search Engine
www.mirago.co.uk

ProFusion
www.profusion.com

Search Engine Colossus
www.searchenginecolossus.com

Search Engine Guide
www.searchengineguide.com/searchengines.html

Search Engine Watch: News, Tips and More About Search Engines
http://searchenginewatch.com

Search Engines - refdesk.com - My Search Engines
www.refdesk.com/newsrch.html

Search Engine Showdown
www.searchengineshowdown.com/features

Search Engines Worldwide (global & local search engines, directories, metasearch, meta, mp3)
http://home.inter.net/takakuwa/search/search.html

SearchUK
www.searchuk.com

Spider's Apprentice - How to Use Web Search Engines
www.monash.com/spidap.html

Starting Point
www.stpt.com

SusySearch (South Africa)
www.susysearch.com

Teoma
www.teoma.com

Thunderstone
http://search.thunderstone.com/texis/websearch

Website Search Tools
www.searchtools.com

Webcrawler
www.webcrawler.com

whatUseek
www.whatuseek.com

Yahoo!
www.yahoo.com

SPECIALIZED SEARCH ENGINES/DIRECTORIES

AgNIC System Engine (Agriculture)
www.agnic.org

Beaucoup! (Arts/Music/Graphics)
www.beaucoup.com/1artseng.html

Beaucoup! (Computers/Internet/WWW/Programming)
www.beaucoup.com/1comeng.html

Beaucoup! (E-mail)
www.beaucoup.com/1emaeng.html

Beaucoup! (Employment)
www.beaucoup.com/1empeng.html

Beaucoup! (Geographically Specific)
www.beaucoup.com/1geoeng.html

Beaucoup! (Health/Medicine/Foods)
www.beaucoup.com/1heaeng.html

Beaucoup! (Media)
www.beaucoup.com/1medeng.html

Beaucoup! (Politics/Government/Law)
www.beaucoup.com/1poleng.html

Beaucoup! (Science/Nature/Technology)
www.beaucoup.com/1scieng.html

Beaucoup! (Social/Environmental/Political Concerns)
www.beaucoup.com/1enveng.html

Beaucoup! (Software)
www.beaucoup.com/1softeng.html

Beaucoup! Reference
www.beaucoup.com/1refeng.html

Bizjournals.com
www.bizjournals.com

BPubs.com – Industry Publications
www.bpubs.com/Industry_Publications/

Business.com - Business Search Engine and Business Directory
www.business.com/index.asp?partner=FT

Computer Science
http://library.albany.edu/subject/csci.htm

Electronic Journal Finder
http://ejournal.coalliance.org/SubSearcher.cfm?subj=Technology

Google Directory
http://directory.google.com

Kellysearch - The search engine for UK industry
www.kellys.co.uk/

MagPortal.com - Magazine Article Search Engine, Directory, and Data Feeds
www.magportal.com

MedNets – A medical search engine and health portal
www.mednets.com

Software

Software found on some of these sites may prove useful in massaging or manipulating business intelligence gathered elsewhere in electronic format.

Adobe Acrobat Reader Download
www.adobe.com/products/acrobat/readstep2.html

CWSApps - 32-bit Internet Agents
http://cws.internet.com/32agents.html

DOWNLOAD.COM: List of Tools & Utilities
www.download.com

FerretSoft - Free Downloads
www.ferretsoft.com/netferret/download.htm

Jumbo! Download Network
www.jumbo.com

Statistics

Statistics of all types are required for building the knowledge base in your company. Information gathered using this data is crucial for making good business decisions, but must be updated periodically. Note that the U.S. government category of this list contains statistics sites at the government department level.

COUNTRY-SPECIFIC STATISTICS SITES

2002 National Industry-Specific Occupational Employment and Wage Estimates
www.bls.gov/oes/2002/oessrci.htm

Occupational Employment & Wage Estimates (U.S.)
http://stats.bls.gov/oes/oes_data.htm

Centraal Bureau voor de Statistiek/Statistics Netherlands
www.cbs.nl

Economic Statistics Briefing Room (US)
www.whitehouse.gov/fsbr/esbr.html

Instituto Nacional de Estadistica (Spain)
www.ine.es

National Statistics Online (UK)
www.statistics.gov.uk/

Statistics Canada
www.statcan.ca/start.html

Statistical Links (Links to many countries)
www.cbs.nl/en/service/links/default.asp

Statistical Office of the Republic of Slovenia (In Slovenian)
www.stat.si/

Statistical Profile of Canadian Communities
http://www12.statcan.ca/english/Profil01/PlaceSearchForm1.cfm

Statistics Bureau & Statistics Center (Japan)
www.stat.go.jp/english/

Statistisk sentralbyrõ (Norway)
www.ssb.no/english/

Sub-Saharan Africa Data and Statistics
http://www4.worldbank.org/afr/stats/cldb.htm

MISCELLANEOUS STATISTICAL SITES

BUBL LINK: Statistical Mathematics
http://link.bubl.ac.uk/statistics

EUROSTAT
http://europa.eu.int/en/comm/eurostat/serven/home.htm

FedStats: One Stop Shopping for Federal Statistics
www.fedstats.gov

FedStats: A to Z
www.fedstats.gov/key.html

GlobalEDGE™
http://globaledge.msu.edu/ibrd/busresmain.asp?ResourceCategoryID=10

International Business Resources: Statistical Data & Information Resources
http://ciber.msu.edu/busres/Static/Statistical-Data-Sources.htm

National Bureau of Economic Research (NBER)
www.nber.org

NSF: Division of Science Resources Studies
www.nsf.gov/sbe/srs/stats.htm

OECD Statistics
www.oecd.org/statsportal/0,2639,en_2825_293564_1_1_1_1_1,00.html

Statistical Sites on the World Wide Web
www.bls.gov/bls/other.htm

Statistical Abstract of the U.S.
www.census.gov/statab/www

Statistical Resources on the Web
www.lib.umich.edu/govdocs/stats.html

Statistics of Income
www.irs.gov/taxstats/content/0,,id=97507,00.html

Standards & Specifications

BUBL LINK: 389.6 Standardisation
http://link.bubl.ac.uk/standards

ISO Online
www.iso.ch/iso/en/ISOOnline.openerpage

Safety Link
www.safetylink.com

World-Wide Web Resources - Shaver Engineering Library - Standards
www.uky.edu/Subject/standardsall.html

Yahoo! Reference: Standards
www.yahoo.com/Reference/Standards

Telephone Information

These tools can be used in every department that makes long distance telephone calls. They save time, thereby increasing productivity.

Area Code Changes LinkPage
www.aim-corp.com/swbull/wwareacode.htm#us

Telephone Area Code Finder by MMIWORLD
http://mmiworld.com/statelis.htm

Telephone Lookups

Locate the correct telephone numbers for clients or competitors using tools such as these.

192.com Free Directory Enquiries
www.192.com/directoryenquiries.cfm

555-1212.com
www.555-1212.com

GTE SuperPages: Interactive Yellow Pages
http://yp.gte.net

Infobel World
www.infobel.com/world/default.asp

International Directories
www.aol.com/netfind/international.html

NumberWay
http://numberway.com

Telephone Directory - Switchboard Internet Yellow Pages and White Pages - Maps
www.switchboard.com

Toll Free Phone Search - Internet Directory for Toll-Free Phone Numbers
www.tollfreephone.com

Trade

All aspects of trade can benefit from one or more of these sites. Locating new sources for raw material may improve your company's bottom line, as could locating new markets for finished products. Government import/export related sites have been included here, as well.

AFTAonline!
www.aftaonline.com/archives01.html

Asian Sources Online
www.asiansources.com

BMI: Global and Emerging Markets
www.businessmonitor.com

Bradford (University) Management Centre
www.bradford.ac.uk/otss/uklinks.htm

Canadian Importers Database
http://strategis.ic.gc.ca/sc_mrkti/cid/engdoc/index.html?he=1

CargoConnect
www.ccx.com/ccsi/vafsr.html

Chamber of Commerce (Israel)
www.chamber.org.il/english/

CBDNet - Fielded Search via GPO Access
http://cbdnet.access.gpo.gov/search2.html

COSMOS
www.industry-portal.com

EURIDILE - Le Registre National du Commerce et des Sociétés (France)
www.euridile.inpi.fr/weur2/init.ow?WRNC

European Union Advanced Information Databases
www.adinfo.com

Exportall.com - the export, import and international business gateway
www.exportall.com

Federal Business Opportunity
www.fedbizopps.gov

Federation of International Trade Associations: Import Export Trade Leads
www.fita.org/fita.html

Federation of Indian Export Organisations (Canada)
www.fieo.com/canada.html

Foreign Trade Statistics
www.census.gov/foreign-trade/schedules/b/

GlobalEDGE
http://globaledge.msu.edu/ibrd/busresmain.asp?ResourceCategoryID=13

Harmonized Tariff Schedule of the United States
http://hotdocs.usitc.gov/tariff_chapters_current/toc.html

IIEINet - Resources - International Trade Links
www.expandglobal.com/library/index.html

IMF International Monetary Fund
www.imf.org

ImportDatabase.coml
www.importdatabase.com

Iceland, Faroe Islands, Finland, Greenland, Latvia, Lithuania, Norway, Sloven
www.randburg.com

India Yellow Pages Indian Business Directory Exporters Importers b2b Manufacturers
http://indiasyellowpages.com

International Trade Administration - Trade Information
www.ita.doc.gov

Journal of Commerce Online
www.joc.com

Schedule B - Commodity Classification - Browse & Search
www.census.gov/foreign-trade/schedules/b

SICE - Foreign Trade Information System
www.sice.oas.org

SignOn (Africa)
www.signonafrica.com

STAT-USA Internet
www.stat-usa.gov

Tdctrade.com
www.tdctrade.com

Tenderseek.com – Business Trade Leads
www.tenderseek.com

Trade Data Online
http://strategis.ic.gc.ca/sc_mrkti/tdst/engdoc/tr_homep.html

Trade Information Center
www.ita.doc.gov/tic

Trade Leads On Line -Argentina - Business Opportunities - Exporting to or Importing from Argentina and the Mercosur
www.tradeline.com.ar

TradePort - International Trade & Export Assistance
www.tradeport.org

The Trading Space
www.mbendi.co.za/a_sndmsg/trade_menu.asp

UK Trade & Investment
www.tradeuk.com/nindex.htm

US Department of Commerce: State Exports to Countries and Regions
http://ita.doc.gov/td/industry/otea/state/

US International Trade Commission: Tariff Database Search
http://dataweb.usitc.gov

U.S. International Trade and Freight Transportation Trends
www.bts.gov/publications/us_international_trade_and_freight_transportation_trends/2003/

USITC: Trade Resources
www.usitc.gov/tr/tr.htm

Websites for Exporters
http://dti.hyperco.net/cgi-bin/Search2.pl

IMPORTS/EXPORTS INCLUDING GOVERNMENT SITES

Bureau of Export Administration Home Page
www.bxa.doc.gov/#index

Canadian Exporters Catalogue
www.worldexport.com

Ex-Im Bank
www.exim.gov

Export Administration Regulations Marketplace (EAR)
http://bxa.fedworld.gov

Export.Gov
www.export.gov/comm_svc/

Export Market Information Centre (EMIC)
www.tradepartners.gov.uk/

Export-Import Bank Home Page
www.exim.gov

Financial Center.com
www.financialsupermarket.com/ies.html

INTERDATA Import Export Publications
www.export-leads.com

Serra International, Inc Freight Forwarder
www.serraintl.com

The Commercial Service of the U.S. Department of Commerce
www.ita.doc.gov/uscs

Travel

If you are in the transportation industry, then these sites may provide the scoop on what deals a competitor is currently offering. If you are not in that industry, you may reduce costs by taking advantage of some of the deals found on these sites.

American Airlines
www.americanair.com

Continental Airlines
www.continental.com

Expedia Travel
http://expedia.msn.com/daily/home/default.hts

Frommer's
www.frommers.com

Orbitz
www.orbitz.com

Southwest Airlines Home Gate
http://southwest.com

Travelocity
www.travelocity.com

US Airways
www.usairways.com

Usenets/Listservs

Monitor these groups to find out what is being said about your company or your competitors. This list of sites will help you to identify lists of interest.

Apple Mailing Lists
http://lists.apple.com

CataList, the official catalog of LISTSERV lists
www.lsoft.com/lists/listref.html

Google Groups
http://groups.google.com

List Resources.com
http://list-resources.com

Tile.Net
http://tile.net

Topica
http://lists.topica.com/dir/?cid=2188

Yahoo! Groups
http://groups.yahoo.com

Resource List

Locating Data, Databases, or Vendors

Finding Who Has What

After awhile, choosing which source to use becomes second nature. You learn which source would work best for the question at hand. There are times, however, when you need to do one of the following:

- Determine (before going online) whether a database file on a service to which you subscribe actually offers the facts you need.

- Find an alternative source for a database file that you know is available on an "expensive" service.

- Validate information already found, using another source.

- Locate pieces of information not explicitly required by the project description, but that will be needed to provide a satisfactory answer.

- Answer the "Friday Afternoon Question."

To librarians, the "Friday Afternoon Question" is that tough question that comes along when they do not have time to spend hours finding the answer or boning up on a new subject or industry. It happens something like this:

> You (or your team, or the Boss) need the information by (fill in blank with short deadline). You are under a time crunch just as you might be on Friday afternoon when your colleagues are leaving for the weekend. There is no "tomorrow" because tomorrow is Saturday, and you cannot work late because you have plans for the evening. Nonetheless, you need the answers quickly.

This Resource List is designed to come to your aid. It contains a **sampling** of the resources available in cyberspace for locating intelligence.

The list is divided into four sections:

- **Data Elements** - Look in the alphabetical list for the type of fact you need, and quickly learn the names of database files that contain that type of data, along with the names of one or more online services that offer that database file.

- **Database Files** - This list provides brief descriptions of the database files mentioned in the Data Elements list.

- **Industry List** - This list provides the names of one or more database files that cover each industry, with the names of the online services where the files can be found.

- **Vendors List** - Here you will find contact information for the database vendors mentioned above and for publishers of print materials mentioned elsewhere in the book.

The Resource List will be updated - where else? In cyberspace, of course, at the Burwell Enterprises website, www.burwellinc.com. Bookmarks & Favorites will be found there, as well.

Data Elements List

The data type is on the left-hand margin in bold. The source/database name is beneath in plain type, with the database provider listed to the right.

The sources listed here are examples; there may be additional data elements available that are not listed here. This information is subject to change.

Accountant (Independent) Voting Results...

LIVEDGAR -- www.gsionline.com

Accountant Opinions...

LIVEDGAR -- www.gsionline.com

Accountants, Change of...

LIVEDGAR -- www.gsionline.com

Advertising /Marketing Firm...

Advertiser & Agency Red Books -- Dialog (File 177, 178)

Marketing & Advertising Reference   Dialog (File 570)
Service (MARS) -- InSite Pro
LexisNexis

Standard Directory of Advertisers -- LexisNexis

Advertising Campaigns...

Globalbase -- Dialog (File 583)

Marketing & Advertising Reference   Dialog (File 570)
Service (MARS) -- InSite Pro
LexisNexis

Predicasts Overview of Markets &   Dialog (File 16)
Technology (PROMT) -- InSite Pro
LexisNexis

Advertising Media...

Business & Industry -- Alacra
DataStar (BIDB)
Dialog (File 9)

Marketing & Advertising Reference
Service (MARS) -- Dialog (File 570)
InSite Pro
LexisNexis

Advertising Spending...

Beverage Marketing -- Dialog (File 770)
Thomson Financial
Profound

Marketing & Advertising Reference
Service (MARS) -- Dialog (File 570)
InSite Pro
LexisNexis

MarketTrack -- LexisNexis (MKTRES)

Advertising Strategy...

Marketing & Advertising Reference
Service (MARS) -- Dialog (File 570)
InSite Pro
LexisNexis

Advertising Techniques...

Marketing & Advertising Reference
Service (MARS) -- Dialog (File 570)
InSite Pro
LexisNexis

Analyst Reports...

Investext Analyst Reports -- Factiva
Dialog (File 545)
Investext (Thomson Financial)

Multex Analyst Reports -- Factiva
www.reuters.com

Analyst Specialty...

Nelsons Specialty Regional
Analyst Coverage -- LexisNexis (NELSPE)

Analysts (Fixed Income/Securities)...

Nelson's Analyst Company Coverage -- LexisNexis (NELANC)

Annual Meeting Proxy Statements...

EDGARPlus - Proxy Statements -- Dialog (File 780)

LIVEDGAR -- www.gsionline.com

Annual Reports...

EDGARPLus - Annual Reports -- Dialog (File 777)

Awards...

Small Business Innovation Research
Awards (SBIRs) -- Knowledge Express

Balance Sheets

MG Financial/Stock Statistics -- Dialog (File 546)

MGFS Common Stock Database -- Alacra

Bank Assets... ... ...

Bankstat -- Thomson Financial

Bankruptcy 8-Ks... ... ...

LIVEDGAR -- www.gsionline.com

Bankruptcy Records...

Bankruptcy File (CBKF) -- FPinfomart.ca

CourtLink -- LexisNexis Courtlink

New Generation Research -- www.turnarounds.com

Banks - Financial Information...

Bankstat -- Thomson Financial

Best Efforts... ... ...

LIVEDGAR -- www.gsionline.com

Betas, Stock...

BARRA Global & Single Country   Alacra
Equity Models -- Barra.com

Financial Snapshot -- Factiva

Board - Classified / Staggered...

LIVEDGAR -- www.gsionline.com

Board Size-Increase...

LIVEDGAR -- www.gsionline.com

Brand Loyalty... ... ...

ABI/INFORM -- Dialog (File 15)
LexisNexis (ABISEL)

Business & Industry -- Alacra
DataStar (BIDB)
Dialog (File 9)

IAC: Newsletter Database -- Dialog (File 636)

Marketing & Advertising Reference   Dialog (File 570)
Service (MARS) -- InSite Pro
LexisNexis

Predicasts Overview of Markets &   DataStar (PTSP)
Technology (PROMT) -- Dialog (File 16)
InSite Pro
LexisNexis

Brand Share... ... ...

TableBase -- Alacra
DataStar (BTBL)
Dialog (File 93)

Bridge Loans... ... ...

LIVEDGAR -- www.gsionline.com

Broker Reports... ... ...

Zacks -- www.zacks.com/research/reports/

Budget Activity...

Jane's Information Group -- Dialog (File 587)
LexisNexis (JANDEF)

Business Partners...

Company Needs/Capabilities -- Knowledge Express

Capital Spending...

Predicasts Overview of Markets &   DataStar (PTSP)
Technology (PROMT) -- Dialog (File 16)
InSite Pro
LexisNexis

Cash Flow...

MG Financial/Stock Statistics -- Dialog (File 546)

MGFS Common Stock Database -- Alacra

Change in Control Tender...

LIVEDGAR -- www.gsionline.com

Collaborative Research & Development Agreements (CRADAs)

Federal Bio-Technology Transfer
Directory -- Knowledge Express

Company History...

ABI/INFORM -- Dialog (File 15)
LexisNexis (ABISEL)

Hoover's Company Profiles -- Hoover's

Company Information...

Canadian Corporate Names (CCCN) -- FPinfomart

Delphes European Business -- DataStar (DELP)
Dialog (File 481)
Questel (DELPHES)

FP Corporate Survey (CFPS) -- FPinfomart

Toolbox -- Hoover's

Company Profiles...

Beverage Marketing -- Dialog (File 770)
Thomson Financial
Profound
www.beveragemarketing.com

Bio Pharma Surveys -- Knowledge Express

Business Communications
Company BCC -- Dialog (File 764)
Thomson Financial
LexisNexis
Profound

Canadian Corporate Profiles (DCCP) -- FPinfomart

Canadian Federal Corporations &
Directors (DCFC) -- FPinfomart

Corptech -- Knowledge Express
www.corptech.com

Hoover's Company Profiles -- Hoover's

IAC Trade & Industry Database -- Dialog (File 148)
InSite Pro
LexisNexis

Marketline International Market
Research Reports -- LexisNexis (MKTLIN)
DataStar (MKTL)

NELCOM Nelson's Public Co. Profiles -- LexisNexis (NELCOM)

Competitive Analysis...

Marketline International Market
Research Reports -- LexisNexis (MKTLIN)
DataStar (MKTL)

Competitive Intelligence...

ABI/INFORM -- Dialog (File 15)
LexisNexis (ABISEL)

Company Intelligence Database -- Dialog (File 479)
InSite Pro
LexisNexis

Competitive Strategy...

Business Trend Analysts (BTA) -- www.businesstrendanalysts.com

IAC Trade & Industry Database -- Dialog (File 148)
InSite Pro
LexisNexis

Competitors...

Asian Business Intelligence -- Dialog (File 568)
LexisNexis (MKTRES)

Business Trend Analysts (BTA) -- www.businesstrendanalysts.com

FIND SVP -- Dialog (File 766)
LexisNexis (MKTRES)

Hoover's Company Profiles -- Hoover's

Toolbox -- Hoover's

Congress (US)...

StateNet -- www.statenet.com

Thomas -- http://thomas.loc.gov

Consumer Research...

Marketing & Advertising Reference Service (MARS) -- Dialog (File 570)
InSite Pro
LexisNexis

Consumer Trends...

IAC: Newsletter Database -- Dialog (File 636)

Predicasts Overview of Markets & Technology (PROMT) -- DataStar (PTSP)
Dialog (File 16)
InSite Pro   LexisNexis

Consumption Figures...

Beverage Marketing -- Dialog (File 770)
Profound
Thomson Financial
www.beveragemarketing.com

Globalbase -- DataStar (EBUS)
Dialog (File 583)

Contract Awards...

Jane's Information Group -- Dialog (File 587)
LexisNexis (JANDEF)

Contract Bids... ... ...

BidAlert -- www.bidnet.com

Contribution Agreements...

Corporate Family -- Dialog (File 513)
FT Profile

LIVEDGAR -- www.gsionline.com

Corporate Governance...

Securities Data Company (SDC) -- LexisNexis (MSTAT)
Thomson Financial

Corporate Name Change...

LIVEDGAR -- www.gsionline.com

Corporate Strategy...

Beverage Marketing -- Dialog (File 770)
Profound
Thomson Financial
www.beveragemarketing.com

Predicasts Overview of Markets &   DataStar (PTSP)
Technology (PROMT) -- Dialog (File 16)
InSite Pro
LexisNexis

Corporate Structure...

Inter-Corporate Ownership (CICO) -- Infomart Online

Securities Data Company (SDC) -- LexisNexis (MSTAT)
Thomson Financial

Cost Analysis...

Business Trend Analysts (BTA) -- www.businesstrendanalysts.com

Country Profiles...

EIU: Country Analysis -- LexisNexis
Profound
Dialog (File 627)
FT Profile
Thomson Financial

Country Risk...

EIU: Country Risk & Forecasts -- LexisNexis
Profound
Dialog (File 627)
FT Profile
Investext (Thomson Financial) (MarkIntel)

Credit Reports...

Creditel Commercial Law Record (CCRE) -- Alacra
Asian CIS
DataStar (AVVC, DVVC, CRCH)
Equifax
FPinfomart
LexisNexis
TransUnion

Decrease Authorized Shares...

LIVEDGAR -- www.gsionline.com

Demographics... ... ...

FIND SVP -- Dialog (File 766)
LexisNexis (MKTRES)

TableBase -- Alacra
DataStar (BTBL)
Dialog (File 93)

Direct Mail... ... ...

Business & Industry -- Alacra
DataStar (BIDB)
Dialog (File 9)

Directories... ... ...

Contact Canada -- http://contactcanada.com

Disclosure... ... ...

Global Access -- Disclosure

Distribution Channels...

Asian Business Intelligence -- Dialog (File 568)
LexisNexis (MKTRES)

Beverage Marketing -- Dialog (File 770)
Profound
Thomson Financial
www.beveragemarketing.com

Business Trend Analysts (BTA) -- www.businesstrendanalysts.com

Corporate & Marketing Intelligence
(CAMI) -- Profound

Marketing & Advertising   Dialog (File 570)
Reference Service (MARS) -- InSite Pro
LexisNexis

Marketline International Market   LexisNexis (MKTLIN)
Research Reports -- DataStar (MKTL)

Distribution Methods...

ABI/INFORM -- Dialog (File 15)
LexisNexis (ABISEL)

IAC Trade & Industry Database -- Dialog (File 148)
InSite Pro
LexisNexis

Investext Analyst Reports -- Factiva
Dialog (File 545)
Thomson Financial

Predicasts Overview of Markets &   DataStar (PTSP)
Technology (PROMT) -- Dialog (File 16)
InSite Pro
LexisNexis

Distribution Networks...

Business Communications Company -- Thomson Financial

Dutch Auction... ... ...

LIVEDGAR -- www.gsionline.com

Earnings & Dividends...

First Call Estimates -- Alacra

IAC Trade & Industry Database -- Dialog (File 148)
InSite Pro
LexisNexis

Earnings Announcement (Time Stamped)

Dow Jones Wires -- Factiva

Earnings Projections...

NELERN Nelson' s Consensus   LexisNexis
Earnings Estimates -- Alacra

Economic Climate...

IAC Trade & Industry Database -- Dialog (File 148)
InSite Pro
LexisNexis

Economic Indicators...

Predicasts Overview of Markets & Technology (PROMT) -- DataStar (PTSP)
Dialog (File 16)
InSite Pro
LexisNexis

Efficiency Levels...

Business & Industry -- Alacra
DataStar (BIDB)
Dialog (File 9)

Emerging Markets...

Emerging Markets -- LexisNexis (WLDSRC)

ISI Emerging Markets -- www.securities.com

Emerging Technologies...

Company Technologies -- Knowledge Express

Globalbase -- DataStar (EBUS)
Dialog (File 583)

Government Technologies -- Knowledge Express

IAC: Newsletter Database -- Dialog (File 636)

International Business Opportunities -- Knowledge Express

Jane's Information Group -- Dialog (File 587)
Dow Jones (PUB LIBRARY)
LexisNexis (JANDEF)

University Technologies -- Knowledge Express

Employee Benefits...

Employee Benefits Infosource -- Dialog (File 22)
Westlaw

Employees - Number Of...

Corptech -- Knowledge Express

Hoover's Company Profiles -- Hoover's

End-User Packaging...

Corporate & Marketing Intelligence (CAMI) -- Profound

Environment...

IAC: Newsletter Database -- Dialog (File 636)

Environmental Impact Statements...

Environmental Impact Statements (EIS) Collection -- `www.library.nwu.edu/transportation/tleis.html`

Euro Currency Conversion...

LIVEDGAR -- `www.gsionline.com`

Executive Changes...

IAC Trade & Industry Database -- Dialog (File 148)
InSite Pro
LexisNexis

Executives By Job Function...

Federal Employer Identification # (FEIN) -- ChoicePoint
LexisNexis
`www.hoovers.com`

(idEXEC) -- `www.idexec.com`

Financial Information...

Corptech -- Knowledge Express

FP Corporate Survey (CFPS) -- FPinfomart

Globalbase -- DataStar (EBUS)
Dialog (File 583)

IAC Trade & Industry Database -- Dialog (File 148)
InSite Pro
LexisNexis

WorldScope -- Factiva

Financial Information - In-Depth...

Hoover's Company Profiles -- Hoover's

Financing Foreign Operations...

EIU: Country Analysis -- LexisNexis
Profound
Dialog (File 627)
FT Profile
Thomson Financial

Financings...

Securities Data Company (SDC) -- LexisNexis (MSTAT)
Alacra

Forecasts...

Asian Business Intelligence -- Dialog (File 568)
LexisNexis (MKTRES)

Beverage Marketing -- Dialog (File 770)
Profound
Thomson Financial
www.beveragemarketing.com

Corporate & Marketing
Intelligence (CAMI) -- Profound

Economagic -- www.economagic.com

EIU Country Risk & Forecasts -- Dialog (File 627)
FT Profile
LexisNexis
Profound
Thomson Financial

FIND SVP -- Dialog (File 766)
LexisNexis (MKTRES)

IAC Trade & Industry Database -- Dialog (File 148)
InSite Pro
LexisNexis

Marketline International Market   LexisNexis (MKTLIN)
Research Reports -- DataStar (MKTL)

Predicasts Overview of Markets &   DataStar (PTSP)
Technology (PROMT) -- Dialog (File 16)
InSite Pro
LexisNexis

Forecasts - Sales & Shipments...

Infotech Trends -- www.infotechtrends.com

Foreign Military Sales...

Jane's Information Group -- Dialog (File 587)
DOW JONES (PUB LIBRARY)
LexisNexis (JANDEF)

Going Concern Opinions...

LIVEDGAR -- www.gsionline.com

Government Policies & Regulations...

Globalbase -- DataStar (EBUS)
Dialog (File 583)

IAC: Newsletter Database -- Dialog (File 636)

Marketing & Advertising Reference   Dialog (File 570)
Service (MARS) -- InSite Pro
LexisNexis

Predicasts Overview of Markets &   DataStar (PTSP)
Technology (PROMT) -- Dialog (File 16)
InSite Pro
LexisNexis

Grants... ... ...

Grants -- Dialog (File 85)
Knowledge Express

Holding Company Information...

LIVEDGAR -- www.gsionline.com

Hostile Tender... ... ...

LIVEDGAR -- www.gsionline.com

Income Statements...

MG Financial/Stock Statistics -- Dialog (File 546)

MGFS Common Stock Database -- Alacra

Increase Authorized Shares...

LIVEDGAR -- www.gsionline.com

Increase Par Value...

LIVEDGAR -- www.gsionline.com

Industrial Production...

Industrial Production & Capacity
Utilization Data -- www.economagic.com

Predicasts Overview of Markets &   DataStar (PTSP)
Technology (PROMT) -- Dialog (File 16)
InSite Pro
LexisNexis

Industry Comparative Data...

MG Financial/Stock Statistics -- Dialog (File 546)

MGFS Common Stock Database -- Alacra

Industry Forecasts...

Current Industrial Reports -- www.census.gov/pub/cir/www/index.html

Globalbase -- DataStar (EBUS)
Dialog (File 583)

TableBase -- Alacra
DataStar (BTBL)
Dialog (File 93)

Industry History...

> IAC Trade & Industry Database -- Dialog (File 148)
>
> Industry Insider -- Thomson Financial

Industry Information...

> Business & Industry -- Alacra
> DataStar (BIDB)
> Dialog (File 9)
>
> Industry Insider -- www.insitepro.com
>
> Toolbox -- www.hoovers.com

Industry Profiles...

> Asia Pulse -- Bloomberg
> Factiva
> LexisNexis
> Profound
> www.asiapulse.com
>
> Business & Industry -- Alacra
> DataStar (BIDB)
> Dialog (File 9)
>
> Investext -- Dialog (File 545)
> Thomson Financial

Industry Stucture...

> Business & Industry -- Alacra
> DataStar (BIDB)
> Dialog (File 9)
>
> Business Communications Co.; BCC -- Dialog (File 764)
> LexisNexis
> Profound
> Thomson Financial

Initial Public Offerings...

> EDGAR Online -- www.edgar-online.com
>
> IPO Central -- Hoover's
>
> LIVEDGAR -- www.gsionline.com
>
> Securities Data Company (SDC) -- Dialog (File 550)
> Alacra
> LexisNexis (MSTAT)

Insider Trading...

> CompanySleuth -- www.companysleuth.com
>
> EDGAR Online -- www.edgar-online.com

Institutional Equity...

Vickers Stock Research -- Alacra

International Arms Acquisitions...

Jane's Information Group -- Dialog (File 587)
Dow Jones (PUB LIBRARY)
LexisNexis (JANDEF)

Inventions...

Federal Bio-Tech. Transfer Directory -- Knowledge Express

Investing... ... ...

EIU: Country Analysis -- Dialog (File 627)
FT Profile
LexisNexis
Profound
Thomson Financial

Investment Research Reports...

Investext Reports -- Dialog (File 545)
Thomson Financial

Reuters -- Factiva   Reuters.com

NELSON (Group File) -- LexisNexis

Nelson's Co. Research Report
Headlines -- LexisNexis (NELREP)

Zacks Investment Research -- www.ultra.zacks.com

Issuer Counsel... ... ...

LIVEDGAR -- www.gsionline.com

Joint Marketing partnerships...

Marketing & Advertising Reference   Dialog (File 570)
Service (MARS) -- InSite Pro
LexisNexis

Small Business Innovation Research
Awards (SBIRs) -- Knowledge Express

Joint Ventures...

Predicasts Overview of Markets &   DataStar (PTSP)
Technology (PROMT) -- Dialog (File 16)
InSite Pro
LexisNexis

Securities Data Company (SDC) -- Dialog (File 554)
LexisNexis (MSTAT)
Alacra

Lawsuits, Major...

IAC Trade & Industry Database -- Dialog (File 148)
InSite Pro
LexisNexis

Predicasts Overview of Markets &   DataStar (PTSP)
Technology (PROMT) -- Dialog (File 16)
InSite Pro
LexisNexis

Lead Finder...

Hoover's Company Profiles -- Hoover's

Leading Players...

Corporate & Marketing Intelligence
CAMI -- Profound

Legislative Tracking (US States)

StateNet -- www.statenet.com

License/Sales Agreements...

BioScan -- Knowledge Express

Fed. Laboratory Technologies FLTDB -- Knowledge Express

Globalbase -- DataStar (EBUS)
Dialog (File 583)

Government Technologies -- Knowledge Express

Marketing & Advertising Reference   Dialog (File 570)
Service (MARS) -- InSite Pro
LexisNexis

Predicasts Overview of Markets &   DataStar (PTSP)
Technology (PROMT) -- Dialog (File 16)
InSite Pro
LexisNexis

University Technologies -- Knowledge Express

Licensing & Trading...

EIU: Country Analysis -- LexisNexis
Profound
Dialog (File 627)
FT Profile
Investext (Thomson Financial) (MarkIntel)

Licensing Opportunities...

Federal Bio-Technology Transfer
Directory -- Knowledge Express

List Generator...

Hoover's Company Profiles -- Hoover's

Lock Up Agreements...

LIVEDGAR -- www.gsionline.com

Management Techniques...

Business Management Practices Dialog (File 13)
BAMP -- XLS

IAC Trade & Industry Database -- Dialog (File 148)
InSite Pro
LexisNexis

Management Theory & Practice...

Trade Industry Database -- Dialog (File 148)
InSite Pro

Manufacturing Capabilities...

Company Needs/Capabilities -- Knowledge Express

Manufacturing Industries...

Business & Industry -- Alacra
DataStar (BIDB)
Dialog (File 9)

Manufacturing Processes, New...

Predicasts Overview of Markets & DataStar (PTSP)
Technology (PROMT) -- Dialog (File 16)
InSite Pro
LexisNexis

Market Analysis...

Investext Reports -- Dialog (File 545)
Thomson Financial

Marketing & Advertising Reference Dialog (File 570)
Service (MARS) -- InSite Pro
LexisNexis

Market Conditions...

Delphes European Business -- DataStar (DELP)
Dialog (File 481)
Questel (DELPHES)

IAC: Newsletter Database -- Dialog (File 636)

Market Contrasts...

IAC Trade & Industry Database -- Dialog (File 148)
InSite Pro
LexisNexis

Market Penetration...

Business & Industry -- Alacra
DataStar (BIDB)
Dialog (File 9)

Business Communications Co. - BCC -- Dialog (File 764)
LexisNexis
Profound
Thomson Financial

Globalbase -- DataStar (EBUS)
Dialog (File 583)

IAC Trade & Industry Database -- Dialog (File 148)
InSite Pro   LexisNexis

TableBase -- Alacra
DataStar (BTBL)
Dialog (File 93)

Market Research...

Investext Reports, Profound -- Dialog (File 545)
Thomson Financial
Profound

Datamonitor -- Alacra
DataStar (DMON)
Dialog (File 761)
LexisNexis (MKTRES)

Market Segmentation...

Asian Business Intelligence -- Dialog (File 568)
LexisNexis (MKTRES)

Business Communications Co. (BCC) -- Dialog (File 764)
LexisNexis
Profound
Thomson Financial

Datamonitor -- Alacra
DataStar (DMON)
Dialog (File 761)
LexisNexis (MKTRES)

Market Share...

Beverage Marketing -- Dialog (File 770)
Profound
Thomson Financial
www.beveragemarketing.com

Business Trend Analysts (BTA) -- www.businesstrendanalysts.com

Computer Product Index -- LexisNexis (MKTRES)

Datamonitor Market Research -- Alacra
DataStar (DMON)
Dialog (File 761)
LexisNexis (MKTRES)

Globalbase -- DataStar (EBUS)
Dialog (File 583)

Marketing & Advertising Reference
Service (MARS) -- Dialog (File 570)
InSite Pro
LexisNexis

Marketline International Market
Research Reports -- LexisNexis (MKTLIN)
DataStar (MKTL)

Predicasts Overview of Markets &
Technology (PROMT) -- DataStar (PTSP)
Dialog (File 16)
InSite Pro
LexisNexis

Register Meal -- LexisNexis (MKTRES)

ScanTrack -- LexisNexis (MKTRES)

TableBase -- Alacra
DataStar (BTBL)
Dialog (File 93)

World Market Share Reporter -- LexisNexis (MKTSHR)
Thomson Financial

Market Size...

Asian Business Intelligence -- Dialog (File 568)
LexisNexis (MKTRES)

Beverage Marketing -- Dialog (File 770)
Profound
Thomson Financial
www.beveragemarketing.com

Corp. & Marketing Intelligence (CAMI) - Profound

FIND SVP -- Dialog (File 766)
LexisNexis (MKTRES)

Globalbase -- DataStar (EBUS)
Dialog (File 583)

Marketing & Advertising Reference
Service (MARS) -- Dialog (File 570)
InSite Pro   LexisNexis

Marketline International Market
Research Reports -- LexisNexis (MKTLIN)
DataStar (MKTL)

TableBase -- Alacra
DataStar (BTBL)
Dialog (File 93)

Market Trends...

Asian Business Intelligence -- Dialog (File 568)
LexisNexis (MKTRES)

FIND SVP -- Dialog (File 766)
LexisNexis (MKTRES)

Marketing Campaigns...

Marketing & Advertising Reference Dialog (File 570)
Service (MARS) -- InSite Pro
LexisNexis

Predicasts Overview of Markets & DataStar (PTSP)
Technology (PROMT) -- Dialog (File 16)
InSite Pro
LexisNexis

Marketing Personnel...

Marketing & Advertising Reference Dialog (File 570)
Service (MARS) -- InSite Pro
LexisNexis

Marketing Strategy...

Business Communications Co. BCC -- Dialog (File 764)
LexisNexis
Profound
Thomson Financial

Marketing & Advertising Reference Dialog (File 570)
Service (MARS) -- InSite Pro
LexisNexis

Merger & Acquisition Data...

Firstlist -- Knowledge Express

Globalbase -- DataStar (EBUS)
Dialog (File 583)

IAC Trade & Industry Database -- Dialog (File 148)
InSite Pro   LexisNexis

Jane's Information Group -- Dialog (File 587)
DOW JONES (PUB LIBRARY)
LexisNexis (JANDEF)

M&A Monitor -- Alacra

Mergerstat -- LexisNexis (MSTAT)
Alacra

Predicasts Overview of Markets & DataStar (PTSP)
Technology (PROMT) -- Dialog (File 16)
InSite Pro
LexisNexis

Securities Data Company (SDC) -- Dialog (File 551)
LexisNexis (MSTAT)
Alacra

Thomson Financial Joint Ventures -- Alacra
Thomson Financial

Thomson Financial Mergers &   Alacra
Acquisitions -- Thomson Financial

Thomson Financial New Issues -- Alacra
Thomson Financial

Thomson Fin. Venture Economics -- Alacra
Thomson Financial

New Technologies...

Business Communications Co. BCC -- Dialog (File 764)
LexisNexis   Profound
Thomson Financial

Business Mgmt. Practices BAMP -- Dialog (File 13)

Cambridge Market Intelligence -- Profound

Non-SEC Offering Circulars (144a & Reg S)...

Non-SEC Offering Circulars
(144a & Reg S) -- www.gsionline.com

Officers & Directors...

Hoover's Company Profiles -- Hoover's

IAC Trade & Industry Database -- Dialog (File 148)
InSite Pro   LexisNexis

idEXEC -- Alacra

Marquis Who's Who -- Dialog (File 234)
LexisNexis

Operating Ratios...

MG Financial/Stock Statistics -- Dialog (File 546)

Orders & Contracts, Major...

Predicasts Overview of Markets &   DataStar (PTSP)
Technology (PROMT) -- Dialog (File 16)
InSite Pro   LexisNexis

Ownership Data - 5% Equity...

The Disclosure/Spectrum Ownership
Database -- Dialog (File 540)

Vickers Stock Research -- Alacra

Ownership Data - Fixed Income...

        Vickers Stock Research -- Alacra

Ownership Data - Insider Equity...

        Vickers Stock Research -- Alacra

Packaging... ... ...

    Beverage Marketing -- Dialog (File 770)
                      Profound
                      Thomson Financial
                      www.beveragemarketing.com

Marketing & Advertising Reference -- Dialog (File 570)
        Service (MARS) -- InSite Pro
                      LexisNexis

Patents... ...

Federal Bio-Tech. Transfer Directory --
    Government Technologies --
      MicroPatent Alert MPA -- Knowledge Express
    University Technologies --

Patents & Copyrights...

Predicasts Overview of Markets & DataStar (PTSP)
    Technology (PROMT) -- Dialog (File 16)
                  InSite Pro
                  LexisNexis

People... ... ...

            BioScan -- Knowledge Express

            CorpTech -- www.corpotech.com

        EDGAR Online -- www.edgar-online.com

Financial Post Directory of Directors
        (DDOD) -- FPinfomart

IAC: Newsletter Database -- Dialog (File 636)

    Magazine Database -- Dialog (File 47)
                  InSite Pro
                  LexisNexis

    Marquis Who's Who -- Dialog (File 234)
                  NEXIS File=MARQUIS

Standard & Poor's Register -Biographical -- Dialog (File 526)

            IdEXEC -- Alacra

Plants & Facilities, New...

Globalbase -- DataStar (EBUS)
Dialog (File 583)

Predicasts Overview of Markets &   DataStar (PTSP)
Technology (PROMT) -- Dialog (File 16)
InSite Pro   LexisNexis

Poison Pills...

LIVEDGAR -- www.gsionline.com

Pooling of Interests...

LIVEDGAR -- www.gsionline.com

Price Histories...

MG Financial/Stock Statistics -- Dialog (File 546)

Pricing...

Datamonitor Market Research -- Alacra
DataStar (DMON)
Dialog (File 761)
LexisNexis (MKTRES)

Private Company Information...

Company Intelligence Database -- Dialog (File 479)
InSite Pro
LexisNexis (COMPNY)

Harris InfoSource -- Alacra

Hoover's Company Profiles -- Hoover's

Standard & Poor's Register - Corporate -- Dialog (File 527)

TableBase -- Alacra
DataStar (BTBL)
Dialog (File 93)

Processes...

International Business Opportunities -- Knowledge Express

Product Brands...

Delphes European Business -- DataStar (DELP)
Dialog (File 481)
Questel (DELPHES)

Product Differentiation...

IAC Trade & Industry Database -- Dialog (File 148)
InSite Pro   LexisNexis

IAC: Newsletter Database -- Dialog (File 636)

Investext Reports -- Thomson Financial

Predicasts Overview of Markets &   DataStar (PTSP)
Technology (PROMT) -- Dialog (File 16)
  InSite Pro
  LexisNexis

Product Evaluations...

IAC Trade & Industry Database -- Dialog (File 148)
  InSite Pro
  LexisNexis

Product Features & Analysis...

Cambridge Market Intelligence -- Profound

International Business Opportunities -- Knowledge Express

Product Forecasts...

TableBase -- Alacra
  DataStar (BTBL)
  Dialog (File 93)

Product Introductions...

ABI/INFORM -- Dialog (File 15)
  LexisNexis (ABISEL)

Globalbase -- DataStar (EBUS)
  Dialog (File 583)

IAC Trade & Industry Database -- Dialog (File 148)
  InSite Pro
  LexisNexis

IAC: New Product
Announcements/Plus -- Dialog (File 621)

IAC: Newsletter Database -- Dialog (File 636)

Marketing & Advertising Reference   Dialog (File 570)
Service (MARS) -- InSite Pro
  LexisNexis

Product Positioning...

Business & Industry -- Alacra
  DataStar (BIDB)
  Dialog (File 9)

Product Pricing...

Corporate & Marketing Intelligence
(CAMI) -- Profound

Product Reviews...

IAC Trade & Industry Database -- Dialog (File 148)
InSite Pro
LexisNexis

Product Search... ... ...

CorpTech -- www.corptech.com

Products...

Datamonitor Market Research -- Alacra
DataStar (DMON)
Dialog (File 761)
LexisNexis (MKTRES)

Products - End Uses...

Predicasts Overview of Markets &   DataStar (PTSP)
Technology (PROMT) -- Dialog (File 16)
InSite Pro
LexisNexis

Products & Services...

Business & Industry -- Alacra
DataStar (BIDB)
Dialog (File 9)

Predicasts Overview of Markets &   DataStar (PTSP)
Technology (PROMT) -- Dialog (File 16)
InSite Pro
LexisNexis

Profitability Analysis...

Business Trend Analysts (BTA) -- www.businesstrendanalysts.com

Prospectuses...

EDGARPLus - Prospectuses -- Dialog (File 774)

Public Offering to Affiliates...

LIVEDGAR -- www.gsionline.com

Rabbi Trusts... ... ...

LIVEDGAR -- www.gsionline.com

Rankings... ... ...

TableBase -- Alacra
DataStar (BTBL)
Dialog (File 93)

Raw Materials, Availability of...

IAC Trade & Industry Database -- Dialog (File 148)
InSite Pro
LexisNexis

Predicasts Overview of Markets &   DataStar (PTSP)
Technology (PROMT) -- Dialog (File 16)
InSite Pro
LexisNexis

Reduce Par Value...

LIVEDGAR -- www.gsionline.com

Registration Statements...

EDGARPlus-Registration/Statements -- Dialog (File 775)

Reincorporation - (Change of State of Incorporation)

LIVEDGAR -- www.gsionline.com

Reorganizations...

Predicasts Overview of Markets &   DataStar (PTSP)
Technology (PROMT) -- Dialog (File 16)
InSite Pro
LexisNexis

Report on Option Repricing...

LIVEDGAR -- www.gsionline.com

Requests for Proposals (RFPs)...

Jane's Information Group -- Dialog (File 587)
Dow Jones (Pub. Library)
LexisNexis (JANDEF)

Research & Development...

BioScan -- Knowledge Express

Company Needs/Capabilities -- Knowledge Express

CORDIS -- www.cordis.lu

Government Technologies -- Knowledge Express

Predicasts Overview of Markets &   DataStar (PTSP)
Technology (PROMT) -- Dialog (File 16)
InSite Pro
LexisNexis

TEKTRAN USDA -- Knowledge Express

University Technologies -- Knowledge Express

Research, Federally Funded...

Federal Research In Progress (FEDRIP) -- Knowledge Express
National Technical Information Svcs (NTIS)

Research firm...

NELRF Nelson's Research Firm Profiles -- LexisNexis

Reverse Stock Split...

LIVEDGAR -- www.gsionline.com

Risk Analysis...

BARRA Global & Single Country   Alacra
Equity Models -- www.barra.com

Risk Assessments...

EIU Country Risk & Forecasts -- Dialog (File 627)
FT Profile
LexisNexis
Profound
Thomson Financial

Sales... ...

Predicasts Overview of Markets &   DataStar (PTSP)
Technology (PROMT) -- Dialog (File 16)
InSite Pro
LexisNexis

Sales By Product...

Computer Product Index --
MarketTrack --
Register Meal --   LexisNexis (MKTRES)
ScanTrack --

Sales Volume...

Beverage Marketing -- Dialog (File 770)
Profound
Thomson Financial
www.beveragemarketing.com

Globalbase -- DataStar (EBUS)
Dialog (File 583)

Marketing & Advertising Reference   Dialog (File 570)
Service (MARS) -- InSite Pro
LexisNexis

TableBase -- Alacra
DataStar (BTBL)
Dialog (File 93)

SEC Filings...

EDGAR Online -- www.edgar-online.com

Hoover's Company Profiles -- Hoover's

Trade Industry Database -- Dialog (File 148)
InSite Pro

Secondary Offering...

LIVEDGAR -- www.gsionline.com

Section 16 Non-compliance...

LIVEDGAR -- www.gsionline.com

Service Industries...

Business & Industry -- Alacra
DataStar (BIDB)
Dialog (File 9)

Service Introductions...

Marketing & Advertising Reference -- Dialog (File 570)
Service (MARS) -- InSite Pro
LexisNexis

Shareholders – Institutional...

Share/World -- www.xls.com

Shelf Prospectuses...

LIVEDGAR -- www.gsionline.com

Shipments...

Predicasts Overview of Markets & -- DataStar (PTSP)
Technology (PROMT) -- Dialog (File 16)
InSite Pro
LexisNexis

Short Interest...

CompanySleuth -- www.companysleuth.com

Spin-off... ... ...

LIVEDGAR -- www.gsionline.com

Stock Performance...

Trade Industry Database -- Dialog (File 148)
InSite Pro

Stock Screener...

Toolbox -- Hoover's

Summary Compensation Tables...

LIVEDGAR -- www.gsionline.com

Suppliers...

Corporate & Marketing Intelligence
(CAMI) -- Profound

Technologies, New...

Predicasts Overview of Markets &   DataStar (PTSP)
Technology (PROMT) -- Dialog (File 16)
InSite Pro   LexisNexis

Technology Analysis...

Business Trend Analysts (BTA) -- www.businesstrendanalysts.com

Technology Needs...

Company Needs/Capabilities -- Knowledge Express

Technology Transfer...

Acquisition, Technology Transfer,
Licensing & Source of Capital
Directory (ATTLAS) -- Knowledge Express

Federal Bio-Tech. Transfer Directory -- Knowledge Express

Ten Year Option Repricing Charts...

LIVEDGAR -- www.gsionline.com

Tenders - Odd Lot...

LIVEDGAR -- www.gsionline.com

Tenders – Self...

LIVEDGAR -- www.gsionline.com

Trademarks...

CompanySleuth -- www.companysleuth.com

Trends... ... ...

EIU Country Risk & Forecasts -- Dialog (File 627)
FT Profile
LexisNexis   Profound
Thomson Financial

Marketline International Market   LexisNexis (MKTLIN)
Research Reports -- DataStar (MKTL)

Trends, Consumer...

Beverage Marketing -- Dialog (File 770)
Profound
Thomson Financial
www.beveragemarketing.com

Trends, Demographic...

Business & Industry -- Alacra
DataStar (BIDB)
Dialog (File 9)

Marketing & Advertising Reference   Dialog (File 570)
Service (MARS) -- InSite Pro   LexisNexis

Predicasts Overview of Markets &   DataStar (PTSP)
Technology (PROMT) -- Dialog (File 16)
InSite Pro   LexisNexis

TableBase -- Alacra
DataStar (BTBL)
Dialog (File 93)

Trends, Industry...

Business & Industry -- Alacra
DataStar (BIDB)
Dialog (File 9)

Globalbase -- DataStar (EBUS)
Dialog (File 583)

IAC Trade & Industry Database -- Dialog (File 148)
InSite Pro   LexisNexis

IAC: Newsletter Database -- Dialog (File 636)

Predicasts Overview of Markets &   DataStar (PTSP)
Technology (PROMT) -- Dialog (File 16)
InSite Pro   LexisNexis

TableBase -- Alacra
DataStar (BTBL)
Dialog (File 93)

Trends, Market...

Beverage Marketing -- Dialog (File 770)
Profound
Thomson Financial
www.beveragemarketing.com

Business & Industry -- Alacra
DataStar (BIDB)
Dialog (File 9)

Corporate & Marketing Intelligence
(CAMI) -- Profound

Globalbase -- DataStar (EBUS)
Dialog (File 583)

IAC Trade & Industry Database -- Dialog (File 148)
InSite Pro
LexisNexis

TableBase -- Alacra
DataStar (BTBL)
Dialog (File 93)

Trends, Pricing...

Business Communications Co. BCC -- Dialog (File 764)
LexisNexis
Profound
Thomson Financial

Globalbase -- DataStar (EBUS)
Dialog (File 583)

TableBase -- Alacra
DataStar (BTBL)
Dialog (File 93)

Underwriter Counsel...

LIVEDGAR -- www.gsionline.com

Venture Capital...

Acquisition, Technology Transfer, Licensing
& Source of Capital Directory (ATTLAS) -- Knowledge Express

Williams Act Filings...

EDGARPlus - Williams Act Filings -- Dialog (File 773)

Year 2000 Compliance Costs...

LIVEDGAR -- www.gsionline.com

Year 2000 Compliance Statements...

LIVEDGAR -- www.gsionline.com

Year 2000 Impact Statements...

LIVEDGAR -- www.gsionline.com

Database Files List

The list below shows some sources for useful business databases. Some of these files may also be available through additional vendor sites or directly from the database producer.

ABI/INFORM
Dialog (File 15)
FT Profile (ABI)
DataStar (INFO)

Includes details on virtually every aspect of business, including company histories, competitive intelligence, and new product development. Database contains bibliographic citations and 25-150 word summaries of articles appearing in professional publications, academic journals, and trade magazines published worldwide. ABI/INFORM indexes and abstracts significant articles from more that 800 business and management periodicals. Full text is included for many of the articles added from January 1991 forward. Twenty-five percent of the journals are published outside the United States.

Acquisition, Technology Transfer, Licensing & Source of Capital Directory (ATTLAS)
Knowledge Express

Contains information on over 2300 international companies, 5200 U.S. companies and 22,000 healthcare executives. Good for identifying sources, acquiring new products, locating financing, expanding distribution and license technologies.

Advertiser & Agency Red Books
Dialog (File 177, 178)
Nexis

Records include company name and address, business description, SIC codes, product types, trade names, sales figures, and phone and fax numbers. Additional details include: types of advertising media used, advertising agencies employed by the company, approximate dollars spent in each type of advertising medium, a breakdown of the products handled by each agency employed by the company, and email addresses for key personnel.

AKTRIN Research
Profound
www.aktrin.com

Databases cover the secondary wood products industry, including all aspects of the furniture industry.

FP Analyzer Company Profiles
FPinfomart

Database provides access to the most popular data items, ratios and financial statement aggregates, as well as the description of business and its operations, current financial statistics, ratios and share price information, address, telephone number, shareholders, names of key officers and number of employees for the top 1,400 Canadian companies.

Asian Business Intelligence
Dialog (File 568)
LexisNexis (MKTRES)

Contains the complete text of detailed local reports focusing on the developing markets, industry and products of Asia.

Asia Pulse
Bloomberg
Factiva
LexisNexis
AsiaPulse.com

Asia Pulse is a real-time business information service geared for business researchers, rather than for use in newsrooms.

Bankstat   Thomson Financial

Database of financial information on 10,000 banks in 190 countries.

Bankruptcy DataSource   LexisNexis (BDS)
                                                Westlaw

Contains information on U.S. companies with more than $50 million in assets that are in bankruptcy. The file contains company profiles, reorganization plans, and other news. Coverage begins in 1989.

Bankruptcy File – Canada   Strategis

Database contains records of all bankruptcies and proposals filed in Canada from 1978 to date. Contains a record of all private and court appointed receiverships filed in Canada from 1993 to date.

BARRA Global & Single Country Equity Models   Alacra

The BARRA United States Equity Model Beta Book provides key risk analysis statistics on over 8000 U.S. publicly traded companies in 55 industries. Beta calculations are based on the S&P 500 index.

Beverage Marketing   Dialog (File 770)
                                                Profound
                                                Thomson Financial
                                                www.beveragemarketing.com

Contains comprehensive beverage statistics, plus analysis of leading companies in the industry.

Bio/Pharma Surveys   Knowledge Express

European Biopharmaceutical Companies Survey - profiles of emerging European pharmaceutical and biotechnology companies; and National European pharmaceutical Companies Survey - profiles of established, small-to-medium size, pharmaceutical companies.

BioScan   Knowledge Express

Lists U.S. and foreign companies actively involved in biotech research and development. Produced by American Health Consultants.

Business & Industry   Alacra
                                                DataStar (BIDB)
                                                Dialog (File 9)

Database contains information with facts, figures, and key events dealing with public and private companies, industries, markets products for all manufacturing and service industries at an international level. B&I coverage concentrates on leading trade magazines/newsletters, general business press, regional newspapers and international business dailies.

Business & Management Practices (BAMP)   Dialog (File 13)

Contains information dealing with the processes, methods, and strategies of managing a business. Coverage focuses on those source publications that deal with management issues or business methodology from a practical approach.

Business Communications Company (BCC)   Dialog (File 764)
                                                LexisNexis   Profound
                                                Thomson Financial

Contains market analysis and technical assessments in areas of advanced materials, high technology, and new technologies.

Business Trend Analysts

Thomson Financial
Profound

Contains macroeconomic data, competitors, market share, distribution channels, demand, as well as descriptions of technologies and the dynamics of technological change.

Cambridge Market Intelligence

Profound

Covers the information technology industry. For individual technologies, provides product information and analysis.

Federal Corporations Data On-Line (Canada)   Strategis

This database contains records for Canadian federally incorporated companies. Searches are available at no cost by Corporation Number, Name, Creation Date, City, Province, Corporation Status or Act.

Canadian Company Capabilities

Strategis

Database is a centrally maintained set of 50,000 Canadian businesses. It includes hundreds of specialized manufacturing, service and product specific business directories.

Canadian Federal Corporations & Directors   FPinfomart

This database contains information on over 300,000 federally incorporated companies. Data is provided by Industry Canada.

Canadian Inter-Corporate Ownership   FPinfomart

The database contains information on the structures of Canadian corporations. Data provided by Statistics Canada. It is compiled from documents filed by companies under the Corporations and Labour Unions Returns Act (CALURA). The database includes every corporation that is carrying on business in Canada or incorporated under a federal or provincial law, whose gross revenues exceed $15 million or whose assets exceed $10 million.

China Business Resources

Thomson Financial
Profound

Provides market share, forecasts, and related data for China, Hong Kong, and Taiwan, covering a number of industries.

ChinaOnline

www.chinaonline.com

Provides business intelligence pertinent to China, including frequently updated industry information, reference materials, government organizational charts, economic news, biographies, and statistics.

Company Needs/Capabilities   Knowledge Express

Contains statements of technology needs, research and development activities from high tech companies in all industries.

Company Technologies   Knowledge Express

Contains abstracts of technologies available for license, collected from emerging high tech companies.

Computer Industry Forecasts   www.infotechtrends.com

Contains sales, shipment market size and growth rate data excerpted from high-technology publications. Hundreds of hi-tech products are covered.

Conference Papers Index (CPI) — Dialog (File 77)

Provides access to records of the more than 100,000 scientific and technical papers presented at over 1,000 major regional, national, and international meetings each year. CPI provides a centralized source of information on reports of current research and development from papers presented at conferences and meetings; it provides titles of papers as well as the names and addresses (if available) of the authors of these papers.

Contact Canada — http://contactcanada.com

Database offers Canadian Biotechnology Directory, Pharma & BioPharma & Nutraceuticals Directory, and the Diagnostics & Biotech Directory.

CORDIS — www.cordis.lu

CORDIS databases provide information about Research and Development sponsored and supported by the European Union.

Corporate & Marketing Intelligence (CAMI) — Profound

So. African business research in food & packaging industries. Database includes market trends, forecasts, pricing, more.

CorpTech
Alacra
Knowledge Express
Thomson Financial
www.corptech.com

Contains company address, telephone number, employment data, key contact and title, primary Standard Industrial Classification (SIC) code, a detailed business description, and annual sales data for over 48,000 U.S. technology companies. When a U.S. technology company has a parent company located outside the U.S., a brief record is provided for the non-U.S. parent. These brief, non-U.S. records do not contain product, history, or performance data.

Datamonitor
Alacra
DataStar (DMON)
Dialog (File 761)
LexisNexis (MKTRES)

Contains market research reports that discuss products, the competitive environment, pricing, market share, and other key issues affecting industries. Most records have tables containing valuable facts and figures on companies and products.

Delphes European Business
DataStar (DELP)
Dialog (File 481)
Questel (DELPHES)

This is considered the leading French database on markets, products, and companies. It contains bibliographic citations and informative abstracts on virtually every aspect of European business.

Disclosure — Thomson Research

Provides company financial and management information using a large collection of real-time and historical company filings; updates and analysis of insider trading; research reports, and business news.

Dow Jones Wires — Factiva

Provides timely access to newswires covering the U.S., Canada, and the rest of the world.

Dun's Market Identifiers
Dialog (File 516)

Contains basic company data, executive names and titles, corporate linkages, D-U-N-S Numbers, organization status, and other marketing information on over ten million U.S. business establishment locations, including public, private, and government organizations.

EDGAR-Online
www.edgar-online.com

Provides SEC electronic corporate filings and related business intelligence tools. Premium subscription offers as real time SEC filings, 144 Insider Transaction filings, the ability to view presentation-quality SEC filings in popular word processor format, and drill-down tools like EDGAR Online People and EDGAR Online Glimpse.

EIU: City Data
Alacra

Database contains pricing information from 123 cities worldwide.

EIU: Country Analysis
Dialog (File 627)
LexisNexis
Profound

Database provides useful background for operating in 180 countries.

EIU: Country Risk & Forecasts
LexisNexis
Profound
Dialog (File 627)

Database contains full text of the EIU's premium Country Risk Service and Country Forecasts. The Country Risk Service provides analysis of the short- and medium-term economic creditworthiness of over 90 countries. Country Forecasts gives a medium-term outlook into economic, political and business trends in 58 countries.

EIU: Country Data
Alacra

Database contains economic indicators and forecasts for 117 countries.

EIU: Market Indicators and Forecasts
Alacra

\Database contains market size and demographics for 60 countries.

Encyclopedia of Associations
Dialog (File 114)
LexisNexis (BUSREF)

Comprehensive source of detailed information on over 81,000 nonprofit membership organizations worldwide. The database provides addresses and descriptions of professional societies, trade associations, labor unions, cultural/religious organizations, fan clubs, groups of all types.

Environmental Impact Statements (EIS) Collection
www.library.nwu.edu/
transportation/tleis.html

The Transportation Library, at holds nearly all the EIS's issued by federal agencies since 1969, often in draft as well as final form, and such related documents as environmental assessments, findings of no significant impact, records of decisions, etc.

Equifax Commercial Law Record
FPinfomart

Equifax obtains public information on commercial legal suits and judgements from courts across Canada. Data provided by Equifax Canada.

Federal Bio-Technology Transfer Directory   Knowledge Express

Contains records about biotechnology and pharmaceutical licensing opportunities as well as technology transfer information on inventions, Collaborative Research and Development Agreements, patent licenses. Describes all federal biomedical basic biotechnology related inventions and technology transfers since 1980.

Federal Laboratory Technologies (FLTDB)   Knowledge Express

Contains descriptions of technologies available for licensing from various government agencies. Also contains historical data on past opportunities.

Federal Research In Progress (FEDRIP)   Knowledge Express
National Technical Information Services (NTIS)

Abstracts describe the basis of the research and recent results. Compiled from input by Federal agencies. Includes title, investigator, contact information, funding agency, award amount, award number, description of research, and project status.

Financial Post Directory of Directors   FPinfomart

Database provides information on approximately 15,500 Canadian business men and women; directors and executives of Canadian companies who reside in Canada. Information is provided by the individuals themselves or by their companies.

FIND/SVP   Dialog (File 766)

Contains the full text of market studies from FIND/SVP and Packaged Facts. Reports cover the current and historical size and growth of the market, forecasts of the future market size and growth, assessments of market trends and opportunities, global market trends, profiles of influential competitors, and other pertinent market-related information.

Firstlist   Knowledge Express

Merger and acquisition opportunities abound here, with profiles of both buyers and businesses available for sale, lists of companies seeking financing, and more.

FP Corporate Survey (CFPS)   Infomart Dialog

Database combines the contents of The Financial Post Survey of Mines and Energy Resources and Survey of Industrials. The database publicly provides detailed corporate and investment information on all companies publicly traded in Canada, as well as information on close to 8,000 subsidiaries and affiliates.

FP Predecessor & Defunct Companies   Alacra

Database provides a comprehensive record of changes to Canadian public corporations since 1929 with details of name changes, amalgamations, takeovers and acquisitions affecting over 21,000 corporate entities. Also includes companies being wound up, dissolved or companies whose charters have been cancelled or struck from the provincial registers.

FreeEDGAR   www.FreeEDGAR.com

Provides convenient searching and navigation features to access SEC filings filed through the SEC's EDGAR system. FreeEDGAR's Watchlist offers email notification of filings. FreeEDGAR generates an Excel spreadsheet from any table in a filing.

Frost & Sullivan Market Intelligence
Dialog (File 765)

Contains in-depth analyses and forecasts of technical market trends. Reports contain five-year forecasts of market size by product category and end-user application. Discusses marketing and distribution strategies, as well as assessments of the competitive and legislative environment. European, U.S., and worldwide coverage. Studies are organized by geographic region and include an Executive Summary, Introduction, Scope and Methodology, Technical Review, Current Product Characteristics, End-user/Application Analysis, Competitor Market Shares and Profiles, Five-Year and Interim Forecast by Major National Market, Product Group and End-user/Application, Trends and Opportunities, and company names and addresses.

Gale Group: Company Intelligence
Dialog (File 479)
DataStar (INCO)
LexisNexis - (CIUS)

Contains current address, financial, and marketing information on more than 140,000 private and public U.S. companies and 30,000 international companies. Good for privately held companies not easily researched elsewhere.

Global Access
Thomson Research

Provides data from the Disclosure database, combined with information from several other sources to help identify investment opportunities, perform competitive analysis, qualify M&A prospects, assess corporate finances, manage investment risk, track insider trading activity, monitor corporate activity, or perform case studies.

Globalbase
Dialog (File 583)
DataStar (EBUS)
FT Profile (GLB)

Contains abstracts with summary of facts and figures from original article. Non-English titles have English language abstracts.

Government Technologies
Knowledge Express

Contains abstracts describing technologies collected from various U.S. federal laboratories.

Grants
Knowledge Express

Contains data on grants from programs supporting disciplines in the sciences, arts, and community development.

Hoover's Company Profiles
Hoover's

Members-only service contains company profiles, lead finder, in-depth financials, full lists of officers, real-time SEC documents, and Power Tool for list creation.

Gale Group: Marketing & Advertising Reference Service (MARS)
Dialog (File 570)
InSite Pro
LexisNexis

Contains abstracts and full-text records on advertising and marketing issues for a wide variety of consumer products and services. Includes market size and market share information. Also used to locate new product or service introductions, evaluate markets for existing products or services, and research the marketing and advertising strategies of competitors.

| **Gale Group: New Product Announcements/Plus** | Dialog (File 621)
DataStar (PTNP)
FT Profile (PRP) |

Contains the full text of press releases from all industries covering announcements elated to products, with a focus on new products and services.

| **Gale Group: Newsletter Database** | Dialog (File 636) |

Contains the full text of specialized industry newsletters providing information on companies, products, markets, and technologies; trade and geopolitical regions of the world. Also covers government funding, rulings, and regulation and other legislative activities which impact the industries and regions covered.

| **Gale Group: PROMT** | Dialog (File 16)
DataStar (PTSP)
FT Profile (PRP) |

Covers business and industry events, trends, issues, and relationships. Trends subject matter includes market, production, shipment, and sales information; major orders and contracts; and imports/exports.

| **International Business Opportunities** | Knowledge Express |

Records describe products and processes available for licensing from 2000 universities, government agencies, research institutes and companies worldwide.

| **International PAtent DOcumentation Center - INPADOC** | Dialog (File 345)
STN |

Brings together information on priority application numbers, countries and dates, and equivalent patents (i.e., patent families) for patents issued by 66 countries and organizations. Legal status information is provided for 22 countries.

| **Investext Analyst Reports** | Factiva
Dialog (File 545)
LexisNexis (COMPNY)
Thomson Research |

Contains the full text of 700,000 company, industry, and geographic research reports written by analysts at more than 300 leading investment banks, brokerage houses and consulting firms worldwide. Provides in-depth analysis and data on approximately 50,000 publicly traded companies, including sales and earnings forecasts, market share projections and research and development expenditures. Other Investext reports analyze specific industries/products and businesses in geographic regions. The reports are useful for market research, strategic planning, competitive analysis, and financial forecasting.

| **ISI Emerging Markets** | `www.securities.com` |

Database contains news, company and financial data direct from emerging markets.

| **IT Product Finder** | `www.gartner.com` |

Database including details on over 97,000 products worldwide, including all the leading vendors in the information technology industry.

| **Jack O'Dwyer's Newsletter** | LexisNexis |

Covers the general news and trends of the PR industry; also provides editorial comment. Special sections of the newsletter cover job changes and promotions of PR professionals; new accounts added by PR firms; news of PR service firms; news of PR counseling firms; honors received by PR people; changes of address of PR firms and PR service firms.

Jack O'Dwyer's PR Services Report
LexisNexis

Provides general news features about the public relations industry. Current trends in PR practice by professionals at PR firms and corporate PR departments are highlighted. News of new PR firms, executive appointments and new products are regular features.

Jane's Defense & Aerospace News/Analysis
Dialog (File 587)

Offers business intelligence involving the defense industry.

JICST-E Plus
DataStar (JIST)
Dialog (File 94)
STN

Database contains English language citations and abstracts covering literature published in Japan in all fields of science, technology and medicine. Also contains "preview" section of non-indexed records that will subsequently be indexed.

LIVEDGAR
www.gsionline.com

Databases provide for search and retrieval of real-time SEC filings, watch service for anticipated filings, and retrieval of exhibits.

MarketTrack
LEXIS/NEXIS
Thomson Research

Provides tracking service for Canadian grocery markets.

Marquis Who's Who
Dialog (File 234)
LexisNexis (Busref, People)

Records can include vital statistics; education; family background; religious and political affiliation; home and office address; career history; creative works; civic and political activities; professional and club memberships.

Media General Financial Services
XLS

Contains financial performance data on 7000+ public companies.

MG Financial/Stock Statistics
Dialog (File 546)
Alacra

Database contains annual and quarterly Balance Sheets, Income Statements and Statement of Cash Flows for over 9000 publicly traded companies on the NYSE, AMEX and NASDAQ (includes National Market & Small Cap Stocks; does not include OTC Bulletin Board or Pink Sheets).

MicroPatent Alert (MPA)
Knowledge Express

Contains summary information from all granted U.S. patents since 1975.

Multex
Factiva
Reuters.com

Multex offers online access to over 850,000 research reports and other investment information from more than 400 leading investment banks, brokerage firms and third-party research providers worldwide. Real-time or delayed delivery are available for multimedia and rich-text research reports, with print, fax, or email options.

NELCOM Nelson's Public Company Profiles   LexisNexis (NELCOM)

Nelson's Public Company Profiles contain brief descriptions of 22,000 publicly traded corporations worldwide and include contact information, key executives and business descriptions. U.S. companies include those traded on the NYSE, and NASDAQ, plus any OTC and NASDAQ small cap stocks with analyst coverage. Non-US companies include ADRs (American Depository Receipts) as well.

NELSON   LexisNexis

Nelson's Investment Research gives you a research edge on over 22,000 stocks worldwide. Complete analyst coverage assignments of over 7500 research firms -representing 1,000 offices and over 9000 security analysts. Profiles of over 9000 U.S. and 13,000 non-U.S. public companies including business description, 5-year operating summary, complete address, phone and fax numbers, plus over 100,000 key corporate executives.

Nelson's Analyst Company Coverage   LexisNexis (NELANC)

Details over 10,000 different equity and fixed income securities analysts who follow more than 22,000 publicly traded corporations worldwide; includes contact information and company and industry coverage.

Nelson's Consensus Earnings Estimates   LexisNexis (NELER)
Alacra

Nelson's Consensus Earnings Estimates Nelson provides consensus earnings estimates and related statistics for over 6000 U.S. and 7,000 non-U.S. corporations. The information is compiled from the individual estimates of hundreds of research firms. Estimates older than 90 days are NOT included in the consensus.

NELSON (Group File)   LexisNexis

Nelson's Company Research Report Headlines is the "Master Index" of nearly every research report published worldwide by more than 700 investment banks, brokers and independent research firms. More than 200,000 reports are catalogued each year - covering more than 14,000 different public companies, 97 different industries and specialties in nine global regions. A description (headline/title) is provided for each report.

Nelson's Research Firm Profiles   LexisNexis (NELRF)

Research Firm Profiles comprise descriptions of over 750 investment banks, brokerage firms and independent research firms worldwide. Information includes contact information, key executives and analysts (research, sales and trading - both equity and fixed income) as well as research service offered.

Nelson's Co. Research Report Headlines   LexisNexis (NELREP)

Nelson's Company Research Report Headlines is the "Master Index" of nearly every research report published worldwide by more than 700 investment banks, brokers and independent research firms. More than 200,000 reports are catalogued each year - covering more than 14,000 different public companies, 97 different industries and specialties in nine global geographic regions. A brief description (headline/title) is provided for each report.

Nelson's Specialty/ Regi. Analyst Coverage   LexisNexis (NELSPE)

Nelson's Company Research Report Headlines is the "Master Index" of nearly every research report published worldwide by more than 700 investment banks, brokers and independent research firms. More than 200,000 reports are catalogued each year - covering more than 14,000 different public companies, 97 different industries and specialties in nine global geographic regions. A brief description (headline/title) is provided for each report.

Nexport Media's Canadian Trade Index   FPinfomart

Nexport Media's Canadian Trade Index contains marketing and business intelligence on Canada's largest 25,000 manufacturers. Each record includes up to 21 functional contacts. Data provided by Nexport Media

ProFile Canada   FPinfomart

ProFile Canada provides marketing and business intelligence on Canada's largest 35,000 companies with a focus on privately owned businesses. Each record includes up to 21 functional contacts. Data provided by Nexport

Small Business Innovation   Knowledge Express
Research Awards (SBIRs)

Contains information on current SBIR award recipients.

Standard & Poor's Register - Biographical   Dialog (File 526)
LexisNexis (SPBIO)

Provides personal and professional data on approximately 70,000 key business executives. Most officers and directors included in the file are affiliated with public or private, U.S. or non-U.S. companies with sales of $1 million dollars or more.

Standard & Poor's Register - Corporate   Dialog (File 527)
LexisNexis (SPCORP)

Covers all public companies and private companies with annual sales greater than $1 million or more than 50 employees. Provides important business facts on over 56,000 leading public and private corporations, including current address, financial and marketing information, and a listing of officers and directors with positions and departments.

StateNet   www.statenet.com

State Net monitors 100% of all pending bills and regulations in the 50 states and Congress. Government affairs managers can track activity on their issues in the 50 states.

TableBase   Alacra   DataStar (BTBL)
Dialog (File 93)

Contains tabular information dealing with companies, products, industries, brands, markets, demographics, and countries from around the world. All records contain a table and the originating textual article when available.

Teikoku Databank: Dialog (File 502)
Japanese Companies   DataStar (TOKU)
Thomson Research

This directory of Japanese Companies provides information for approximately 220,000 Japanese companies. Information for these companies includes current address, telephone number, financial and employment data, and executive officer information. Full and condensed Balance Sheets and Income Statements are available for about 120,000 companies.

TEKTRAN/USDA   Knowledge Express

Contains summaries of the latest research results and pre-publication abstracts from USDA's Agricultural Research Service.

TFSD Ownership Database   Dialog (File 540)

Contains public corporate ownership information generated from the Disclosure (File 100) database and from three publications containing data produced by CDA/Spectrum: Spectrum 3 (institutional holdings), Spectrum 5 (5% ownership holdings), and Spectrum 6 (ownership by insiders). This database details the common stock holdings of major institutions, corporate insiders, and 5% beneficial owners for over 6000 companies. The data indicate specific institutions and individuals, their relationship to the company, their holdings, and their most recent trades.

The Toolbox   `www.hoovers.com`

Free version of the Hoover's database. Contains company name and address, company type, key numbers, employees, key personnel, IPO Central, Stockscreener, List of Lists, Industry Zone, more.

Trade & Industry Database   Dialog (File 148)
                                             InSite Pro
                                             LexisNexis

Provides strong intl. coverage of over 65 major industries, including companies, products, and markets.

University Technologies   Knowledge Express

Contains abstracts of collaborative research and license opportunities from 150+ U.S. and foreign universities and non-profit research institutes.

Vickers Stock Research   Alacra

Includes Institutional Equity and Fixed Income Ownership data, 5% Equity Ownership data, and Insider Equity Ownership data, delivers single security report with information from a variety of sources, including 13F Filings, voluntary filings, share registers, 13D&G, forms 3, 4 and 144.

World Market Share Reporter   Thomson Research

Market share data for industries or services, by SIC code with indexes to products, companies, brands.

Worldscope   Factiva

Contains financials on 11,000 non-U.S. companies, offering either profiles or snapshots of companies.

Database File Coverage of Industries

Accounting ... ...

ABI/INFORM -- Dialog (File 15)

Advanced Materials ...

Business Communications Company (BCC) -- Dialog (File 764)
LexisNexis
Profound
Thomson Financial

FIND/SVP -- Dialog (File 766)

Aerospace & Defense ...

Frost & Sullivan Market Intelligence -- Dialog (File 765)

Agriculture / Agribusiness ...

Business & Industry -- Alacra
DataStar (BIDB)
Dialog (File 9)

TEKTRAN/USDA -- Knowledge Express

Agriculture Products ...

Asian Business Intelligence -- Dialog (File 568)

Apparel ...

IAC Marketing & Advertising Reference -- Dialog (File 570)
Service (MARS) -- InSite Pro
LexisNexis

Automotive ... ...

ChinaOnline -- www.chinaonline.com

Banking ... ...

Bankstat -- Thomson Financial

Beverages ... ...

Beverage Marketing -- Dialog (File 770)

Biotechnology ... ...

BioScan -- Knowledge Express

Contact Canada -- http://contactcanada.com

Federal Bio-Technology Transfer Directory -- Knowledge Express

Globalbase -- Dialog (File 583)

Chemicals ...

Corporate & Marketing Intelligence (CAMI) -- Profound

Chemistry ...

Conference Papers Index (CPI) -- Dialog (File 77)

Communications ...

Communications Industry Forecast -- www.vss.com/publications/

Computer Hardware ...

Computer Industry Forecasts -- www.infotechtrends.com

Consumer Products & Services ...

Marketsearch Directory -- www.marketsearch-dir.com

Datamonitor -- Alacra
DataStar (DMON)
Dialog (File 761)
LexisNexis (MKTRES)

Data Communications ...

Cambridge Market Intelligence -- Profound

Defense ...

Jane's Defense & Aerospace News/Analysis -- Dialog (File 587)

Trade & Industry Database -- Dialog (File 148)

Energy ... ...

FP Corporate Survey (CFPS) -- FPinfomart

Engineering ...

Federal Research In Progress (FEDRIP) -- Knowledge Express

Financial ... ...

Disclosure -- Factiva

Dow Jones Wires -- Factiva

Dun's Market Identifiers -- Dialog (File 516)

Global Access -- Thomson Research

Food & Beverage ...

Marketline Intl. Market Research Reports -- DataStar (MKTL)

Furniture Industry ...

AKTRIN Research -- Profound
www.aktrin.com

Healthcare ...

Acquisition, Technology Transfer, Licensing
& Source of Capital Directory -- Knowledge Express

High Technology ...

Company Needs/Capabilities -- Knowledge Express

Company Technologies -- Knowledge Express

CorpTech -- Knowledge Express

Information Technology ...

Infotech Trends -- www.infotechtrends.com

Law ... ...

StateNet -- www.statenet.com

Medicine ... ...

JICST-E Plus -- DataStar (JIST)

Multi-Industry ...

Advertiser & Agency Red Books -- Dialog (File 177, 178)

Asia Pulse -- Bloomberg

Bankruptcy DataSource -- LexisNexis (BDS)

Bankruptcy File (CBKF) -- Infomart Dialog

BARRA Global & Single Country Equity Models -- Alacra

Business & Management Practices(BAMP) -- Dialog (File 13)

Canadian Corporate Names -- FPinfomart

Canadian Federal Corporations & Directors -- FPinfomart

CORDIS -- www.cordis.lu

Delphes European Business -- DataStar (DELP)

EDGAR-Online -- www.edgar-online.com

EIU: Country Analysis -- LexisNexis

EIU: Country Risk And Forecasts -- LexisNexis

Encyclopedia of Associations -- Dialog (File 114)

Environmental Impact Statements Collection (EIS) -- `www.library.nwu.edu/transpor tation/tleis.html`

Federal Laboratory Technologies (FLTDB) -- Knowledge Express

Firstlist -- Knowledge Express

FreeEDGAR -- `www.FreeEDGAR.com`

Government Technologies -- Knowledge Express

Grants -- Knowledge Express

Hoover's Company Profiles -- Hoover's

IAC New Product Announcements/Plus -- Dialog (File 621)

IAC Newsletter Database -- Dialog (File 636)

IAC PROMT -- Dialog (File 16)

IAC: Company Intelligence -- Dialog (File 479)

Canadian Inter-Corporate Ownership -- FPinfomart

International Business Opportunities -- Knowledge Express

INternational Patent Documentation Center -- Dialog (File 345)

Investext Analyst Reports -- Factiva

Investext: Research Bank Web -- Thomson Financial

IPO Data Systems -- Ipodata.com

ISI Emerging Markets -- `www.securities.com`

LIVEDGAR -- `www.gsionline.com`

Marquis Who's Who -- Dialog (File 234)

Media General Financial Services -- Alacra

MG Financial/Stock Statistics -- Dialog (File 546)

MicroPatent Alert (MPA) -- Knowledge Express

Multex -- Factiva
Reuters.com

NELCOM Nelson's Public Company Profiles -- LexisNexis (NELCOM)

NELSON -- LexisNexis

NELSON (Group File) -- LexisNexis

Nelson's Analyst Company Coverage -- LexisNexis (NELANC)

Nelson's Co. Research Report Headlines -- LexisNexis (NELREP)

Nelson's Consensus Earnings Estimates -- LexisNexis (NELERN)

Nelson's Research Firm Profiles -- LexisNexis (NELRF)

Nelson's Specialty/ Regi. Analyst Coverage -- LexisNexis (NELSPE)

Profile Canada -- FPinfomart

Standard & Poor's Register - Biographical -- Dialog (File 526)

Standard & Poor's Register - Corporate -- Dialog (File 527)

TableBase -- Alacra
DataStar (BTBL)
Dialog (File 93)

Teikoku Databank: Japanese Companies -- Dialog (File 502)

The Disclosure/Spectrum Ownership -- Dialog (File 540)

The Toolbox -- Hoover's

University Technologies -- Knowledge Express

Vickers Stock Research -- Alacra

World Market Share Reporter -- Thomson Research

Pharmaceutical ... ...

Bio/Pharma Surveys -- Knowledge Express

Public Relations ...

Jack O'Dwyer's Newsletter -- LexisNexis

O'Dwyer's PR Services Report -- LexisNexis

Publishing ... ...

Globalbase --Dialog (File 583)
DataStar (EBUS)
FT Profile (GLB)

IAC Marketing & Advertising Reference Dialog (File 570)
Service (MARS) --InSite Pro
LexisNexis

Pulp & Paper ... ...

Business & Industry --Alacra
DataStar (BIDB)
Dialog (File 9)

Real Estate ... ...

ABI/INFORM --Dialog (File 15)
FT Profile (ABI)
DataStar (INFO)

ChinaOnline --www.chinaonline.com

Restaurants ...

IAC Marketing & Advertising Reference Dialog (File 570)
Service (MARS) --InSite Pro
LexisNexis

Retailing ... ...

Business & Industry --Alacra
DataStar (BIDB)
Dialog (File 9)

FIND/SVP --Dialog (File 766)

Marketline Intl. Market Research Reports --DataStar (MKTL)

Trade & Industry Database --Dialog (File 148)
InSite Pro   LexisNexis

Science & Technology ... ...

JICST-E Plus --DataStar (JIST)
Dialog
STN

Security & Access Controls ...

Frost & Sullivan Market Intelligence --Dialog (File 765)

Software Development ...

Cambridge Market Intelligence --Profound

Subassemblies & Components ...

CorpTech --Knowledge Express
www.corptech.com
Thomson Research

Taxation ... ...

ABI/INFORM --Dialog (File 15)
FT Profile (ABI)
DataStar (INFO)

Telecommunications ... ...

ABI/INFORM --Dialog (File 15)
FT Profile (ABI)
DataStar (INFO)

Asian Business Intelligence --Dialog (File 568)
LexisNexis (MKTRES)

Business & Industry --Alacra
DataStar (BIDB)
Dialog (File 9)

Cambridge Market Intelligence --Profound

China Business Resources --Thomson Financial
Profound

ChinaOnline --www.chinaonline.com

Frost & Sullivan Market Intelligence --Dialog (File 765) XLS

Globalbase --Dialog (File 583)
DataStar (EBUS)
FT Profile (GLB)

Marketline Intl. Market Research Reports --DataStar (MKTL)

Trade & Industry Database --Dialog (File 148)
InSite Pro LexisNexis

Telecommunications & Internet ...

CorpTech --Knowledge Express
www.corptech.com
Thomson Research

Test & Measurement ... ...

CorpTech --Knowledge Express
www.corptech.com
Thomson Financial

Textiles ...

Frost & Sullivan Market Intelligence --Dialog (File 765) XLS

Tobacco & Cigarettes ...

Corporate & Marketing Intelligence (CAMI) --Profound

Toiletries & Cosmetics ...

Corporate & Marketing Intelligence (CAMI) --Profound

Transportation ... ...

ABI/INFORM --Dialog (File 15)
FT Profile (ABI)
DataStar (INFO)

Asian Business Intelligence --Dialog (File 568)
LexisNexis (MKTRES)

Business & Industry --Alacra
DataStar (BIDB)
Dialog (File 9)

China Business Resources --Investext (Thomson Financial)
Profound

ChinaOnline --www.chinaonline.com

CorpTech --Knowledge Express
www.corptech.com
Thomson Research

Veterinary Medicine ...

Frost & Sullivan Market Intelligence --Dialog (File 765) XLS

TEKTRAN/USDA --Knowledge Express

Waste Management ...

FIND/SVP --Dialog (File 766)

Water Treatment ...

FIND/SVP --Dialog (File 766)

Wood Products ...

AKTRIN Research --Profound
www.aktrin.com

Online Vendors & Publishers

Database Producers

Addresses and contact information are provided for North America, with other addresses included if a U.S. or Canadian office could not be located. For additional locations in other parts of the world, please visit the website provided.

A.C. Nielsen Corporation
ACNielsen
770 Broadway
New York, NY 10003
Tel: +1 646 654 5000
Fax: +1 646 654 5002
www.acnielsen.com

AKTRIN Research Institute, Canada
151 Randall St.
Oakville ON
Canada
(905) 845-3474
Fax: (905) 845-7459
www.aktrin.com

AKTRIN Research Institute, NC
64 S. Main St. (Radio Bldg.)
P.O. Box 898
High Point, NC, 27261, USA
Tel.: (336) 841 8535
Fax.: (336) 841 5435

Asian CIS (Asian Credit Information Service)
886 2 28754355
Fax : +886 2 28754360
www.asiancredit.com/Home/wh
atmakeusdifferent.cfm

Beverage Marketing Corporation
850 Third Ave.
New York NY 10022
(212) 688-7640
Fax: (212) 826-1255
www.beveragemarketing.com

Business Communications Company (BCC)
25 Van Zant St.
Norwalk CT 06855
(203) 853-4266
Fax: (203) 853-0348
www.buscom.com

Business Trend Analysts
2171 Jerico Turnpike
Commack NY 11725
(516) 462-1842
Fax: (516) 462-1842
www.businesstrendanalysts.com

Cambridge Scientific Abstracts
7200 Wisconsin Avenue
Bethesda MD 20814
301-961-6727
800-843-7751
Fax: 301-961-6720

Collector Trends Analysis, Inc.
900 Watkins Glen Dr
Spring Valley, OH 45370
937-885-9649

Corporate Technology Information Services, Inc (CorpTech)
300 Baker Avenue
Concord, MA 01742
978-318-4300
Fax: 978-318-4690
www.corptech.com

Databank SpA
Via dei Piatti 11
20123 Milano
39 2-809556
Fax: 39 2-8056495

Datamonitor
245 Fifth Ave, 4th Fl
New York, NY 10016
212-686-7400
Fax: 212-686-2626
www.datamonitor.com

Decision Resources
260 Charles St.
Waltham MA 02453
781-296-2500
Fax: 781-296-2550
www.dresources.com

Drewery Shipping Consultants Ltd.
11 Heron Quay
London E14 9YP England
44 171-538-0191
Fax: 44 171-987-9396

Economist Intelligence Unit
The Economist Building
111 West 57th Street
New York NY 10019
212-554-0600
Fax: 212-586-1181
www.eiu.com

Electric Power Research Institute (EPRI)
3412 Hillview Avenue
Palo Alto CA 94304-1395
650 855-2000
www.epri.com

Elsevier Science USA
360 Park Avenue South
New York, NY 10010-1710
888-437-4636
Fax: 212- 462-1974
www.elsevier.com

Engineering Information Inc (Ei Village)
1 Castle Point Terrace
Hoboken NJ 07030-5996
800 221-1044 U.S. & Canada
Fax: 201 216-8532
www.ei.org

Espicom Business Intelligence
Lincoln House
City Fields Business Park
City Fields Way
Chichester England P020 2FS
44 1-243-533-322
Fax: 44 1-243-533-418

Espicom USA Inc.,
116 Village Boulevard,
Princeton Forrestal Village,
Princeton, NJ 08540-5799
609-951-2227
Fax: 609-734-7428

Euromonitor Plc.
122 South Michigan Ave, Suite 1200
Chicago IL 60603
312-922-1115
Fax: 312-922-1157
www.euromonitor.com

Federal Laboratory Consortium
950 N. Kings Highway, Suite 208
Cherry Hill NJ 08034
609-667-7727
Fax: 609- 667-8009
www.federallabs.org

FIND/SVP Research Publications
625 Avenue of the Americas
New York NY 10011-2002
212-645-4500
Fax: 212-807-2676
www.findsvp.com

The Freedonia Group, Inc.
767 Beta Drive
Cleveland OH 44143-2326
440-684-9600
Fax: 440-646-0484
www.freedoniagroup.com

Frost & Sullivan
2525 East Charleston Road
Mountain View CA 94043
650-961-9000
Fax: 650-961-5042
www.frost.com

Gartner Group
56 Top Gallant Road
Stamford CT 06904
203 964 0096
www.datapro.com

Groupe DAFSA
117, quai de Valmy
75010 Paris, France
33 1-55-45-26-00
Fax: 33 1-55-45-26-35
www.dafsa.fr

Houlihan Lokey Howard & Zukin
1930 Century Park West
Los Angeles CA 90099-5098
800-455-8871

infoUSA, Inc.
5711 South 86th Circle
Omaha NE 68127
800-321-0869
Fax: 402- 331- 0176
www.infousa.com

International Foundation of Employee Benefit Plans INFOSOURCE (Employee Benefits Database)
18700 W. Bluemound Rd.
Brookfield WI 53008-0069
414- 786-6700
Fax: 414-786-8670
www.ifebp.org

J.R. O'Dwyer Company
271 Madison Avenue
New York NY 10016
212-679-2471
Fax: 212-683-2750
www.odwyerpr.com

Japan Science and Technology Corporation, Information Center for Science and Technology (JICST)
1800 K Street N.W. Suite 920
Washington D.C. 20006
202-659-8190
Fax:: 202-659-8199

Key Note Ltd.
Field House
72 Oldfield Road
Hampton Middlesex TW12 2HQ
England
44 181-481-8750
Fax: 44 181-763-0049
www.keynote.co.uk

Killen & Associates
1212 Parkinson Avenue
Palo Alto CA 94301
650-327-2312
Fax: 650-289-0505
www.killen.com

Lafferty Group
The Graybar Building
420 Lexington Avenue, Suite 2531
New York NY 10170
212-557-6726
Fax: 212-557-7266
www.lafferty.co.uk

Leatherhead Food Research Association
Randalls Road
Leatherhead Surrey
England KT22 7RY
44 1372-376-761
Fax: 44 1372-386-228
www.lfra.co.uk

Market & Business Development (MBD)
Barnett House, 53 Fountain St
Manchester M2 2AN
United Kingdom
44 161-839-2739
Fax: 44 161-839-9320
www.mbdltd.co.uk

Marketdata Enterprises, Inc.
2807 West Busch Blvd., Suite 110
Tampa FL 33618
813-931-3900
Fax: 813-931-3802
www.mkt-data-ent.com

Marketing Intelligence Service
6473 D Route 64
Naples NY 14512
800-836-5710
Fax: 716-374-5217
www.productscan.com

Mintel Marketing Intelligence
Mintel International Group Ltd,
213 W. Institute Place
Chicago, IL 60610
312-932-0400
Fax: 312 932 0469
www.mintel.co.uk

Moody's Investors Service
99 Church Street
New York NY 10007
212-553-0300
www.moodys.com

MSI Marketing Research for Industry
Viscount House, River Lane
Saltney Chester CH4 8QY
44 1244-681-186
Fax: 44 1244-681-457

OCLC Public Affairs Information Service (PAIS)
521 West 43rd Street, New York
New York NY 10036
800 288 7247 (Toll-Free in U.S. and Canada)
Fax: 212 643 2848
www.pais.inter.ne

PIRA International
Randalls Road
Leatherhead Surrey KT22 7RU
44 1372-802-000
Fax: 44 1372-802-238
www.pira.co.uk

Political and Economic Risk Consultancy, Ltd.
233 Hollywood Rd, Rms. 1603-1604
Hollywood Centre
Hong Kong
852 2541-4088
Fax: 852- 2815-5032
www.asiarisk.com

PR Newswire
810 7th Ave., 35th floor
New York, NY 10019
212-596-1500
800-832-5522
www.prnewswire.com

Standard & Poor's Corporation
25 Broadway
New York NY 10004
212-770-4000
Fax: 212-770-0275
www2.standardandpoors.com

Strategic Directions International, Inc.
6242 Westchester Parkway, #100
Los Angeles CA 90045
310-641-4982
Fax: 310-641-8851
www.strategic-directions.com

Taylor Nelson Sofres plc
AGB House - Westgate
London W5 1UA England
44 0 20 8967 0007

Fax: 44 020 8967 4060
www.huginonline.com

Teikoku Databank Ltd.
747 Third Avenue, 25th Fl.
New York NY 10017
212-421-9805
Fax: 212-421-9806
www.teikoku.com

Thomson Gale
27500 Drak Rd
Farmington Hills MI 48331
248-699-4253
www.galegroup.com

VerdictSearch/The New York Jury Reporter
128 Carlton Avenue
East Islip NY 17730
516-581-1930
www.verdictsearch.com

Database Vendors - Internet

Alacra
88 Pine Street, 3rd Fl.
New York, New York 10005
212 363 9620
Fax: 212 363 9630
www.alacra.com

Asia Pulse Pte Ltd.
Level 7, 9 Lang Street
Locked Bag 21, Grosvenor Place
Sydney NSW 02000
61-2 9322 8634
Fax: 61-2 9322 8639
www.asiapulse.com

AutoTrackXP
ChoicePoint Inc.
4530 Conference Way South
Boca Raton, FL 33431
800-279-7710
Fax: 561-982-5363
www.dbt.net

BizAdvantage
973-605-6441
companyreports@dnb.com
www.bizadvantage.com

Burrelle's /Luce
75 E. Northfield Road
Livingston NJ 07039
800-631-1160
www.burrelles.com

ChoicePoint
1901 E. Alton Avenue, Suite 200
Santa Ana CA 92705-5847
(949)222-7700
www.choicepointonline.com/cdb/

Companies House
21 Bloomsbury Street
London WC1B 3XD
www.companieshouse.gov.uk/

The Conference Board
845 Third Avenue
New York NY 10022
212-836-9740
Fax: (212) 980-7014
www.conference-board.org

CorpTech Information Services, Inc.
300 Baker Avenue
Concord, MA 01742
978-318-4300
Fax: 978-318-4690
www.corptech.com

DCS Information Systems
500 North Central Expressway
Ste. 280
Plano TX 75074
800-299-3647
Fax: 972-422-3642
www.dnis.com

Dialog Profound
11000 Regency Parkway, Suite 400
Cary NC 27511
888 809-6193
www.dialog.com/products/pro
found/

Dun & Bradstreet
The D&B Corporation
103 JFK Parkway, Short Hills, NJ
07078 U.S.A.
800-234-3867
www.dnb.com

Economist Intelligence Unit
The Economist Building
111 West 57th Street
New York NY 10019
212-554-0600
Fax: 212-586-1181
www.eiu.com

EDGAR Online
50 Washington Street, 9th Floor
Norwalk, CT 06854
800-416-6651
203-852-5666
Fax: 203-852-5667
www.edgar-online.com

Equifax (Consumer Credit Reports, Geo-Demographic & Econometric Information)
PO Box 740241
Atlanta GA 30374-0241
800-997-2493
www.equifax.com

Environmental Data Resources
440 Wheelers Farms Road
Milford, CT 06460
1-800-352-0050
www.edrnet.com

Experian
475 Anton Blvd.
Costa Mesa, CA 92626
714 830 7000
www.experian.com

Factiva
105 Madison Avenue
10th Floor
New York, NY 10016
800-369-0166
www.factiva.com

FPinfomart
CanWest Interactive Inc.
333 King St East
Toronto, Ontario M5A 4R7
CANADA
800-661-7678
416-350-6500
Fax: 416-350-6501
www.FPinfomart.ca/

Global Securities Information (GSI)
419 Seventh St. NW
Suite 202
Washington DC 20004
800-669-1154
Fax: 202-628-1133
www.gsionline.com

H.W. Wilson (Abstract & Full Text Databases, Indexes)
950 University Avenue
Bronx NY 10452-4224
800-367-6770
www.hwwilson.com

HighBeam Research
360 North Michigan Avenue, #1320
Chicago, Illinois 60601
Phone: 312-782-3900
Fax: 312-782-3901
www.highbeam.com

Hoover's Online
Hoover's, Inc.
5800 Airport Blvd.
Austin, TX 78752
512-374-4500
Fax: 512-374- 4501
www.hoovers.com

IBM Patent Server
Intellectual Property & Licensing
North Castle Drive
Armonk, New York 10504
914-765-4420
www.patents.ibm.com

Internet Database Service
CSA -- 7200 Wisconsin Ave, #601
Bethesda, Maryland 20814
301-961-6700

Fax: 301-961-6720
www.csa.com/csa/ids/ids-main.shtml

Informus Corporation
2001 Airport Road, Suite 201
Jackson MS 39208
800-364-8380
www.informus.com

IPO Data Systems
74-16 Roosevelt Avenue, Suite 141
Jackson Heights NY 11372
www.ipodata.com

ISI Emerging Markets Internet Securities, Inc.
225 Park Avenue South
New York, New York 10003
888-ISI-4-INFO
212- 610- 2900
Fax: 212-610-2950
http://securities.com

Jane's Information Group
110 N. Royal Street, Suite 200
Alexandria, VA 22314,
800-243-3852
www.janes.com

Knowledge Express Data Systems (KEDS)
3000 Valley Forge Circle, Suite 3800
King of Prussia PA 19407
800-529-5337
www.KnowledgeExpress.com

KnowX
See ChoicePoint

LexisNexis
PO Box 933, Dayton OH 45401
800-227-4908
www.nexis.com/research

Manning & Napier Information Services
1100 Chase Square
Rochester NY 14604
800-278-5356
Fax: 716- 454-2516
www.mnis.net

MicroPatent
250 Dodge Avenue
East Haven CT 06512
800-648-6787
www.micropat.com

National Library of Medicine
8600 Rockville Pike
Bethesda MD 20894
(888) FIND-NLM
(301) 594-5983
301-594-5983 (local and international calls)
www.nlm.nih.gov/databases/

NERAC
One Technology Drive
Tolland, CT 06084
860 872-7000
www.nerac.com

NTIS
Springfield, Virginia 22161
703-605-6000
www.ntis.gov

Ovid Technologies
333 Seventh Avenue
New York NY 10001
(800) 950-2035
Fax: 646-674-6301
www.ovid.com

PACER
PO Box 780549
San Antonio TX 78278
800-676-6856
http://pacer.psc.uscourts.gov

Proquest UMI
300 N. Zeeb Road
PO Box 1346
Ann Arbor MI 48106-1346
800-521-0600
www.umi.com/proquest

QUESTEL-ORBIT, Inc.
7925 Jones Branch Drive
McLean, VA 22012
703-873-4700
Fax: 703-873-4701
www.questel.orbit.com

Skyminder
2701 North Rocky Point Drive, #110
Tampa FL 33607
813 636 0981
Fax: 813 637 8451
www.skyminder.com

State Net
2101 K Street
Sacramento CA 95816
916 447-1886
www.statenet.com

STN International
Chemical Abstracts Services
2540 Olentangy River Road
Columbus OH 43210
800-753-4227
http://stnweb.cas.org/

Stock Smart
PO Box 191408
Dallas TX 75219
www.stocksmart.com

Strategis
Industry Canada
C.D. Howe Building
235 Queen Street
Ottawa, Ontario K1A 0H5
613-954-5031
800-328-6189 (Canada)

Superior Information Services
300 Phillips Blvd.
Trenton NJ 08650
800-848-0489
609-883-7000
www.superiorinfo.com

Teltech Resource Network
Corporation
2850 Metro Drive
Minneapolis MN 55425-1566
612-851-7500
Fax: 612-851-7744
www.teltech.com

Thomson & Thomson
(Trademark & Copyright w.
Domain Name Search)
500 Victory Road

North Quincy MA 02171-1545
800-692-8833
www.thomson-thomson.com

Thomson Delphion
901 Warrenville Road Suite 20
Lisle, IL 60532
630-799-0600
Fax: 630-799-0688

Thomson Derwent
3501 Market Street
Philadelphia, PA 19104
800-336-4474
Fax: 215 386 2911
www.derwent.com

Thomson Dialog
11000 Regency Parkway, Suite 400
Cary NC 27511
800-3-Dialog
919-462-8600
Fax: 919-468-9890
www.dialog.com

Thomson Financial
195 Broadway
New York NY 10007
646-822-2000
www.thomson.com/financial/f
inancial.jsp

Thomson Research
195 Broadway
New York NY 10007
646-822-3500
Fax: 646-822-3530
http://research.thomsonib.com

Thomson Scientific
3501 Market Street
Philadelphia PA 19104
800-336-4474
Fax: 215-386-2911
www.isinet.com

Trans Union Corporation (Credit
& Fraud-Prevention Data)
555 W. Adams St.
Chicago IL 60661-3601
800-899-7132
www.transunion.com

UCC Direct Services
2727 Allen Parkway, Suite 1200
Houston TX 77019
800-833-5778
713-864-7639
www.uccdirect.com

USIS Transportation Services
P.O. Box 33181
Tulsa, OK 74153
800-381-0645
www.usis.com

Westlaw / Thomson West
610 Opperman Dr.
St. Paul MN 55123
800-328-9352
www.west.thomson.com

Document Delivery Services

The list that follows includes both general and industry-specific document delivery services on several continents. Many major university libraries also offer this service.

A Google search using "document delivery services" as the search string will retrieve many of these.

The British Library
St Pancras
96 Euston Road
London, NW1 2DB
mailto: dsc-customer-services@
bl.uk+44 (0)1937 546060
   or
British Library Newspapers
Colindale Avenue
London, NW9 5HE
www.bl.uk/services/bsds/dsc
/delivery.html

Canada Institute for Scientific & Technical Information (CISTI) | National Research Council of Canada
Montreal Road, Jac, E. Brown Building
Ottawa ON K1A 0S2
800-668-1222\
www.cisti.nrc.ca/cisti

CAS Document Detective Service
2540 Olentangy River Rd.
P.O. Box 3012
Columbus, OH 43210-0012 USA
800-678-4337 (North America)
(614) 447-3670 (elsewhere)
Fax: 614- 447-3648
www.cas.org/Support/dds.html

Infotrieve
US Account Services
11755 Wilshire Blvd., 19th Floor
Los Angeles, CA 90025
800-422-4633
310-445-3001 ext. 0
Fax: 310-445-3003
service@infotrieve.com

Kinetica
The National Library of Australia
Parkes Place, Canberra ACT 2600
1800 026 155
Fax: 02 6273 1180
kinetica@nla.gov.au
www.nla.gov.au/kinetica/doc
del.html

National Agricultural Library Document Delivery Service
National Agricultural Library, rm. 300
Beltsville, MD 20705
301-504-6503
Fax: 301-504-7593
www.nal.usda.gov/ddsb/

Federal Court Records Online

The advent of the Internet has prompted many government agencies to go "online." The Federal courts – U.S. District and U.S. Bankruptcy – are leading the way in making their case records searchable on the Web. A few sites offer free searching, but the number is diminishing. In this section, you will find web addresses for all types of records available online from federal courts.

While some of the courts offer electronic access only through the dial-up PACER systems, more and more of them are making their records available online. In most cases, one must have a PACER membership in order to access the records. Visit http://pacer.psc.uscourts.gov to sign up for PACER. For those courts where dial-up PACER is your only option, you can begin your search using the U.S. Party/Case Index. Most U.S. Courts participate in the U.S. Party/Case Index.

More and more courts offer alternatives to PACER, primarily ECM-CF, for access to their electronically-filed records. ECM-CF equipped courts provide the opportunity to file and access cases online. Like PACER, fees do apply to ECM-CF online documents.

Before Using PACER, Search the National Index

Rather than dialing in to each PACER system to determine if a record exists, you can search the U.S. Party/Case Index – a national index of the U.S. district, bankruptcy and appellate court records. The U.S. Party/Case Index is available via the Internet and through traditional dial-up methods.

You can search using party name, Social Security Number, and/or nature of suit. National and regional searches are available. The results are comprised of a list of case numbers, filing locations and filing dates for any records that match your search criteria. Once you have that information, you may access the PACER system for the particular location of the record you are seeking.

The Internet site for the US Party/Case Index is http://pacer.uspci.uscourts.gov. The toll-free dial-up number for the US Party/Case Index is 800-974-8896. For more information, call the PACER service center at 800-676-6856.

Accessing PACER Using the Internet

PACER access requires that you use a PACER login name and password. Visit http://pacer.psc.uscourts.gov for more information and sign up.

RACER and Other FREE Internet Court Systems

RACER (an Internet-based PACER-Imaging system) as well as several other online case records systems are accessible via the Internet. You may search for free at:

Arkansas – District - Western
`www.arwd.uscourts.gov/CaseInfo.htm`

> Only pending case list is available free at this website.

Delaware - Bankruptcy
`http://206.96.0.130/wconnect/WCI.DLL?usbcn_racer~main`

> Free searching of Chapter 11 filings for 2003-4; format is pdf lists.

Idaho - Bankruptcy
`www.id.uscourts.gov/wconnect/wc.dll?usdc_racer~main`

Idaho - District
`www.id.uscourts.gov/wconnect/wc.dll?usdc_racer~main`

Indiana – District – Southern
`www.insd.uscourts.gov/casesearch.htm`

Minnesota - Bankruptcy
`www.mnb.uscourts.gov/ers-bin/mnb-651-main.pl`

New Mexico - District - Bankruptcy
`www.nmcourt.fed.us/web/DCDOCS/files/accountrequest.html`

> You may submit a written request for an ACE (Advanced Court Engineering) user name and password in order to freely access court records, docket reports, and court opinions.

North Carolina - Bankruptcy - Eastern
`www.nceb.uscourts.gov/access_to_data.htm`

> Even though the URL above is similar to PACER URLs, the site is indeed a RACER site.

Pennsylvania - District - Eastern
`www.paed.uscourts.gov`

Electronic Filing

Electronic filing of Federal court documents – ECM-CF – is becoming more widespread. The following federal courts offer electronic filing for law firms and practitioners. Keep in mind that if searching is available it consists *only* of a search of cases that were filed electronically, *not* all cases.

Courts Accepting Electronic Filings

U.S. District Courts

Alabama Southern District Court
`www.als.uscourts.gov/cmecf/main22.html`

California Northern District Court
`https://ecf.cand.uscourts.gov/cand/index.html`

Connecticut District Court
www.ctd.uscourts.gov/cmecf/

District Of Columbia District Court
www.dcd.uscourts.gov/ecf.html

Florida Northern District Court
www.flnd.uscourts.gov

Indiana Northern District Court
www.innd.uscourts.gov/ecf.shtml

Indiana Southern District Court
www.insd.uscourts.gov/ecf_info.htm

Iowa Northern District Court
www.insd.uscourts.gov/ecf_info.htm

Kansas District Court
www.ksd.uscourts.gov/cmecf/index.php

Maine District Court
www.med.uscourts.gov/Site/cmecf/cmecf.htm

Maryland District Court
www.mdd.uscourts.gov/CMECF/cmecfstart1.asp

Massachusetts District Court
www.mad.uscourts.gov/CaseInfo/CM_ECF.htm

Michigan Western District Court
https://ecf.miwd.uscourts.gov

Missouri Eastern District Court
https://ecf.moed.uscourts.gov

Missouri Western District Court
www.mow.uscourts.gov/dc_cmecf.htm

Nebraska District Court
www.ned.uscourts.gov/cmecf/index.html

New Jersey District Court
http://pacer.njd.uscourts.gov/njdc/cm-ecf/njdc-cmecf.htm

New York Eastern District Court
www.nyed.uscourts.gov/CM_ECF/cm_ecf.html

New York Northern District Court
www.nynd.uscourts.gov/cmecf/

New York Southern District Court
www.nysd.uscourts.gov/cmecf/cmecfindex.htm

New York Western District Court
www.nywd.uscourts.gov/cmecf/index.php

Ohio Northern District Court
www.ohnd.uscourts.gov/Electronic_Filing/electronic_filing.html

Ohio Southern District Court
www.ohsd.uscourts.gov/cmecf.htm

Oklahoma Western District Court
www.okwd.uscourts.gov/cmecf.htm

Oregon District Court
www.ord.uscourts.gov/ECF/CMECFHomePage.htm

Pennsylvania Eastern District Court
https://ecf.paed.uscourts.gov

Pennsylvania Middle District Court
www.pamd.uscourts.gov/ecf.htm

Puerto Rico District Court
www.prd.uscourts.gov/cmecf/Main.asp

South Dakota District Court
www.sdd.uscourts.gov/sdecf.html

Texas Eastern District Court
www.txed.uscourts.gov

Washington Western District Court
www.wawd.uscourts.gov/wawd/cm-ecf.nsf/main/page

Wisconsin Eastern District Court
www.wied.uscourts.gov/ECF/ECF.htm

Court of Federal Claims
www.uscfc.uscourts.gov/CMECF.htm

U.S. Bankruptcy Courts

Alabama Middle Bankruptcy Court
www.almb.uscourts.gov/cmecf/index.htm

Alabama Southern Bankruptcy Court
www.alsb.uscourts.gov/EFiling.htm

Alaska Bankruptcy Court
www.akb.uscourts.gov

Arizona Bankruptcy Court
www.azb.uscourts.gov/azb/documents.nsf/1

Arkansas Bankruptcy Court
www.arb.uscourts.gov/CM-ECF/cm-ecf.htm

California Northern Bankruptcy Court
www.canb.uscourts.gov

California Southern Bankruptcy Court
www.casb.uscourts.gov/html/frontcounter.htm

Colorado Bankruptcy Court
https://ecf.cob.uscourts.gov

Delaware Bankruptcy Court
www.deb.uscourts.gov

Florida Middle Bankruptcy Court
www.flmb.uscourts.gov

Florida Northern Bankruptcy Court
www.flnb.uscourts.gov/CMECF/index.htm

Georgia Northern Bankruptcy Court
www.ganb.uscourts.gov/cmecf/ecf.html

Hawaii Bankruptcy Court
www.hib.uscourts.gov/cmecf

Illinois Southern Bankruptcy Court
www.ilsb.uscourts.gov/cmecf.htm

Indiana Northern Bankruptcy Court
www.innb.uscourts.gov/cmecf.htm

Iowa Northern Bankruptcy Court
www.ianb.uscourts.gov/ecf/index.asp

Iowa Southern Bankruptcy Court
www.iasb.uscourts.gov/courtpages/home/homepage.asp?sPage=ECF

Kentucky Eastern Bankruptcy Court
http://207.41.15.180/kyeb/CMECF/cmecf.htm

Kentucky Western Bankruptcy Court
www.kywb.uscourts.gov/fpweb/cm_ecf/cmecf.htm

Louisiana Eastern Bankruptcy Court
www.laeb.uscourts.gov/ECFINFO/cmecf.htm

Louisiana Middle Bankruptcy Court
www.lamb.uscourts.gov/cmecf.htm

Louisiana Western Bankruptcy Court
www.lawb.uscourts.gov/CMECFlinks.htm

Maine Bankruptcy Court
www.meb.uscourts.gov/mebcmecf.html

Maryland Bankruptcy Court
www.mdb.uscourts.gov/cmecf/cmecfframe.asp

Massachusetts Bankruptcy Court
www.mab.uscourts.gov/CMECFSignUp/ecf_default.htm

Michigan Western Bankruptcy Court
www.miwb.uscourts.gov/content/cmecf/

Missouri Eastern Bankruptcy Court
www.moeb.uscourts.gov/cmecf/cmecf.html

Missouri Western Bankruptcy Court
www.mow.uscourts.gov/bk_cmecf.htm

Montana Bankruptcy Court
www.mtb.uscourts.gov

Nebraska Bankruptcy Court
https://ecf.neb.uscourts.gov

Nevada Bankruptcy Court
www.nvb.uscourts.gov

New Hampshire Bankruptcy Court
www.nhb.uscourts.gov/CMECF_Home_Page/cmecf_home_page.html

New Jersey Bankruptcy Court
www.njb.uscourts.gov/ecf/

New York Eastern Bankruptcy Court
www.nyeb.uscourts.gov/cm_ecf.htm

New York Northern Bankruptcy Court
www.nynb.uscourts.gov

New York Southern Bankruptcy Court
www.nysb.uscourts.gov/ecf.html

New York Western Bankruptcy Court
www.nywb.uscourts.gov/ecf/ecf-manual/ecf.htm

North Carolina Western Bankruptcy Court
www.ncwb.uscourts.gov/ecf/ecf.html

Ohio Northern Bankruptcy Court
www.ohnb.uscourts.gov

Ohio Southern Bankruptcy Court
www.ohsb.uscourts.gov

Oklahoma Northern Bankruptcy Court
www.oknb.uscourts.gov/CMECF/Index.htm

Pennsylvania Eastern Bankruptcy Court
www.paeb.uscourts.gov

Pennsylvania Western Bankruptcy Court
www.pawb.uscourts.gov/cm_ecf.htm

Rhode Island Bankruptcy Court
www.rib.uscourts.gov/cmecf/cmecf2/cmecf2.htm

South Carolina Bankruptcy Court
www.scb.uscourts.gov/cmecf/cmecf.htm

South Dakota Bankruptcy Court
www.sdb.uscourts.gov/CaseInformation/CMECF.htm

Tennessee Western Bankruptcy Court
www.tnwb.uscourts.gov/ECF/NewIndex/index.html

Texas Eastern Bankruptcy Court
www.txeb.uscourts.gov/cmecf/cmecf.asp

Texas Northern Bankruptcy Court
www.txnb.uscourts.gov/ecf/index.jsp

Texas Southern Bankruptcy Court
www.txs.uscourts.gov/ecf/index.html

Texas Western Bankruptcy Court
www.txwb.uscourts.gov

Utah Bankruptcy Court
www.utb.uscourts.gov/cm_ecf/cmecfstart.htm

Vermont Bankruptcy Court
www.vtb.uscourts.gov/cmecf.html

Virginia Eastern Bankruptcy Court
www.vaeb.uscourts.gov/ecfnew/ecf.htm

Washington Western Bankruptcy Court
http://www2.wawb.uscourts.gov/ecfhome/index.html

West Virginia Northern Bankruptcy Court
http://207.41.17.85/ecf_support/

West Virginia Southern Bankruptcy Court
www.wvsd.uscourts.gov/bankruptcy/index.htm

Wisconsin Western Bankruptcy Court
www.wiw.uscourts.gov/bankruptcy/CM_ECF.htm

Wyoming Bankruptcy Court
https://ecf.wyb.uscourts.gov

Appendix A

SEC Filings, Defined

Part of the challenge in business intelligence lies in understanding the implications as well as the content of what you read. This is definitely true when dealing with the myriad filings made by public companies with the Securities & Exchange Commission.

Although terms like 10K, 10Q, etc. are commonly understood, many other SEC forms may be much less familiar. Companies do not always wish to broadcast the news that is contained in certain mandatory filings. Knowing what to watch for, and understanding the content of certain filings, therefore, can provide you with some interesting insights into the goings-on over at Company X.

Various commercial vendors of EDGAR SEC filings have been mentioned elsewhere in this book. The list of form definitions below is reprinted, with permission, from EDGAR ONLINE at `www.edgar-online.com/formdef.htm`.

Registration Statements

S-1: This filing is a pre-effective registration statement submitted when a company decides to go public. Commonly referred to as an "IPO" (Initial **Public Offering) filing.**

S-1/A: This filing is a *pre-effective* amendment to an S-1 IPO filing.

S-1MEF: Registration of up to an additional 20% of securities for any offering registered on an S-1.

POS AM: This filing is a *post-effective* amendment to an S-Type filing.

S-2: This filing is an optional registration form that may be used by companies which have reported under the '34 Act for a minimum of three years and have timely filed all required reports during the 12 calendar months and any portion of the month immediately preceding the filing of the registration statement.

S-2/A: This filing is a *pre-effective* amendment to an S-2 filing.

S-2MEF: Registration of up to an additional 20% of securities for any offering registered on an S-2.

S-3: This filing is the most simplified registration form and it may only be used by companies which have reported under the '34 Act for a minimum of three years and meet the timely filing requirements set forth under Form S-2. The filing company must also meet the stringent qualitative tests prescribed by the form.

S-3/A: This filing is a *pre-effective* amendment to an S-3 filing.

S-3MEF: Registration of up to an additional 20% of securities for any offering registered on a S-3.

S-3D: Registration statement of securities pursuant to dividend or interest reinvestment plans which become effective automatically upon filing.

S-3D/A: Amendment to a previously filed S-3D.

S-3DPOS: This filing is a *post-effective* amendment to an S-3D filing.

S-4: This filing is for the registration of securities issued in business combination transactions.

S-4/A: This filing is a *pre-effective* amendment to an S-4 filing.

S-4EF: Filed when securities are issued in connection with the formation of a bank, savings and loan, or holding company.

S-4EF/A: This filing is a *pre-effective* amendment to an S-4EF filing.

S-4 POS: This filing is a *post-effective* amendment to an S-4EF filing.

S-6: Initial registration statement for unit investment trusts.

S-6/A: This filing is a *pre-effective* amendment to an S-6 filing.

S-8: filing is required when securities are to be offered to employees pursuant to employee benefit plans.

S-8/A: Amendment to a previously filed S-8.

S-8 POS: This filing is a *post-effective* amendment to an S-8 filing.

S-11: Filing for the registration of securities of certain real estate companies.

S-11/A: This filing is a *pre-effective* amendment to an S-11 filing.

S-11MEF: Registration of up to an additional 20% of securities for any offering registered on a S-11.

S-20: Initial registration statement for standardized options.

S-20/A: Amendment to a previously filed S-20.

SB-1: An optional filing for small business issuers for the registration of securities to be sold to the public.

SB-1/A: This filing is a *pre-effective* amendment to an SB-1 filing.

SB-1MEF: Registration of up to an additional 20% of securities for any offering registered on a SB-1.

SB-2: An optional filing for small business issuers for the registration of securities to be sold to the public.

SB-2/A: This filing is a *pre-effective* amendment to an SB-2 filing.

SB-2MEF: Registration of up to an additional 20% of securities for any offering registered on a SB-2.

POS AM: Post-effective amendments.

POS AMI: Post-effective amendments.

424A: Contains substantive changes from or additions to a prospectus previously filed with the SEC as part of the registration statement.

424B1: A form of prospectus that discloses information previously omitted from the prospectus filed as part of a registration statement.

424B2: A form of prospectus filed in connection with a primary offering of securities on a delayed basis which includes the public offering price, description of securities and specific method of distribution.

424B3: A form of prospectus that reflects facts or events that constitute a substantive change from or addition to the information set forth in the last form of prospectus filed with the SEC.

424B4: A form of prospectus that discloses information, facts or events covered in both form 424B1 and form 424B3.

424B5: A form of prospectus that discloses information, facts or events covered in both form 424B2 and form 424B3.

DEL AM: Delaying amendment.

497: Definitive materials filed by investment companies.

497J: Certification of no change in definitive materials.

487: Pre-effective pricing amendment.

10-12B: A general registration filing of securities pursuant to section 12(b) of the Securities Exchange Act.

10-12B/A: Amendment to a previously filed 10-12B.

10-12G: A general registration filing of securities pursuant to section 12(g) of the Securities Exchange Act.

10-12G/A: Amendment to a previously filed 10-12G.

10SB12B: Filed for the registration of securities for small business issuers pursuant to section 12(b) of the Securities Exchange Act.

10SB12B/A: Amendment to a previously filed 10SB12B.

10SB12G: Filed for the registration of securities for small business issuers pursuant to section 12(g) of the Securities Exchange Act.

10SB12G/A: Amendment to a previously filed 10SB12G.

18-12B: Registration of securities filed pursuant to section 12(b) of the Securities Exchange Act.

18-12B/A: Amendment to a previously filed 18-12B.

18-12G: Registration of securities filed pursuant to section 12(g) of the Securities Exchange Act.

18-12G/A: Amendment to a previously filed 18-12G.

N-8B-2: Registration statement for unit investment trusts.

N-8B-2/A: Amendments to a previously filed N-8B-2.

N-1: Registration statement for open-end management investment companies.

N-1/A: Amendments to a previously filed N-1.

N-1A: Registration statement for Mutual Funds.

N-2: Registration statement for closed-end investment companies.

N-2/A: This filing is a *pre-effective* amendment to an N-2 filing.

N-3: Registration statement for separate accounts (management investment companies).

N-3/A: This filing is a *pre-effective* amendment to an N-3 filing.

N-4: Registration statement for separate accounts (unit investment trusts).

N-4/A: This filing is a *pre-effective* amendment to an N-4 filing.

N-5: Registration statement for small business investment companies.

N-5/A: This filing is a *pre-effective* amendment to an N-5 filing.

N-14: Registration statement for investment companies business combination.

N-14/A: Pre-effective amendment to a previously filed N-14.

F-1: Registration statement for certain foreign private issuers.

F-1/A: This filing is a pre-effective amendment to an F-1 filing.

F-1MEF: Registration of up to an additional 20% of securities for an offering filed on an F-1.

F-2: Registration statement for certain foreign private issuers.

F-2/A: Amendment to a previously filed F-2.

F-2D: Registration of securities pursuant to dividend or interest reinvestment plans (foreign).

F-2DPOS: Post-effective amendments to a previously filed F-2D.

F-3: Registration statement for certain foreign private issuers offered pursuant to certain types of transactions.

F-3/A: Amendment to a previously filed F-3.

F-3D: Registration statement for certain foreign private issuers offered pursuant to dividend or pursuant to dividend or interest reinvestment plans.

F-3DPOS: Amendment to a previously filed F-3D.

F-4: Registration statement for foreign private issuers issued in certain business transactions.

F-4/A: Amendment to a previously filed F-4.

F-6: Registration of depository shares evidenced by American Depository Receipts. Filing to become effective other than immediately upon filing.

F-6/A: Amendment to a previously filed F-6.

F-6 POS: Post-effective amendment to a previously filed F-6.

F-6EF: Registration of depositary shares evidenced by American Depository Receipts. Filing to become effective immediately upon filing.

F-6EF/A: Amendment to a previously filed F-6EF.

20FR12B: Registration of securities of foreign private issuers pursuant to section 12 (b) of the Securities Exchange Act.

20FR12B/A: Amendment to a previously filed 20FR12B.

20FR12G: Registration of securities of foreign private issuers pursuant to section 12 (g) of the Securities Exchange Act.

20FR12G/A: Amendment to a previously filed 20FR12G.

24F-1: Registration of securities by certain investment companies pursuant to rule 24f-1. Notification of election.

24F-2EL: Registration of securities by certain investment companies pursuant to rule 24f-2. Declaration of election.

24F-2EL/A: Amendment to a previously filed 24F-2EL.

24F-2NT: Registration of securities by certain investment companies pursuant to rule 24f-2. Rule 24f-2 notice.

24F-2NT/A: Amendment to a previously filed 24F-2NT.

POS462B: Post effective amendment to proposed Securities Act Rule 462(b) registration statement.

POS462C: Post effective amendment to proposed Securities Act Rule 462(c) registration statement.

8-A12B: Registration of certain classes of securities pursuant to section 12(b) of Securities Exchange Act.

8-A12B/A: Amendment to a previously filed 8-A12B.

8-A12G: Registration of certain classes of securities pursuant to section 12(g) of Securities Exchange Act.

8-A12G/A: Amendment to a previously filed 8-A12G.

8-B12B: Registration of securities of certain successor issuers pursuant to section 12(b) of the Securities Exchange Act.

8-B12B/A: Amendment to a previously filed 8-B12B.

8-B12G: Registration of securities of certain successor issuers pursuant to section 12(g) of the Securities Exchange Act.

8-B12G/A: Amendment to a previously filed 8-B12G.

8A12BEF: Registration of listed debt securities pursuant to section 12(b) - filing to become effective automatically upon filing.

8A12BT: Registration of listed debt securities pursuant to section 12(b) - filing to become effective simultaneously with the effective of a concurrent Securities Act registration statement.

8A12BT/A: Amendment to a previously filed 8A12BT.

485A24E: Registration statement for separate accounts (management investment companies). Post-Effective amendment filed pursuant to Rule 485(b) with additional shares under 24e-2.

485A24F: Registration statement for separate accounts (management investment companies). Post-Effective amendment filed pursuant to Rule 485(b) with additional shares under 24f-2.

485APOS: Registration statement for separate accounts (management investment companies). Post-Effective amendment filed pursuant to Rule 485(a).

485B24E: Registration statement for separate accounts (management investment companies). Post-Effective amendment filed pursuant to Rule 485(a) with additional shares under 24e-2.

485B24F: Registration statement for separate accounts (management investment companies). Post-Effective amendment filed pursuant to Rule 485(b) with additional shares under 24f-2.

485BPOS: Registration statement for separate accounts (management investment companies). Post-Effective amendment filed pursuant to Rule 485(b).

Registration, Withdrawal & Termination Statements

RW: Request for a withdrawal of a previously filed registration statement.

AW: Amendment to a previously filed RW.

15-12G: Certification of termination of registration of a class of security under Section 12(g) or notice of suspension of duty to file reports pursuant to Section 13 and 15(d) of the Securities Exchange Act. Section 12 (g) initial filing.

15-12G/A: Amendment to a previously filed 15-12G.

15-15D: Certification of termination of registration of a class of security under Section 12(g) or notice of suspension of duty to file reports pursuant to Section 13 and 15(d) of the Securities Exchange Act. Section 13 and 15 (d) initial filing.

15-15D/A: Amendment to a previously filed 15-15D.

15-12B: Certification of termination of registration of a class of security under Section 12(g) or notice of suspension of duty to file reports pursuant to Section 13 and 15(d) of the Securities Exchange Act. Section 12 (b) initial filing.

15-12B/A: Amendment to a previously filed 15-12B.

24F-2TM: Registration of securities by certain investment companies pursuant to rule 24f-2. Termination of declaration of election.

Proxies and Information Statements

PRE 14A: A preliminary proxy statement providing official notification to designated classes of shareholders of matters to be brought to a vote at a shareholders meeting.

PREC14A: Preliminary proxy statement containing contested solicitations.

PREC14C: Preliminary information statement containing contested solicitations.

PREN14A: Non-management preliminary proxy statements not involving contested solicitations.

PREM14A: A preliminary proxy statement relating to a merger or acquisition.

PREM14C: A preliminary information statement relating to a merger or acquisition.

PRES14A: A preliminary proxy statement giving notice regarding a special meeting.

PRES14C: A preliminary information statement relating to a special meeting.

PRE 14C: A preliminary proxy statement containing all other information.

PRER14A: Proxy soliciting materials. Revised preliminary material.

PRER14C: Information statements. Revised preliminary material.

PRE13E3: Initial statement - preliminary form.

PRE13E3/A: Amendment to a previously filed PRE13E3.

PRRN14A: Non-management revised preliminary proxy soliciting materials for both contested solicitations and other situations. Revised preliminary material.

PX14A6G: Notice of exempt solicitation. Definitive material.

DEF 14A: Provides official notification to designated classes of shareholders of matters to be brought to a vote at a shareholders meeting. This form is commonly refered to as a "Proxy."

DEFM14A: Provides official notification to designated classes of shareholders of matters relating to a merger or acquisition.

DEFM14C: A definitive information statement relating to a merger or an acquisition.

DEFS14A: A definitive proxy statement giving notice regarding a special meeting.

DEFS14C: A definitive information statement regarding a special meeting.

DEFC14A: Definitive proxy statement in connection with contested solicitations.

DEFC14C: Definitive information statement indicating contested solicitations.

DEFA14A: Additional proxy soliciting materials - definitive.

DEFN14A: Definitive proxy statement filed by non-management not in connection with contested solicitations.

DFRN14A: Revised definitive proxy statement filed by non-management.

DFAN14A: Additional proxy soliciting materials filed by non-management.

DEF13E3: Schedule filed as definitive materials.

DEF13E3/A: Amendment to a previously filed DEF 13E3.

DEFA14C: Additional information statement materials - definitive.

DEFR14C: Revised information statement materials - definitive.

Quarterly Reports

10-Q: A quarterly report that provides a continuing view of a company's financial position during the year. The filing is due 45 days after each of the first three fiscal quarters. No filing is due for the fourth quarter.

10-Q/A: Amendment to a previously filed 10-Q.

10QSB: A quarterly report that provides a continuing view of a company's financial position during the year. The 10QSB form is filed by small businesses.

10QSB/A: An amendment to a previously filed 10QSB.

NT 10-Q: Notification that form type 10-Q will be submitted late.

NT 10-Q/A: Amendment to a previously filed NT 10-Q.

10-QT: Quarterly transition reports filed pursuant to rule 13a-10 or 15d-10 of the Securities Exchange Act.

10-QT/A: Amendment to a previously filed 10-QT.

13F-E: Quarterly reports filed by institutional managers.

13F-E/A: Amendment to a previously filed 13F-E.

Annual Reports

ARS: An annual report to security holders. This is a voluntary filing on EDGAR.

10-K: An annual report which provides a comprehensive overview of the company for the past year. The filing is due 90 days after the close of the company's fiscal year, and contains such information as company history, organization, nature of business, equity, holdings, earnings per share, subsidiaries, and other pertinent financial information.

10-K/A: Amendment to a previously filed 10-K.

10-K405: An annual report that provides a comprehensive overview of the company for the past year. The Regulation S-K Item 405 box on the cover page is checked.

10-K405/A: This filing is an amendment to a previously filed 10-K405.

NT 10-K: Notification that form 10-K will be submitted late.

NT 10-K/A: Amendment to a previously filed NT 10-K.

10KSB: An annual report that provides a comprehensive overview of the company for the past year. The filing is due 90 days after the close of the company's fiscal year, and contains such information as company history, organization, nature of business, equity, holdings, earnings per share, subsidiaries, and other pertinent financial information. The 10KSB is filed by small businesses.

10KSB/A: Amendment to a previously filed 10KSB.

10-C: This filing is required of an issuer of securities quoted on the NASDAQ Interdealer Quotation System, and contains information regarding a change in the number of shares outstanding or a change in the name of the issuer.

10-C/A: Amendment to a previously filed 10-C.

10-KT: Annual transition reports filed pursuant to rule 13a-10 or 15d-10 of the Securities Exchange Act.

10-KT/A: Amendment to a previously filed 10-KT.

10KSB40: An optional form for annual and transition reports of small business issuers under Section 13 or 15 (d) of the Securities Exchange Act where the Regulation S-B Item 405 box on the cover page (relating to section 16 (a) reports) is checked.

10KSB40/A: Amendment to a previously filed 10KSB40.

10KT405: Annual transition report filed pursuant to Rule 13a-10 or15d-10 of the Securities Exchange Act.

10KT405/A: Amendment to a previously filed 10KT405.

11-KT: Annual report of employee stock purchase, savings and similar plans. Filed pursuant to rule 13a-10 or 15d-10 of the Securities Exchange Act.

11-KT/A: Amendment to a previously filed 11-KT.

18-K: Annual report for foreign governments and political subdivisions.

18-K/A: Amendment to a previously filed 18-K.

11-K: An annual report of employee stock purchase, savings and similar plans.

11-K/A: Amendment to a previously filed 11-K.

NT 11-K: Notification that form 11-K will be submitted late.

NT 11-K/A: Amendment to a previously filed NT 11-K.

NSAR-A: Semi-Annual report for management companies.

NSAR-A/A: Amendments to a previously filed NSAR-A.

NSAR-AT: Transitional semi-annual report for registered investment companies (Management).

NSAR-AT/A: Amendments to a previously filed NSAR-AT.

NSAR-B: Annual report for management companies.

NSAR-B/A: Amendments to a previously filed NSAR-B.

NSAR-BT: Transitional annual report for management companies.

NSAR-BT/A: Amendments to a previously filed NSAR-BT.

NSAR-U: Annual report for unit investment trusts.

NSAR-U/A: Amendments to a previously filed NSAR-U.

NT-NSAR: Request for an extension of time for filing form NSAR-A, NSAR-B or NSAR-U.

NT-NSAR/A: Amendments to a previously filed NT-NSAR.

N-30D: An annual and semi-annual report mailed to shareholders. Filed by registered investment companies.

N-30D/A: Amendments to a previously filed N-30D.

20-F: Annual and transition report of foreign private issuers filed pursuant to sections 13 or 15 (d) of the Securities Exchange Act.

20-F/A: Amendment to a previously filed 20-F.

ARS: Annual report to Security Holders.

Statements of Ownership

SC 13D: This filing is made by person(s) reporting beneficially owned shares of common stock in a public company.

SC 13D/A: An amendment to a SC 13D filing.

SC 13G: A statement of beneficial ownership of common stock by certain persons.

SC 13G/A: An amendment to the SC 13G filing.

SC 13E1: Statement of issuer required by Rule 13e-1 of the Securities Exchange Act.

SC 13E1/A: Amendment to a previously filed SC 13E1.

SC 13E3: Going private transaction by certain issuers.

SC 13E3/A: Amendment to a previously filed SC 13E3.

SC 13E4: Issuer tender offer statement.

SC 13E4/A: Amendment to a previously filed SC 13E4.

SC 14D1: Tender offer statement.

SC 14D1/A: Amendment to a previously filed SC 14D1.

SC 14D9: Solicitation/recommendation statements.

SC 14D9/A: Amendment to a previously filed SC 14D9.

SC 14F1: Statement regarding change in majority of directors pursuant to Rule 14f-1.

SC 14F1/A: Amendment to a previously filed SC 14F1.

Insider Trading

3: An initial filing of equity securities filed by every director, officer, or owner of more than ten percent of a class of equity securities. Contains information on the reporting person's relationship to the company and on purchases and sales of equity securities. This form type is not required to be filed with the EDGAR system.

3/A: An amendment to a 3 filing. This form is not required to be filed with the EDGAR system.

4: Any changes to a previously filed form 3 are reported in this filing. This form type is not required to be filed with the EDGAR system.

4/A: Amendment to a previously filed 4.

5: An annual statement of ownership of securities filed by every director, officer, or owner of more than ten percent of a class of equity securities. Contains information on the reporting person's relationship to the company and on purchases and sales of equity securities. This form type is not required to be filed with the EDGAR system.

5/A: Amendment to a previously filed 5.

144: This form must be filed by "insiders" prior to their intended sale of restricted stock (issued stock currently unregistered with the SEC). Filing this form results in each seller receiving an automatic exemption from SEC registration requirements for this one transaction. A Form 144 is NOT an EDGAR electronic filing; each 144 is filed by the seller in paper during the day at the SEC. *EDGAR Online* cumulates and adds all of the current day's 144 paper filings to our electronic database at the END of each business day.

The value of the *EDGAR Online* end-of-day listing of 144's is that the first notification of a 144 filing sometimes is the precursor of other 144 filings. 144 sales frequently come in clusters caused by events such as the end of a "lock-up" period or stock options being exercised and can be used to successfully project the onset of increased "sell side" activity in the stock of the target company.

Other uses of 144's include targeting individuals who will be coming into money and may wish to deploy such funds. Thus this timely information is the source of myriad business intelligence uses.

144/A: Amendment to a previously filed 144.

Filings pursuant to the Trust Indenture Act

305B2: Initial statement filed pursuant to the Trust Indenture Act.

305B2/A: Amendment to a previously filed 305B2.

T-3: Application for qualification of trust indentures. Filed pursuant to the Trust Indenture Act.

T-3/A: Amendment to a previously filed T-3.

Filings Pursuant to the Public Utility Holding Company Act

U-1: Application of declaration under the Public Utility Holding Company Act.

U-1/A: Amendment to a previously filed U-1.

U-13-1: Application for approval for mutual service company filed pursuant to Rule 88 of the Public Utility Holding Company Act.

U-13-1/A: Amendment to a previously filed U-13-1.

U-12-IB: Annual statement pursuant to section 12(i) of the Public Utility Company Act or by a registered holding company or a subsidiary thereof.

U-13-60: Annual report for mutual and subsidiary service companies filed pursuant to Rule 94 of the Public Utility Holding Company Act.

U-13-60/A: Amendment to a previously filed U-13-60.

U-33-S: Annual report concerning Foreign Utility Companies pursuant to section 33(e) of the Public Utility Holding Company Act.

U-3A-2: Statement by holding company claiming exemption from provisions of the act pursuant to Rule 2.

U-3A-2/A: Amendment to a previously filed U-3A-2.

U-3A3-1: Twelve-month statement by bank claiming exemption from provisions of the act pursuant to Rule 3 of the Public Utility Holding Company Act.

U-3A3-1/A: Amendment to a previously filed U-3A3-1.

U-57: Notification of Foreign Utility Company Status under section 33(a)(2) of the Public Utility Holding Company Act.

U-57/A: Amendment to a previously filed U-57.

U-6B-2: Certificate of notification of security issue, renewal or guaranty filed pursuant to Rule 20(d) of the Public Utility Holding Company Act.

U-7D: Certificate concerning lease of a utility facility filed pursuant to Rule 7(d) of the Public Utility Holding Company Act.

U-7D/A: Amendment to a previously filed U-7D.

U-R-1: Declaration as to solicitations filed pursuant to Rule 62 of the Public Utility Holding Company Act.

U5A: Notification of registration filed under section 5(a) of the Public Utility Holding Company Act.

U5B: Registration statement filed under section 5 of the Public Utility Holding Company Act.

U5B/A: Amendment to a previously filed U5B.

U5S: Annual report for holding companies registered pursuant to section 5 of the Public Utility Holding Company Act.

U5S/A: Amendment to a previously filed U5S.

35-APP: Statement concerning proposed transaction for which no form of application is prescribed filed pursuant to Rule 20(e) of the Public Utility Holding Company Act.

35-APP/A: Amendment to a previously filed 35-APP.

35-CERT: Certificate concerning terms and conditions filed pursuant to Rule 24 of the Public Utility Holding Company Act.

35-CERT/A: Amendment to a previously filed 35-CERT.

Miscellaneous Filings

8-K: A report of *unscheduled* material events or corporate changes which could be of importance to the shareholders or to the SEC. Examples include acquisition, bankruptcy, resignation of directors, or a change in the fiscal year.

8-K/A: Amendment to a previously filed 8-K.

N-14AE: Initial statement with automatic effectiveness for investment companies business combination.

N-14AE/A: Pre-effective amendment to a previously filed N-14AE.

N-30B-2: Periodic and interim reports mailed to shareholders. Filed by registered investment companies.

2-E: Reports of sales of securities pursuant to Regulation E. Filed by investment companies.

2-E/A: Amendment to a previously filed 2-E.

SP 15D2: Special financial report pursuant to Rule 15d-2 of the Securities Exchange Act.

SP 15D2/A: Amendments to a previously filed SP 15D2.

NT 15D2: Notification of late filing Special report pursuant to section 15d-2.

NT 15D2/A: Amendment to a previously filed NT 15D2.

6-K: Report of foreign issuer pursuant to Rules 13a-16 and 15d-16 of the Securities Exchange Act.

6-K/A: Amendment to a previously filed 6-K.

8-K12G3: Notification of securities of successor issuers deemed to be registered pursuant to section 12(g) of the Securities Exchange Act.

8-K12G3/A: Amendment to a previously filed 8-K12G3.

8-K15D5: Notification of assumption of duty to report by successor issuer.

8-K15D5/A: Amendment to a previously filed 8-K15D5.

Current Industrial Reports

The U.S. Bureau of the Census makes available statistical data on the industries listed below. This data can be downloaded in various formats for manipulation using spreadsheets or other software. The Internet address for this material is: `www.census.gov/pub/cir/www/index.html`.

311 - Food Manufacturing

M311J, Fats and Oils: Oilseed Crushings

M311K, Fats and Oils: Production, Consumption, and Stocks

MA311D, Confectionery

MQ311A, Flour Milling

313 - Textile Mills

M313P, Consumption on the Cotton System

MA313F, Yarn Production

MA313K, Knit Fabric Production

MC313T, Broadwoven Fabrics (every 5 years)

MQ313D, Consumption on the Woolen System

MQ313T, Broadwoven Fabrics

314 - Textile Product Mills

MA314Q, Carpets and Rugs

MQ314X, Bed and Bath Furnishings

315 - Apparel Manufacturing

MA315D, Gloves and Mittens

MQ315A, Apparel

316 - Leather and Allied Product Manufacturing

MA316A, Footwear

MQ316A, Footwear (Discontinued)

321 - Wood Product Manufacturing

MA321T, Lumber Production and Mill Stocks

325 - Chemical Manufacturing

M325AT, Titanium Dioxide (Discontinued)

MA325A, Inorganic Chemicals (Discontinued)

MA325B, Fertilizer Materials (Discontinued)

MA325C, Industrial Gases (Discontinued)

MA325F, Paint and Allied Products

MA325G, Pharmaceutical Preparations

MQ325A, Inorganic Chemicals

MQ325B, Fertilizer Materials

MQ325C, Industrial Gases

MQ325F, Paint, Varnish, and Lacquer

327 - Nonmetallic Mineral Product Manufacturing

M327G, Glass Containers

MA327A, Flat Glass

MA327C, Refractories

MA327E, Glassware

MQ327D, Clay Construction Products

331 - Primary Metal Manufacturing

M331D, Aluminum Ingot and Mill Products (Discontinued)

M331J, Inventories of Steel Producing Mills

MA331A, Iron and Steel Castings

MA331B, Steel Mill Products

MA331E, Nonferrous Castings

332 - Fabricated Metal Product Manufacturing

MA332K, Steel Shipping Drums and Pails (Discontinued)

MA332Q, Antifriction Bearings

MQ332E, Plumbing Fixtures

333 - Machinery Manufacturing

MA333A, Farm Machinery and Garden Equipment

MA333D, Construction Machinery

MA333F, Mining Machinery

MA333J, Industrial Air Pollution Control Equipment (Discontinued)

MA333L, Internal Combustion Engines

MA333M, Refrigeration and Heating Equipment

MA333N, Fluid Power Products

MA333P, Pumps and Compressors

MA333U, Vending Machines (Discontinued)

MQ333W, Metalworking Machinery

334 - Computer and Electronic Product Manufacturing

MA334B, Selected Instruments and Related Products

MA334M, Consumer Electronics

MA334P, Communication and Other Electronic Equipment

MA334Q, Semiconductors and Electronic Components

MA334R, Computers and Office

MA334S, Electromedical and Irradiation Equipment

335 - Electrical Equipment, Appliance, and Component Manufacturing

MA335A, Switchgear and Industrial Controls

MA335E, Electric Housewares and Fans

MA335F, Major Household Appliances

MA335H, Motors and Generators

MA335J, Insulated Wire and Cable

MA335K, Wiring Devices and Supplies

MA335L, Electric Lighting Fixtures (Discontinued)

MQ335C, Fluorescent Lamp Ballasts

336 - Transportation Equipment Manufacturing

M336G, Civil Aircraft and Aircraft Engine

M336L, Truck Trailers (Discontinued)

Appendix C

Periodicals' Special Issues

Economic Overviews, Previews, and Forecasts

What are "Special Issues?" Many journals and magazines include, in their December or January issues, feature articles covering economic information. This economic information often takes the form of forecasts, outlooks, reviews/previous of the past/present year, state-of-the industry reports, etc. The two lists presented on the following two pages are reprinted with permission, from *Directory of Business Periodical Special Issues*, edited by Trip Wyckoff, and published by The Reference Press.

See the "For Further Enrichment" Appendix E of this book for additional details, and additional sources of published information in newspapers, magazines, articles, and books.

Economic Outlooks - Business Services

ABA Journal

Ad Age's Creativity

Advertising Age

Association Management

Bank News

Barron's

Business Facilities

Business Geographics

Cablevision

Canadian Printer

Canadian Underwriter

California Real Estate

Card Marketing

CCM - The American Lawyer's Corporate Counsel Magazine

Chicago Daily Law Bulletin

Collections & Credit Risk

Commercial Investment Real Estate Journal

Communications Industries Report

Contingency Planning & Management

Counselor, The

Credit Card Management

Direct

Editor & Publisher

Expo

Financial Service Online

Financial World

Flexo

Government Product News

Graphic Arts Monthly

Incentive Magazine

Industry Week

Insurance Journal: The Property Insurance Magazine of the West

Health Insurance Underwriter

Journal of Business Strategy

Marketing News

MC

Mediaweek

Meetings In the West

Mortgage Banking

Nation's Business

National Mortgage News

National Real Estate Investor

Pensions & Investments

Print & Graphics

Printing Impressions

Printing News East

Printing Views

Promo

Publishers Weekly

Public Relations Tactics

R&D Magazine

Real Estate Forum

Real Estate New York

Real Estate News

Real Estate Weekly

Registered Representative

Report on Business Magazine

Research

Resource

ResponseTV

Risk Management

Rough Notes

Russian Magazine

School Planning & Administration

Security

Security Distribution & Marketing

Security Sales

Site Selection

Skylines

Southern Graphics

T H E Journal

Teleprofessional

Television Broadcast

Today's Realtor

Tradeshow Week

Trusts & Estates

Tuned In

US News & World Report

Variety's On Production

Economic Outlooks - Business Journals

Alaska Business Monthly

Arizona Business Magazine

Bellingham Business Journal

Birmingham Business Journal

Business Examiner

Business Journal Serving Charlotte & the Metro Areas

Business Journal Serving Phoenix & the Valley of the Sun

Business Journal Serving San Jose & the Silicon Valley

Business Journal Serving Sonoma & Marin County

Business News Serving the Dayton-Miami Valley Region

Business Life Magazine

Business News New Jersey

Business NH Magazine

Business Times (CT)

BusinessWest

Capital District Business Journal

Caribbean Business

Cecil Business Ledger

Central Penn Business Journal

Colorado Business Magazine

Colorado Springs Business Journal

Corporate Report Minnesota

Crain's Chicago Business

Crain's Cleveland Business

Crain's Detroit Business

Crain¹s New York Business

Daily Business Review

Daily Record, The

Detroiter

Eastern Pennsylvania Business Journal

Everett Business Journal

Florida Trend

Georgia Trend

Grand Rapids Business Journal

Greenville Business & Living

Hartford Business Journal

Houston Business Journal

Illinois Business

Ingram's For Successful Kansas Citizens

Inland Empire Business Journal

Inside Tucson Business

Island Business

Journal of Business

Journal Record

Long Beach Business Journal

Long Island

Los Angeles Business Journal

Memphis Business Journal

Metro Journal

Minneapolis/St. Paul CityBusiness

Nashville Business Journal

Nevada Business Journal

New Castle Business Ledger

North Carolina Magazine

Pacific Business News

Providence Business News

Puget Sound Business Journal

Sacramento Business Journal

San Francisco Business Times

San Gabriel Valley Business Journal

Seattle Daily Journal of Commerce

State Journal

Tampa Bay's The Maddux Report

Triangle Business Journal

Washington CEO

Wenatchee Business Journal

Appendix D

The Society of Information Professionals

The Need for a CI Community

We all know that information is not enough anymore. Managers need skilled professionals to turn a sea of data into actionable intelligence that will provide the company with a competitive edge. Just as satellites and radar allow ships to reexamine their course at any moment, so too does CI employ the latest tools and techniques coupled with cutting-edge technology and resources to carefully sketch out the constantly changing competitive terrain. In a world where one right decision can make millions of dollars or one wrong choice can destroy you, wouldn't you want to have the most sophisticated tools at your disposal?

As an organization of individual CI professionals from countries across the globe, the Society is dedicated to providing the training and knowledge to pilot companies towards competitive success while maintaining the highest ethical standards. From educational seminars to networking opportunities, the Society emphasizes the need for CI professionals to learn from each other and stay abreast of the latest developments in information gathering, analysis, and dissemination. Through their special events and publications, members are made aware of the changes in the business environment and know before anyone else what lies ahead.

SCIP Benefits and Dues

The fee to join the Society of Competitive Intelligence Professionals is $155 per year, in return for which you receive the following key benefits:

Contacts

The SCIP Membership Directory (members receive one per year, published in mid-July) is the primary tool for reaching other CI practitioners, consultants, vendors, and academics to share professional experiences.

The Society also has an active program of chapters around the country and overseas where members meet and exchange valuable techniques with counterparts in other companies and with service firms that specialize in CI.

Skills

Through educational programs, CI products, and professional contacts, members have the opportunity to increase skills in every aspect of CI — from data gathering and database management to analysis and strategy development. Members receive advance notification of all CI programs and products, and, of course, enjoy reduced rates at conferences and meetings.

News and Views

Members receive the quarterly publications *Competitive Intelligence Review* and *Competitive Intelligence Magazine*. These excellent journals not only contain full-length articles and timely tips, but also regular columns, book and product reviews, and much more. Members also receive the monthly newsletter, *Actionable Intelligence*, which keeps members informed of CI happenings and programs scheduled throughout the regions and chapters.

How to Join

An electronic membership application is available at www.scip.org. You can call or write SCIP at:

Society of Competitive Intelligence Professionals
1700 Diagonal Road, Suite 600
Alexandria, VA 22314
(703) 739-0696, fax (703) 739-2524

Frequently Asked Questions

The following information is taken from SCIP's website and reprinted with permission.

Is CI espionage?

No. Espionage is the use of illegal means to gather information. In fact, economic espionage represents a failure of CI. Almost all the information a CI professional needs can be collected by examining published information sources, conducting interviews, and using other legal, ethical methods. Using a variety of analytical tools, a skilled CI professional can fill by deduction any gaps in information already gathered. Promoting CI as a discipline bound by a strict code of ethics and practiced by trained professionals is the paramount goal of the Society.

Are CI and counterintelligence the same thing?

No. The term counterintelligence describes the steps an organization takes to protect information sought by "hostile" intelligence gatherers. One of the most effective counterintelligence measures is to define "trade secret" information relevant to the company and control its dissemination.

Why is CI important?

The pace of technological development and the growth of global trade mean that today's business environment changes more quickly than ever before. Executives can no longer afford to rely on instinct or intuition when making strategic business decisions. In many industries, the consequence of making one wrong decision may be to see the company go out of business.

Does CI really make a difference to the bottom line?

Yes. Research shows that companies with well-established CI programs enjoy greater earnings per share than companies in the same industry without CI programs.

Isn't it true that CI is only important for big businesses?

No. Executives at many global companies like Xerox, IBM, and Motorola have already realized the importance of CI and have developed their own operations. But small businesses, like large corporations, must compete in the marketplace. It is just as important for decision makers in small businesses to know what lies ahead as for CEOs at Fortune 500 companies.

Is it possible for a company to practice some form of CI without realizing it?

Yes. Any employee that visits a trade show, reads a newspaper, or talks to friends in the same industry is doing research (one of the components of CI). Other components of CI are often missing in businesses today. CI adds value to information gathering and strategic planning by introducing a disciplined system not only to gather information, but also to perform analysis and disseminate findings tailored to the needs of decision makers.

How does the Society of Competitive Intelligence Professionals enter the picture?

The Society (SCIP) is a global, nonprofit organization providing education and networking opportunities for business professionals working in the rapidly growing field of CI.

Does SCIP have an impressive membership?

Yes. SCIP is rapidly becoming the association of choice for CI professionals. Currently, its membership is more than 6000 (and has been increasing at a rate of 40% annually). Many SCIP members have backgrounds in market research, government intelligence, or science and technology. They work in a broad variety of industries. There are more than 40 SCIP chapters around the world, with more than 1500 members from 44 countries outside the USA. The growth in the Society's membership reflects the growing awareness of the value of CI in the global business community.

Is CI truly valued in the business community?

Yes. In companies all over the world, SCIP members are enabling executives to make the informed decisions that keep companies responsive, well positioned, and profitable. Robert Flynn, the former CEO and chairman of NutraSweet, said in a keynote address to the Society's ninth annual conference that CI was worth up to $50 million each year to his company. The demand for CI professionals suggests that other CEOs agree: a recent study by SCIP finds that salaries for CI professionals have increased.

What is SCIP's standpoint on the "spy" perception that stigmatizes CI?

CI is not spying. It is not necessary to use illegal or unethical methods in CI. In fact, doing so is a failure of CI, because almost everything decision makers need to know about the competitive environment can be discovered using legal, ethical means. The information that cannot be found with research can be deduced with good analysis, which is just one of the ways CI adds value to an organization. By joining SCIP, a member agrees to abide by the Society's code of ethics. The code of ethics forbids breaching an employer's guidelines, breaking the law, or misrepresenting oneself.

Appendix E

For Further Enrichment...

Important Reading for the Online Searcher

Magazines/Newspapers

Business Information Alert. Alert Publications, 401 W Fullerton Pkwy, Ste. 1403E, Chicago, IL 60614-2857, 312-525-7594.

Econtent. Online: a Division of Information Today Inc., 213 Danbury Road · Wilton, CT 06897-4007, (203) 761-1466, (800) 248-8466 · Fax (203) 761-1444, · custserv@infotoday.com.

Information Advisor, The. Information Today Inc., 143 Old Marlton Pike, Medford, NJ, 07055-8570. 609-654-6266, Fax: 609-654-4309, www.infotoday.com.

Information Today. Information Today Inc., 143 Old Marlton Pike, Medford, NJ, 07055-8570. Telephone: 609-654-6266, Fax: 609-654-4309, www.infotoday.com.

Searcher. Information Today Inc., 143 Old Marlton Pike, Medford, NJ, 07055-8570. Telephone: 609-654-6266, Fax: 609-654-4309, www.infotoday.com.

The Cyberskeptic's Guide to Internet Research. Information Today Inc., 143 Old Marlton Pike, Medford, NJ, 07055-8570. 609-654-6266, Fax: 609-654-4309, www.infotoday.com.

Books

Bates, Mary Ellen. *Super Searchers Cover the World: The Online Secrets of Global Business Researchers.* Information Today Inc, 143 Old -Marlton Pike, Medford, NJ 07055-8570; 2001. Telephone: 609-654-6266, Fax: 609-654-4309, www.infotoday.com.

Berinstein, Paula. *Business Statistics on the Web.* Information Today Inc, 143 Old -Marlton Pike, Medford, NJ, 07055-8570 : June, 2003. Telephone: 609-654-6266, Fax: 609-654-4309, www.infotoday.com.

Berkman, Robert Irving. *Finding Business Research on the Web.* Research Publications Group, 625 Avenue of the Americas, New York, NY, 10011-2002. 800-346-3787, (outside the US 212-807-2657), Fax: 212-645-7681.

Carr, Margaret Metcalf. *Super Searchers on Competitive Intelligence: The Online and Offline Secrets of Top CI Researchers.* Information Today Inc, 143 Old -Marlton Pike, Medford, NJ 07055-8570: June, 2003. Telephone: 609-654-6266, Fax: 609-654-4309, www.infotoday.com.

Fulltext Sources Online. Information Today Inc., 143 Old Marlton Pike, Medford, NJ, 07055-8570. Telephone: 609-654-6266, Fax: 609-654-4309, www.infotoday.com.

Hock, Randolph. *The Extreme Searcher's Internet Handbook.* Information Today Inc, 143 Old -Marlton Pike, Medford, NJ, 07055-8570: January 2004. Telephone: 609-654-6266, Fax: 609-654-4309, www.infotoday.com.

Lane, Carole A. *Naked in Cyberspace: How to Find Personal Information Online.* 2nd Edition. Information Today Inc, 143 Old -Marlton Pike, Medford, NJ, 07055-8570: 2002. Telephone: 609-654-6266, Fax: 609-654-4309, www.infotoday.com.

Lanza, Sheri R. *International Business Information on the Web.* Information Today Inc, 143 Old -Marlton Pike, Medford, NJ, 07055-8570: 2001. Telephone: 609-654-6266, Fax: 609-654-4309, www.infotoday.com.

Mintz, Anne P. *Web of Deception: Misinformation on the Internet.* Information Today Inc, 143 Old -Marlton Pike, Medford, NJ, 07055-8570: 2002. Telephone:\ 609-654-6266, Fax: 609-654-4309, www.infotoday.com.

Sankey, Michael; Weber, Peter J., *Public Records Online, 5th ed.* Facts on Demand Press, PO Box 27869, Tempe, AZ 85285, 2004. Telephone: 800-929-3811; Fax: 480-829-8505, brb@brbpub.com

Schlein, Alan M. *Find It Online*, 4th ed. Facts on Demand Press, 2004. ISBN 1-889150-45-2. PO Box 27869, Tempe, AZ, 85285. 800-929-3811; Fax: 480-829-8505, brb@brbpub.com

Sherman, Chris and Gary Price. *The Invisible Web: Uncovering Information Sources Search Engines Can't See.* Information Today Inc, 143 Old -Marlton Pike, Medford, NJ, 07055-8570: 2001. Telephone: 609-654-6266, Fax: 609-654-4309, www.infotoday.com.

Berkman, Robert. *The Skeptical Business Searcher: The Information Advisor's Guide to the Evaluating Web Data, Sites, and Sources.* Information Today Inc, 143 Old -Marlton Pike, Medford, NJ, 07055-8570 : September 2004. Telephone: 609-654-6266, Fax: 609-654-4309, www.infotoday.com.

Villamora, Grace Avellana. *Super Searchers on Madison Avenue: Top Advertising and Marketing Professionals Share Their Online Research. .* Information Today Inc, 143 Old -Marlton Pike, Medford, NJ, 07055-8570: 2003. 609-654-6266, Fax: 609-654-4309, www.infotoday.com.

A Selected CI Reading List

Articles

Barson, Donna. *Competitive Intelligence Returns* Global Cosmetic Industry 170 no9 68, 70 S 2002

Barson, Donna. *Competing Intelligently* Global Cosmetic Industry 170 no6 26, 28 Je 2002

Breitstein, Joanna. *Toward competitive intelligence.* Pharmaceutical Executive 22, #9(9/2002) p. 110

Breitzman, Anthony and Patrick Thomas. *Using patent citation analysis to target/value M&A candidates.* Research Technology Management 45, no. 5 (Sep/Oct 2002): p. 28-36

Burdette, Scott. *Customer Intelligence* Chain Store Age 78 no1 133 Ja 2002

Centralized Intelligence At Work; Companies are creating business-intelligence competency centers staffed with experts who establish standards and work with employees and vendors. Information Week (4/19/04)

Competitive Intelligence: a strategic imperative. Business Owner 27, no. 1 (January 2003): p. 13

Competitive intelligence in action: how do organizations use competitive intelligence, and what can it mean to their success? Two case studies illustrate different approaches and results. Information Management Journal 38, no. 2 (March 2004): p. 64

Competitive intelligence, corporate security and the virtual organization. Advances in Competitiveness Research 11, no. 1 (January 2003): p. 20

Competitive intelligence in UK firms: a typology. Marketing Intelligence & Planning 20, no. 6 (6/2002): p. 349

Coakley, Debbie. *Market Research Plays Prized Role in Competitive Market Roundtable* Agri Marketing v. 41 no10 (Nov./Dec. 2003) p. 40-1

Conover, Gerry & Susan Day, *Mining Your Competition,* Automotive Industries 182 #3 32-3 3/02.

Fitzpatrick, William M. *Uncovering Trade Secrets: The Legal and Ethical Conundrum of Creative Competitive Intelligence.* Advanced Management Journal v. 68 no3 (Summer 2003) p. 4-13

Fleisher, Craig S. *Competitive Intelligence Education: Competencies, Sources, and Trends.* Information Management Journal v. 38 no2 (Mar./Apr. 2004) p. 56-8, 60-2

Gonzales, Angela. *STRATEGIES: COMPETITIVE INTELLIGENCE, Valley EAP provider relishes vigorous competition.* Business Journal 22, no. 52 (Sep 20, 2002): p. 24

Hall, Lee *CI CONFIDENTIAL* Atlanta Business Chronicle 24, no. 53 (Jun 07, 2002): p. B1.

Jarvis, Lisa. *Gauging the Competitive Threats in China and India.* Chemical Market Reporter v. 264 no17 (Nov. 17 2003) p. 10, 12

McGonagle, John J. *Competitive Intelligence in Action.* Information Management Journal v. 38 no2 (Mar./Apr. 2004) p. 64-5, 67-8

Ojala, Marydee. *Online relevance for competitive intelligence. (The Dollar Sign).* Online Magazine 27, no. 4 (July 2003): 41

A perfect blend. An effective market intelligence program joins MR, competitive info. Marketing News 37 no19 32-3 S 15 2003

Ray, Linda C. *Navigating Minefields OF INTELLIGENT INFORMATION.* Business Leader 13, no. 9 (Mar 01, 2002): p. 18.

Smith, Robert W. *Going Beyond Competitive Intelligence.* Adhesives Age v. 45 no3 (2/2002) p. 39

Sounding off on CI. KMWorld 13, no. 2 (February 2004): 24

The use of an online commercial database as a source of competitive advantage for developing marketing strategies and tactics. Competitiveness Review 13, no. 1 (January 2003): 35

Vedder, Richard G. and C. Stephen *Guynes CIOS' PERSPECTIVES ON COMPETITIVE INTELLIGENCE* Information Systems Management 19 no4 49-55, Fall 2002

A Vendor-Provided Case Study: Rapid Competitive Intelligence Strengthens Global Sales Teams. T+D v. 57 no6 (June 2003) p. 66-7

Wray, Barbara. *Portelligent dissects a slew of tech gadgets.* Austin Business Journal 21, no. 49 (Feb 22, 2002): p. A22.

Books

Dutka, Alan. *Competitive Intelligence for the Competitive Edge*. NTC Contemp Pub Co, 1999.
ISBN: 0-8442-0293-2

Fleischer, Craig S. and Bensoussan, Babette. Strategic and Competitive Analysis: Methods and Techniques for Analyzing Business Competition. Prentice Hall, 2002. ISBN: 0130888524

Fuld, Leonard M. *The New Competitor Intelligence: The Complete Resource for Finding, Analyzing, & Using Information about Your Competitors*. Wiley, 1994. ISBN: 0-471-58508-4 EDITION: 2nd ed.

Gilad, Benjamin. *Early Warning: Using Competitive Intelligence to Anticipate Market Shifts, Control Risk, and Create Powerful Strategies*. AMACOM, 2003. ISBN: 0814407862

Herring, Jan P. *Measuring the Effectiveness of Competitive Intelligence: Assessing & Communicating CI's Value to Your Organization*. Society of Competitor Intelligence Professionals, 1996.ISBN:0-9621241-2-5

How to Find Business Intelligence in Washington. Washington Researchers, 1997.
ISBN: 1-56365-053-3 EDITION: 12th ed.

Jenster, Per, and Hussey, David. *Company Analysis: Determining Strategic Capability*
John Wiley & Sons, 2001. ISBN: 0471494542.

Kahaner, Larry. *Competitive Intelligence*. Simon & Schuster, 1998. ISBN: 0-684-84404-4

Loshin, David. *Business Intelligence: The Savvy Manager's Guide*. Morgan Kaufmann, 2003.
ISBN: 1558609164

McGonagle, John J. and Vella, Carolyn M. *Bottom Line Competitive Intelligence*. Quorum Books; (September 30, 2002. ISBN: 1567205054.

McGonagle, John J.; Vella, Carolyn M. *The Internet Age of Competitive Intelligence*. Greenwood, 1999.
ISBN: 1-56720-204-7

Prescott, John E., ed., Miller, Stephen H.ed., and The Society of Competitive Intelligence Professionals.
Proven Strategies in Competitive Intelligence: Lessons from the Trenches. John Wiley & Sons, 2001.
ISBN: 0471401781.

Shaker, Steven M.; Gembicki, Mark P. *The WarRoom Guide to Competitive Intelligence*. McGraw, 1998.
ISBN: 0-07-058057-X

Tyson, Kirk W.M. *The Complete Guide to Competitive Intelligence*, 2nd ed. - Leading Edge Pub. 2002.
ISBN: 0966321928.

Vitert, Conor. *Competitive Intelligence: A Framework for Web-Based Analysis and Decision Making*.
South-Western Educational Publishing, 2003. ISBN: 032420325X

Glossary

More Terms Used in Online Competitive Intelligence

The following are explanations of *some* of the terms used in this book. Some terms pertain to the vocabulary of the Internet, while others are related to business intelligence. Terms defined within the text of the book are not included here.

Adverse items – Issues, or filings with government offices, which could be considered to have a negative impact on the individual or company in question. These items often involve financial obligations or possible violations of laws or regulations.

Alert services – Services offered by information vendors whereby requestor is informed when particular subject matter is published in specified sources such as news media, trade publications, government materials, etc. (Sometimes called Current Awareness Services).

Analyst reports – In-depth studies of companies or industries, created and published by financial institutions such as brokerage houses. Reports help determine the status and to make forecasts regarding the financial performance of a company or industry.

ASCII – (American Standard Code for Information Interchange) an encoding scheme used by PC's for the exchange (or interchange) of information between programs. ASCII files can be read by machines or humans, without any special handling.

Background checks – The system of investigating the credentials of an individual such as a job applicant, to verify information on topics such as education, previous employment, criminal record (or lack thereof), etc.

Bias factor – The knowledge that information found on an Internet website expresses the views of those who created the site, and that although these views may be one-sided, the site may contain useful information.

Bookmark – The process of saving to a computer file (and possibly organizing) the web addresses of sites to which you plan to return. Bookmarks may be managed by your browser or by specialized products available from software producers. The Internet Explorer browser calls these *Favorites*.

Chat rooms – Places on the Internet where people conduct synchronous line-by-line communication in real time, as opposed to email.

Current awareness services – Services offered by information vendors whereby requestor is informed when particular subject matter is published in specified sources such as news media, trade publications, government materials, etc. (Synonym for Alert Services)

Cyberspace – A popular term used to describe the range of information resources available through computer networks.

Database – A computer file consisting of fielded information, arranged consistently in the form of individual records. Some fields in a database record may contain brief amounts of information or data, while others could include the full text of a document.

Defendant-Plaintiff tables – Listings of cases filed in a given jurisdiction. These listings indicate pending cases as well as those that have been heard or settled. They are a useful source of information that may not appear in LEXIS or Westlaw or in other case law databases.

Document retrieval service – A commercial service that obtains copies of specified documents from government or other sources, by request. Such services usually pay copyright and other costs as applicable, and bill these back to their clients.

Download – The process by which files or data is saved or pulled down from a remote computer.

EDGAR – (Electronic Data Gathering, Analysis, and Retrieval system) An automated system used for the collection, validation, indexing, acceptance, and forwarding of submissions by companies and others who are required by law to file forms with the U.S. Securities and Exchange Commission (SEC).

Email – (Electronic mail) Messages, usually in the form of text, that are sent from one individual to another individual or group of individuals on a network or over the Internet.

FTP – (File transfer protocol) A means for transferring files from one computer to another. Anonymous FTP is used to transfer public files from a computer where you don't have a password or account. With the increased popularity of the World Wide Web, FTP is used less frequently than in the past.

Insider trading – Every director, officer, or owner of more than ten percent of a class of equity Securities is considered an "insider". Prior to their intended sale of restricted stock (issued stock currently unregistered with the SEC), insiders must make certain filings with the SEC. These filings contain information on the reporting person's relationship to the company and on purchases and sales of equity securities. Filing this form gives the seller an automatic exemption from SEC registration requirements for this one transaction.

Lag time – The time between when information is published in hardcopy and the date when it appears in electronic databases. Lag time varies from a day or so to several weeks, depending upon the publication involved. It is usually included as part of a licensing agreement between print publishers and database vendors, and is sometimes used to help retain circulation levels for print subscriptions.

Mailing list - A way of having a group discussion or distribution of announcements by electronic mail. You join the list and then receive other people's postings by email. You may respond to the list, where all can read your comments, or you may simply read what is posted by others. This process is handled automatically by programs called mailing list managers or mail servers.

Meta-search engines – Hybrids of search engines and subject directories that allow you to search several sites at once. Popular examples of meta-sites include Dogpile, Mamma, Vivisimo, ProFusion or Kartoo.

NAICS – A hierarchical classification system that uses a six-digit coding system versus the four digits in SIC. (See below.) Industries and types of businesses are assigned NAICS codes based on their principal activity. The classification scheme breaks down categories from very broad to very narrow.

Push technology – A popular distribution method for providing information over the World Wide Web. Periodic updates are scheduled and automatically sent to the user's PC screen or window.

Real time – A method used online for providing information is being broadcast at the present time, live, not delayed or recorded.

Search tools – The tools used to search the Internet. They include search engines, which are a type of software that creates indexes of databases of Internet sites and allows you to type in what you are looking for and it then gives you a list of results of your search. Other tools include subject directories, which are catalogs of resources, collected and ranked by human beings, and meta-tools, which allow you to search several search tools at once.

SIC – (Standard Industrial Classification) A classification system that assigns a four-digit numeric code to industries and types of businesses, based on their principal activity – commonly referred to as an SIC code.

URL – (Uniform Resource Locator) The address for a resource or website.

Usenet – A collection of newsgroups and a set of agreed-upon rules for distributing and maintaining them.

Web browser – Software that provides a (usually) graphical interface for searching the Internet's World Wide Web. The browser searches for and displays documents specified in a search request.

Web page – A document created with HTML (HyperText Markup Language) that is part of a group of hypertext documents or resources available on the World Wide Web. It usually contains hyptertext links to other documents on the Web. Collectively, these documents and resources form what is known as a website.

Page Index

Note: sub-entries to each index item may not be listed in alphabetical order or numerical order.

B

F

Hoover's, 92, 210; industry information, 210

Hoover's Pro, 231

hospitals: bookmarks, 326

HotBot, 171; features, *176*

hotlinks: broadcast resources, 68; international publications, 64; newspaper, 64; for fast access, 22; from a company directory, 37; to key people, 29

Houston Chronicle, 60; online version, 60

human resources department, 73, 108, 216

HyperText Markup Language, 472

I

identifying: companies and executives, 230; experts, 80; science/technical experts, 85; officers and directors from public records, 30

IdEXEC, 197, 231

illegal corporate donations, 78

image: patent or trademark, 30

iMorph Inc, 196

import penetration data, 258

imports/exports, 258

imports/exports: bookmarks, 376

Inc. Magazine, 154

incorporation or limited partnership records, 103

incubator, local, 3

IncyWincy, 183

Indonesian Commercial Newsletter, 41

industrial espionage, 14

industrial reports: current, 457

industries: high-tech, 88

Industry Analysis Report: example form, 249

industry and profession: bookmarks, 318

Industry Forecasts, 209

industry forecasts: bookmarks, 332; incorrect, 205

industry history: resources for, 255

Industry Insider, 75, 256, 257, 263, 264; The Trade Association Database, 75

industry links: bookmarks, 318

industry profiles, 210

industry reports: pre-packaged, 208

industry research: bookmarks, 332; good starting place, 210

industry specific: bookmarks, 282

industry studies, 208, 209

industry trends: resources for, 256

industry: analysis and trends, 27, 70, 73, 75, 80, 92, 256, 257; awards, 216; developments, 203; example analysis, 249; filings, 106; government data, 204; keyword search, Hoovers', 210; laws and regulations, 30, 106; identifying trade literature, 70; issues affecting your company, 79; information packages, 75; laws and regulations, 79;

organizations, 73; news, 66, 70, 82; newspapers and magazines, 35, 70; search tips, 209; statistical data lists, 457; studies, 208; studies, 255; study template, 269; tracking, 188; what information is available, 255; watchers and regulators, 75, 144; your company, 3, 35; directories. *See also* experts; industry.

industry databases, lists of, 423

industry directories, 227; names in publications, 228

IndustryLink, 211

InfoGrid, 175

Infominder, 196

INFOMINE, 184

information broker, 13; bookmarks, 333

information professional, independent, 13

information supermarket, 48

Information Technology Department, 82

information: packages, 75; public, 95; science, 13

Inktomi search engine features, *176*

Inside Conferences, 81

insider trading information, 100

Insider Trading Monitor, 100

insider trading sites: bookmarks, 309

insider trading: definition of, 471

insiders. *See* company insiders

insiders: financial filings, 224; industry monitors, 70

inspections: OSHA, 133

Institution Directory (ID), 134

institutions: financial. *See* financial; institutions

insurance industry: alerting service, 194

insurance related: bookmarks, 326

Integrity in Science Internet Database, 227

intellectual property, 30, 31, 134, 135; assets of a company, 135; bookmarks, 351

Intelligence Organizer, The, 169

intelligence: from conference papers, 80; from environmental data, 79; where found within your company, 73

Intelliseek, 202

interactive manuals, 88

interfaces: advantages and disadvantages of, 52

Internal Revenue Service. *See* IRS

international organizations: bookmarks, 333

international: business online sources, 163; business resources, 167; comparisons, 139; copyrights, 134; job search, 61

internet ads: sources of, 69

internet directories: bookmarks, 366

Internet Guide to Engineering, Mathematics, and Computing, 175

Internet Intelligence Index, 169

internet resources: for faculty, students, and research staff, 184

Internet Searching Tip Sheet, 169

M

O

P

NOTES

NOTES

Additional titles from
Facts on Demand Press

The Safe Hiring Manual

The Safe Hiring Manual goes far beyond the typical reference-checking handbook. A comprehensive blueprint for developing a safe hiring program, *The Manual's* 30 chapters detail how to properly verify educational credentials and past work histories, to find and interpret public records, and update your current programs to comply with recent changes involving the EEOC, FCRA, Patriot Act, and other legal concerns -- and it includes new information on how to identify terrorists and perform international background checks. This new book, which lets you audit the effectiveness of your current hiring program, provides all the whys and how-to's for implementing the necessary employment practices that will keep your business safe -- and keep you out of court.

Les Rosen • 1-889150-29-0 • June 2004 • 360 pages • $24.95

The Criminal Records Manual   2nd Edition

The Criminal Record Handbook is an important reference manual for anyone who uses criminal records when making business or hiring decisions. Author Hinton analyzes the compliance issues connected to complicated federal and state laws that employers, financial institutions, attorneys, corporate security centers, private investigators and others must abide by when obtaining and using criminal records. Sixteen practical, easy-to-read chapters are combined with an incredibly in-depth study of each state's restrictions and policies regarding the release of all types of criminal and incarceration records, including locations and explanations of the states' and federal specific citations and statutes. A timely publication for today's world of heightened interest in security and correct hiring procedures.

Derek Hinton • 1-889150-43-6 • June 2004 • 360 pages • $28.95

Find It Online   4th Edition

Are you using the Internet to the best of your ability? *Find It Online* provides the tools and techniques you need to master online research. Learn how to effectively use numerous search tools, manage and filter information, then evaluate the accuracy and credibility of that information. *Find It Online* teaches you how to search more effectively and profiles over 2,000 reliable websites . . . including the best links to government, news, and business resources. The 4th edition contains tips from 20 industry experts and is totally revised to include specifics on spyware, popup blockers, and spam killers as well as the most current online search tools.

Alan Schlein • 1-889150-45-2 • Aug 2004 • 580 pages • $21.95

Available at your favorite bookstore.

Facts on Demand Press • 1-800-929-3811 • www.brbpub.com

Annual Public Record Titles From
BRB Publications, Inc.

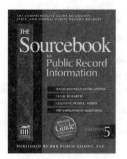
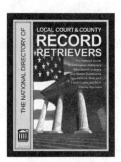

Helen P. Burwell

Author and online expert Helen Burwell is well known for providing consulting and research services to the information industry and the international business community. Since 1984, as President of Burwell Enterprises, Inc., she has helped corporate clients develop successful strategies for electronic retrieval of competitive intelligence information. Her master work, *Online Competitive Intelligence*, was first published in 2000.

Helen is principal of the Information Professionals Institute, which presents seminars nationwide on business information and online topics, providing expert guiadance to information professionals and those in the broader corporate market.

Ms. Burwell is editor and publisher of the *The Burwell World Directory of Information Brokers*, a directory of companies who provide information retrieval and consulting. *The Burwell Directory* is widely used by business and industry for outsourcing information research. *The Directory* is also available on the Internet at www.burwellinc.com.

Ms. Burwell holds a Master's Degree from Louisiana State University's School of Library and Information Science, which named Helen its 1996 Outstanding Alumna for her contributions to the information profession.

In 1998, the Association of Independent Information Professionals – an international organization comprised of information consultants, online searchers, document delivery services, and other information professionals – presented Ms. Burwell with the President's Award for Outstanding Service to the Profession.

In recent years Ms. Burwell has been an invited guest speaker both at the European Information Brokers Meeting in Frankfurt, Germany and at the First Asian and Pacific Rim Conference and Exhibition on Electronic Commerce in Shanghai, China.

Regular speaking engagements in the U.S. include national conferences and large trade shows such as The National Online Meeting, Online World, and The Society of Competitive Intelligence Professionals.

Helen makes her home in Dallas, Texas with her husband Ed. She can be reached by email at helen@burwellinc.com. Her website is www.burwellinc.com